THE FABRIC OF
THE ANCIENT THEATRE

THE FABRIC OF
THE ANCIENT THEATRE

*Excavation Journals from Cyprus
and the Eastern Mediterranean*

Diana Wood Conroy

MOUFFLON PUBLICATIONS LTD.

Moufflon Publications Ltd.
20 Costi Palama
Aspelia Buildings, Apartment E1
1096 Lefkosia, Cyprus
publishing@moufflon.com.cy

Copyright © Diana Wood Conroy 2004
All rights reserved.
No part of this book may be reproduced or transmitted
in any form by any means, electronic, mechanical,
photocopying, recording, or otherwise, without the
prior written permission of the publisher.

Typeset by Toby Macklin, Co-create Ltd., Cyprus
in Hoefler Type Foundry Requiem.

ISBN 9963-642-14-4

Printed and bound by Imprinta Ltd., Lefkosia.

For my parents,
Marion Carment Wood
and David Roy Vernon Wood

CONTENTS

Acknowledgements *x*
Map of the Eastern Mediterranean *xii*
Preface *xiii*

PART I ❊ *The Orchestra: The Paphos Theatre, 1995-1999*

1 The First Season *17*
2 Fragments from the Excavation *24*
3 Wreaths of String and Sacred Stones *43*
4 Flesh and Stone: the Theatre *54*
5 Finding Things: Dolphins,
   a Carved Hand, a Sandalled Foot *60*
6 Dreaming on site *68*
7 The Village *73*
8 Invisible Worlds: Easter *80*
9 Necropolis *86*
10 The Tomb of the Garlands *90*
11 Mosaics *92*
12 A.H.S. Megaw and the Seventh Century *104*
13 Thread and Cloth *118*

PART II ❊ *The Cavea: The Arc of the Mediterranean, 1999-2000*

1 Coptic Fabrics *131*
2 City of Memory: Alexandria *141*
3 Ikingi Mariut *155*
4 Athens *165*
5 Vergina *176*
6 The Hellespont *185*
7 Pergamon *199*
8 Ephesos *208*
9 Muses *217*

INTERLUDE ❊ *Art Works* Following page 225

PART III ❦ *The Theatres of Southern Turkey, 2000*

1. In Southern Turkey:
   Pamphylia, Lycia and Pisidia *243*
2. Perge and Side *247*
3. Antalya Museum *255*
4. Aspendos *260*
5. Lycia: Olympos *268*
6. Lycia: Myra *273*
7. Pisidia: Termessos *277*
8. Selge *282*
9. Isparta and Sagalossos *285*
10. Water *292*

PART IV ❦ *Theatre and Tomb: Cyprus, 2001-2002*

1. Dionysos and Ariadne in Cyprus *297*
2. The Labyrinthine Theatre *302*
3. The Procession: the Pompe *304*
4. Layers *310*
5. Fragments *315*
6. The Fifth Century *319*
7. The Painted Wall Uncovered *322*
8. Emerging Colour and Spectacle *326*
9. The Divided City: Nicosia *331*
10. The Street *336*
11. Within the Walls *338*
12. Winter Paphos *343*
13. Amathus *348*
14. The Seventh Season *351*
15. Chances *352*
16. The Terebinth Tree *355*
17. The Tomb in Ikarou Street *358*

NOTES, BIBLIOGRAPHY
AND INDEX OF PROPER NAMES   Following page *365*

ACKNOWLEDGEMENTS

Australian archaeologists and artists are in Cyprus through the invitation of the Department of Antiquities. Professor Vassos Karageorghis first suggested exploring the Paphos theatre site to Professor Richard Green, and Dr Demos Christou gave permission to excavate, beginning in 1995. Dr Sophocles Hadjisavvas, the current director of the Department of Antiquities, and Dr Eustathios Raptou, the director of the Paphos District Museum, have greatly helped both the Australian excavation from the University of Sydney and my individual researches. The assistance of the staff of the Paphos District Museum has been invaluable, especially that of Neoptolemos Demetriou and Andreas Michaelides. The collegial environment and library facilities of the Cyprus American Archaeological Research Institute in Nicosia, under Dr Nancy Serwint and Dr Robert Merrillees, with Vathoulla Moustikki and Diana Constantides, have been crucial. I am grateful to Barbara Lyssarides for highlighting my writing. Professor Demetrios Michaelides of the University of Cyprus encouraged my research into frescoes.

In Turkey Professor Hüsamettin Koçan of the University of Marmara, Istanbul, smoothed my path to southern Turkey, while Edip Ösgür at the Antalya Museum gave expert advice and Dr Enis Tan from Suleyman Demirel University, Isparta, translated and facilitated remote journeys. Dr Norbert Zimmerman of the Austrian Archaeological Institute at Ephesos engaged me in a memorable conversation about Roman fresco painting. Jan Casson Medhurst gave great assistance at the Australian Institute of Archaeology in Athens. Professor Janis Jefferies arranged a visiting fellowship at the University of London.

The Australian team in Paphos has been the essential ingredient that brought the theatre back to life. Professor Richard Green of the University of Sydney, through his initial invitation to me in 1995 to join the team and re-awaken my archaeological training has been the pivot of the Paphos Theatre Excavation. My deepest thanks are due to him for offering me such a transformative experience. Fellow team members Josephine Atkinson, Craig Barker, Grahame Bond, Holly Cook, Anita Cvijanovic, Amanda Dusting, Dr Jonas Eiring, Glynnis Fawkes, Smadar Gabrieli, Anthea Garrod, Celeste Goulding, Brush

Gordon-Smith, Patti Henderson, Anne Hooton, John Kennedy, Dr Estelle Lazer, Jennie Lindbergh, Fran Keeling, Marcie McConville, Dr Ian McGrath, Robert Miller, Sam Moody, Patricia Priestley, Helen Joy Suliman, Anna Sophocles, Dr Edna Stern, Geoff Stennett, Archondia Thanos, John Tidmarsh, Kristina Winther Jacobsen, Christie Waddington and Robert Wood, among many others, all contributed key observations. Ian Arcus helped me greatly with his artistic expertise. Richard Anderson, Professor Pascale Ballet, and Dr John Hayes enlarged my understanding of antiquity. Mr A.H.S. (Peter) Megaw's kindness and deep knowledge were a source of wonder.

George and Crystalla Christodoulou of the Pyramos Hotel in Kato Paphos have provided constant guidance to Paphos village life, and essential support. To Kyria Athina Sophronio, Kyrie Costas Economou, Kyrie Antonios Koushis, and Dr Th. Theophilos warmest thanks. David and Marion Neville, and Dr Paul Croft, with members of the Paphos Archaeological Society, offered loyal support to the team.

For crucial help in Australia I was encouraged by the close friendship of artists and writers Professor Kay Lawrence, Liz Jeneid, and Dr Kurt Brereton. Dr Dorothy Jones discussed the intricacies of Ariadne in literature. Kate Llewellyn offered constant support and a perceptive reading of the manuscript. Jasleen Dhamija, Dr Ivor Indyk and Dr Evelyn Juers gave me generous critical insights. Dr Guy Warren encouraged me and gave me the indispensable travelling watercolour set used throughout my travels. I would like also to acknowledge Anton Veenstra, Hilary Rhodes, Hsiu-li Kuo, Emma Rutherford, Terrance Henningsen, Paul Kelly and Lycia Trouton for help with research and collegial support. Toby Macklin and Stephanie Amos provided invaluable editorial expertise.

My journeys were supported by study leave grants from the University of Wollongong. Without grants from the Australian Research Council, work in Paphos would not have been possible.

To my wonderfully loving family, my sons Nicholas and Rowan, my nephew Simon, my parents David and Marion Wood, greatest thanks. My mother's passionate interest has been an inspiration for my journeys. And much gratitude to my niece Alyson Wood, whose enthusiasm turned out to be vital.

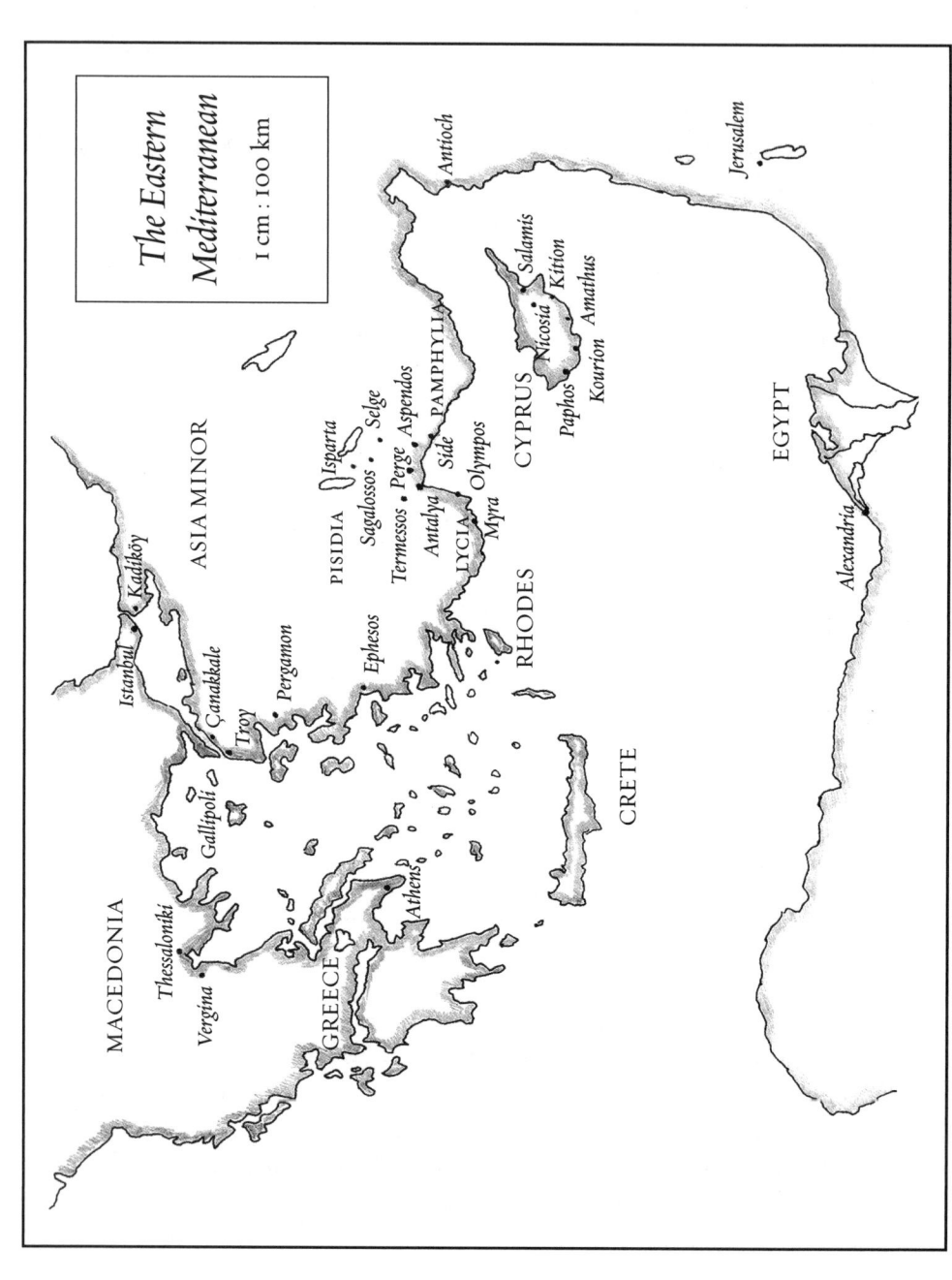

PREFACE

My journals of the Paphos theatre excavation in Cyprus extend over seven years, a span of time in which, it is said, all the cells of the body are renewed. In this time, the site reveals the shape of its hybrid past from under blankets of earth and a new performance begins in the ancient theatre. I, too, as one of the performers who bring the Hellenistic theatre to life again, am changed by this process of interacting every season with the site, and with the intricate unravelling of the strands of the excavation that open up the breadth and detail of forgotten histories. The past becomes as complex as the present, and intertwined with it. Tracing the threads of connection from the Hellenistic and Roman theatre led me eventually to travel from Cyprus across the eastern Mediterranean, to Anatolia, to Macedonia and to Alexandria, the curved edge of the landmass between Europe and Asia that was the original theatre for Alexander's almost mythical journeys.

PART I

The Orchestra:
The Paphos Theatre, 1995-1999

Charoupía or carob leaves from the Paphos theatre. Watercolour, 1997.

I. THE FIRST SEASON

Prelude, 1995

Midday. The car drove off and I was left alone at the site of old Paphos. The place seemed oddly familiar – perhaps the light reminded me of the jigsaw puzzle of the Mediterranean coast that I had so obsessively put together as a child, and then scattered to be reassembled again. The puzzle was called 'The villa garden'. Now an encompassing light poured down over a wide open landscape, gold with scattered olive trees in terraced slopes pierced by the occasional dark gaps of tombs.

The hot sun blazed silently, after the noise and racket of the road – just a few slow walkers wandering over the fragmentary mosaic floors, whitened by light. I felt so tired, so comfortable to be amongst these particular stones, that I lay down with my bag for a pillow under a solitary pine at the edge of the ruins, near a vast battered stone, and fell deeply asleep. On waking, refreshed, I looked carefully around – noting the sun on the stones, lizards, ants, sensed a cool breeze, and saw the dome of the low church in the village rising like a breast from beyond the bony ribs of the site. The once renowned sanctuary of Aphrodite is now occupied by the village of Kouklia on a high hill just inland from the coastal plain, with the sea a long blue ribbon winding around the horizon. Sleeping in sanctuaries was always considered auspicious in the ancient world, as the god may send a healing vision. The gift of that sleep to me was a sense of hope, of coming in sight of some dimly remembered home, of wonderful possibility, an augury perhaps of working years to come. This dreamless sleep on the ground was the beginning, foreshadowing a long engagement with the earth of Paphos, an obsessive assembling of fragments that would absorb me with an intentness like that of the child on the puzzle.

As I got to my feet a young Russian peering at the remains with a guidebook came over to me to ask urgently: 'Why was it all ruined? Why did people here destroy the past? The Greeks are as bad as my people.' His intensity was unusual, as if he really wanted to know, as if these questions were of fundamental importance and as if there could be some unofficial story that was not to be found in the guide. My ability to sleep on site seemed to imply I had some inner understanding of the place. But I had no answers.

I went to a small *kafeneion* in the village square of Kouklia. The only woman amongst all the men seated drinking coffee was the tired proprietor, who smilingly brought me egg, potatoes and salad, which I ate beside the men, who watched the empty square intently as if a performance were about to begin.

May 1995

My presence here is astonishing to me. As a visual arts lecturer in an Australian university, in Wollongong on the east coast south of Sydney, I have been invited by Professor Richard Green of the University of Sydney to come to the dig as an artist-in-residence, and to help with the management of the large team brought from Australia. My first degree had been in classical archaeology, with Richard as one of my lecturers, and as a young woman I had studied in Athens and worked as an archaeological illustrator in the Museum of Archaeology in Florence, Italy, and in the British Museum in London. On returning to Australia I had married and become an artist, a tapestry weaver, eventually taking up teaching in a university. Now my two sons were older, I dreamed of reconnecting with the ancient world so intensively studied as a young woman. A friend had said with insight that after my marriage ended I was mourning not only the end of a long relationship but also the loss of my early passionate connection to archaeology.

This invitation to Paphos is revealing a whole area of knowledge, the unknown island of Cyprus, distinct from Greece and yet haunted by their mutual history and language. In coming back to an archaeological site in the Mediterranean I unearth my own past as well as that of the site. As a young woman graduate in archaeology, Mediterranean antiquity was intensely familiar. I had lived in Athens and tried to speak and understand Greek. After many years the ancient past is again a fresh field to reconsider, its objects and sites have a new poignancy, a different fragility, at the end of the century. And I am returning to the sites of the ancient world with an orientation towards land and relationships gained through long work with Aboriginal artists. This may change the way I understand the rituals of the classical past.

Because of his expertise in the area of classical theatre imagery, Richard has been invited by the director of the Department of Antiquities in Cyprus to excavate the ancient theatre set into a hill in Paphos on the west coast of Cyprus. The theatre was built about 300 BC and was in use until around AD 400 when it fell into ruins and was used as a quarry. Substantial evidence of medieval walls and pottery show the site also to have been occupied into the nineteenth-century Ottoman period. Now the theatre is part of the prosperous tourist town of Kato (or Lower) Paphos, among old farmhouses and newer apartment blocks, on the edge of the World Heritage site where the antiquities of the Hellenistic city lie preserved, many of them still under the ground. Nothing can be removed from Cyprus, so foreign archaeologists abroad can only study the material through photographs and drawings.

The Australian excavation team of the Paphos theatre is made up of students and staff from the University of Sydney, several other Australian universities, and colleagues from international institutions. They will work for a six-week season each year to uncover sections of the seating, the *orchestra*, the stage structures and the associated road and buildings. The size of the team can swell to nearly sixty people, or shrink, in study seasons when there is less excavation, to ten or twenty. Each season there are groups of paying 'volunteers', usually mature professional people (doctors, lawyers, educators, engineers, artists) whose enthusiasm for archaeology helps to fund the excavation.

The half circle of the theatre is on the edge of the hill called Fabrika, which is part of the open grassy space around the port which must in antiquity have held all the old town of Paphos. Remains of the city wall are in place on the east, and Roman houses have been excavated to reveal exquisite mosaics of the second century AD. Earthquakes have shaken the old structures, theatre and sanctuaries were mined as quarries for building materials in the confused times after the fall of Rome. The theatre is hardly perceptible in its full semicircular form, as the *orchestra* is buried under debris to the depth of two or three metres.

The dig house for the Australians in Nea or New Paphos (new because it was founded in the fourth century BC, to be nearer to a functional port than the old Paphos) turned out to be an old four-bedroom house of some elegance. Inside are high ceilings and a curved bay window, with an irregular iron-trellised area outside the kitchen door, where you can sit to eat looking out at the theatre site. This became the outdoor eating area for up to fifty people. Together with another old farmhouse across the road, the house had been set aside by the Department of Antiquities for use by archaeological teams, such as the Italians and the Poles, involved in excavating different areas of the ancient city. Both houses were long abandoned by their owners, overgrown with the teeming plants of a wild garden – I found small almond and lemon trees, hibiscus, guavas and artichokes hidden by weeds and tumbled stones.

Housecleaning is fundamental. Four people including myself arrived ahead of the main team to organise the living quarters. John Tidmarsh, the field supervisor, was intent and organised, and Monica and Roz from luxurious Sydney suburbs were mature postgraduates in archaeology and ready to take on the task. Monica and I shopped in the Paradise Supermarket a few streets away for all kinds of cleansers. (It turns out to be well named, as every variety of item is available, as if the owners had uncannily predicted what a group of archaeologists might need – everything from disinfectant to tissue paper, cutlery to alcohol and goat's cheese). Roz attempted the bathroom, and together we worked all day, a sunny blue day, to make spaces habitable. John collected the camp beds, loaned by the army, and tried to find and purchase essential tools. Fortunately the water seemed to be flowing in the taps, and the gas stove was finally persuaded to light. We cleaned out the deeply encrusted fridge, which appeared to be still functioning, and then started on the garden, working very hard to clear waist-high weeds and garbage – old chairs, rags, containers. I found useful things – a file, a screwdriver, a rubbish scoop; what pleasure to make a functioning house out of such desolation.

In breathing spaces between tasks I observe my companions, who are very experienced in excavations. John is a medical specialist with a practice that he sometimes sets aside to engage with his other life as an archaeologist. He had been excavating at Pella in Jordan, and had recently discovered bodies crushed by earthquakes, with gold coins in their pockets. He told us as we waded through the debris of cleaning up, 'I think the past in its essentials is no different from the present – certainly needing spaces to live in and essential tools and utensils.'

In the surrounds of our two houses luxuriant date palms, an olive and a bay tree tangle with a pink rose bush and lean over towards the remains of an apricot orchard in a wilderness of prickly pear. A fragmentary domed oven contains a mummified cat. I stumble over a column base in the weeds in the garden, near old font-like stones carved to hold water. Could it be part of a well? Inside, the dim shuttered rooms are heaped with old clothes, broken furniture, plastic toys and containers. I mop the lovely worn marble floors for temporary sleeping quarters while John removes spider webs and makes a shelf. He comments, his mouth full of nails, 'We need to see the titles for this house – it's probably in the middle of a *temenos* or sanctuary. Really, we should dig here as well.' The place seems protean, each stone full of a possible meaning in an unshaped past. Later Richard says he has a 'mad hope' that what will be beneath the garden of the old house will be the sanctuary of Aphrodite. I read Mimnermos from the seventh century BC in my worn book of Greek poetry. 'What would life be, what pleasure without golden Aphrodite?' Paphos was her birthplace and her domain.[1]

The marvel is that both old houses are built right beside the theatre, at the base of Fabrika Hill. At the height of the season twenty women will camp in the 'Villa Aphrodite', while the squarer farmhouse where the men have their dormitory becomes known as 'Sodom and Gomorrah'. The five smaller rooms opening on to a verandah are designated 'Palm Court' and are set up for the office, as a photographic and conservation laboratory, as a room for drawing and as areas for sorting and cataloguing finds. Activities spill out of the rooms all around, with stone architectural fragments used as seats. Other smaller houses in various states of decay are lent to the excavation, and there will be constant emergencies with plumbing, and a chronic shortage of hot water. Many of the older team members, including myself, choose to pay extra and stay in the simple hotel, the Pyramos, five minutes walk away, owned by George and Crystalla, whose generosity and local knowledge become essential to the welfare of the team.

It occurs to me how ironic it is for Australians to be discovering old 'new worlds'. To be returning to classical Europe is in itself a reversal of the nineteenth-century movement to colonise and 'civilise' the distant Antipodes. Walking and wondering along the dark road from the village shops to the theatre for the first time that evening (a walk made innumerable times in succeeding years) – I asked Richard, 'Why bring Australians to excavate a Hellenistic theatre?'

'It's good training for classical archaeologists to dig,' he said, 'and we can't do this kind of work at home. The Ptolemaic Alexandrian theatre is very significant in the history of theatre and Paphos obviously had close connections to her sister city of Alexandria, which was founded at about the same time in 320 BC.' The road was very dark and rough under our feet with a smell of dust, and ultramarine clouds pricked with stars were just visible moving across the sky.

He went on: 'Not many theatres of this early Hellenistic period are known, and the place of the theatre within the town of Paphos itself is of great significance. We don't know the exact shape of the seats and their angle to the *orchestra* – the theatre is not the typical Hellenistic horseshoe, but a semicircle.' The dig house loomed up by the road. We lit candles in the dark rooms, and fell into our canvas beds.

I sleep well in my creaky bed in the one swept room, without sheets. Waking suddenly at dawn with great excitement I rush first to look at the theatre ruin, in the pale gold clarity of early light. The stones of the tiered seats are covered with long meadow grass, poppies, asphodels and yellow daisies. I search for and find the few engraved letters, iota, theta, pi, omega, delta, etched but still inscrutable in the first rays of sun. These letters are crucial in the dating of the site. The low, raking light of dawn and dusk can reveal secret markings, odd dimples, faded indications of past use in battered stones that seem to have no secrets in the harsh light of midday. Richard was already there, in his old hat, kneeling on the stones peering intently at the lie of the land, planning his strategy of uncovering the past like any general.

He and John were talking of key approaches for digging – first removing the baulks or walls from Grimm's trench. (The German archaeologist Grimm had made an attempt to dig the site in the 1980s, but had not persisted.) Several more exploratory trenches would be placed to the east, to get down to the lower level of the seats and clear them. There's too much 'overburden', they said, on the top of the *orchestra* (the flat circular area in front of the stage building), including a terraced wall three metres high in places. There's also a small stone house where a farmer lived until recently, and most strikingly a giant terebinth tree growing in the centre of the theatre's semicircle, spreading over the site. It must have been planted a hundred years ago, during the Ottoman period, for its mastic, and for its oily berries which can be used as a poor substitute for olive oil.

To excavate is like planning an artwork, the results are never certain, it's a risk, and there is an element of chance, even luck, involved in such choices. Looking at the bare traces of the ancient theatre with new companions in a whole new terrain, I feel like an explorer seeing an unknown land emerging on the horizon.

2. FRAGMENTS FROM THE EXCAVATION

19 March 1996

A windy dawn, with eucalyptus trees outside the hotel roaring. It's still cold, and the whole site has a cooler aspect than during my brief sojourn in the previous season. It is such a pleasure to have gained permission from my institution to be here, this time bringing students from my university and also my two sons, Nicholas, who is nineteen, and Rowan, who is fourteen, to work as team members. My nephew Simon, seventeen years old, is also here to complete the family.

The village is so inconsequential within the greater town of Paphos – winding streets with small buildings, and amongst them, ruins, and low Byzantine churches. It's hard to imagine what it might have looked like in antiquity, the surface of the earth has received such a battering.

The beautiful old terebinth tree in the middle of what may have been the stage area is just coming into leaf. In all the pockets and crevices of the cut rock that formed the base of the seats, tiny white and pink cyclamens are in flower. The asphodels have nearly finished, the yellow daisies, black-centred vermilion poppies and wild grasses are abundant, as well as tiny purple irises. I've noticed how ruins attract flowers as if the debris of so much past life formed a kind of natural fertiliser. People are gone, but the flowers come up every year, despite the site being cleared so thoroughly, scoured and brushed for excavation only a year ago.

The process of excavation could appear like a kind of ceremony. The team consists of thirty-five people, mostly students from the University, both very young and mature and it is amazing what can be done in an hour with so many. Everyone is here in distant Cyprus after much planning, through the connivance of families and friends. The site is approached with reverence and hope, the soil and stones probed for signs that may reveal what is beneath. The earth is the repository of secrets and the only way to decipher the layers and debris is through meticulous excavation. The earth, as the trowels begin to scratch the surface, is full of potsherds, bones, varying textures from gravel to sticky clay.

Only when the scientific apparatus, the grid, the intricate measuring devices that form the basis of this whole archaeological process, are clearly in place can the earth be read with any degree of certainty. In pits and trenches the diggers scrape and shovel, with great attention – from the chaos of the earth tiny fragments of information can be gleaned. Indigenous people in Australia make large clearings on the ground and construct ditches and mounds, around which they spend a great deal of time performing rituals whose intensity forms a curious parallel to the devotion of archaeologists to their trenches.

Theatres and sanctuaries are inextricably connected in the Hellenistic world. To wear the mask of theatrical performance is to take on another persona, which allows the actor to come to the edge of normal reality, and this must be sanctioned by the deity. Sanctuaries of Dionysos are common to theatres, but it is also possible that Aphrodite may have had a sanctuary close to the performance area.

So many people excavating the site make a considerable impact even in a day. Six trenches are being dug, some continuing from last season, with some new ones being started at the top of the site where the wind is strong, and at the sides, with the hope of determining the full extent of the seating cut into the rock.

21 March

A venerable archaeologist came for lunch yesterday, Peter Megaw, who has worked in Cyprus since the 1930s. As the weather turned from overcast and raining to a beautiful spring afternoon, I took him to the top trench with its wonderful view of the whole spread of Paphos. He pointed out the cyclamens in the white rocks, as we went slowly up the hill. Here the diggers are uncovering medieval walls – a lovely crenellated fragment of blue turquoise pottery came to light, which my friend with his acute eye identified as medieval. This trench will go down to bedrock, to see what may be found. Just beyond, the large cuttings in the rock at the top of the hill form a rectangle and are supposed to belong to a temple of Aphrodite – 'but if we wanted to discover anything there, it would have been too late even a thousand years ago,' said Peter. This is because the hill has been washed away by earthquake and rain, and the great measured stones of the Greek and Roman temples long ago quarried for other buildings. In the Second World War the vast underground tombs and quarries of Fabrika Hill were used as a military hospital. My friend remembered the earliest museum of Paphos, begun in 1936 when he first came to Cyprus. A young school teacher from the then village of Paphos went to the city of Nicosia to see him when he was working as director of the Department of Antiquities in the British Government, and a museum was set up in a corner of the Paphos High School.

The site looks as if a small earthquake has taken place – mounds of earth, stripped to bedrock in many places. The terebinth tree seems the only firmly rooted and stable element in the whole scene. Little meadows of wild grains, poppies and daisies wave in the cool wind, despite the fact that they are imminently threatened by their position on the site. The trenches are like wounds, revealing the bony depths, walls and inarticulate bedrock, beneath the outer flesh of the soft earth with its layer of ephemeral flowers.

Paphos has beautiful skies and sunsets, I noticed on my evening walks, great heaped cumulus clouds, and clarity of air, sometimes lacking in Attica now. An almost new moon at the moment, and a large planet hanging in the unfamiliar western sky – could it be Venus? Lawrence Durrell claims the Aphrodite of Paphos to be a 'symbol, not of licence and sensuousness, but of the dual nature of man – the proposition which lay at the heart of the ancient religions from which she had been derived and to which her legend itself was the most enduring and poetic of European illustrations. She belonged to a world of innocence outside the scope of the barren sensualities which are ascribed to her cult.'[2]

24 March

The issue of philosophical meaning is not really discussed among archaeologists; what is important are the logical connections across the site in the process of excavation and analysis. Beautiful and accurate description can result from this emphasis on material and factual evidence. But the ideas of French structuralism have opened out the rigid discipline I knew as a student, bringing in elements from literature and poetry. To understand the place of the theatre, according to Richard, is to reevaluate the underestimated importance of festivals in ancient Greek life, particularly the element of sacrifice. In the great ceremony of leading the animal to sacrifice, the animal must consent, and in order to be killed must nod its head to grant permission. Water was thrown gently to make the beast nod and shake its head.

After a week I now have the storeroom set up – the window reveals a neglected garden of prickly pear and old almond trees. I scrubbed the room with harpic and bleach to try and get rid of the smell of cat. (The handsome shoddy builder told me in his thick accent that a cat had been inadvertently locked in the room for a week.) The walls are disintegrating and stained in an interesting way – it's the old kitchen, and rain comes down the chimney into the raised fireplace. An old woman who made yoghurt for the whole village used to live here, a nice spirit to have around. I put a column capital as a support for the improvised table top where it will now be possible to draw. All the finds from last season are in boxes on the other side, on shelves put up by Ken, the thin and energetic volunteer who comes to archaeology after a career as a forensic policeman.

The finds are very interesting – yesterday a bit of terracotta dog figurine with traces of a hair pattern, and a part of a large marble bowl, with claw chisel marks. I love the tiny *tesserae* from mosaics and the jewels of glazed earthenware of the Byzantine period. The lingua franca of the site is red unglazed earthenware, from Late Roman to medieval times – almost eight hundred years.

Yesterday was bitterly cold, despite the sun, with an icy wind. It's too cold for drawing outside, though I scrutinise the site as usual – it has a compelling quality for me, even while I am working inside. I have made a list of plants growing on the site that I can recognise: almond, lemon, terebinth, carob, pomegranate, prickly pear, olive, bay and palm. The smaller plants are yellow daisies, poppies, asphodel, wormwood, a few orchids, white clusters of wild garlic, a small yellow pea, a tiny pink pea, purple irises, and in rock crevices, cyclamens. Also I've found sorrel and rocket, and a bluebell. Pythagoras believed that the asphodel and mallow offered the perfect natural food, such as the gods might have eaten, and therefore humans who ate these plants, or who offered them as a sacrifice, showed their affinity with the deities.

The mosaics of the Roman palaces about fifteen minutes' walk to the west of the site offer another dimension. I am overwhelmed by the flickering stony images of the birth of Dionysos from the fourth century in the House of Aion, and the optical patterns in the ruined basilica close to the port, open to the sky. Pagan and Christian seem to mingle. The Byzantine period is the longest – as in Greece, there's been no Renaissance, but a medieval period that extended to the nineteenth century. As I write this, the long drawn-out chant wafts over the town from the basilica church, St Mary Covered with Cloud, a block away. I see it from my hotel balcony rising above the hotch-potch backyards like an indomitable small mountain. The round curves and domes of these Greek Orthodox churches seem to relate them closely to mosques. There's a closed and disintegrating mosque in the upper town, among small poor houses in what was once the Turkish quarter. It's a good place to find cardboard boxes from the food warehouses to store finds.

Winckelmann, who first described and wrote of the antique past, is supposed to have exalted the plain frame, 'his most beloved perfect order of divisions'.[3] The way we impose order on the ungovernable fragments and layers of the site is through the grid, the measure, which would not have surprised Winckelmann, who had understood the mathematical model as the underlying force in architectural harmony. There's great satisfaction in this grid. From large grids of metres to tiny grids of millimetres – I drew a centimetre grid yesterday for the photographer to place beside objects – this net holds it all together to give structure and significance to seemingly unrelated finds. The mosaic is another kind of grid where positive and negative spaces are of equal importance.

A sunny morning on site except when a great cloud crossed the sky, and we all grew chill. I did a rubbing of a newly discovered marking in the rock, faint lines and a circle, and made another diameter chart. A coin found in the trench to the side of the seats is as yet unidentified, and some vivid medieval ware came from the top trench. The Garden trench from which so much is expected has foul-smelling black soil with large animal bones. So many textures and colours of soil – what must it contain? Rowan (my son) painted a flower like an asphodel, but with tube-like leaves – it must be a smaller species – he did it quite exquisitely. He is learning, as a fourteen-year-old, to work in a disciplined pattern. Relationships in this team of diverse people are complex, it's a network that encompasses this very strange activity of stripping back the earth, of unstitching, and unpicking the fibrous soil to reveal its solidities of bone, ceramic and stone.

26 March

Today a small bronze figurine of Athena turned up in the Garden trench, together with lovely architectural stones from a Roman architrave, possibly Julio-Claudian. Such a tremor of excitement went through everyone on the site. Her helmet is visible through all the encrustations, her hand raised to hold a spear. And in the huge cut that traces the steps of the seating carved from the hill, the round of a column appeared, and a tiny fragile glass perfume vessel. It is miraculous to see these objects being lifted from the soil – the gems of the unconscious earth. What I am noticing is the enormous richness of vision, how looking goes from the wide view, the huge picture, the vast sky, to tiny detail, to pixels of information. The difficulty of teaching students to draw pots emphasises this – vision is as complex as language.

27 March

I compiled a list of known earthquakes over a thousand years, so that we can see if our fallen walls and tumbles of fragments are related. A cold grey day, lots of earth moving and lifting of rocks and column fragments, with a large mechanical crane lent by the Paphos Municipality poised above the Garden trench.

29 March

So nice to get out of Paphos to the village of Fiti, into the striated chalky hills, patterned with terraces and twisted vines not yet in leaf. Fiti is small with winding streets and many empty houses, but charming. We drove just beyond the village and found a hill with a vast view over mountains to a distant snow-covered peak and had a delicious lunch of fresh *horiatico* or country bread, fetta, fat black olives from Athens, tomatoes and cucumbers. Up where it's higher and cooler the asphodels are marvellously abundant (though I'm not at all tempted to eat any, despite Pythagoras) and there are green new crops — but few of the hedge plants in full leaf. The yellow flowers of a rocket-like plant were profuse. Rocket, says my plant guidebook, is a well-known medicinal plant and 'is esteemed to be an excellent aphrodisiac. As Dioscurides in this respect stresses "being eaten raw in any quantity doth provoke venery".'[4]

The deep silence of that profound space was a relief. One hawk hovering. But so many terraces abandoned, the intimacy of this once fervently cultivated landscape is going back to asphodel and thistle. We looked at an abandoned farmstead just on the edge of the village — a roof had collapsed, a loom once strong lay outside a barn, a piece of fine cotton still tied to an upright. In the village found a café with a loom being used, but the owner who had returned from South Africa after forty years said there were only a few old women doing it now — it wasn't being passed on. 'Only pensioners in Fiti,' he said, 'only a few old people out of a town of formerly six hundred, and all the young ones gone.' Then on to a small church high in pine forests — Nicholas and Rowan wanted forests. So quiet, with the colours of the pines forming a kind of blue mist. Hyacinths, occasionally.

30 March

Today is overcast and cool, but with sunny patches. In the work spaces of our old peasant house, I love the continually shifting tables of sherds with their glints of colour and whole forms — a loom weight, a bowl from a Turkish pipe, a handle. There are discussions about the most minute variations of colour in the fabric of a clay, on whether the mica atoms are silvery gold or gold coloured, indicating a different origin. From such minutiae archaeologists reach conclusions about the wide patterns of material culture. The ability to remember a host of textures, colours and details of construction creates a mnemonics of vision that is the basis of the discipline.

Today there is a delicate light on the sides of buildings, like a Morandi painting, blurring the soft gold of sandstones. The Garden trench has uncovered, one and a half metres down, an extraordinary road paved with huge slabs worn smooth with traffic. Underneath the road there appears to be a substantial drain, and the large stone with a hole bored through it with a fitting lid indicates even a toilet. The diggers complain there is still an awful smell. It is amazing that smells should last so long — like finding a sound, a voice from the past captured in a vacuum. But the drain area is rich in coins not identified because so corroded, as well as rich in odours.

Athina the Paphiot cook made a wonderful pork dish cooked with cinnamon and spices, flavoured with bay, and cracked wheat pilaf with yoghurt. Every day I meet her to discuss cooking lunch for the team within our budget. She gives me marvellous lists of foods written in Greek for me to buy in bulk at the supermarket.

4 April

I walked on the Fabrika Hill early, so radiant with all the flowers, clusters of cyclamens like white flames going down into the dark entrances of tombs.

Scylla, that creature of unresolved contradictions, seems appropriate to my mood today, so I went to the House of Dionysos and looked at the strange Hellenistic image made in tiny black and white pebbles. She has the majestic head and breast of a goddess, regally holding a trident, but her body below the waist divides into the foreparts of three leaping dogs and attached to her back is the serrated body of a sea serpent. Apparently, she was made a monster through excess of loving. The guidebook says: 'This horrid monster was once a girl. Glaucus loved her but she did not return his affections. For this reason he sought the help of the sorceress Circe. Unfortunately, Circe herself was in love with Glaucus and on finding her love rejected she tried to eliminate her rival. She mixed magic herbs and juices and poured them into the little bay where Scylla used to rest when the day was at its hottest. Scylla came to the bay and descended into the water up to her waist when the lower part of her body was suddenly transformed into that of a horrid monster. Scylla never left the bay again and gave vent to her misery by sinking all the ships that came her way.'[5] So Scylla's monstrosity was entirely the product of other people's machinations. Her lack of response made her 'monstrous' from the waist down. *Skylla* in modern Greek is a female dog.

The animals on the site are poignant somehow – I at last found the mysterious camel that had appeared like a hallucination on the site. He was shut in an empty tomb on Fabrika, staring out from the ramshackle barrier rather morosely. The lovely long-faced sheep, so tame, roam over the grassy ruins near the sea with the weather-beaten shepherd. The sheep are the same colour as the battered rocks. From the sea wall I also saw a huge bull grazing, like another remnant of dark tomb rock. There's so much untidiness and haphazard building in the rapidly growing tourist areas. Yet still there are overgrown, silent patches of greenery which are found to contain an old blocky house, deeply enshrouded in almonds and figs, with giant artichokes showing above piled-up rocky walls. These are the abodes of the old women in black, still around, still entrenched in old traditions – the open doors reveal pictures of saints, rows of rush-bottomed chairs, a flowery plastic tablecloth. They must be the ones who keep the candles burning in the innumerable tiny churches. They are almost invisible among the bustle and money making of the tourist streets, fragments of another life, like the Turkish fountains, and odd bits of Frankish wall.

5 April

It has been hot and sunny the last three days, so that I have walked early on Fabrika, until breakfast at seven. The light is brilliant and the whole landscape intensely cultured – nothing is 'natural'; everything has been built on, or dug into, layer upon layer, and the process repeated after each earthquake. The flowers and grasses soften this waste – but even the trees are cultivated rather than wild, pomegranate and almond, terebinth and mulberry.

Our hotel, Pyramos, is named after the Pyramos and Thisbe mosaic in the House of Dionysos, in another section of the palatial apartments. Ovid's story is the origin of the Romeo and Juliet motif of two beautiful young people from hostile families falling in love. They met in secret by a mulberry tree that grew by a spring. One day Thisbe arrived first and while she was waiting for her lover a lioness came to drink at the spring, her jaws dripping blood from an animal she had just killed. Thisbe ran in great fear to hide, but dropped her veil, which the animal tore to pieces. When Pyramos arrived he found the torn and bloody veil and in great despair ran his sword into his side, spraying the mulberries dark red. When Thisbe emerged and found him dead, she also took her own life, and in memory of the fated lovers the mulberry fruit has stayed purple ever after. The Pyramos and Thisbe story was repeated almost as a farce by Shakespeare in *A Midsummer Night's Dream*, and something of this ineptitude is found in the mosaic, where Pyramos, wreathed in water weeds is mistakenly represented as a river god, holding a cornucopia. Perhaps the artist mistook the character for another Pyramos, a river in Asia Minor. This charming mistake, in all the diversity of mythological characters, makes the mosaicist seem very present.[6]

Today I went out along the sea wall of the old city, a cloudy indigo pale morning, with touches of cerulean in the sky. A party of English birdwatchers with very complicated equipment were staring at the empty sea. The flock of sheep streamed past me, followed slowly by the shepherd in ancient clothes, his jacket moulded to him. He seemed to be collecting long shoots from within the thorn bushes that grow everywhere. I drew the rectangular cistern, a mirror reflecting the sky set in a rather desolate landscape of piles of earth and gravel, and heaps of old stones. The scene evokes early nineteenth-century drawings – the melancholy 'pleasure of ruins'. The new desolation is the endless unplanned streets of concrete hotels and tourist shops, so much larger in scale than anything in antiquity that has survived. The ruins are valued because the tourists want to see them, they are a potential source of income. Yet the same cycle could just conceivably occur – a devastating earthquake, new heaps of rubble to be built over. The pattern of earthquakes is so consistent over the past two thousand years. The seismic centre is appropriately situated off Petrou tou Romiou, the rocks on the coast where Aphrodite is supposed to have come from the foam.

7-8 April

Looking at the depths of the past in our newly opened trenches, how transient our individuality is, the great commonplaces are really all that we will be remembered for – being born, doing some particular activity, having families, dying at a particular time. Perhaps that's why I find stories so engrossing that give glimpses into people's lives, details that are missing from the archaeological record. In the small family taverna where we sometimes eat, the fisherman owner told me in his slow voice, his great spade-like hands placing home-made wine in brandy bottles on the table, that he came to Paphos from the north coast of Cyprus twenty years ago. He never went to school, he told me, but sailed with his father on fishing trips. 'Often we would look over the side of the boat into the clear water and see ruined cities deep below.'

Later Nicholas, Kylie, Rowan, Simon and I went off to Kourion near Limassol, squeezed into a tiny rented car – on this day of intense light and blueness, with a cold wind. We stopped at the Temple of Apollo poised on cliffs above the sea and sat on the steps of the 'display area' to eat the delicious picnic lunch I had brought. (Ruins do seem to bring on the appetite.) Rowan loved this site – set in a young pine forest scattered with rock roses. Apollo here was called Apollo Hylates, the god of the forest, and there has been a sanctuary here since Mycenaean times – high up, looking out over the great blue arc of the sea. 'If one had to build a temple, this is certainly the place,' said Simon. The Queen Anne's lace is flowering everywhere, 'like little doilies on stalks,' he said. They muck around like young puppies, hugging and pushing. Despite the frantic growth of the coastal towns the old sites are often abandoned, in such wild, windy and remote places that people no longer live there.

Kourion itself, on a cliff edge, is spectacular. There are haunting images in the House of Eustolios built in my favourite late-Roman period which juxtaposes pagan and Christian images with a pervasive ambivalence. The mosaics must have been installed while most of the Roman city still lay in ruins from an earthquake, never to be rebuilt. They are very beautiful – fish and birds enclosed by geometric panels and a touching mosaic inscription – 'In place of big stones and solid iron, gleaming bronze and even adamant, this house is girt by the much venerated sign of Christ.'[7]

The delicacy of the imagery suggests a refinement of choice, a large vocabulary of form, and also an interiority, a philosophical approach, as the Roman world slowly disintegrated. Devastating earthquakes helped in the late fifth and sixth centuries. Another inscription reads 'The sisters Reverence, Prudence and Piety tend the platform and this fragrant hall.'[8] In the meticulously constructed bathhouse is the memorable mosaic bust of a woman – named KTISIS – the founding spirit of creation, large eyes, and an expression full of longing. Eustolios constructed the bathhouse as he says in another mosaic inscription – how curiously longlasting these tiny *tesserae* are, though exposed to sun, rain and wind – 'Eustolios, having seen the Kourians, although previously very wealthy, were in abject misery, did not forget the city of his ancestors but first having presented the baths to our city, he then took care of Kourion as once did Phoebus Apollo, and built this cool refuge sheltered from the winds.'[9]

I drew the pink convolutions of the wild rose in the garden during a pause in a very busy and fragmented day, rather cold and grey. I looked at the wonderful engravings of the sixteenth to eighteenth centuries in a book of classical architecture, and absorbed the depth of nuanced tone. This contrast of light and dark is the most satisfying element in drawing ruins and makes a repetitive order out of even a fragment – a column, a row of steps – in the general chaos of the landscape.

Le Corbusier, that essential modernist, claims classical antecedents – 'It is the Acropolis made a rebel of me. One clear image will stand in my mind forever: the Parthenon. Stark, stripped, economical, violent; a clamorous outcry against a landscape of grace and terror. All strength and purity.'[10]

Poetics and rhetoric were the backbone of classical culture and I realised again how this included visual forms. Rhetoric was both 'to instruct and persuade' at a time when oral skills were vital. Aristotle discussed the *techne*, the skill, of composition so that the results could be applied to any subject, any class of thing. Poetics (from *poiein*, to make) dealt universally with the ordering and distribution of matter, the place to which each thing is to be assigned within the order of the whole. 'The whole,' states Aristotle, 'is tripartite; it has a beginning, a middle and an end.' In other words, say Tzonis and Lefaivre, all classical works, whether in words, sounds or shapes, are identifiable by their strict adherence to the schema that demarcates a realm of departure, a central realm and a realm of arrival.[11] How different this is from our aesthetic of fragmentation and shifting meanings.

10 April

A concert 'Lament and Praise' in St Paul's Basilica, the tiny barrel-vaulted church – with of all things, Dido's 'Lament,' and another haunting piece by Purcell, 'Man that is of woman born'. Despite musical flaws I enjoyed it immensely, such a marvellous sound, there is a remorseless grid from the bass underneath Dido's flowing range, which I had not picked up before. Classical music well named, the same *taxis* in place, the same grid with variations. The rounded heavy stone roof seemed to bring the sound down around one. I watched the inconostasis, the icon-stand in front of the altar. There is the popular Archangel Michael, with the crucifix above, and small panels of Mary – always in a red cloak here – and St John, both in attitudes of mourning.

Every day I pass by the little solid chapel in the main square. It's a mess inside, old candle wax, bottles of fuel for lamps and the icons are covered in lace curtains, because of Easter, possibly. The Panayia, the Virgin, is an old nineteenth-century print – a sentimental but charming face, holding a little man somewhat apart on her lap. Always, candles burn with the heavy smell of incense, which reminds me of being young. The same print appears in all the old churches. And there's a little shrine to the Panayia strangely built into the side of a pub bar, run by an Australian Cypriot, just near the chapel.

A very odd and rather repellent shrine is in part of what may have been the south-east face of the ancient city wall – an odd rock formation jutting from the old site, like a cave, with rags pushed in all the crevices. Inside, the usual organised clutter of old wax and plastic bottles of fuel, and disintegrating paper images of saints and the Virgin. On the floor a large crude image in wax of half a body, other organs – liver? heart? – hung up nearby. Who looks after and goes to these chapels? It must be those secretive black-clothed women, living in their leafy one-room houses.

11 April

The team is stressed by the amount to be done in the next two weeks. The conservator is absorbed, sitting at the end of a long table covered in bottles and containers, delicately prodding coins and the little bronze Athena who fizzes in her electric cleansing bath, so that details gradually emerge. A very large deposit of coins turns up near bedrock in the Garden trench. An intricate pattern of drains, soundly constructed under the main street-paving suggests a largeness of planning not evident in the Byzantine period, where walls are scrappy and recycled. Just the way a stone is cut can indicate a broadness of vision, implying complex equipment to lift and cut, cranes and pulleys, and skilled men. The beautiful wall in the western trench may well indicate the original retaining wall.

A very strange feeling looking into the two complete Garden trenches, like binoculars into a buried and forgotten past. Custom continues, individuals are forgotten – the road and the shrines are aligned today in a similar direction, but individual achievements and possessions have irretrievably faded. The lost objects of the drain of late antiquity are the treasures of the late twentieth century. I am moved by the innumerable boxes of small finds, the crusty bone, the glinting and tarnished glass of such fineness, heavy unreadable bronze coins (now over one hundred of them).

The museum attendant, Demetrios, and the bulldozer driver say to cook the artichokes that are growing in the garden either boiled with only a little lemon, or baked whole with meat and potatoes in the oven.

12 April

Yesterday was slightly cloudy and overcast, though warm. Tensions are building as the need to order the mass of material, and reach the bottom of trenches becomes imperative in the next two weeks. The sherds continue to spread out across the whole garden in an irregular grid, attracting many tourists. Fascinating pieces – some intriguing glazed fragments with figures, a little Roman moulded dolphin from the rim of a vase.

Peter Megaw visits the site – to my great pleasure. His presence calls up the almost vanished world of colonial archaeology, in his tweed coat and tie and the precision of his speech. His understanding of Cypriot archaeology is profound, though he tells us that knowledge of this dark-age area we seem to be in, this period from AD 500 to 700, is very uncertain. He speaks with fervour of an earthquake in the mid-seventh century, around the time of the Arab sack of Paphos, when the little harbour church was turned into a mosque. Bending over a tray of sherds he says the ring-handled amphorae may possibly be Arab, from Palestine, and the slipware starts coming from Egypt after the decline of Rome about AD 500 – but that Roman types of wares continue to be made until the seventh century. The churches mostly hold the cultural record for this dark period, so new evidence from a theatre site may be of great importance. It may be that there are remnants of a small chapel in the Garden trench – a cross on a cylindrical stone comes up in a new trench.

Conservation techniques are stripping the encrustations from several of the coins so that strong images emerge – an arrogant profile, a deity seated with a lyre. So moving to have images out of that foul and greasy dirt, such vivid signs.

14 April

The feast of Paskha (Easter) approaches in overcast and rainy weather. Church bells toll all evening, and a constant stream of black-clothed women head towards St Mary Covered With Cloud, the church I can see from my hotel balcony. (Built in 1923 on the site of a much older one, the former church was miraculously saved by the Lord from Arab invaders in the seventh century by being covered in a thick mist.) On a late walk I find the beautiful mosaic fragments of St Paul's basilica, just behind the hotel. Earthquake tremors take place at night and also at four in the afternoon.

19 April

The increasing furor of digging is matched by turbulent weather, occasional heavy rain and a bleak east wind. Someone told me that the bombing of Lebanon by Israel (so close by) had disturbed the normal patterns of air over Cyprus, resulting in this chilly and inauspicious atmosphere, a fearful tension. Pindar writes of the 'liquid sky' as a vault above aspiring humanity, and insists on what seems an impossible hope. 'But human excellence grows like a vine tree, fed by the green dew, raised up among wise men and just, to the liquid sky.'[12]

26 April

Of particular wonder to me are the painted plaster fragments from the fine retaining wall – there seem to be plant tendrils in a pure emerald, smudges of indigo and madder. To find colour after so much time is like finding a smell. And one of the heavy Roman coins from the drain has been cleaned by the conservator and reveals a word, FELICITAS, a sign from the past that we must surely take seriously.

The site has been swept, tidied for photography, and the digging has stopped, just when it seemed more tantalising features of the *orchestra* might be uncovered. It looks like a strange earthwork tiered with rough stone steps and with geometric trenches carved meticulously from the earth. Flowers and green grasses have almost disappeared. The trenches have destroyed the ordinary curve of the land in giving birth to this stony, ruined but so evocative theatre, this centre for the imagination both then and now. The passion of the diggers for the site and its processes reminds me of sculptors handling clay or metal, except this is a sculpture in reverse – subtraction of substance and absence are the signs of this artwork.

The little bronze Athena is finally revealed intact, except for her shield and spear, mistress of *techne* above all, of stratagems and skills against the untamed forces that so often gather against reason. She was goddess of war, as well as of weaving. Perhaps this unique combination explained her continued popularity as Minerva. She could even provide a role model in the digital age. After all, computer circuit boards are descended from the punch cards of complex drawlooms, and her helmet, shield and spear all give her a cyborg compatibility.

Like an earth sculpture or a ground prepared for a specific ritual event, the site is now frozen and static, its brushed surfaces photographed and drawn. As I prepare to leave at the end of the excavation season, the shapes, textures, light and shadow of this remnant of a theatre is engraved on my memory. There's a glimpse of the architectural daring of that precise, measured half-circle set into the hillside, where the still engrossing conundrums of fate, fortune, and the arbitrariness of chance were once played out. In setting out to discover the sanctuary behind the theatre what was in fact revealed was the old road, with its drains and toilet. Tyche or Chance must be smiling ironically as those potent drains are uncovered, rather than the much desired sanctuary. Despite continuing adherence to the grid, to meticulous systems of excavation, the past here comes to light as elusive and unresolved fragments, without the satisfaction of completion or any final ordering.

3. WREATHS OF STRING AND SACRED STONES

Palaepaphos, 26 March 1996

On a violently windy grey afternoon I take the three young women, Anna, Lynne and Robin from Wollongong, to visit Aphrodite's temple at Palaepaphos – the sun a lurid disk behind tearing clouds as we fight the wind to walk up to the ruins.

Paphos is Aphrodite's town, and her legendary birthplace from the sea is still visited by hundreds of tourists at Petrou tou Romiou, where white rocks emerge from the pebbly beach south of Paphos. This site of old Paphos, where I began the journey, is on a high hill above the sea, fifteen kilometres from the theatre site in New or Nea Paphos. It is conjectured that there was a pilgrims' way between the eastern gate of the city of Nea Paphos, just at the edge of the theatre, and the temple, famous throughout the ancient world. Its pointed roof and columns sheltered a remarkable 'aniconic' stone, a stone 'without an image'. This roughly triangular stone appeared on coins inside the portico of the temple, which must have been visible to ships approaching land. Aphrodite was the goddess of sailors, as she was born from the sea, from the semen of the genitals of Uranus, thrown into the sea by the Titan, Cronus. Her image sometimes appears painted on the prow of ships.

I remember how, not long ago in the looming ruins of Acrocorinth in Greece, I had climbed to the site of the Aphrodite temple above the old city, again on a dark cold day, with grey showers of rain. The great walls of the fortified peak enclosed a wild and silent enclave, with stepped streets still visible leading up to a little ruined mosque. I walked up to the highest point in the drifting mist to the temple of Aphrodite, finding only some beautiful square blocks and a column base. The silence was absolute, but I met partridges, gentle hen-like birds, and everywhere almond and thorns were just coming into blossom. Scattered among the rocks and ruins the brilliant yellow euphorbia offered clusters of tiny yellow bowls, like miniature votive vessels. The two Aphrodite sites in Greece and Cyprus have the same panoramic vistas over the coast to the sea, and a quiet underlying sense of presence, despite all the devastation. They also share the condemnation of St Paul, as Aphrodite worship seems for him to have symbolised the worst aspects of pagan beliefs.

Old Paphos is a tattered, battered site, as if the extent of its fame in antiquity had to be paralleled by the devastation of its ruin after the advent of Christianity. The old temple site was used as a sugar cane factory in the medieval period, with recycled stones from the temple complex, perhaps a metaphorical remnant of the sweetness of Aphrodite. The mosaic floors of the Roman temple are spread out in the unshadowed light, exposed to wind and rain, looking very pale and lovely. It is said that St Paul denigrated Aphrodite in Paphos – he harried the Paphiots just as he did the Corinthians, because of the rumours – or truths – about temple prostitution.

The rumour of prostitution started with Herodotus writing in the fifth century BC. He gives a vivid picture of the crowds around a temple.

> Every woman born in the country must once in her life go and sit down in the precinct of Venus, and there consort with a stranger. Many of the wealthier sort who are too proud to mix with the others drive in covered carriages to the precinct, followed by a goodly train of attendants, and there take their station. But the larger number seat themselves within the holy enclosure with wreaths of string about their heads – and here there is always a great crowd, some coming and others going; lines of cord mark out paths in all directions among the women and the strangers pass along them to make

their choice. A woman who has once taken her seat is not allowed to return home till one of the strangers throws a silver coin in her lap, and takes her with him beyond the holy ground. When he throws the coin he says these words – 'the goddess Mylitta prosper thee' (Venus is called Mylitta by the Assyrians.) The silver coin may be of any size; it cannot be refused, for that is forbidden by law, since once thrown it is sacred. The woman goes with the first man who throws her money and rejects no one. When she has gone with him, and so satisfied the goddess, she returns home, and from that time forth no gift, however great, will prevail with her.'

This custom was called 'the abomination of the Babylonians' by Herodotus, who observed that 'a custom very much like this is found also in certain parts of Cyprus'.[13]

In any case the Palaepaphos temple is eastern in concept, not a closed *temenos* but an open structure for an Astarte/Mylitta kind of goddess. Aphrodite is a hybrid, not truly enclosed in the classical frame. She was a goddess of many aspects, heavenly, oceanic, and even underground. There are two rather haunting statuettes of draped women on the same base found in the Roman House of Theseus not far from the Paphos theatre and now in the Paphos Museum. The smaller figure is of dark grey marble inscribed with stars – perhaps Aphrodite Ourania (Heavenly) – and the other, slightly taller, may be Aphrodite Chthonia (Underground, or from a cave). The significance of the goddess is doubled. Sometimes the Heavenly Aphrodite is represented in vase paintings perched on a rustic ladder such as you would see leaning against an olive tree even today, poised between heaven and earth. The Olympians blur into relationships with older, eastern deities in Cyprus, and become slightly altered, so that in some guises it seems likely that Apollo Hylates, the Apollo of the Forest, may also be the same deity as Adonis, under another name, the lover of Aphrodite, slain by a boar. And Aphrodite herself takes on some of the roles of a chthonic, underground deity, as a partner in the rock-cut sanctuary of Apollo Hylates in Paphos. It takes concentration to keep up with the intricacies of the ancient soap opera of the gods.

The old Paphos site looked so different from the serene summer day in May when I first visited it. The odd selection of objects in the museum seemed to give the place another significance on this dark day. Here was a little loom warped up with loom weights, and a clay bowl with eggs still in it as an offering to the dead. The bird is the soul, it was thought, and with wings the soul flies. I remembered that the surrealist artist Meret Oppenheim once said, 'Creativity is the hatching of the thousand-year-old egg'. These tomb eggs are possibly two thousand years old, so hatching them would bring marvels. New life of a kind, of course, may just possibly come from the observations of Antipodean wanderers such as myself, remote and unimaginable entities to the person who originally dedicated the grave offering.

And I found another creative egg story: from Homer comes the myth that black-winged Night, at the beginning of the world, was courted by the Wind and laid a silver egg in the womb of Darkness. From the egg came Eros, to set the world in motion.[14] The power of erotic love is Aphrodite's most powerful weapon. (One of her statues in the Paphos Museum has her literally armed, her hand upraised to hold the sword.) The poet Sappho's prayer to Aphrodite begins: 'Immortal Aphrodite on your richly decorated throne, beguiling daughter of Zeus, I beg you, honoured goddess, do not crush my heart with pain and anguish.'[15]

I suddenly thought of my grandfather while wandering around the site. (Old sites bring up almost forgotten images in the walking reverie induced by moving on uneven ground through a maze of walls and foundations.) The vivid memory appeared of a tall and angular man who was very ill, lying on what was to be his deathbed, in a dark corner calling to me, a child on the other side of the room momentarily alone there. He pressed my arm with his horny, arthritic hands. 'Remember, you must always remember,' he said, 'God is love.' I reflected then, greatly disturbed by his intensity, I don't know what that means. But he may have liked the idea of Eros hatching from a silver egg.

The huge cornerstone of the earliest remains of the temple, one of just a few fragments still standing from the original sanctuary, is overwhelming in its weight and size, and pitted inexplicably with small cavities. Remnants of this ancient sanctuary wall extend for twenty-eight metres, with stones so twisted and frayed by time that they look like meteoritic stones such as I once saw in central Australia, fallen from outer space. How this 'orthostat' stone of two metres by five metres was moved and lifted is unknown. If stone can be living, as Buddhists believe, this stone would have a grave eminence. Maria, the thoughtful museum official, told me, lifting her eyebrows and smiling, that the stone was a 'singing' stone and that offerings were still made in the little weathered grottoes that pit its surface. The small guidebook said: 'And until today young mothers offer candles to the Panayia Galatariotissa, the milk-giving Virgin, at a conspicuous stone in the old temple wall: a last trace of the age-old fertility cult.'[16] Colin Thubron observed in his walking travels of Cyprus in the fateful year of 1974 a 'nest of expired candles in the temple cornerstone.'[17] The great stone had a heavy presence, an aura, enhanced by the winter day. Perhaps there was a faint sighing in the cold wind, but no singing was audible to me.

The dark green conical stone representing Aphrodite is still on the site, kept in the medieval manor house that is now the museum. After archaeologists had removed a sacred stone from the temple, says Thubron, 'they found it shiny with olive oil: for the young mothers of Kouklia village, when the milk was running dry at their breasts, had for centuries anointed it as a petition to the Lady of the Place.'[18] I noticed that the metre-high stone of basalt in the dim room was indeed still slippery with oil – someone was keeping up this old tradition. I felt that the stone was outside the conventional classical canon, so often described in naturalistic terms. It had more likeness to the *xoanon*, the wooden 'plank' goddess whose simple roughness was venerated and adorned long after naturalistic statues were in place. This was the stone at the heart of the Paphos cult, not a 'made' art object, but a natural one, 'found' by a myth that no one remembers. It seemed like a Djankkawul sacred stone such as people avert their eyes from in Yirrkala in northern Australia, a sign from the creation ancestors.

Anna from the Cypriot suburbs of Wollongong, whose father had emigrated to Australia from Paphos when she was tiny, seemed overwhelmed by the aura of the stone as we all stood around it in the museum, and leaned forward with her fingers outstretched: 'I must touch it because I need so much love.' She had to be gently restrained.

7 April

On an impulse I drive the fifteen kilometres to Palaepaphos one evening after seeing a coin representing Aphrodite's temple that turned up in the theatre excavation. It shows with wonderful detail the 'horns of consecration' on top of the central doorway, framing the triangular sacred stone. Two standing lamps are displayed in the two lower side doors, and there even seem to be paired birds on the roof, while a semicircular enclosure curves in front of the *temenos*. All this is modelled with great clarity on a coin the size of a penny – each element entire and succinct, as the images on a coin have to be able to communicate a message in a flash. Tradition says that the stone was so sacred that it never got wet, despite being in an open courtyard.

This is a very old site. The pointed Aphrodite stone probably dates from the Chalcolithic period, the 'age of stone', about 2400 BC. The more famous *omphalos* or navel stone is of course central to the cult of Apollo in Delphi, and Apollo Hylates was his representative in Cyprus. Paphos was said by Hesychius, writing a lexicon in the first century AD, to have been another navel of the world parallel to that of Delphi in Greece, the centre of the earth.[19] My more recent lexicon has beside the word *omphalos* 'Anything like a navel can be called an *omphalos*, such as the raised knob or boss in the middle of a shield, or a knob on the horse's yoke to fasten the reins to. Calypso's island Ogygia is called the navel of the Sea.'[20]

The king Nikokles of Paphos, who founded Nea Paphos just before our theatre was built, described himself as a 'priest of Anassa'. One of his coins has a head of Aphrodite, crowned with flowers, and on the reverse, Apollo seated on a netted *omphalos*. The navel stone in Delphi was often decorated with woollen roving from the fleece, a harvest offering. It is not known how Nikokles set about planning the city of Nea Paphos in 320 BC, but later on the Romans believed that in order to found a city a central point had to be established called the *umbilicus*, a navel for the town corresponding to the navel of the body. Richard Sennett described how the planners also pinpointed the *umbilicus* of the city by studying the sky. 'The passage of the sun seemed to divide the sky in two; other measurements of stars at night appeared to cut this division at right angles so that the heavens were composed of four parts. To found a town, one sought on the ground a spot that reflected directly below the point where the four parts of the sky met, as if the map of the sky were mirrored on the earth.' Two streets bisected to form a quadrant with the *umbilicus* at the centre. From this reference point, this belly button, all the measurements for the roads and buildings (the arms and legs) of the city were set out. Just as in the sequence of a child's birth the navel separates the world of the unborn from the light of day, so the significant *umbilicus* point was the dividing point between the realm of the infernal gods in the ground and the gods of light in the heavens. The city could be born after a hole called the *mundus* was dug where offerings to the chthonic deities were put. After it had been covered over, and a fire was lit, the city was 'born'.[21]

The conical Aphrodite stone on the coins does look like an *omphalos*, like those shown so often beside graves. The unknown qualities of the image tease, and speculations about its meaning are intriguing, if unknowable. The traditions of old Paphos point to a dominant goddess whose god-king husband was sacrificed, like Adonis. The *omphalos* may have been a sign of the maternal emblem, marking the site of that knot, that tie, in the middle of one's body. The navel knot stands between the dark territory of the womb and the light of the sun. The great Python, the snake that came out of similar clefts and holes in the earth, was associated with the *omphalos*. At some point in mythological history, the goddess was shifted from her pre-eminence, and the god Apollo takes over these dark forces as a site for prophecy and truth – but the shield boss was still called an *omphalos*, and served as a protective device to turn away evil.[22]

Navels and oracles seem to go together – the influential Sybil made her prophecies in a cleft below the temple of Apollo at Delphi where an *omphalos* stone still stands beside the path. Just near this chamber is a great rock shown to tourists, where the Sybil is supposed to have sat. And at Paphos it is likely that the oracle of Aphrodite used the entrails of animal offerings to divine the future (*haruspicium*), and perhaps also the flight of birds (*oionismos*) gave prophetic insights.[23]

I set off on the wandering track that leads around the top of the hill from the temple site to the ruins of a Roman villa to look at the House of Leda overlooking the sea, past great *charoupia* or carob trees. Leda is represented here in an image of undying popularity, which is seen on every rack of postcards in association with nude girls photographed beside the sea at Aphrodite's birthplace. Here she is in a lovely mosaic pavement in a summer dining room, the *triclinium*, shown standing between a pilaster and a fountain beneath a tree. She has her back to the viewer, turning her head to look over her shoulder, her wonderful pear-shaped buttocks revealed by her slipping drapery which the swan is catching in his beak. The mosaic has a soft glitter from its many-coloured stones, all local, of rose red, ochre, grey green and a kind of lapis blue. The Romans, who regarded themselves as descended from Venus-Aphrodite through their ancestor Aeneas, greatly admired the Paphian Venus. She is hauntingly represented, mourning Adonis, in the paintings of the Villa of Boscotrecase near Pompeii.

So many of these allusions to the multiple aspects of the deity can only be glimpsed – as in the small exquisite terracotta head of a Hellenistic Aphrodite from the sanctuary, with a heavy-lidded gaze and a nearly suppressed smile. The terracotta painted Bronze Age goddess figurines from tombs near here have necklaces and string-like ornaments around their necks. These may have been more than ornaments. 'Woollen garlands,' writes Artemidorus, 'signify witchcraft and spells because they are intricate and multi-coloured.'[24]

I see old houses with roofs caved in, where pigeons now nest, or rooms used as a stall for animals on the outskirts of the village of Kouklia (from the French Lusignan word 'couvoucle', the name of the thirteenth-century chateau) near the temple site. Waist-high weeds full of rubbish grow near a great arched room with a wooden ceiling, its floor covered in leaves.

Near here, at the derelict edge of the village is the small twelfth-century church with a ruined cloister, on the edge of the temple precinct, called the Panayia Katholiki. It sinks into the earth, behind a fragmentary wall, long tufts of wild iris growing beside the steps down. Above the barrel vault is a rusty red dome that can be seen from the temple site; its uneven curved surface evokes either breast or navel, but from a weathered and wrinkled body. In the early twentieth century the church was called the Khrysopolitissa, substituted for the earlier name Panayia Aphroditissa – so that the goddess still retained a ghostly, if chastened presence. How could Aphrodite, whose modus vivendi was erotic love, ever be confused with the Virgin? But so it is. Both have a concern for nurturing the newborn, both have a compassionate aspect. Old stones with inscriptions from the ancient site are built into the church walls and the guidebook pointed out that offerings are still made to Aphrodite at a stone by the west wall of the church.

Most astonishingly, the church is entirely wrapped with a white cotton warp, many threads in a coil as thick as my arm, a coil that must be seventy-five metres long, twining and twisting around each wall. The church is still used daily, the paths are swept, though I saw no one. I remembered the 'wreaths of string' and 'lines of cord' mentioned in connection with the women serving the goddess by Herodotus. Perhaps this warp thread looped around the old church was an almost forgotten sign meaning 'in the service of the goddess' or at least acknowledging the Lady of the Place and her powers to avert evil, between the heavens and the dark underground.

The persistence of dim memories of navels, breasts and of a powerful Virgin is also to be found in the remarkable many-domed church of Ayia Paraskevi at Yeroskippou, a village standing on the forgotten pilgrims' road between old and new Paphos. This sculptured, asymmetrical church is in a square surrounded by shops making and selling Cyprus Delight, *loukoumi*, in every imaginable flavour – that sweetness again, reminding me that Palaepaphos had been a centre for the powerful medieval sugar industry. The varieties of *loukoumi* replace the cakes in the shapes of flowers, fruit and phalluses that were sold along the ancient pilgrims' route. 'Yeroskippou' means a 'sacred garden', the *ieros kepos* associated with Aphrodite. The story is that Friday, Paraskevi, the name of the church, was the feast day of Aphrodite. Saint Friday, Ayia Paraskevi, is a female saint whose story is lost. All we know is that she holds an icon of Christ suffering on Good Friday – so Aphrodite holds on to her mourning for Adonis. The church is ninth-century, and spaced around it in the square, like fence posts or bollards, are marble Corinthian capitals intricately carved with acanthus, the remnant of some Roman temple. I have also found all kinds of baskets in the little shops around the square. Sweet foods and woven objects are suitable offerings for the pilgrim to buy. It is as though a coded language were superimposed on the forbidden Aphrodite customs, so that they became something else officially, but within the same ancient framework and calling up the same emotional pattern.

If you draw a 'wreath of string' you get a sign like the letter 'O'. The first indications of a date for the Paphos theatre were given by the mysterious letters engraved into the rock-cut seats – iota, theta, omega, delta, pi. All these Greek letters have become symbols in later arts and sciences, in algebra, in physics, even in psychiatry. (The letters I D are actually engraved side by side into the stone steps, so appropriate to a theatrical subjectivity).

As I drive back to Paphos in the dusk I muse that the 'I' is the sign of the outgoing and roving intelligence, in classical times of course, mostly male – the letter 'I' seems to have the courage of an individual subjectivity which was so outstanding in that Greco-Roman culture. It is, too, the sign of the symbolic phallus, the location of power. For many women still, that confident 'I' is always a particular achievement. But the sign of the omega is curved, turning in on itself, and looks like a navel, the end and the beginning, like a wreath of string. It does not have the one-point perspective, the outward ranging movement of the 'I', but is part of a wider pattern where self is not differentiated from the community. Both letters are cut inscrutably into the curved seats of the Paphos theatre. How intriguing to imagine both 'phallic' and 'omphalic' sensibilities intersecting and interacting in the long time span of the Greco-Roman theatre, carrying a sign for us, if we could read it.

4. FLESH AND STONE: THE THEATRE

15 March 1997

Returning to Paphos a year later on a cool spring evening, after the long flight from summer Australia, is like arriving in a different time, as well as space. The theatre site is indistinct with blurred tones of almond and pear blossom, leafless trees. The archaeologists strip the earth of its prolific daisies and poppies (like shaving before an operation) so that the site can be measured and surveyed for the new trenches, and photographed before the excavations begin. Every atom of that earth during the course of the digging is sifted, rubbed and fingered. Nothing will return the way it was – the earth is not put back, but piled into 'spoil heaps', and it is the nature of archaeology that evidence is destroyed as we remove the layers. Those layers packed down with all their fibrous tangle of broken artefacts and debris over millennia can't be reconstituted once pulled apart.

Is it elegiac, remembering and mourning the past, this scouring the grounds for traces of people long dead, a way of postponing our own end as the present grips us? Why do we come from so far away? I had brought with me a catalogue of an exhibition from the vast archives of the Paul Getty Institute in Los Angeles, *Irresistible Decay: Ruins Reclaimed*. It begins with a quote from Marcel Proust: 'The past is hidden somewhere outside the realm, beyond the reach of intellect, in some material object (in that sensation which that material object will give us) of which we have no inkling. And it depends on chance whether or not we come upon this object before we die.'[25] Even on a scientific excavation, chance is a potent element, as is the character of the excavator.

Our reason for excavation is scholarly and practical in the pursuit of knowledge, and elegiac feelings are hardly conscious, except perhaps in the sense of inarticulate longing that I see in the faces of people who desire to be part of the excavation team. There is a certain passion to being here which is not entirely explained by clear reasoning. Michel de Certeau points out that people travel to explore 'the deserted places of memory', to repopulate the imagination with legends that have disappeared from their own localities.[26] And for me there is a notion that we return from the colonial 'utopias' at the periphery of known worlds in the eighteenth and nineteenth centuries to look again at the old European centre, to find an ancient utopia that might lessen our melancholy about our violent origins in Australia.[27]

The past can be re-imagined and re-interpreted through an inner journey. Claude Levi-Strauss wrote in 1955:

> Journeys, those magic caskets full of dreamlike promises, will never again yield up their treasures untarnished. A proliferating and over excited civilization has broken the silence of the seas once and for all. The perfumes of the tropics and the pristine freshness of human beings have been corrupted by a busyness with dubious implications, which mortifies our desires and dooms us to acquire only contaminated memories.[28]

The dimly known Greco-Roman past, the site of so much of our culture – this offers our energetic curiosity a spark, a possibility of new perceptions. The people from those no longer utopian tropics come back to re-invent European landscapes, to find an almost invisible utopia in the past.

Australians are so sportive – our team works in a physical way to win back the past, to uncover trophies and 'pristine and uncontaminated' treasures from a provincial ancient city as if it might redeem our own history.

17 March

Today in interrupted sun and a cold wind Richard delivers an impromptu lecture on the origins of theatre, while people stand silently, sheltering from the sudden shower. He emphasises the fact that it was the tremendous response of audiences that shaped both the intense development of the dramatic form itself and the architectural form – the fierce competition to excel from actors, from patrons and from playwrights in Athens, a city that had a population comparable to Wollongong, perhaps 100,000 people. Texts developed because people needed to remember the words for re-performance. Playwrights such as Sophocles only wrote for the one performance. A sheet of papyrus cost a day's pay.

The theatre of Hellenistic Alexandria was distinctive for being built on a flat terrain without hills to form the slope of the seats. Seats must have been built up on supporting walls, prefiguring the later Roman theatres which are self contained structures without reference to the landscape. The Paphos theatre is partly caught and engaged in the side of the hill, partly built out at the sides, a transitional type. But the seats that remain are cut into the bedrock itself. What happens when bodies are disengaged from sitting on the actual substance of the rock, hoisted on architectural structures to watch a performance? A subtly different kind of understanding of the drama?

I am still reflecting on our presence here for six weeks, concentrating entirely on a tiny area of land, this site, to know it, to destroy it as it presently is and transform it back to some indication of its past. But which past? So many levels of habitation, which one will be chosen? Not only Hellenistic Greeks, but also Romans, Arabs, Lusignan French, Venetians and Ottomans added layers to Paphos. The medieval walls, merely a thousand years old, are documented and carefully removed as less significant in the history of the theatre. The most permanent structures will remain, the blocky base of the retaining wall that held the tiered seats, and the foundations of the Roman stage building. We are constructing a particular past for the needs of the twenty-first century. As developers of an ancient theatre property we are unable to fully encompass all the languages and histories of the theatre's eight-hundred-year span with an equal emphasis.

In the evening I read Italo Calvino, who writes of the city and memory, of its 'relationships between the measurements of its space and the events of its past', as if it were a living organism.

> The city, however, does not tell its past, but contains it like the lines of a hand, written in the corners of the streets, the gratings of the windows, the banisters of the steps, the antennae of the lightning rods, the poles of the flags, every segment marked in turn with scratches, indentations, scrolls.[29]

In Paphos the theatre is like the trace of a rib cage, and from this trace we try to reinstate and re-imagine the breathing entity.

26 March

I spend days in the tiny drawing office, putting order into the boxes of the inventoried fragments by listing them and scanning the drawings onto the computer. There are sometimes seven people working in these cramped conditions – mostly with patience and good humour. A swallow continually flies in and out of the door to build a nest, and bird droppings fall on the drawing boards.

Data entry is time consuming, and I even need to learn the scanning programs. I try to draw directly onto the computer screen, but the irregular curved section line proves extremely difficult to plot. Even with the new technologies, the human eye is more accurate. There's endless detail in putting together the comprehensive visual record by aligning drawings and plans with conservation and photography. Archaeology is about infinite detail, and we don't really know what will turn out to be significant in the unknotting of the strands of the site. There is a plan of the theatre on the wall of the office. Joy, my Honours student of Egyptian and Lebanese ancestry, sits at the computer below it, her dark hair curling around her ear (punctured with several earrings) – the theatre too is the shape of an ear, an ear which listens to multiple voices, the sounds playing out individual fates.

Today as I took a walk to get warm in the middle of the morning, Heather showed me an extremely smooth pebble found in the medieval layers – surely from someone's pocket. The pebble still exists to be touched but the hand that fingered and selected it is lost. The most inconsequential objects – a pebble dropped in a courtyard – are more lasting than human flesh. Signs of a fire were found in greasy black dirt, a cooking fire perhaps, as there were animal bones nearby – just a moment in a busy day, but that is what survives. The intense feeling of self, the thoughts and emotions that hurtle through the mind in the course of a day, leave no material traces.

Nicholas Poussin watched marble statues being unearthed in Rome in the late seventeenth century. He observed the classical forms but reconstituted them in his painting with no concessions to archaeological accuracy, seeking another kind of synthesis, a poetic ordering to bring the past to bear on the present. The poet Rainer Maria Rilke wrote about a ruin:

> There it lies, yard upon yard, only fragments one beside the other ... And yet the more closely one looks, the more deeply one feels that all this would be less of a whole if the individual bodies were whole... One feels suddenly that it is rather the business of the scholar to conceive of the body as a whole and much more that of the artist to create from the parts new relationships.[30]

18 April

Finally there is sun and the cold wind has dropped. The warmer weather brings an ease of moving and working, people sing and laugh from their trenches. The fresh flowers and green leaves die away almost overnight to dessicated brown; white dust and grit is everywhere. I climb down the tumbled stones of the baulk (the cut edge of the trench) to sit in the warm sun in the deep trench at the western entrance, to document the plaster fragments still attached to the stone. Saffron gold, faience green, madder on cream – wriggles of colour swirl in a lozenge pattern while white light saturates every tiny atom of paint. I half listen as I measure the stone to the banter from the trenches nearby, to the excavators scraping, shovelling, or considering whether a new deposit is needed, whether an area might be 'contaminated' by sherds infiltrating it from another level. Joking, teasing, bodies sweating from the hard work, enjoying the sun, the possibility of a swim in the clear sea later, an ice cream, a beer. There was a constant faint twittering of swallows circling and diving above. The wonderful momentum of physical energy feels everlasting, as natural as the day.

Often I feel suspended between two modes: that of the artist who is driven by the emotion of experience, and the codifying and ordering mind of the archaeologist. For me, archaeological documentation is held in the context of a wider imaginative sense that relates our time to this dimly perceived Greco-Roman past. Considering this fragmentary theatre is like being pregnant, and looking for the first time at the ultrasound image of the breathing foetus: a range of unforeseen possibilities may emerge at its eventual uncovering, its birth.

5. FINDING THINGS: DOLPHINS, A CARVED HAND, A SANDALLED FOOT

2 April 1997

A walk on the hill above the excavation reveals one astonishing discovery. The medieval name of this hill was Fabrika, 'the making place'. It was once within the city walls, and is honeycombed with caves and tombs that are still fertile with surprises. A child playing beside the path in the winter, scrabbling in the shallow earth above bedrock, finds the little stones in a pattern, and uncovers a rare Hellenistic pebble mosaic with black dolphins, a hero figure and a snake on a white ground. It must be part of the floor of a sophisticated house, perhaps the *triclinium* or dining room, built about the same time as the foundation of the theatre. I see it first in the brilliant rays of the setting sun (just about to dip into the western sea), making each individual rounded stone distinct, with its own curved shadow. The dolphins leap in a precise choreography above a frieze of voluptuous spirals as if pleased to be in the open air once more. Last year it was still hidden – I must actually have been sitting on those dolphins as I drew the rock-cut temple plinth only metres away from this place.

What chance there is in the discovery of such artworks. Our site seems to have been picked over and ransacked in antiquity, in contrast to the Roman villas nearby where the Polish excavators found whole sculptures within two hours of starting to dig. Out of the earth came that armed Aphrodite holding a spear with arm raised as if to bring it down, menacing above her flawless body. Such differences can be seen in the Paphos Museum in the way the nude deities are represented – Artemis is boyish and muscular with small breasts, while Aphrodite is sinuous and long limbed. The satyr, the boy with tiny goat's horns, is sensual, recording a moment in late adolescence. Dionysos is almost a hermaphrodite, with a pinched waist and a rounded chest and a languorous stance. Nudity is a convention, but also a language here.

7 April

A water diviner wanders on site with two little twitching wires that indicated holes or water beneath. He looks rather distracted, even slightly mad, but said he had been an electrical engineer in England whose company kept losing equipment so he had turned to divining in order to find lost cables. There is a large hole under the terebinth tree, according to him. But large holes are everywhere in Cyprus, tombs are everywhere – sacred is underground.

I realised today that all this digging and trowelling will not result in any predictable crop. Our harvests are broken sherds, taken from the earth which is sifted and pulverised, heaped up so that it becomes just dust and stones rather than a living entity. Once its contents are removed, it is formless, amorphous, getting in the way of the cultural structures emerging from it. Shapeless old mother, full of detritus. Yet next year, those spoil heaps will be covered in flowers and grasses.

10 April

A team scraping in the prickly pears to the west of the ancient retaining wall that held the curve of the seats locates the corner of this vital wall structure, just beside and even under the present road. This indicates a larger circumference than had been imagined. Possibly more than five thousand people might have crammed in for the seasonal dramatic festivals. On a day when heavy clouds were blown across the sky in a rushing cold wind, with gleams of sun and then a hail storm, a beautiful piece of heavy dark basalt was found with a hand carved on it, probably Egyptian. It came from unstratified rubble against this massive wall, near the western theatre entrance, where the vivid fragments of painted plaster were also found. The director said excitedly, 'This is the most beautiful stone wall in Paphos.' Its sandstone blocks are more than a metre long, measured exactly to align together. Some tantalising sculptural fragments of marble from the same area show a draped shoulder, a few letters from a Greek inscription.

Near here, another trench was dug to the stone floor, the Roman floor of the theatre entrance, with a long white marble threshold at one end. The trench is nearly two metres deep, the sides cut straight, and cut into the floor is a circular pit, perhaps a cistern or a grain storage pit, so that it looks like an earth sculpture. This pit was dug at the end of the Roman period in the early sixth century when the whole theatre seems to have been used as a place for squatters. It must have been a heap of disintegrating walls and stairs, half destroyed by the earthquake around AD 365, and used after that as a source for ready-cut building materials for the new churches. The drawings of Piranesi in Rome in the seventeenth century capture something of the monumental mystery and scale of such ruins, inhabited by shepherds, hermits and the destitute.

While this trench is underway, winter returns with an icy wind blowing dust and grit, even over the carefully swept bones of a donkey found squashed absolutely flat, fused to the stone floor – perhaps pinned down by tons of earthquake rubble. People must have made shelters and cooked amongst the impressive remains of the theatre, that towering retaining wall as high as a telegraph pole, with their donkeys and sheep tied up outside the little rooms constructed out of the ruins. The evidence for these small squats is very moving – the ashes of the fire, cooking debris, a few poor possessions dropped in the dirt while the disintegrating theatre must have loomed all around, with its useful fallen stones and still upright walls. A glass earring was found in this area, and it is almost possible to sense the ancient annoyance at its loss. The earring comes to light while its possessor is untraceable. A network of relationships remains hidden by the arbitrariness of such finds.

As well as keeping meticulous archaeological records in the vital dig book, noting all the complexities of stratigraphy and different deposits, the mature women Holly, Fran and Patricia working this trench also construct a whole imaginative narrative around these discoveries. For a moment all their responsibilities drop away and they make up stories like children making play houses in mud and sand with rooms for all the characters, and little tea sets and beds. Hands in dirt, open to sun, wind, cold, heat, they are happy – the process itself is as absorbing as those radiant infant days of play. Uncovering a deposit of animal bones left near a medieval wall above the stage building, I hear Holly say, 'This bone doesn't look right for a donkey. I think they must have had a moufflon' – the native sheep of Cyprus – 'for dinner, or perhaps they had a pet one and it was squashed by that wall falling.'

The constant and devastating effect of earthquakes is very evident in the tumble of fallen masonry on the theatre site. Last week in the museum at Episkopi, not far away, I saw the entwined skeletons of a mother, baby and father who perished in the catastrophic earthquake of the late fourth century. The man sheltered the woman and baby with his arm in such a familiar gesture. Some exquisite Hellenistic Aphrodite figurines in a case nearby seemed to watch the embracing skeletons. White slip and red paint were still in evidence, and a despairing and anguished glance could be discerned in the features of the face above the lovely nudity. This little museum also had a marble sculpture of a plump boy with a dolphin, and a wave-washed marble of Dionysos, patron of theatre, a melting image with just a haunting out-of-focus stance visible.

The full extent of the theatre stage wall emerges slowly, great slabs of stone with cuts for later structures stretching across the site behind the *orchestra*, still overlaid by medieval walls. Hearing cries of excitement I go to watch a piece of sculpture being very slowly lifted after careful scraping and brushing, and photographs – it is a fragment of a marble foot in a fine sandal, possibly second century, perhaps from a statue dedicated beside the stage. (When something significant is about to emerge the trench leader calls out, and those of us who have some excuse to be moving around go to watch.) This looks like an authoritative masculine foot, well tended and shod, perhaps from a dedicatory statue, creamy marble against the umber of the gritty earth. And worked stone, possibly similar to Alexandrine architectural ornament, appears in another trench. The formal functions of the theatre become a little more evident in these visual clues.

12 April

Every day I watch the progress of a particularly mesmerising trench, just metres away from the drawing office. Suddenly, after ten days of meticulous digging they reach a paved road, with narrow wheel ruts that must have passed behind the stage building. The worn stones are smooth from treading feet and carts. Where did the road lead? Who travelled on it? Probably it was part of the Hellenistic grid of roads connecting the theatre to the agora and the areas of government around the port. A road connects communities, permitting journeys, arrivals and departures, and without roads communities stop functioning, as happened after the great roads, ports and skilled trades of the Roman empire slowly decayed in the seventh century. To see stone worn and rutted by so many feet and wheels makes one look freshly at the invisibility of our own everyday surfaces, walls, roads, expressways, with an eye that overlays these familiar surfaces with inevitable disintegration.

During the season Andrea the field supervisor gave a talk with many diagnostic objects from the dig spread out over the great sorting table, which is partially sheltered by an overhanging roof, but not really protected from wind and rain. In a satisfying grid she laid out sequences of pottery from different periods, glass and small finds such as coins, bone pins, and clay spindle whorls, in a semblance of order. Although there were only a few textile artefacts, as a weaver I found them very absorbing, and longed to give them a voice. The six objects I was drawn to comprised three stone spindle whorls, two of marble, and one of soapstone incised with concentric circles, a bone pin or spindle, and an oval loom weight. The loom weight was found in a Late Roman building towards the top of Fabrika Hill, above the seating of the theatre. In the trenches near the site of the ancient road, spindle whorls and bone pins emerged together with fragmentary Roman pottery and coins. It was near here, beneath the paved Roman road that the small bronze figurine of Athena, or Minerva, had come to light, the goddess of weaving, crafts and strategies of war. The textile artefacts were not dropped by the theatre audience, but were part of the layers of destruction of buildings next to and associated with the theatre. Ancient textiles hardly survive in the clammy clay and limestone soils of Cyprus, except in imprints on soft clay, or occasionally caught up in a metal tomb vessel.

So later I asked the excavators Holly and Craig about the whorls and the bone pins and consulted their dig books, in which excavators record the progress of each layer and deposit. As so often, it's the drains which are rich in finds; a rather splendid drain flowing beneath the road contained the textile artefacts as well as many fine pieces of Roman glass. Earthquake and burning activity were evident in the composition of the soil, with 'lenses of burning and decomposed mud brick', and the trench was also disturbed by root activity from the vigorous terebinth and fruit trees of later gardens. It is like unravelling a complex tangle to understand so many threads. It seems clear that the three spindle whorls and the bone awl or spindle are late in the life of the theatre.

The fresco fragments are beginning to spread out across the table and are rather outside anyone's expertise. Their brushed patterns show such verve. I hover over them in fascination, as the calibre of finds such as these suggests complexities of thinking and feeling. The painting indicates a connection with the rich iconography of

Greco-Roman art, and is also a reflection of the decorative textiles that have not survived. The painted plaster is very fragile. As the conservator crouches on the site for days picking at the encrustations of the plaster on a limestone slab, soft colours emerge, red, indigo, madder, the elusive turquoise. It is a pleasure to make gouache drawings of these plaster fragments, which Richard asked me to do as a matter of urgency.

14 April

On a windy day with chill undercurrents a visiting pottery expert, John Hayes, spends the morning examining our sorting tables and talking pot fabrics. This dedicated man, a thin sprightly figure, seems driven by his desire to understand a particular facet of the past. How admirable, I think, to be able to make a living as a freelance consultant on eastern Mediterranean Late Roman pottery. His hands move rapidly as he bends over the table, intensely curious as to what we might have, speaking in an intense low undertone. I catch words – 'This one is flaky and soft, this has a better clinky kind of fabric, reddish rather than brown – you can tell Cypriot *sigillata* by its crumbling more powdery firing.' On one part of the table there's a pit full of Byzantine ware laid out, the 'botch ware' from Gaza in ancient Syria (now the Gaza Strip), which the excavators get fond of because they say it is so awful, nearly like mud. Sometimes you find a fingerprint in the soft clay where the handle or spout has been pinched together. Piles of these pinkish brown fragments are heaped up all over the tables and sorting mat. His hands flicker over the potsherds, sorting, collecting little piles to one side, amazingly finding joins from different heaps, knowing each fabric and its shape from all the countries so active in antiquity – Egypt, Syria including Palestine and Lebanon, Africa, Italy – the wares from these places all came to Paphos. The pottery, which must have been a relatively unnoticed and disregarded necessity of life, has become the one material sign that survives war, catastrophe, and earthquake. Pottery is the essential ingredient of the dig, enabling sequences and connections across countries to be established as a fact, rather than a supposition.

The plain cooking ware speaks – round and red, charred black, patterned with incised designs, in swelling shapes. Like the amphorae, these cooking pots must have been as common as our everyday table settings are to us – imbued with the power of the ordinary, the pot over which conversations flowed at meals or in the kitchen, there on the table when bad news came, or when a marriage or a funeral took place. The little girl learning to cook becomes the grandmother: and the same small bowl is used to break eggs into. The tenuous order of domestic life was constructed around these anonymous potsherds.

A marvellous Roman pottery fragment from a mould has a woman beside an altar, lighting the fire that curls upward. On the other side of the altar is a gnarled olive tree. This image is vivid with swirling drapery. More coins are found, nearly every hour it seems, with fierce beaked Roman profiles. The coins offer moments of clarity – so much coded information on a tiny surface. Diocletian emerged, a heroic profile, and Constantine veiled, from near the stage wall. I made graphite rubbings of the coins and scanned them into the computer. How the Romans understood power, the same power abroad today – a commercial, quotidian, practical and hedonistic will is evident in these heads.

Among many intriguing pottery fragments a small votive vase of the type made as a dedicatory offering, unglazed, turns up near this road, of Hellenistic or Roman type. It is miraculously intact, soft red terracotta. It may be a sign that the elusive sanctuary is somewhere close, the temple that is always found near to theatres.

Probably we should encourage the little boy who found the Hellenistic dolphin mosaic to make further efforts, or perhaps the child obsessed with archaeology (who persistently attaches himself to the pot washers after school in the afternoon). As he sits on the ground playing with the spoil from the trenches, perhaps he could with his uninhibited vision indicate where exactly to search for clues to the enigma of the theatre.

6. DREAMING ON SITE

16 March 1997

Often, travelling impels dreams – and many people on the excavation comment on the vivid dreams they have, sleeping in physical exhaustion after a long day's digging. The prolific traces of ancient life brought up into the open seem to draw a kind of resonance from the unconscious. The self too was a site, Freud intimated, with its dark holes, forgotten earrings, coins, and vestiges of lost loves. Dreams, as the excavation unfolds, seem to contain a mirroring of the fragments uncovered, perhaps a repressed knowledge of the future waning of my own full material life. This season I am keeping a dream diary of small drawings to try to manage the flow of images, documenting them as if they were just more material evidence from the excavation.

Artemidorus, writing in the second century AD, at the same time as the renovations to our theatre, was part of a long 'oneirocritic' tradition that tried to discover a uniform set of laws for dreams that would allow them to be categorised. First he established what was 'normal' in everyday life: 'These, then, are common customs: to venerate and honour the gods, to nurture children, to yield to women and to sexual intercourse with them, to be awake during the day, to sleep at night, to take food, to rest when tired, to live indoors and not in the open air.' Artemidorus then made a parallel list of common events in the dream life of different levels of people, and ascribed specific meanings to dream images. Dreams might then be used to foretell possible future events, depending on the age, gender and status of the dreamer.[31]

The dream of tumultuous water is frequent. Last night I dreamt of falling from a narrow bridge into the depths of an immensely turbulent and powerful river, churning and seething. I am carried down and emerge finally, utterly fatigued. The earth that we dig became liquid and transparent as water in my dream. Despite all our careful grids and measurements, the earth shifts and changes.

The theatre site itself seems like a body, worked on day to day, with a life of its own. Corrugated limestone seats and cut bedrock are like the vertebrae and curved rib cage, though the softer and more transient flesh around this bony core has vanished into the sticky earth – such as the impermanent wooden stage buildings with painted walls and textiles. Peggy Phelan writes about Elizabethan theatres as conforming to the convoluted shape of a stomach, into which the audience was ingested, and from which it was excreted.[32] The entrances and exits of ancient theatres are known as *vomitoria*, because they eject the audience from the curved solar plexus of the *cavea* seats.

29 March

If the theatre can be a metaphor of the body, in dreams the house or the building stands for the self. Visiting the stony ruins of the city of Kourion not far from Paphos, uninhabited since the seventh century, Grahame, a well-known theatre personality from Sydney, starts a conversation about a mutual, once dear, friend, an actor. He is now very ill – 'Not AIDS, arthritis? A very sick boy, but what a voice.' To talk about him is almost like remembering the dead, in this dead city washed with light, perched on the cliff above the great arc of the sea. Its joints also are lying in pieces. To be remembered for a voice is something, a resonant voice of great power that seemed to promise so much. Its reverberations moved the listener in a subliminal way without any reference to content, deeper than the deepest tones of a normal voice. Looking at the dismembered city, shops, streets, marketplace and temples disentangled from the earth and open to the light is like looking at an old love affair. The white eggcup-shaped flowers with black centres, like flickering bits of paper blowing over the old city are *ranunculus orientalis*.

I dream too of betrayal. A lover unexpectedly arrived to see me. He seemed as fond as ever, but when I went to meet him at his hotel he was with a Miss Radich (Root, obviously), who smirked at me. This dream lover said, 'I have spent an entirely satisfactory night with Miss R.' I was furious with her (but why not with him?) – I shouted to the crowds in the assembled ancient theatre, 'She's a slug! A slimy slug!' and tried to hit her broad cheek, but my hand would not move despite the passion of anger. Such a dream could be fittingly played out in masks, with a satirical narrative. I consulted Artemidorus and he commented that theatrical dreams were frequent. According to him my dream may be a warning of turmoil and gossip to come:

> If a man dreams that he is dancing in a theatre wearing make-up ... that he is held in high esteem and praised, it signifies for a poor man riches that will not however, last until his old age. For on stage the dancer plays the part of a king and is surrounded by many attendants. But after the performance, he is left alone. For a wealthy man on the other hand the dream predicts turmoil and many lawsuits because of the intricate complications that arise in the plot. We have observed however, that this dream is good neither for a rich nor a poor woman. For they will be involved in great and notorious scandals.[33]

30 March

I become absorbed in the entrancing brevity of ancient love stories, hardly ever ending in 'happy ever after', found in the mosaics of the Roman House of Dionysos, a short walk from the theatre site. An image of Narcissus, poised on a rock, is at the entrance, gazing into a pool at his reflection, which looks out quite wisely, like a separate self. Around him is a border of interlacing, framing the uncontrollable love of self. My old friend Scylla is just to the left of him, six hundred years older, quite majestic in her monstrosity, quite accepting of her serpent's tail and dog's heads, given to her because unwittingly she loved Circe's lover. How important animals were. Scenes of fated love ended often in metamorphosis – Pyramos and Thisbe, changed into a mulberry tree, Apollo and Daphne, already with leaves and twigs branching from her limbs. These scenes are interspersed with narratives of hunting wild animals, with wonderful fierce tigers, and more intricate geometric patterns. The largest room has a tapestry-like mosaic of a vine twining across the floor, with birds, fruits, and plump *erotes* helping to harvest the grapes. Around this central panel coils a richly waving spiral of vegetation, with a mask caught up in it, and birds, prefiguring the grotesque vegetal masks of the baroque more than a thousand years later. Next to this is a Bacchic procession, with individual figures of maenads and musicians dancing against the cream mosaic background, and Dionysos in a chariot pulled by leopards in the centre.

This I found in *The Bacchae* of Euripides, like a dream of orgiastic abandonment:

> And [the women] all slept, sprawled out, some leaning back against the branches of fir trees, others just letting their heads fall on the oak leaves on the ground... And your mother, when she heard the lowing of the horned bulls, stood up in the middle of the Bacchants and called out to them to shake the sleep from their eyes... And first they let their hair loose upon their shoulders, and fastened the fawn skins – with snakes that licked their jaws; those who were young mothers, whose breasts were still swollen and who had left their

infants, held in their arms a fawn or the wild cub of a wolf, and gave them their white milk to suck.[34]

8 April

The slow processes of drawing can encourage a lapse into a kind of waking reverie, as I find when weaving. The drawers sit absorbed in their work, headphones connected to a tape or CD. Memories of other homes, other obsessions with place are stirred up in the trenches of memory. Looking at the new areas revealed each day and the increasing mounds of earth, uncovers old sites in the psyche, old gardens. I dreamt I was back in Bellingen, that small town on the north coast of New South Wales, looking at a deserted house set out like a Cypriot blocky farmstead – rows of vines, a neglected orchard, riotous flowers and weeds, a dark and empty interior. In the dream I asked myself, could I re-inhabit it?

The sense of layers of kin, layer upon layer of generations with their ties to land and garden reminds me of the tenacity of Aboriginal friends. I dream of being in Yirrkala in the Northern Territory with a Yolngu friend – a sense of home not unlike a Cypriot village. She wishes me to sew dresses for her, and I said we'd go shopping first. A vista filled with shining tropical light, a red road and a small building remains with me after I wake.

There is a constant knowledge working with ruins that, as those hundreds of centuries have passed over the site, all those to whom this theatre was the highpoint of a festival, a crux of living, are now dead. In the night I frequently woke with a start, dreaming that there had been an earthquake, and I was buried alive amid great heaps of rubble, and that no one would ever be able to find me, as none of them has ever been found. In fact, there are often small quakes at Paphos. I dreamt a restless cat had jumped on my bed, not realising that the building itself had slightly shaken.

The dream drawings tell me how constant the old myths are,

recurring dressed up in contemporary mode, but still recognizable. Sleeping heavily, descending to those other worlds is the counterpoint to all those hours of disciplined observation as part of the larger entity of the team.

7. THE VILLAGE

20 March 1997

The dawn light falls on the flat white roofs of the village and the occasional ferny top of a terebinth tree. Just audible below the noise of traffic is the peeping of innumerable sparrows, making bushes and trees alive with their fluttering and constant sound. I can catch a glimpse from my room of the pale gold site with its purplish greyish stones – the seats at the top of the *cavea*, hardly visible between the satellite dishes, solar panels and water tanks of the rooftops all around. The harsher cries are crows perhaps, or herons flying over. The tourist world goes into abeyance in the early morning: the village life swells up and lingers in unvisited corners – there are still brown hens in the small square house opposite the Turkish baths, even though the very old woman who lived there two years ago has gone. It's just on the edge of demolition, waiting to be noticed and swept away. There is an unchanging figure with a broom, sweeping the street. The sparrows remind me of my first journeys in Greece as a young woman, while the sound of roosters is quintessentially the early morning village sound. Villages change – these sparrows flutter in the satellite dish above the hotel. Even so there is a glimpse of that archetypal village underneath the tarty tourist town, the folkloric utopian village which everyone in Cyprus once came from, where animals and humans mingle around church and café. Such villages are safely in the past; the prosperous restaurant owners and business men in Paphos recall their villages of origin with nostalgia, but also with relief that those times are over, times which offered few choices.

Fabrika Hill is a point of reference for the whole of Lower Paphos. (I just discovered that the Italian word *fabbrika* means the working place of artisans, the *homo faber*, often associated with the building of sanctuaries in the medieval world – a word has archaeological layers too, especially an Italian word in a Greek Cypriot context).[35] Early this morning I arrived at the site, and an engineer from Public Works was waiting, not speaking English, but there to tell us about the surveyors coming to co-ordinate the surveying points or stations across the hill behind the theatre. My technical Greek is not so good (some confusion, as the word for 'bus stop' and 'surveying point' is the same) but I accompanied them to every point on the hill, translating as best I could for our Australian surveyor. A can of red spray paint was used to refresh the faded letters of the survey points, even on the rock-cut temple platform. We went down into tombs and caves to find the points. One large cave a little to the north of the theatre had been reused as a byre for animals. A round chimney to the surface was full of bats, with a pile of droppings beneath – these were pointed out to me as the source of deadly disease.

The Cypriot surveyor knew every cave and tomb in the hill as he had once lived in the old house on the theatre site that had been pulled down to make way for our excavation – it had belonged to his uncle. His father had owned land to the east of Fabrika. A short stocky man of great energy, dark, fiery, he told me his grandmother knew a story about a young man who had heard about the gold of Aphrodite, and went down into an opening in the ground, near the present lighthouse. But the air was so bad down there, he died three days after he emerged, without revealing anything. The gold is still buried in Paphos, his grandmother believed. 'Perhaps you will find it!' Looking at our battered excavation, the three of them doubled up laughing.

Neighbours come and talk about what the site was like years ago, with a puzzled and reflective look on their faces, as they see the chaos of the excavation in process. The thick Cypriot dialect is often impenetrable, but the faces are memorable. Kyriakos, who runs the Halkyon, 'Kingfisher', restaurant where we sometimes eat told me his grandfather lived to be a hundred and five, and was a goatherd all his life, but all his grandchildren are educated and live in cities. Kyriakos is an upright and very courteous man whose bearing reminds me of a university professor. He works until all hours in the tourist season, and looks after a large family without being married himself. He orders a *kafethaki*, a coffee for me, and we talk briefly about the menu for the evening meal. Afterwards I ask him about his village. 'We like to keep the house in the village, so we can go back, on Sundays and feast days, and of course anyone born in my village comes and eats here.' People talk about place in terms of genealogies: 'My mother's family came from here', 'My uncle had a house there', 'My grandmother remembers that well'. A sort of indestructible village is hidden just below the surface, despite the urbanisation of Paphos.

In the cold evening I heard an eery honk about five in the chill afternoon, and looking up saw to my amazement an arrow of migrating cranes flying to the north in a geometric formation – a great mark in the sky, an arrow of direction and significance. Apparently it is a rare thing to see the cranes migrating. Later, on the way to the harbour restaurant near an unfinished shopping centre, a large pool of rainwater had collected, which resonated with loudly croaking frogs, insisting on their presence despite the inhospitable concrete. The birds and the frogs have congregated around Paphos through patterns as permanent as the mosaic interlaces on the Roman floors.

23 March

The importance of place, of families passing down knowledge

becomes obvious on another visit to the village of Fiti. We filled a car to make the short journey from Paphos with Ian, a theatre technologist, Joy, the Honours student of Egyptian ancestry, and Rowan. As we went into the crowded *kafeneion* in the main square, Efterpi Christodoulou, the weaver, greeted us in delighted recognition, her loom in a corner of the room, semi warm with a kerosene stove, men playing backgammon, a blue robed priest watching. We had coffee, looked at her weavings and bought some. To celebrate our purchases her husband brought his own wine from the Fiti vineyards, light red, zesty. I was moved to see how Evreti wove on the old loom exactly as I do on mine, swinging to the the rhythmic bang of the beater, the boat shuttles flying through the open space between the two sets of warp threads in archaic movements.

In ancient Greece the warp, so stretched and taut, was masculine, while the soft and accommodating weft thread that passes through it was feminine. Both together made up the fabric of the state, according to Plato.[36] Weaving was also the sign of matrimony. The designs do mean something quite definite, but I lost the language, and could not understand the idiosyncratic Cypriot dialect as Efterpi mentioned the long threads tied around the church I'd seen in Palaepaphos. Her mother taught her, she taught her daughters. The Greek language is about connectedness, each word has to have the correct ending according to its relationship to the subject – a network of tiny bonds, obligations, conventions, in which kinship is central.

I talked to the father of Eleni, our kind neighbour, who was slowly walking over the site at dusk staring into the trenches. The bulldozer had just removed the asphalt road so that the buildings beneath it could be dug. His pleasant house is just a step away from the excavation. I asked him if he was born here, no, but his wife's family was. He told me there used to be a church in what is now the garden of the men's sleeping quarters (a carved stone with a cross has been found exactly where he pointed out). He kept saying, 'Many many things lie beneath the ground.' It must be very disturbing for the local people to see the tarred road that crossed the site being removed to allow for excavation, in a country where public works can be erratic.

Antonios the retired musician came and railed at me, talking of the past, of his children, the difficulty of life – I understood only a fraction, but watched his solid carved face with the crumbling surface of the wall behind, flickering with shadows of leaves, and listened to the husky guttural Greek. His face was not smoothed by an easy life but solid and weathered like olive wood, bringing to mind the people who have lived here over so many generations, when Paphos was just a remote village pierced with ruins. He walks up and down the road beside the site, a short stout figure bent over with arthritis, his flute tucked into the jacket of his old suit. Once it was a living, to play the flute at weddings and ceremonies.

At sunset after work I went to the lighthouse and watched the turbulent and magnificent scene of the sun sinking into the wide sea. I saw the full moon rise in the east over the town, which all at once looked quite African with its blocky white houses, palm trees, and faint chalky light. On a freezing night the sun drops like a red coin below the shivering wall of the sea. A flock of sheep was all around me, each animal with curved and pleated horns, tiny feet beneath their shaggy coats, and many lambs. A warm woolly smell permeated the cold evening air, but the sheep were strangely, completely silent.

3 April

Sometimes change brings a revival to the countryside. I bought lavender oil from a Cypriot English woman who had a herb farm near Dali, once Idalion, a site from the Bronze Age. She inherited the abandoned land from her father, and had revitalised it by setting up a business of essential oils and medicinal dried herbs and teas – she showed me a photo of a sea of blue lavender. There are so many derelict terraces in the villages: Cyprus is full of recent ruins as well as ancient ones. It is always a scented landscape, even when deserted.

Athina, who had cooked for the team, is the same age as I am, her children grown up and one away in America, while she is still living in a small house near the theatre. '*An thelei o theos*, what God wills', says Athina. God and family is what we talk of; the weather, water and food. She calls me *koukla mou, koritsaki mou*, doll, little girl, perhaps because she is teaching me so much. She is a sweet natured woman, not bitter that her husband left her to bring up her children alone. He went to sea, and never came back, settling somewhere else, and she still works hard as a cleaner in the hospital. To please her I went with her to her favourite restaurant to watch some dancing.

People of all ages dance, some old and unbending but moving with dignity, drinking wine, peeling fresh fruit and nuts. One young man was very beautiful, lithe, moving with impossible agility, dark eyes and face like those prancing young men on Mycenaean vases. He did tricks, showing off by dancing to the bouzouki with a table, chairs, and even a girl in a chair balanced in his mouth. The way he flirted extravagantly with an older British woman made Athina look disapproving. She danced with me very modestly, restrained by the old steps, but with a light in her eyes. As we sat drinking brandy she told me that when she was a child her father had worn vraka, the baggy Turkish trousers. She had twelve brothers and sisters – seven sisters, one dead now – and family all over Cyprus, a *mega* family. They all go back to the family home in the village on Sundays. The young don't have to work hard she said, and now there is so much to eat; when she was young bread was scarce, just a little bit left for her mother after feeding so many. 'Despite this the young ones aren't happy, they seem to be bored.' She shrugged, 'What can we do?'

After a day on the site, the night outside my room hums with people and music, children calling, a mother shrieking '*Ela, ela,* come inside.' People sit musing on balconies, or under trees with a collection of ancient tables and chairs, and pots and tins bursting with flowers. Soon there will be shouts from the bar as the squaddies from the British base get steadily drunker. I walked to the black arc of the harbour wall, to have a coffee. The water was still and softly luminous, the old square fort lit up and reflected in the dark sea – cars and people surge up and down the waterfront. The palms are rhythms of small explosions of fronds, pale against the dark water. Last night when I woke, suddenly sleepless, I read a phrase in Sophocles, 'the circle of night'. This still resonates.

Sitting at dusk at a blue table in a restaurant with a rush ceiling and yellow walls, I watched the faces of friends, so well-known now from seasons of working as a team. Crystalla and George were taking us for dinner in Crystalla's sister's fish restaurant, which is built next to the Pyramos Hotel on land once owned by their mother, a farm thirty years ago. Crystalla's heavily pregnant cat Sofila lay, a heap of soft fur, under the table and was about to have rather plebian kittens, as she had been very 'naughty', Crystalla said, with the common tomcats. These same 'bad' cats tiptoed around the tables, having emerged from their hideouts in the basilica ruins, pretending to be invisible and taking the tidbits meant for the spoilt housecat. Tourists walk up and down the street in their casual clothes in the fresh night, half a moon hanging above, looking for excitement, and restaurant owners call to them enticingly as they pass. *Rembetica* or *zeimbekiko* music, said to have its roots in ancient tragedy, flowed beneath all the voices, that characteristic poetic singing evoking Byzantine melodies, but also sympathetic to the outcast and the rascal.

While listening to the lament, a strange and spectacular looking woman at a table opposite suddenly seemed like a courtesan from Alexandria, and as if by a magical transformation, everyone looked like someone in the past. I saw languorous faces from Roman paintings, or sharp carved features from an archaic gravestone.

7 April

Occasionally it seems possible to find the folkloric village. Today, a pristine spring day, I drove with a full car-load of diverse people by a roundabout route to Kourion, and we got lost in a little valley, as if driving into another time. There appeared suddenly in the windscreen of the car a perfect composition, a blocky stone ruin, a date palm, a taverna with a few tables beside the blue sea, nothing else, like a medieval painting without the hermit. The hushed hills around were covered with low heath and starred with flowers. Following the dirt track, knowing it would lead somewhere, and looking for irises we came unexpectedly to a barbed-wire fence with a handwritten notice clumsily tied to the wire: 'Bloodhound Camp'. This fence surrounding British army territory was the reason for the undeveloped peace of the hills around. So much for utopias, for the search for the perfect village in an undisturbed landscape – history makes so many painful complexities in Cyprus.

8. INVISIBLE WORLDS: EASTER

4 April 1997

Old women zigzag down the street to church. 'Good morning,' I said to a distracted elderly woman yesterday just after dawn as I walked to the site. 'Are you coming to church?' she asked, peering into my face: 'No, I'm going the other way.' 'Oh well, I'll go to the upper church too,' and she turned and walked in my direction. Ayios Prodromos, Ayia Marina – I visited all the small chapels and was relieved to find everything unchanged since the previous year, all in order, candles burning before the icons, the churches trustfully open. (*Ayíos* or *ayía* means 'holy' or 'saintly'.) The icon of Ayios Prodromos – the 'forerunner', St John the Baptist – looks like St Francis of

Assisi, small, thin, and vulnerable. Once I saw a baptism take place in his tiny barrel-vaulted church. St John the Evangelist is supposed to help children who are late in learning to speak. It is customary to bring a wax model of a tongue and hang it up in front of the saint's icon. Offerings of afflicted parts of the body are found beside many icons – hearts, livers, feet, eyes, ears, all of wax or tin, so that the saint may intercede. This is exactly as votive offerings were made in antiquity.

The churches are still central to village life and I've counted seven very old churches within a short walk from the site, including cave and catacomb shrines, not to mention the large modern cathedral. The intricate interiors of the Orthodox churches offer a glimpse into a much older world, as the pigments and techniques of decoration have an affinity with the processes of ancient frescoes and mosaics. Christianity came so early to Cyprus (through the apostles Paul and Barnabas in AD 45) that there is a seamless blurring between pagan and Christian imagery. Greek Orthodoxy has only one answer for art, so reducing, yet for all that powerful in its narrow focus – the icon is a way of looking at an invisible transcendent world, 'a window into eternity' through the faces of saints who peer out from heaven.[37]

A strange and melancholy shrine just to the west of the theatre is in a series of underground chambers that may date to the same period as the building of the theatre, to Hellenistic times. It is very dark in the passage, which leads down to water so still that it is invisible. After visiting once, and looking down into this sacred healing well, I found I avoided the place despite remnants of hieratic figures painted on the wall. This is the chapel of Ayia Solomoni, who was a Jewish Maccabee martyr of pre-Christian times, killed with her seven sons, and honoured by the early Christians. The small stone rooms seem to have layers of repressed sound, layers of events captured mutely like archaeological strata – it's suggested that there may have been a tragedy in what was probably a secret Christian catacomb. Medieval visitors were told that this was the Chapel of the Seven Sleepers, seven Christian youths walled up alive for their faith who emerged two hundred years later – a Rip van Winkle story. Above Ayia Solomoni grows a spreading terebinth tree tied with a myriad of fluttering rags: handkerchiefs, socks, even shoes belonging to those in need of the succour of the saint.[38]

And just on the other side of the theatre, not far from the old north-east gate of the city, where pilgrims once set out on the road to the temple of Aphrodite, is a whitewashed church from the fifteenth century, with a belfry, dedicated to Ayia Marina. She is famous for her ability to subdue demons – in the icon in the church they scurry about her like unruly children. She is the protectress of small children, as well as being able to cure insomnia. Often I see women I know from the village darting into this peaceful church to light a candle. The remarkable seventh-century painting of Ayia Marina in the Byzantine Museum in Paphos is dark and passionate, an 'orans' type with arms raised in prayer and scenes from her life in small pictures, almost like cartoons, around the main figure. Mostly these depict the tortures that led to her martyred death – being boiled in a cauldron, and attacked with prongs while naked, but always she has her arms upraised and a steadfast expression, her large eyes turned to heaven.[39]

Returning late from the site I noticed a light in the small Latin, or Catholic basilica (Ayia Kyriaki), and the chant of plainsong. I went in, the priest and three men in white surplices were preparing to wash the feet of two older men, while the singing went on, some in Latin, some in English, very formal. It seemed very modest, the gestures archaic – the priest stood with hands apart in the old praying stance seen in the Ayia Marina painting. The icons glimmered, the unaccompanied voice sang in the dense air. It was like looking at an ideal past: the village congregation in its simple humanity. What a comfort, I thought, to tie the dead to the living through belief in a heavenly afterlife, in the harsh times this town has lived through.

Looking at the images arrayed on the icon-stand in the uneven light of the churches is such a different experience from viewing them in an art gallery. The structure of the icon-stand, like a stage set before the congregation, displays the saints, apostles, angels, Christ and the Virgin to maximum effect in hierarchical rows one above the other, almost like the images in the crowded galleries of the old Royal Academy. The dark sad heads, shadowy-ringed eyes, tiny mouths, seem to look out with infinite sadness at the frailty of humans. The saints seem to look at me without judgement, quite kindly, just seeing me as another middle-aged woman with the usual baggage. They reflect back at me a stern world of virtue, of knowing how to manage the huge forces of loss. I thought to myself that the dragon St George would have to fight today is the monster of doubt that undermines serene trust in the work to be done.

In the twenty minutes or so that I stood before the carved screen that supports the icons, several older women came in. One moved heavily, with a wrinkled sad face and grey hair dyed orange. She kissed each of the images in the long row of the iconostasis, crossed herself, and departed. The Panayia, the Holy Virgin, had a lily, still fresh, stuck in the edge of the frame. Almost immediately, four elegant women hurried in, went up to the Panayia and kissed her, made the sign of the cross, rushed out and drove off in a little red car. It was like a visit to the ATM I thought, to get a little spiritual sustenance in the middle of a busy day. So many angels, or cherubs with eight wings float around the turquoise skies of the icons, or are entangled in the glittering carved vegetation of the vivid collections of figures in the icon screens. Often the churches are in semi-darkness and smoky with incense. The icons indicate a possibility of personal transcendence and become worn away with kisses so that glass screens have to be placed over the kissing areas. (Nobody kisses the images in an art gallery.) The Orthodox priests say that the icons radiate an angelic energy, which has a positive effect on viewers.[40] Rupert Gunnis, writing in the 1950s, observed that the icon of the Virgin was more likely to offer blessings as she was especially sacred, but because of this 'more subject to wear and tear (through intensive touching) than any of the others.'[41]

20 April

Archondia, the Greek 'princess' of the archaeological team (because of her distinctive bearing), is fasting in the weeks before Easter and looks pale and withdrawn – but she says 'I am sure of heaven!' The great festival of Paskha erupts into the routine of the archaeological season. From Panayia Theoskepasti (which means 'covered by God') a crescendo of chants is broadcast over the village by loudspeaker, building up through the last days of Lent. The church stands on a high rock, rebuilt many times since the seventh century when it was hidden by divine providence from marauding Arabs.

The structured grammar of mourning in the archaic language and ritual of Greek Orthodoxy seems to refer back to ancient rituals. On Good Friday night four armed soldiers with metal helmets stood at each post of the bier of Christ set up in the middle of the church of Panayia Theoskepasti, a guard of honour with formidable machine guns. Standing anonymously in the packed crowd, I watched the line of people laying roses, lilies and carnations on the bier. Each approached the curtained image of the Virgin Panayia, and kissed the icon through a slit in the crocheted lace. Overlaying the murmur of conversation and the shuffling of the standing congregation was the formal chanting of the priest in the rhythmic flow of Byzantine Greek, his red vestment resplendent with gold double eagles. Sparks of comprehensible words came through to me: light, cross, death, life, suffering. It's impersonal and encompassing, I felt, individual sadness sternly reminded of the vastness of human loss in the rhetoric of an almost military spirituality. The bier, heaped with vegetation, could have been the bier of Adonis, a much older deity who also died tragically young.

The next evening, at midnight on Easter Saturday, the square in front of the church was filled with a thousand people. The priests' chant was inescapable throughout the streets, crackly and magnified by the sound system. At midnight the flame flickers from the altar across the rows of people, each one lighting a candle from the person in front in fragile points of light almost snuffed out in the strong wind from the sea. 'Christ is risen!' 'Indeed he is risen!' is the greeting. Two old people kissed, shielding their candles. Prodromos the fisherman, and his wife, their faces absorbed and unseeing, walked past, the flame vanishing into his huge hand, lighting it up like a lantern. I noticed delicate girls, dressed up, and laughing. Boys beside the bonfire were throwing bangers and sparklers. The street was jammed with dark figures, lit only by candles. The flow of people in old Paphos must have been like this, warm bodies passing quickly over the paved road, transient but vital presences that evoke that most intangible aspect of the past, the irreplaceable people, just able to be dimly imagined in moments like this.

Such gatherings are very intense. Seeing the priests in their embroidered vestments with incense holders swinging, chanting from large books on stands it is impossible not to think of Byzantine and medieval paintings. It also occurs to me that this intensely theatrical and visual feast is descended from an even more ancient theatrical tradition, where the layered scene building held images of heroes and deities, while the chorus sang before it and actors in distinctive flowing garments entranced the audience. In some ways the church replaces the theatre. The tiers of the iconostasis of the church are parallel to the storeys of the scene building of the theatre, with the gods in heaven, lesser deities in the middle layers, and human heroes at the base, forming a backdrop to the performances.

St Augustine, who was born in AD 354 in the Roman province of Africa at a time when the Paphos theatre was coming to the end of its life, loved the theatre as a young man, because it was a world 'full of the reflections of my own unhappiness, fuel to my raging fire', where he could watch the emotional parting of lovers. 'And I, an unhappy young man, loved to weep; and I went out of my way to find something to make me weep.'[42] It was passionate Christians like St Augustine, brought up in a world still half pagan, who saw the slow demise of the theatre. The deep emotion and theatrical presentation of both 'pagan' theatres and religious pageants became encompassed by the *ecclesia*, the church, as the temples and theatres faltered.

I met George coming back to the hotel after midnight. Easter is the turning point of the year. '*Christos onesti!*, Christ is risen', and, he said, the central heating must be turned off.

9. NECROPOLIS

23 April 1997

Today was an exquisite spring day, cloudless and fragile green. We were reminded in the middle of a busy morning that the fast growing tourist city of Paphos is built over parts of the old necropolis to the west of the city, closing off access to many tombs of the ancient city of the dead.

A Cypriot artist, Kostas Economou, had told me he did not mind that all the antiquities were still in their tombs and sealed beneath the packed new buildings and concrete roads. 'Then there are still things to be found thousands of years in the future, and they may see things that we would not even recognise, as we see more, or differently to the nineteenth century.' During the construction of yet another large concrete apartment building not far from the theatre site, on the busy Tombs of the Kings road, a dark hole appeared – the workmen had inadvertently broken through the top chamber of a tomb. Neoptolemos from the museum arrived on the site and asked Richard if he could borrow five people to do a rescue dig, to excavate and document the gaping hole in the forecourt of the new building. The need to examine the tomb was obviously holding things up for the developers, and great pressure was being put on the museum to finish excavating.

The underground structures of ancient Paphos are often better preserved than the great public buildings of the *polis*, the urban domain of power. In the extraordinary rock-cut formations of the Tombs of the Kings the plan of the tombs mimicked the domestic home with small rooms for sleeping and storerooms with containers of vital substances set around a courtyard with a well, and the daily shrine. The tomb courtyard and its little spaces mirrored the site of the child's memories and the woman's life. I had been reading how in ancient theatre the scene of the domestic drama, the primal scene of the Oedipal tragedy was performed in the courtyard outside the family house. So the people of Paphos came back in death to this first house plan, they went 'home'. In some ways the spaces of the tomb are the negative structures, dark and damp, the hollow underside to the full sun and heat of the city's public architecture.

In my search for signs of the feminine in the ancient Mediterranean I had discovered that the Greeks thought that coldness, wetness and passivity indicated the female, even from the earliest moments of conception. If the foetus was well heated in the womb it became male, others lacking such heat became female 'more soft, more liquid, more clammy-cold.' The qualities of the male were heat, dryness and light, but male and female represented 'two poles of a bodily continuum'.[43] In the architecture of a town, heat and light were found in the monuments of the public spaces, the place of male activity, while private houses were dark and cool, the domestic feminine realms.

I went to help Bob Miller, the photographer, in the awkward space of the tomb. It is an uncanny feeling lowering oneself into a rock-cut tomb which has been closed since the second century – yet quite intimate once one was there, with three stone sarcophagi the size of small beds. In the thick quietness of the space – about three metres square, and just high enough to stand up – filtered light came through the jagged hole at the top. Women had been buried here, as was evident from the items discovered so far – the fragile glass perfume vessels, a gold earring, and a tiny gold ring. In all the fragments of the site and the museum I had been trying to place women in the confusing hierarchies of the many facets of ancient society. It was in this tomb that I had a sense of the feminine as sharply significant in ancient life, even though the writings of women are scant in the texts that have survived. Fragments of plaster still adhered to the rough surface – had the tomb been painted? The air was dense and moist, with crumbling surfaces, pockmarked ochre sandstone and a faintly unfamiliar smell, earthy, but as though strange substances had gone into its making.

I remembered all the stories of poisoned air, of people looking for Aphrodite's gold and dying from the polluted vapour of the cave or tomb. The perfume vessels are frequently found with their stoppers removed, so that those entering the tomb to place another body would not be troubled by odours of decomposition. Heaps of yellow and crumbling bones had already been removed by the time I arrived, to wait for further examination in the museum storerooms. This is the tradition of classical archaeology, and no modern Paphiot claims kinship with the ancient dead, but I could not help thinking how Yolngu people in Northern Australia would be appalled at disturbing the dead like this, after merely eighteen hundred years. Aboriginal people still maintain the responsibilities of kinship after twenty or thirty thousand years.

Literary references reverberate sitting in a tomb; Antigone buried alive, or the 'devouring grave' of seventeenth-century Europe. The sheer sense of the transience of bodily vitality is overwhelming when you sit in that dank chill. Perhaps it is wise to seal over these secret spaces below the ground of the city and get on with the hotel life, the busy life of the street and the market, away from that fearful stop, that silence. To experience the freshly discovered tomb is to be in an entirely unfamiliar atmosphere, and to feel like an intruder. We no longer have that close relationship with the physicality of death, yet its intimate spaces, containers, traces and stains, speak of moments of living.

After so many centuries it was absurd that suddenly time was short, almost a violation that the tomb must be excavated rapidly so that the new building could continue without interruption. An entrance of sorts would be left so that it might be revisited, a concrete trapdoor, looking like the entrance to the city drains. In the irregular space of the small chamber I helped to hold equipment for the photographer in the faint light and watched the museum archaeologist excavate the sticky clay at the stepped entrance, or dromos. Sandra, the architect, made rapid measurements of the asymmetrical spaces for her plan drawing. Again and again Neoptolemos scraped at the resistant ground with a sharp pick. Suddenly he stopped and handed through to us a fragmentary piece of painted plaster about the size of a plate, clearly painted in terracotta red on cream. Above some lettering was a sandalled foot, and two birds' feet. In my first astonishment I read the Greek letters ΜΗΤΗΡ, 'mother', flaming out of the dirt, not read since the second century.

This painted word, 'mater' or 'mother', appeared to flash in the dark space of that moment of discovery like a sign from the dreaming unconscious, as though the dense air of the tomb trembled. The ostensible fact of the inscription from the plaster fresco indicated that 'Demetrios' was perhaps a family name of those buried here. But to me, the visual impact and freshness of the red painted word with its pristine serifed letters was like a spoken sound, giving a voice to the unvoiced, the reverberation of the word 'mother' echoing around the tomb.

10. THE TOMB OF THE GARLANDS

10 April 1997

Winter has returned with an icy wind that blows dust and grit. The conservator, Bronwyn, crouches on the site all day in these miserable conditions, picking at the thick salt encrustations that obscure the painted plaster on a limestone slab from the entrance to the theatre. It is very slow and tricky work, to remove the encrustation without lifting the surface of the paint, using a fine dental tool. Soft pure colours emerge, red, indigo, madder, and a vivid turquoise in swirls and scallops, interspersed with petal-like blobs. The paint marks look almost like a text, and I felt a wave of excitement, as if a voice spoke from the past, to find such vibrant colour and sophisticated pattern in the ground. I finally realised after making a meticulous gouache drawing of the image, that the pattern was part of a 'fake marble' motif, so common on the lower panels of painted Roman walls. Painted marble was much less costly than the real thing, which had to be expensively imported.

The fresco fragments are becoming part of my responsibility, as pottery is the main emphasis for most of the archaeologists, and my training lies equally in art history. Geoff, the architect, is concerned to reconstruct a possible space for these intriguing frescoes that are turning up on isolated blocks near the great wall that supported all the tiers of seats, with some remaining fragments still attached to the wall itself. Because of its precisely measured level stones, this is the wall that Richard calls 'the most beautiful in Paphos.'

John, whose expertise is in Hellenistic sites, told me there was a remarkable painted tomb a short walk away, which may be helpful in placing the fresco painting of the theatre. So in late afternoon after work four of us set off into the cutting wind and biting light to walk across Fabrika Hill to the east of the old city site to look at the Hellenistic tomb. Waving grasses go down to the sea, over the unexcavated bumpy ground where the old city lies, interspersed with the dark entrances to tombs and a few ruined walls. Sheep and goats were grazing, turned away from the wind, the sea a brilliant line of light just beyond. I found a few tiny white anemones and miniature purple irises, despite the cold.

The tomb entrance was barred but looking through the grille we could see the painted rock-cut chamber about four metres square and barely two metres high. In decorative loops and swags blue-green garlands of myrtle and bay, tied with red ribbons, formed a frieze around the walls, with deep red bands making a border above panels of imitation marble. The colours were the same palette exactly as the painted plaster fragments I had just been drawing from the theatre. The bows were so cheerful and almost rococo in their waving lines; yet on the stone niche below, remains of the skeleton were still in place. The roof must once have been a deep blood red. The wreaths and the decorative marble in stripes of red and yellow were very sensitively painted. The conjunction of the haunting refinement of the painting with the darkness of the tomb catches the breath. Whose bones are they, so open to view? The tomb is probably from the first century BC, a time of shifting allegiances and wars between the dynasties of Alexander's generals, but also a time that valued a more intimate individuality, celebrating the transience of flowers, the crinkly fabric of a girl's dress, or even, for the first time, poignant portraits of old age.

The contrast between the delicacy of the painted garlands and the violence of that Hellenistic age, the same dire elegance, can be seen in the cracked and haunting terracotta portraits from the cenotaph of Nikokreon, the last king of Salamis (now in the Turkish-occupied north of Cyprus) defeated by Ptolemy. It seems that leading members of the royal family committed suicide in 310 BC to avoid capture, and their unfired clay masks were burnt on their funeral pyre, becoming 'fired' and permanent through the intense heat of the pyre. This is exactly the moment at which the Paphos theatre was being built, in all the restructuring of power after the death of Alexander. Slightly distorted, these heads (now in the Cyprus Museum in Nicosia) are astonishing and haunting images that seem to capture the extremes of emotion in their heavy-lidded eyes, the slightly open mouths, and tousled hair, which of course are also attributes of Alexander in his numerous portraits. The portraits show the essence of *pothos*, desire or longing.

I had just been reading Menander, the renowned Hellenistic dramatist and comedian who combined a love of the detail of ordinary life with a certain melancholy. He wrote: 'When you want to find out who you are, look at the tombs as you walk along. Inside them are the bones and fine dust of men who were kings and tyrants, wise men and proud of their noble descent, their wealth, of their glory and of the beauty of their bodies. And then, afterwards, not one of these things protected them against time.'[44]

How still and timeless the small tomb chambers are – I wondered at the vanished personalities of the occupants of the tomb, and at their need to be accompanied in the sealed chamber by the beauty of everlasting garlands and red ribbons. I noticed that rags, a coke can, a plastic water bottle and fast-food wrappers had been dropped into the stone sarcophagus in front of the entrance by previous visitors. Through its cracked lid I could see a humerus, a leg bone, sticking out amongst all the garbage.

Inside the tomb it became very dark as the first stars appeared in the windy sky, torn with cumulus clouds. The paintings disappeared into the shadows.

11. MOSAICS

2 April 1998

On the first free day after arriving in Paphos for the new season I sat on the old stones of Ayia Khrysopolitissa (also known as Ayia Kyriaki) and drew weaving, twining motifs from the mosaics washed clean by the rain, lit up by the early sun.

A convoluted ruin of walls, extensive mosaic floors, and beautiful column fragments in Ionic and Corinthian orders makes this one of the most evocative sites near the theatre. It feels like a place dense with the fervour of ritual, indicated by fragments with impassioned images. This may have been the site of the Roman forum, and the early Christian Paphiot bishopric considered it an apt setting for the huge basilica, which had seven aisles to hold the congregation. It was first built in the late fourth century, the time our theatre was ending its life, and was remodelled in the sixth century, only to be destroyed in AD 653 by Arabs. Arab inscriptions show they had a continued presence here, in what must have been the centre of town. The small fifteenth-century church of Ayia Kyriaki perches on the northern aisle of the once vast basilica or cathedral, in a sea of mosaics, so that you have to enter it over a wooden bridge above the flow of twining rosettes and ribbons. Fragments of a Gothic cathedral add to the intricacy of the ruins. Now the site is overshadowed by eucalyptus trees and rather hidden behind the new Woolworths building, which rises where once the water of the harbour would have lapped the edge of the cathedral precinct.[45]

The mosaics are muscled and complicated patterns continually entangling and parting with an underlying structure which is geometrical and repetitive. Known as carpet mosaics, the designs reflect the textiles that have vanished. The five-petalled rosette, originally an attribute of Demeter, is pierced here by a Christian cross. The patterns are all about connection and the interchangeability of positive and negative space. You can read the same element differently according to which part of the pattern is in the foreground. As you gaze at these intricate designs they seem to move, to shimmer, while revolving around fixed certainties of form, such as grids and circles, ellipses and lozenges. Interlaced rosettes form larger patterns in optical waves, with shimmering grids, chequers and scale or feather patterns in a graduated measure. The scholar Richard Sennett suggests that in times of uncertain and fluctuating security Roman societies found a particular pleasure in these optical patterns.[46] The passion for complex intertwining arises at that moment of late antiquity when there was an overlap between paganism and Christianity. Islamic patterns are descended from this fertile mix.

The mosaics are made of tiny cut pieces of coloured stone, unable to fade even in that unmitigated white light. In the 1950s it was thought that there were few ancient mosaics in Cyprus, but since then many extraordinary discoveries have been made. The earliest mosaics are made of small black and white pebbles (like Scylla) and then the great period for floor mosaics starts in the Hellenistic period, about 150 BC, with monochrome and sometimes irregular pieces of cut stone. Suddenly there is a great flowering of floor mosaics in the second century AD under the Severan emperors, and the *tesserae* include brilliant glass as well as multicoloured stones, so that great detail in figures and patterns can be realised.

6 April

A strange chance has given me the opportunity to design a new 'mosaic' floor. Richard was asked by Dr Theophilos of the Royal Artemis Hospital in Paphos if there were artists who could help with the 'mosaic' decorations of his swimming pool project. So every afternoon after my usual work drawing and documenting on site, I come to the covered pavilion behind the hospital which holds a swimming pool, still under construction, with a wide paved stone floor around it where Dr Theophilos wants mosaic designs of mythologies, to give 'peace and strength' to his patients. We discussed which mythological characters he would like to see, and I have made a scale drawing. Aphrodite emerging from the sea with nereids, Heracles, Cheiron the Centaur, Artemis (of course), Apollo,

Poseidon, Demeter and Persephone, Adonis and Hermes, with animals and plant ornaments will frame the pool. With the help of colleagues from Wollongong, Ian and Celeste, I am drawing the lifesize and challenging figures in charcoal on the stone. Two Sri Lankan workmen Hamid and Samah engrave the drawn line into the stone with a noisy machine that fills the air with stone dust. Into the engraved stone groove, black cement is poured. This is not a true mosaic, but the images do form part of the substance of the stone flooring.

The hospital and its staff are another microcosm within the town of Paphos. I am astonished to discover that many of the nurses, cleaners, carpenters and ground staff are from Sri Lanka, another former British colony. Dr Theophilos and the other doctors could not manage without their hardworking Sri Lankans – what a strange result of the mingling and shifting processes of colonisation.

Samah is small and sturdy with bits of brown skin showing through the covering of white stone dust. We communicate in a mixture of pidgin Greek and a few English words. He is immensely fascinated with the images in my drawings and expressed a desire for peacocks, somewhere. So I found a place next to the goddess Hera, as she is always associated with the bird of immortality. Samah said, rather wistfully, that peacocks are also beautiful to eat in Sri Lanka, his own land. Also, he wants some nereids or mermaids as women with fish tails who come out of the sea are familiar to him. The Sri Lankans work tirelessly, twelve hours a day, in a cloud of gritty dust, fixing machinery that constantly breaks.

Dr Theophilos' father had little education and few opportunities, he told me. He was a farmer on the headland above the old port, and while ploughing the stony soil more than forty years ago he discovered the now famous mosaics of the House of Dionysos just below the topsoil. Dr Theophilos has broken the pattern of families tied to the land – he studied obstetrics in London – but has a determined strong-featured face rather like one of the vital

Roman figures in those same mosaics found beneath his family's ancestral fields. As it is spring he is delivering many babies, sometimes even dashing away while talking to me. He shrugs, 'Obstetrics is easy: the woman does it all.' A man of great energy, he comes out for a short break each afternoon to look at our work as we crouch on the pavement, covered in dust, ordering a cool drink or a coffee for us from the little café.

18 April

The mythological stories so vividly represented in the ancient mosaics preoccupy me, and underline the stories that emerge from the people in the archaeological team. Travelling in a strange country always makes people talk about their own lives, as if distance and strangeness clarified and gave a shape to experience; although Ian quoted wryly from John le Carré – 'The trouble with travelling is that I come too'.

    The puzzle is to reconstruct the past from the arbitrary material evidence. The complexities of lived life as we know it are reduced to the impersonal evidence of plates, bowls and cooking pots. Each person becomes absorbed in assembling an almost talismanic significance from particular objects. Ian was excited about some lead discs which he hoped might be theatre tickets. We are all involved in slow processes of documentation and sorting around the theatre, which can seem almost like fairytale occupations. Phillippa, a graduate from Sydney, is endlessly dividing up large and small fragments of different kinds of marbles, while Marcie and Gina are cataloguing the glass finds, with tiny fragments of glinting irridescence spread out over the table. Mounds of just excavated pottery have to be sorted every afternoon – with people from each trench stooped on the large green mat identifying the 'diagnostic' fragment, making lists of closed and open vessels, feet, lips and handles of all the pots of daily life that are layered through the excavation. Bones come up in a deposit laid out on the mat and the young trench supervisor almost wails in despair, 'They shouldn't be there!' Craig is making a large study of Rhodian amphorae for his doctoral thesis, amphorae which have been described as the cardboard boxes or plastic bags of antiquity, used throughout the Hellenistic period for transporting oil, wine and grain. He carefully makes a rubbing over the delicate impressed inscriptions on the handles with a soft pencil and a cigarette paper, to identify period and type. An ancient logo of a rose is associated with the inscriptions on the jars.

Thinking of the odd stories and the almost surreal associations of the things we find it was very moving to visit Khirokhitia yesterday, a Neolithic site out in the dry country on the road to Nicosia. The steep rocky hill of carob and olive is layered with wild grasses, probably like those simple grains of 9,000 years ago that must have provided sustenance for the settlement. The stone foundations of the houses are set into the hill like a honeycomb, with tiny womblike dwellings nestled together, where people were either very small, or slept in the foetal position. There was hardly room to stretch out. Those who died were buried under the floor, so that generations must have lain one above the other. Querns and mortars, curved and rubbed stones for grinding grain were lying everywhere. The site seemed curiously vulnerable even though the stone walls were so thick. Now without their mud-thatched roofs, these earliest houses are exposed to the harsh light, in circular foundations so old as to appear like a natural formation, the dark inner life gone.

We drove through pale ochre terraced hills, light against the sombre grey sky. Wind blew grass over the windscreen of the car. Layers of loss were also evident in the landscape – a sign proclaimed 'To the forest of the disappeared.' There is always a need for a 'new' land – but lands are seldom new.

The textured and scratched stones of the walls of the Turkish baths near the theatre are like pages, laid out in a sequence to be read, if that were possible.

25 April

Dr Theophilos is a chanter in the cathedral church, the Mitropoleos in Paphos, and he showed me a great electric organ that he keeps near his waiting room for music practice. He sings frequently, he told me, to his patients while they are in labour. The bishop of Paphos has been interested in his swimming pool pavilion and came a few days ago to inspect the work of engraving the mythological images. He wanted to know why there were no saints amongst all the figures. Dr Theophilos said, persuasively, 'If we had saints around the pool we would have to walk on them, and how could we walk on figures so close to God?'

'Of course, this is not possible,' the bishop agreed.

It is remarkable to think how long there has been a bishop in Paphos, ever since the fourth century AD, at the basilica of Ayia Khrysopolitissa. And Dr Theophilos' family has lived in Paphos near the theatre for generations. As a child, he remembers staying in the small house that once existed near the beneficent terebinth tree, with his grandmother, without ever realising that the slope of the hill was a theatre. She was born, lived and died there. His grandfather died after finding a tomb and going down into the polluted air, repeating a variant of that old fairy story I have heard before.

27 April

Today I made archaeological drawings of glass at the Paphos Museum. Neoptolemos, the museum official, went into the depths of the storerooms, unlocking door after door. He found small boxes from the Tombs of the Kings (the ancient necropolis to the west of the old city), boxes full of tiny glass vessels with a rainbow opalescent crust over the fragile surfaces. Very slowly and carefully he took them out of their nests, as small shavings of glass clung to the yellowing cotton wool. He gave a group of the small cardboard boxes, material excavated in the 1970s, with dusty faded labels, to Anita, who is in charge of cataloguing all the glass from a sequence of tombs. One piece was a perfect unguentarium or perfume vessel, with the surface encrusted with iridescence in extraordinarily subtle shades. 'Blue-green or green-blue?' asked Anita, pausing over her notebook. Infinitely patient descriptions of each object are necessary. These vases used to be called *lachrymatoria* because, I was told as a young student, they were held up to the eye to collect the tears of mourning which were then offered at the grave. The little glass vessels are sometimes shaped like tears.

'Don't disturb the inside. That dust may be the residue of substances that can be identified,' Anita told me. In the rock-cut chamber tombs such fragrances kept the air perfumed. These haunting groups of vessels are the true *nature mort*, true still lifes – what essences did they contain? These are the vessels that may have been left open, full of scented oils and perfumes, to counteract the odours of decay in the 'Mother' tomb.

The stone garden at the museum is very lovely with its grid of stone paths interspersed with oleanders, hibiscus and pine – with an astonishing series of Ionic and Corinthian capitals geometrically arranged on plinths. They looked as if they might sprout with fresh arabesques of spiraled foliage.

I found a sentence from Rhea Galanaki: 'I determined that one day I would write the invisible story of that evening in a manner dictated by things visible.'[47] This is what archaeology does: precise descriptions of what is visible, which is all we have to encompass and frame what is not seen and can never be known.

30 April

Up at the Royal Artemis Hospital all the conversation is about Adonis, that blighted young lover of Aphrodite who, it is said in one version of the story, was gored to death by a wild boar. Adonis is 'wild for the girls,' the doctors tell me, and the English matron is also very keen on images of the young deity. She has put Adonis on the banner of her English club. 'Very little on, just a fig leaf.' An older doctor tells me he has written a novel about a German woman travelling around Cyprus, a novel that includes all the local legends of Adonis. He insisted that the Cypriot Adonis had his own story, different to that of the Greek Adonis, in that he came from the valley near the Kykko monastery. Adonis' rival was Hermes, who was also a 'friend' of Aphrodite and the real story was that they fought each other and Hermes killed Adonis. (In the versions I have read the rival to Adonis is Ares, god of war, not Hermes, the messenger, but myth is always slippery.) The poppies in the valley near Kykko came from Adonis' blood. 'The river is mentioned in Homer,' he told me. His sources are also folk stories – village girls used to be called Berengaria before they married, a name from the Lusignan French period. Berengaria was a mythical queen who used to reign over the island. The doctor said, 'Mothers call their sons Adonis but look at his face! Does he know what a face he has! But it's true that ugly dark parents can have beautiful children.'

Now he wants me to make the Cypriot story of Adonis and Hermes. 'Show Adonis in rivalry for Aphrodite with Hermes – it's important that it's right'. They talk about these stories as if they were recent history. All the doctors admired my Aphrodite, poised naked with just a twist of flying drapery, on a scalloped shell. Dr Theophilos has kindly promised to contribute a substantial sum to the excavation for my work, and that of my helpers, Ian and Celeste.

4 May

A very hot afternoon, a white still sky is a foretaste of summer. Samah and Hamid, the workmen at the hospital, have slowly cut the stone around the lines of Narcissus and filled the grooves with black pigment. They have finished Apollo. Today I drew Myrrha, the mother of Adonis, Persephone and Demeter, and a mermaid/nereid, with flowers and a pomegranate. 'But who is Demeter?' Dr Theophilos asked rhetorically. 'Who's Persephone? People will want to know – I'll put a plaque in the floor with the stories.'

'These *rodi*, pomegranates, are everywhere,' he said, pointing to all my floating fruits. 'There are too many.' He had forgotten why pomegranates were important, so I reminded him about Persephone eating the three pomegranate seeds in Hades, and being forced to return to the underworld for three months of every year. I love the vivid red flowers of the sharp green pomegranate trees, and the way the memory of the star shape of the flower remains on the rosy fruit like a little collar.

There's such a pleasure in this dreamy drawing on a large scale: the images come now without having to use the models. I've learnt from the old mosaics how each of the deities has his or her specific gesture and pose, and once you have learnt this basic vocabulary the composition becomes easy. Celeste and Ian become absorbed in drawing ornamental motifs adapted from the theatre frescoes, and Ian has included some dolphins. These are gentle linear narratives – the genre of an Aristide Maillol or Raoul Dufy, unobtrusive, light-hearted decorations around a swimming pool.

Dr Theophilos' daughter is ten, he tells me, and his older daughter who is seventeen doesn't know what she wants to do, and won't tell him – he just pays the bills. He makes an indescribable face, lifting his eyebrows, and shrugging. Today he requested the image of an amphora with wine spilling out. He loves the figures – but did not like the lyre floating in the coil of vine leaves; he needed a person attached to it. He now suggests I decorate the walls as well, but there is hardly any time left in our season.

Each afternoon he rushes out to see what I'm doing. The death of Adonis is his favourite of all the stories – I composed Adonis lying broken in the lap of Aphrodite – but now he likes Demeter nursing her daughter Persephone (my own invention with some help from classical models.) 'This is excellent, very nice.' Other doctors come and look.

11 May

Cutting the line of my drawing in the stone floor is difficult and often the line becomes distorted, but Samah is deeply interested in the process and tells me in Greek he is a sculptor himself. His English hardly exists, perhaps because he is very young, born long after the British left Sri Lanka. For the spa room beside the pool he is making a plaster frieze of provocative nubile women – most of them are Zeus' lovers, with impossibly curved hips and breasts that seem to belong to the voluptuous temple deities of South India. It is such a bizarre conjunction, a woman from Wollongong in Australia and a man from Sri Lanka, working on Dr Theophilos' vision of old/new mythologies to restore his patients' sense of well-being. Such strange alliances have no doubt happened many times before in the long tradition of Cypriot art, where East and West mingle in so many combinations. How remote from 'high art' this project has been, grounded in a specific locale. I have become engrossed in drawing large figures on this stone pavement, and in the stories they represent. Everyone wants to tell stories about the images; and that's what the doctors talk to me about, strolling out for a smoke, wandering around the pavilion. They always come back to Adonis, the Cypriot Adonis – is it the doctors' younger, virile selves? 'We were all Adonis for a brief little while,' says Dr Theophilos. What an enigma he has organised for future archaeologists to puzzle over.

A walk by moonlight to the theatre, so shattered and ruined in its present existence, so that it is hardly possible to imagine its glory. The moon shines on the tiers of seats, with two figures sitting talking, their cigarettes points of light, their voices murmuring in the clear acoustics of the curved hill. The theatre's present ruin is now more permanent than its other lives – but the time of its supposed perfection in the glorious fourth century BC haunts all the other stages;

a mirage really, as that period is so overlaid with later reconstructions. There is no perfect past, the theatre is a hybrid of many buildings, and this is its great value and fascination. To get to some sense of the original Hellenistic theatre, the evidence of Late Roman kilns, of medieval farmsteads or pottery workshops must be destroyed. Many pasts exist together, not sequentially. The old walls around the site of the north-east gate of the city seem to be of all periods. The mythical stories continued over the centuries, linking generations, and even becoming transformed into new life in the Christian mosaics. The life of these fragmented monuments of Paphos may take on a vigorous momentum in the present, revitalised by the strange concerns of archaeology. Earthquakes left the great basilica of Ayia Khrysopolitissa and the castle of Saranda Kolones with a real life that was quite short. As ruins they have another life, continually evoking the small intense moment of actual habitation, but also it seems causing a new generation of mythical stories in the concrete buildings of modern Paphos.

12 May

Working at the Royal Artemis Hospital has shown me what chance connections may bring an artwork into existence, through the odd pathways of a colonial history. Surely the past was just as complex as my present experience of the hospital. The artisans of the theatre may have come from widely separate provinces of Rome around the eastern Mediterranean, speaking the common Greek language within the Pax Romana.

A perfect dawn on the last day of the season. The raking light reveals the theatre ruin scoured by wind and light, crackling with dry gold plants. The hill of Fabrika behind is bony and stark, as if nothing more could ever be revealed – but the mere presence of those cut and tunnelled stone platforms intrigues and questions certainties, brings up to consciousness new variations on old stories of love and loss.

12. A.H.S. MEGAW
AND THE SEVENTH CENTURY

18 April 1998

One late spring day when the caper bushes are beginning to push up through the cracks in the walls with their tight round buds and silky tasselled flowers, I walk up the hill to Peter Megaw's house in upper Paphos, not expecting him to be there. But he welcomes me warmly into the cool house and gives me orange juice as it is so hot. His garden is already brown and drying in the heat despite the banksia rose profusely flowering. I take him a small offering, a jar of Australian honey.

Sometimes, looking at an archaeological section cut through the earth two distinct layers can become blurred. Occasionally it happens that an individual also seems to exist in several layers of time at once, with nuances of language and gesture from an earlier age that coexist, almost invisibly, with the concerns of the present moment.

A constant and kindly presence in Paphos, A.H.S. or Peter Megaw, born in 1911, had been the director of the British School of Archaeology in Athens when I had been a student there. It is wonderful to me that someone I knew so long ago in another country, Greece, is rediscovered here. Now, after half a century of excavating sites, he lives in an old house poised on a hill looking out over the site of the ancient city that he had managed to preserve for archaeology, despite the pressures of tourist development.

The high rooms – the main living room with a charming gallery – were full of beautiful traditional things; spoons and farm utensils, woven and embroidered textiles, and old carved furniture gathered from all over the island in the days before it was divided in 1974. This collection speaks of the vigorous delight in Cypriot ethnicity by the English who governed Cyprus before the Second World

War, a group of highly educated and much travelled people who come alive in Lawrence Durrell's *Bitter Lemons*. On the walls, riven with earthquake cracks, were his wife Electra's delicate and precise watercolours of places and plants in colonial Cyprus, in her fine Slade School technique. Electra Mangoletsi, of Albanian ancestry, had married Peter in Athens in 1937, and was famous in Cyprus for her exquisite botanical record of the flowers of the island. Her work had been included in the magazine *Cyprus Review* edited by Lawrence Durrell in the 1950s. I remembered Peter as the sturdy, ruddy man from the British School of Archaeology in Athens thirty years ago How terrifying I had found the vibrant Electra as a hostess, entertaining the residents of the School with her formidable party games, whose terms of reference were remote to me.[48]

As director of Antiquities for the British Government in Cyprus after the Second World War, Peter was instrumental in encouraging and organising not only early excavations in Paphos but also the beginnings of a museum in the town. Lawrence Durrell described him as 'a quite exceptional archaeological officer.'[49] Before 1974, Paphos was very remote and unexplored archaeologically compared to the spectacular sites on the north coast of Cyprus, such as Salamis. But after the Turkish invasion, the rich northern sites were inaccessible, and Paphos was opened up, not only by Cypriot archaeologists but also by Polish and Italian archaeological missions.

Knowing that he was living in Paphos, I contacted him with some shyness when the Australians first began their excavation of the theatre. But he was delighted that we were in town, and curious about the excavation strategy. (He has always talked about excavations as a military exercise; perhaps in a kind of historical recollection of so many colonial explorations and battles, when the by-product of a British presence might well have been an archaeological site.) I explained how few tools we had for the tough work of clearing the site. 'I may be able to help you there,' he said with that courteous formality I remembered so well. 'I believe I have wheelbarrows, spades and perhaps buckets stored in an underground tomb on Fabrika Hill.' And so it turned out, as if that were the most natural and inevitable place for storage.

He seemed to be deeply preoccupied with the intricacies of the past, almost as if in some way he 'remembered' the seventh century. Saranda Kolones, 'Forty Columns', the ruined Crusader castle near the port of Paphos, was an immensely complicated puzzle, and Peter had been thinking about it since 1957 when he first started excavating it. Early travellers assumed from the scattered granite columns that the ruin might be an ancient temple, perhaps another temple of Aphrodite. But it turned out to be a medieval building, built long after the passing of the Greco-Roman world. The castle evolved during a period of flux in the eastern Mediterranean, as Byzantine Constantinople and the eastern Orthodox church tried to balance the competing interests of the 'Latin' Crusader countries of France and England against the constant threat from the Islamic East.

'"Triple-harboured Paphos",' Peter commented. 'Strabo said it all, succinctly.' The Franks built the castle on the middle lobe of the harbour around 1205; what was the harbour is now a parking lot on reclaimed land. It appears the castle was never finished as they intended. Richard Anderson, the excavating architect also working at the Agora in Athens, gave the archaeologists from the theatre a site tour of Saranda Kolones. 'It was lost to memory, this huge building, it was just a mound.' He told us that on 7 May 1191, Richard the Lionheart defeated Isaac Comnenius, setting up an independent Cyprus, and was declared Emperor of Cyprus. Byzantium regarded him as a troublemaker in their area of influence. When he left for the Crusades Cyprus was put in the hands of the Knights Templars, and from them the island passed to Guy de Lusignan. These 'Latins' or Franks ruled Cyprus for three hundred years. Destroyed in an earthquake of 1222, the castle may have been in use for barely thirty years. The grey granite columns from Egypt were first used in the Roman buildings in the agora, such as the Odeon, or small theatre, and recycled by the Lusignans in the thick walls. Military architecture needed speed and economy, and it is thought that as the builders did not have the technology to cut the hard stone they placed the old Roman columns horizontally through the walls, like giant nails.

Peter told me about first starting to dig at Saranda Kolones, through the generosity of the mayor of Paphos, who gave him access to the land in those days when Paphos was a distant village far from the tourist itinerary. They used the farmer Hassan's mud-brick house as a base, he said, but there was no proper storage, and bora beetles ate the shelves. Things got lost, labels got eaten too. The so-called Tombs of the Kings were also dug in these early years, first of all cleared out by convicts from the prison. The austere tomb courtyards and *loculi* had been used as shelters for animals and shepherds, and centuries of manure had to be removed. He wondered, 'Where is the material from the medieval kiln in the Tombs of the Kings?' The archaeological record is fragile when there is no secure building for storing and recording finds. It was his example that gave value and importance to the Byzantine and Ottoman pottery, so that now these eras are recognised as vital in revealing complicated histories.[50] The captivating quality of these previously denigrated periods became clear to me as I listened to his rapid identifications while bending over a table of Late Roman and early Byzantine potsherds from the theatre site – 'I think this type is from Lapithos, and this is a kind of proto-majolica from Italy.' He selected a beautiful piece with a blue petal: 'This blue and white is from Venice and this is from Florence probably about 1500, but this is Ottoman, really very late, it could even be nineteenth-century.' There's evidence for all periods in this tumbled and ruined theatre: he finds this so valuable and seemed keyed up with excitement looking at what had emerged from the ground.

The castle was built over an earlier fort, which may have been the first overseas Arab position in the seventh century. Peter talked of a well of that date which was much earlier than the castle, which he had excavated. In the well was a group of strange coins re-issued in the later seventh century, after the Arabs had come and gone. At first, he thinks, the Arabs came to negotiate only and the Cypriots tried to keep on friendly terms with each of their large armed neighbours, the Byzantines and the Arabs. Once again, Peter spoke of that Arab garrison down by the port as if he had been there. Cyprus was almost completely occupied by the Arab raiders until the tenth century, he thought. Traces of archaeological evidence such as the well seemed to give a glimpse of this Arab presence. 'I think we can place the very severe earthquake that set life back for a generation to about AD 680,' he observed in a lunchtime discussion.

Saranda Kolones was destroyed in a comprehensive earthquake, and there is haunting evidence of the catastrophe to be gleaned from archaeology. After the first shock of the great quake most people probably escaped from the castle, but one man came back to rescue an exceptionally lovely glass flask, and then a larger shock came – he was caught, but managed to get down into the substantial drains beneath the castle. Unfortunately, iron grilles covered their entrances to protect against subversive attacks, and although alive, he could not get out and died there, with the masonry collapsed above him, holding his treasure. 'Poor chap,' said Peter. 'We found part of his sword and scabbard.' A girl student from the Australian team ran through these dim tunnels, and knocked her head so badly she was concussed for days, as if there might still be an uneasy presence in the labyrinth of this great ruin.

So often as I wander over the Saranda Kolones site in the dusk I see the herd of sheep and the shepherd, collecting herbs, or sitting on a stone. Richard Anderson told us he was not some timeless peasant as nostalgia might suggest but Iperides the shepherd, son of the headmaster of the American School in Larnaca, and could well have a mobile phone in his pocket.

21 April

A few weeks into the season a remarkable find turns up at the eastern entrance area of the theatre, which was also the northeast gate of the walled city. A student leaning over the sieve picks out what she thought was a sliver of gold foil, and yells out as if bitten. One of the youngest members of the team, this is her first time away from home. She is so excited. 'I imagined it was a bit of rubbish that must have blown into the trench from the road.' But it was a solid gold coin, miraculously unscathed and gleaming, the head identified as a portrait of Constantine IV, around AD 688. Peter came to the theatre site with a thick book, a rare catalogue of Byzantine coins that had the exact match to our coin. It comes from the same period as that provoking Arab well below Saranda Kolones, and the gold coin could have belonged to soldiers from the Arab garrison, as such coins were used by all countries even a long time after issue, like the American dollar today.

The excavators made up stories about the loss of the valuable coin, no doubt a disaster for its owner in that turbulent time, when established order was collapsing. One version had it that a woman was fleeing from her elderly rich husband out of the northeast gate, taking the opportunity of earth tremors to break her stultifying routine and run off with her lover. A coin falls as she runs, but she's being pursued and she can't stop to find it. Or a courtesan has pleased a rich man in a house in the narrow street behind the theatre that leads to the northeast gate and he pays her lavishly. But perhaps in the confusion of an Arab raid, the coin slips between the fissures of the road, to be retrieved in another millennium by people from a part of the world unimaginable to Europe when the coin was lost.

It was likely that by 688 the Arabs had left their base because of a severe earthquake around the same time. Byzantium negotiated with the Arabs to take over the island, although isolated raids continued, forcing the population to live away from the coast. Looking at the coin in his palm, Peter thought that possibly the Arabs may even have sacked Paphos and Kourion, as these cities were getting too friendly with Byzantium. Even the great basilica of Ayia Khrysopolitissa in Paphos was made into a mosque for a time, as Arabic inscriptions indicate both in the basilica and in the smaller church at the port. The terminology of this hardly known period is contentious – archaeologists do not always agree even on the term 'Byzantine'. When does 'Roman' become 'Byzantine'?

Smadar, one of the archaeologists, looked up from her Late Roman domestic ware at the other end of the table and observed that transitional periods are the most fascinating, especially that blurring between Islam and Christianity. (For her doctorate, she is studying the often crudely fired but very evocative domestic pottery impressed with simple and repetitive patterns.) The two religions were more similar than different in the seventh century, when many sects flourished. Muhammad's religion was taken for yet another form of Christian heresy when it first appeared around AD 640 and was for a time treated by the Christians as a related sect.

Peter Megaw's other great Cypriot project has been the uncovering of the great early Christian basilica at Kourion south of Paphos. He told me he'd 'had a good campaign' excavating the Kourion basilica in 1964, about the time of Independence, when there was much unemployment, and he had got some money to pay workmen. He was now documenting the first excavations of G. McFadden from the Pennsylvania University Museum, begun in 1934.[51] All the material excavated from the early years seemed to have been lost, except for the coins, 'and they seem to be alright.' McFadden had tragically drowned, and there had been little money, even though Peter had been asked to take it on. He talked about his nearly finished book on the Kourion Byzantine excavations, and was choosing a plan of all the structures, drawn by Richard Anderson as a frontispiece. The building was really an *episkopeion*, a bishopric with a church and living quarters.

I had not realised that Peter has a close understanding of Egypt, as he had worked with A.B. Wace in the upper Nile on Coptic churches. He has gained a vast knowledge of artefacts and sites, building on his original training as an architect with many decades of practical experience in the field. How much, how widely he has published – I must have read his *Reports on Archaeological Work* in Greece first in 1962.

Richard Anderson, the Athenian Agora architect, has reconstructed the plans of Kourion, as well as those of Saranda Kolones. The Kourion episkopeion was built on the Roman foundations of the town basilica which fell during the vast earthquake of AD 363 that may even have generated a tsunami or tidal wave, and then another earthquake in 688 destroyed it, never to be re-inhabited. The fourth-century earthquake documented in Kourion may also have affected the Paphos theatre, as evidence for the use of the theatre subsides at that time. In the usual Cypriot mode of recycling, all the material from Kourion was taken to build the subsequent town of Episkopi. Kourion was excavated in sections over a long period from the 1930s to the present – baptistery, forecourt, bishop's palace all emerged, perched above a great vista of sea and coastline. Some of the complex has fallen down the cliff hundreds of metres to the beach below. It seems that wherever Peter Megaw digs he finds major catastrophe and earthquake ruin. (For this reason his military terminology in describing excavation is appropriate.) The past may be disastrous, the present full of political revolution, accident and war, but the disciplined excavation of the earliest Christian communities in Cyprus continued through all those years.

10 April 1999

Almost a year later I call on Peter to borrow some books on coins, and to keep him up to date on our seasonal progress on the theatre site. This time he offers me Keo Supreme sherry (only with my father and Peter do I drink sherry) and a little plate of *píkro*, shrivelled local black olives. He seems unchanged, a little more hesitant in his movements perhaps, but still in jacket and tie, and as alert as ever. He goes on to say he wasn't much good in the kitchen and how marvellous a cook his mother-in-law had been, Electra's mother. I ask him to tell me about that time. His parents-in-law had been poor Albanian Greeks who had come first to Salonica, Thessaloniki, to work in textiles and had then gone to the USA and learnt about cotton, setting up factories in England but constantly travelling to Athens, to Albania, and to Crete. Electra had been educated in England and went to the renowned Slade art school – 'It must have been in the late 20s or early 30s.' Her parents had lost a great deal in the stock market crash and slump at this time and decided to move to Athens and consolidate what they could, and Electra went too, not being able to find work in the UK. She was introduced to Peter by Humphrey Payne, the young director of the British School in Athens, where Peter was already the deputy director at the age of twenty-five.

I had admired Humphrey Payne's writing very much as a student in Sydney, for his work on the exquisite Corinthian *aryballoí* or archaic perfume vessels, and for the excavation of Perachora in the Corinthian Gulf. Sadly he died suddenly of blood poisoning, as people could then, aged only thirty-three. His wife was Dilys Powell, 'sent down' from her university for climbing into Humphrey's college window, who later became a prominent journalist and writer.

As he sat in a chair covered with red kilims and embroideries, the sun coming through from a high window, he looked suddenly frail despite his intellectual energy, the bones of the head vulnerable in the soft light. But I know from my own family that old age can be very tough and persistent.

Peter accepted the post as head of the newly formed Antiquities Service in Cyprus as the War started, working of course for the British Government. He said that things were very difficult in the

War, particularly after the invasion of Crete by the Germans, when it was expected that Cyprus would fall next. Women and children were evacuated to South Africa by ship, as Egypt was too full of refugees. But Electra managed to get back to Egypt after eight months in Capetown, and because of new emergencies and the retreat of the Germans in the eastern area she was employed in censorship.

Gently insisting I stay for some lunch, he got out tomatoes, ham and bread. I left after a three hour conversation, laden with books on Byzantine ware for Holly, who is now the excavation's medieval pottery expert. Having observed such tumultuous histories in the eastern Mediterranean, he seemed unconcerned about death. 'I may need five years to see these publications through.'

13 April

There's a discussion over the sorting table about the fifth-century coins found outside the perimeter of the theatre, near the ancient road. The severe earthquake about AD 360 may really have finished off the theatre so that it was never reconstructed, Richard thinks. In the early fifth century it would have been a great ruin, and a rich source of ready-cut building material for recycling in the great Christian churches nearby.

Later on after work I walk to Ayia Khrysopolitissa, the church ruin with its spreading carpet mosaics half a kilometre from our theatre site, also dug over years with the hovering presence of Peter Megaw. This is the place where the Arab obituaries were found, where people have worshipped since the church was first built in the fourth century. An apocryphal story that St Paul was tied to a particular Ionic column and beaten by devotees of Aphrodite is still told to tourists. I sat under an arch with my back against a stone and drew an extraordinary medieval capital lying on the ground among pink hollyhocks – with a relief carving like uncurling fern fronds. Another similar capital has been re-used in an Ottoman fountain around the corner – nothing stays in its proper period but migrates and transforms into new structures.

What a magnificent building this basilica must have been; as big as a cathedral, intricately decorated with marbles and mosaics. Despite the official declaration that paganism was dead by Emperor Theodosius in the late fourth century, the wonderful infrastructure of public buildings and roads, the elaborate transport of goods and food across the Roman Empire must have seemed everlastingly in place after more than five hundred years of Empire. Yet in a few generations it was all lost, in a combination of natural and human disaster – earthquakes and consequent plagues, and then famine combined with political uncertainty. I remembered a conversation exploring the idea that technologies can retreat; that knowledge and expertise can be irretrievably lost, after a lecture by an Oxford coin expert in Nicosia.

Traumatic events repeat themselves. The excavators have discovered traces of temporary huts in the ruins of the fourth century theatre, just as people more recently have camped in the dusty remains of the great buildings of Sarajevo and Kabul, making do with what is to hand, as if memory could reconstruct the stones and re-imagine the transient comforts of daily life. Looking at the television news is like seeing a mirror image of ancient devastation and survival. Homes remain a simulacrum of home in all the stony dust, and broken shrines like the vast cornerstone of the old *temenos* of Aphrodite still receive offerings because the memory of a place outlasts stone.

Tonight I sit with George and Crystalla in the hotel and watch the Greek news of the Balkan War, bombs falling and flames roaring at night. People stream doggedly over hard mountains carrying crying babies, or in primitive trucks on pitted roads. Here is Libanius writing about a revolt against the emperor in the late fourth century in his town, Antioch, a city closely related to Paphos: 'So death came upon the children, some from exposure on the bare ground, some even falling from the arms of those who carried them, and death from starvation afflicted them all... We all hear the news that everywhere is full of the bodies of the dead – fields, roads, hills, ridges, caves, hilltops, groves and gullies – some a feast for birds and beasts, others borne by the river down to the sea.'[52]

After that I dreamt that the old drains of the theatre ran with blood and effluent, but the team do not notice, or pretend not to, despite my protestations.

14 April

It is nearly the end of the season and Peter comes for lunch on the site and spends an hour with me first, looking around the recently dug trenches. For the first time he negotiated the rough ground using a stick, but seemed to find everything full of interest. He pointed out that in 'my' trench on the western *parodos* or entrance, the stones had fallen not in a typical earthquake scatter, but as if they had been partially toppled by an earthquake and then the destruction was completed by trying to make a level area.

He looked again at the layers of Late Roman and glazed ware, and I knew it was the last period of the theatre that was of most interest to him, the time of the mysterious Arab garrison down by the port. For me he represents worlds that are gone, a colonial world of service and discipline. Even his voice has an archaic quality of reticent gentleness, very clearly enunciated, but modest. He speaks Greek with ancient overtones, and an English accent, which is apparently perfectly understood by Cypriots, who know an archaic dialect. Scholars are still speculating about the great silence of the post-Roman era – trade seems to come to a standstill, roads and cities remain in ruins. By the eighth century even coinage was rare, and it is likely the small population lived with difficulty among the abandoned ruins and devastated roads of empire. This is the fascination of Peter Megaw's area of research over nearly half a century. To bring to light the so-called 'dark' ages and the early eras of medieval Christianity with all its uncertainties has been an extraordinary enterprise.

Further up the road from the theatre site, a little beyond Fabrika Hill lives Antonios, a contemporary of Peter Megaw, so often to be seen sitting outside his simple block house, his hands shaking around an old recorder. As I pass, he calls to me in his thick deep voice, but I understood very little through his accent. He learnt his idiosyncratic and expressive English from Indian troops stationed in Cyprus in 1940, under the British. For his livelihood he had been a well digger, a stone cutter, a violin maker, and a musician at festivities. He grew table grapes in Paphos after he was able to buy some land, and exported them all over Europe, while never leaving Cyprus. His small house just near Fabrika Hill has a concrete floor, a huge TV, and is surrounded by a fertile market garden. A cemetery, derelict and overgrown, lies opposite, on the other side of the road. (Every stone was broken or defaced; I could find only one date, 1946.)

Antonios Theodoros Kousios, known as Koushis, was born in 1920. Working on the theatre site is Anthea Garrod, a niece of Antonios, although his family is so immense that he hardly knows the ones that have left Cyprus, as Anthea has, marrying an Englishman. Anthea and I visit him to find out what he knows about any earthworks in the Fabrika area over the last forty years. Two of the excavators, Mel and Craig, want to know if he can think of any digging or building activity near the theatre site to account for the inexplicable plastic bag found metres below the surface in a seemingly stratified trench. He only remembered that in the 1940s some of the tombs on Fabrika had been dynamited to make building stone for the vast carob warehouses just down the road, now long empty of carobs, although the charoupia trees with their sweet pods are everywhere still.

Remembering all the treasure stories I asked him, 'Have you ever come near the "gold of Aphrodite"?' 'No, I was unlucky!' He told me a story of how he had found a tomb while ploughing a muddy field. He waited until the earth was dry and went back in summer, and was excited to find the stone sarcophagus in perfect condition. He told me he lifted the lid with great anticipation, but there was no gold, just bones. 'And when I looked in, I was so disappointed. "Hey," I said, "you're even poorer than I am!" and I slammed down the lid.'

In his life, he said, he had dug two hundred and fifty wells, some very deep, with only a pick and shovel. All his life he has been fit and well, until recently. As he had five daughters and only one son, he had many *preka* or dowries to organise, to give each daughter the house that they expected on getting married. He has nothing for himself now except his twenty violins in a tin chest and a well under the floor of his room, marked by a stone on the floor. He shoved the stone aside with his stick. 'It reminds me that the well is there, full of beautiful water.'

He first learnt music when he was ten, learning to play and to make the violin and the bamboo flute. Antonios said his flute needed mending but he played me a bar or two – to him music is as instinctive as talking, and he sings that familiar rhythm still heard in the Orthodox liturgy. Everyone knows him, as he sits by his house with his musical instruments, and people even come from Athens to make videos and record his old songs. His grandson is in a band, still playing some of the same music, a youngish man with large eyes, brown complexion, every plane smooth and convex, an easy physique. There must have been so much interconnection and even intermarriage in the village, resulting in 'linen and cotton' unions, *linobambaki*. Peter Megaw told me he had both Turkish and Greek Cypriots working for him in Kourion in the early 1970s, and they all spoke each other's languages.

Antonios comes to the site to inspect us, moving so slowly, shaking and bent double, using his bicycle as a walking stick. Sitting on a stone beside the stage building trench, he plays on his flute – Arab, Turkish and Greek music he told me, he knew them all. He sings a song about a postman, about letters that never came, in a lilting melody. His hands are like rocks, his eyes kind but rogueish. He sings tremulous love songs, I think as a kind of courtesy to me. It is moving to hear that wavering old music in the theatre, where all the sounds that must have filled it are now silenced, beyond excavation. The young, lithe students smile at him tolerantly. Leaping in and out of trenches, they are another species, rather impatient with the wandering old and their musings over the site. To Antonios it seems mad, to come all the way across the world to dig up old walls.

This was the second old man with a stick to visit the site in my company, but with what disparate histories. Their connection is through the ground of Paphos that they have both worked in so intently, and so differently. In both men there is a notion of decorum in relationships, that allows resilience through war and the turbulent times they've lived through, and which seems to me to echo much older patterns of settled and ceremonious living.

13. THREAD AND CLOTH

2 April 1998

Set into the steep slopes of a narrow valley looking out over the encroaching town of Paphos to the sea, the monastery of Ayios Neophytos was once remote and isolated. I was intrigued to discover that the twelfth-century saint Neophytos is supposed to have woven his own shroud (as well as cutting his own tomb out of the rock while living in his hermitage). After work I drove to the monastery to look at the remarkable, detailed paintings in the saint's rock-cut shrine, looking for representations of textiles. In the intensity of the late-afternoon light the church with its astonishing relics and iconostasis, the serene courtyard garden give the monastery an otherworldly atmosphere, as if it might still be a refuge. The saint made a hermitage in a cave in a cliff, above and apart from the main buildings. Inside, its curved and asymmetrical walls are covered with frescoes of clustering holy men and an image of the Virgin floating against a visionary blue. As I went into in the narthex, or entrance to the shrine (the *enkleistra*) I saw the figure of a girl spinning, poised above the door, sitting on a low stool in a blue-purple dress with gold trim at the neck. She draws out the red thread from a small pot – it must be linen fibre, made wet by the water in the pot, in order to spin better. The archangel Gabriel is waiting nearby to tell her something important should she lift her eyes from her work.[53]

Spinning was a constant activity in the ancient and medieval world, so necessary to both comfort and economy, when all thread had to be spun by hand for the innumerable textiles of clothing and bedding, not to mention ropes, sails and awnings. As a young woman travelling in the distant settlements of Crete and the Pindos Mountains, I saw in mountain villages the women sitting on doorsteps or grazing goats and cows on the hills, with long spindles and distaffs, spinning continuously. Moving through the market, pausing to gossip at the baker's oven, tending young children, the deft spindles never stopped, the distaffs crooked in the arm holding clouds of teased wool. In their cloak-like brown or black clothes they were like Rembrandt women or reminiscent of fairy godmothers. Sometimes the eyes of the old women were milky white, blind with cataracts, but they still produced thread in movements that were as unconscious as breathing. Storytelling and spinning always went together. (I was like a visitor from another world; wearing pale purple flared jeans with a zip down the front – children followed me calling out, '*Eisai yunaika ei andres?* Are you a woman or a man?').

I was taught to spin in Andros on a wooden spindle that was the same in every dimension as the eighth-century BC spindles excavated on the headland of Zagora, where I was working. 'Take my old spindle,' said the tired woman I met in a tiny house in a ruined olive terrace high above the village where we stayed. 'Take it, it's no use to me any more.' The spinning movement was difficult at first, keeping the teased wool drawing out in an even thread, and not letting the spindle touch the ground. Yet there's a delight in seeing the energetic motion of the small whorl transferred to a twist that moves up the formless fibre like something alive and becomes thread. The Andros spindle and its whorl (three centimetres in diameter and conical in shape) were carved from olive wood, polished by contact with the slightly greasy wool. Although of lighter wood, its shape is a shadow in every way of the soapstone spindle whorls dropped near the old road and houses of the Paphos theatre in the fourth century AD. Like our hammers and knives, needles and scissors, the shape of tools hardly changes across millennia, immune to the unimaginable innovations in other areas of technology.

10 April

The inland road from Mamonia into the Troodos Mountains is a long green valley, with occasional clustered villages, old people sitting in the cool sun by houses worn from the winter. Intense brittle greens flash by, rocket flowers yellow beside the road. There is still almond blossom at high Platres, as well as peach and apricot just emerging, while lower down the mountains the fruit trees already have new green leaves. A thread of a river divides the floor of the valley, with orange orchards and grain, wild terraces further up, ancient and crumbling, a few olives clinging to life. At Kidasi a mosque tower leans over the tiny village, while not far away two other villages are derelict and ruined in this valley. Blackbirds and hawks hover and dive. Wonderful vine terraces are embroidered over a whole hill. It's easy to drive quickly through and not to see that this quiet country is the fundamental element of old Cyprus, *to chorio*, the village, the heart of it all, where crafts like textiles are remembered by older people, but hardly central any more.

What flourishes are the crafts of food preparation, and basket making. We were all invited to visit the hilly village of Drousia near Polis, north of Paphos to watch, the making of *houloumi*, the delicious goat's-milk cheese that I so often eat fried, with cucumber and caper salad. The milk for the *houloumi* is stirred over a low fire, with a slow elaborate process, tiny details of care evident in the milking, the preparation of utensils and ovens – frugality and sparsity as a way of life. Lovely cylindrical baskets are woven from a narrow reed, to hold the cheeses. Sustenance was difficult but just possible from very little, a few goats, a small crop of grain, a variety of fruits and vines.

We watched the kneading of the Easter bread, *flaounda*, sitting in the dappled shade of a courtyard. Under the pomegranate tree eggs were being dyed with madder root – the women sweated at the round ovens, sliding in the risen bread on long trays. In the street nearby, a sieve maker sold flat circular traditional metal sieves punched with patterns in soft copper or tin. I remembered Kyriakos, now a restaurant owner, and Theophilos, the doctor, reiterating: 'How poor we were as children, how little we had.' Village life itself is a constant pattern of tasks – to escape to the city must feel liberating – and yet the successful professional people never forget this other world of custom and binding relationships.

16 April

I've been searching the folk museums for textile artefacts and have found some resonant objects at Yeroskippou. *Uphantike* means 'weaving'. Flax, wool and silk were all grown on the island and exported. The *adrachtos*, a rope spinner, was formed of a cross of two pieces of elliptical wood; a photograph showed a team of men twisting thick fibres, the second-quality flax fibres, into a great coil with the aid of this rope spinner. In the reconstructed kitchen were round sieves made of silk, even mended silk, and of skin tightly stretched over a wooden frame, while the grain sieves were of pierced metal. Swelling gourds were cut into many shapes as containers, and dried pomegranates lined up on the chimney mantelpiece. The big flat baskets were used for breeding silkworms, and huge storage pots were grouped in the courtyard under a mulberry tree. Exquisite woven textiles of white linen and cotton with patterned borders draped the bed. Each object speaks of hard work, of unremitting labour for a minimum of comfort – bread boards of concave shells scooped out of a plank in a row, threshing boards set with stone flints, squat amphorae for carrying water.

When I look at the immensely old Chalcolithic tools – the stone whorls and loom weights, the grinding stones and querns in the Paphos Museum – they seem to relate in a clear line to that artisanal life. A row of odd, rough round stones and some smooth ovoid ones emerged from the trenches around the stage building. This was the area where people built simple shacks in the rubble after the theatre was abandoned. 'They're Chalcolithic, re-used,' said Paul Croft, the prehistorian. 'They could be the stoppers of big jars.' Useful things are endlessly recycled. Chalcolithic hand tools – mortars and pestles – were still being used in the thirteenth century to mash and to pound.

The basic forms of tools persist, as unchangeable as buttons.

25 April

The giant fennel stalks with their branches of yellow flowers are withering as I drive through a lonely landscape of white calcareous hills (the rock-roses are still out) to the villages of Kato Drys, Kato Lefkara and Pano Lefkara. Looking down on them from the road the distant villages are scattered like islands of brown and white mosaic in the waving flow of terraced slopes, gold and green with patches of crops. In the narrow streets of Pano Lefkara, with all its lace shops, it is apparent that there are more old people than young ones. The hills above wait unchanging while the old stone terraces disintegrate, and the new waves of people are tourists, not small farmers and lace makers.

I asked two women, Melanie and Andrea, who were sitting embroidering in a large shop, about the textiles for which this village is so famous. Lefkaritiko work is a form of cutwork embroidery, or needle lace, probably influenced by the Venetian presence in Cyprus in the fifteenth and sixteenth centuries. There is a legend that Leonardo da Vinci himself visited Cyprus and later presented an embroidery from Lefkara to the cathedral in Milan. During the nineteenth century and up until about 1950 the men of Lefkara sold embroideries in Alexandria, Smyrna, Constantinople and western Europe. In my own family a set of exquisite embroidered table mats from Lefkara came to Australia after being purchased in Scotland by my great grandmother, probably about 1910. The patterns on these linen pieces could read like a musical notation, a secret text or even a map. A dominant motif is the ripple of tiny diamond holes cut diagonally into the square of linen, called a *potamos*, a river. A broad row of these zigzag holes is the *potomotos*, after the raging winter river. A delicate latticed grid of threads sometimes set in the *potamos* is an *arvali*, which is a coarse sieve for larger seeds. Intricate segments of satin stitch form the petals of the *sourafotee* daisy.[54] Such an array of signs are like the paintings of 'country', of sacred sites made in central Australia by Aboriginal artists. The whole cloth is edged with a double row of little rounded arches with decorative knots.

Kyria Melanie told me that a tablecloth of such work might take eighteen months, 'and I would only make about eleven pounds for a week of constant work.' She said that younger women and girls were not interested in learning the arduous skill: her daughter works in a clothing shop in Limassol, where she makes that much money in a day. It was no longer necessary to bring a chest of embroidered handmade textiles as part of a marriage settlement. Andrea was making table-mats for a German couple in Limassol who had come here to work for a few years and could pay the high price of handmade embroidery. She makes one every few weeks, then they come and buy it from her. The old patterns are dying out – the complicated cutwork is nearly forgotten. Her auntie, who is seventy-eight, knows, but she can hardly see any longer. 'It will die out in a few years.' Her father sold lace from a suitcase and then settled in England for years. The six basic designs of the 'Leonardo' patterns are still being made, each design varying slightly with the individual embroiderer. There are copyright problems with work 'made in Taiwan' being sold to tourists as Lefkara lace. 'We get no help from the Government to protect us, and the only tools we need are just needles and small sharp scissors.'

Ceremonial and ornate fabrics like those from Lefkara, which do not survive in the archaeological record, are most tantalising to imagine. The delicate painted plaster of the theatre frescoes may dimly reflect the wall hangings and fabrics lost to us, as music has been lost. The great artefacts of women were textiles, so perishable that only glimpses remain. Textiles are still hidden, except when reflected in sculpture, mosaic or painting, yet the work of spinning and weaving was the main work of women, an immense work, and in myths often stands for the 'voice' of women.

29 April

With Christie's help (the finds co-ordinator) I found the inventoried spindle whorls, the clay loom weight and the bone pins amongst all the stored finds from the theatre, and drew them all with great attention. I'd been delighted to find a tiny set of scales in a shop in the upper town to weigh the whorls, because weight was an indication of what kind of fibre might have been spun – heavier whorls for coarser yarns of wool and linen, and lighter, smaller whorls for silk thread. Looking at the scratched and worn surfaces under a magnifying glass is like opening out a whole tissue of associations and everyday use. The loveliest whorl is the grey-green highly polished soapstone one, from a 'surface deposit'. It has four little concentric circles or 'god's eyes' engraved on the flat surface. The decoration seems to show that it may have been someone's treasure. What stories it must have heard, I thought, remembering the pervasive sound of the voice in all its modes that is the background murmur to life in Cypriot villages. Also very evocative is the round clay loom weight that held the warp threads taut for weaving, which has traces of burning on one side. It seems likely that loomweights may have been handed down from mother to daughter as a set. None of these objects can be dated clearly, but they probably come from the later life of the theatre, from the third or fourth century.

The role of Greco-Roman women reflects an emphasis that is blurred to our world, an emphasis on genealogy and generation – the identity of your father; whether you had children in a legal union was central to identity. Despite the seeming voicelessness of women in ancient texts, such a vitality of gesture is evident in sculpture, ceramic and mosaic of women as deities, active in ritual and myth, that it is hard to imagine how such feminine energy was contained within a mute domestic world. Of course, not all women were restricted within the house. Other inscriptions from the wider Roman world give a vivid picture of the life of the streets for ordinary women, freed women or even slaves. Directly relating to the pervasive task of textiles are inscriptions mentioning wool-workers, seamstresses, weavers and spinning girls. In grave inscriptions we have women also described as sesame seed sellers, grocers and salt vendors, horse tenders, perfume vendors, musicians, honey and frankincense sellers, shoe sellers, gilders of helmets, as well as concubines, procuresses, wet nurses, harp and lyre players. Those clusters of ivy, myrtle and olive painted in the tombs reflected the daily work of women garland weavers.[55]

5 May

So few actual textiles survive from antiquity in the clammy soils of Cyprus that I was astonished to find on the shelves of the Paphos Museum a tiny piece of woven cloth dated through coins to the second century AD. A few weeks ago I asked permission from the Department of Antiquities to examine and publish it – as the survival of any fragment of textile is so rare. And today a fax came through to the Paphos Museum giving me that permission. With great ceremony Neoptolemos and Demetrios accompanied me to the glass case, unlocked it, and gave the object to me for drawing and photography.[56]

I did a meticulous watercolour drawing of each thread of the fragment, feeling a contained excitement to see the slight wobble in the spin of the linen fibre, and its blue-green colour. Tiny metal particles of bronze, remnants of coins, were still partially entangled in the fabric.

The archaeologist Dr Kyriacos Nicolaou found the tiny scrap of cloth in 1967 when excavating the House of Dionysos. He described the scene, almost like the scene of a crime – 'When the wall was removed the skeleton of a man was found under it just as he had died when the wall collapsed on him. Clasping his hands above his head, he had sought protection of the wall but the tremor was too strong to spare him.'[57] The little fragment of cloth had been part of the man's pocket or tunic, and had survived because it had been suffused with metal compounds from the bronze coins. This coarse linen cloth looked like the linen tea towel in my kitchen and was remarkable in being so ordinary – not the ritual cloths or elaborate carpets that were translated in mosaics and paintings, but the cloth of everyday life worn close to the body.

This understanding that textiles were part of the bodily realm appears in an influential book by the fourth-century philosopher Porphyry on the 'Cave of the Nymphs', a mythical cave in Ithaca mentioned by Homer. To the souls of nymphs 'that are occupied in corporeal energies' what symbol can be more appropriate than the tools of weaving? asked Porphyry. As flesh covers the bones of the body, so the purple webs of weaving are made on looms of stone in the cave of the nymphs. Their stone looms are like the bones of animals and 'purple woollen garments are tinged from blood; and wool is dyed from animal juice.' Also he points out, 'The body is a garment with which the soul is invested' just as the 'heavens are called by the ancients a veil' because they are like 'the vestments of the celestial Gods.'[58]

Like relationships, like sound and smell, textiles such as those described by Porphyry are merely traces in the archaeological record. They can be seen indirectly through an imprint on a harder material, a kind of negative casting. In a tomb near the village of Sanida in Cyprus knives were found that had been wrapped in another series of plain linen cloths – the grid of the cloth is now corroded into the knives as the fibres of the linen became permeated with the metallic oxides from the bronze.[59]

In the excavation of tombs, the presence of weapons indicates a man's burial, while a woman is always identified by items like a mirror, spindle whorls or jewellery. These textile-embossed knives are like strange, cross-gendered objects.

The colour and richness of textiles that we've lost can be glimpsed in remnants from Egypt, where the dry climate allowed cloth to survive. My fascination with early textiles began when I was working in the British Museum, as an illustrator, and in the Victorian clutter of the Department of Medieval and Later Antiquities I was asked to tidy a cupboard. Inside were boxes sent from a 1950s excavation in Egypt, and as far as I could see, never opened. I was permitted to unpack them, and among painted pottery sherds, out came tiny fragments of Coptic tapestry – an ivy leaf, a staring head, a vivid bird woven in a style known as 'eccentric' to tapestry weavers. An indistinct madder, indigo blue, olive green and saffron seemed to be telling me something, urging me to some new understanding.

Now in Paphos, it's those glimpses of colour in the ancient fresco on the walls of the theatre that conjure up the lost momentum of ancient life and may be just about to reveal a new insight. Archaeologists are like artists, driven on by an inarticulate longing, an intuition that in the next box of potsherds or in the uncovering of a fragmentary wall, there will be a clue that leads to revelation. The fresco fragments from the theatre – a painted red flower, a fillet, a swag of cloth laid on in subtle blues and creams – are related to those vibrant Coptic cloths which were made only a hundred miles to the south of Paphos, perhaps even in Alexandria, her sister city. Just as the red spinning thread of the girl painted in the Ayios Neophytos sanctuary is implicated in the layered story of the Annunciation, so these fresco fragments are part of a hidden iconography, the obscure signs of the language and myths of the theatre.

PART II

The Cavea:
The Arc of the Mediterranean, 1999-2000

Coptic ceramic, fourth century AD. British Museum. Indian ink on card, 1969.

I. COPTIC FABRICS

17 April 1999

Now I'm sitting in bed in the Victoria Hotel in Cairo, where Bertrand Russell once stayed. Voices and laughter come from the street even though it is well after midnight. The ceiling is immensely tall, with the looped bulbs of a flickering chandelier, and the old fashioned furniture appears rather looming and oddly shaped in the dim light, while even inside with the air conditioning on the room smells faintly polluted with exhaust and smoke. Coming in to land after the short flight from Cyprus, the city was like brilliant clusters of beads, points of light spread to the horizon.

Flying tonight from Larnaca in Cyprus to Cairo is the culmination of long planning. Cyprus to Egypt is such an ancient route – about 675 kilometres, a few days by ship. It is the same distance to Rhodes, another vital trading partner. Both Ephesos in Anatolia and Constantinople were closer to Paphos than Athens, and closest of all were the coasts of southern Turkey, once the rich provinces of Pamphylia and Lycia, and ancient Antioch, now in Syria. Cyprus has been a crossing point between East and West since earliest times – but edges towards the East, geographically. To make this journey, I am imagining Paphos at the centre of a ring of vital ancient cities, Paphos as the character standing in centre stage, while the cities around the arc of the Mediterranean coast are the audience seated in the curved auditorium, the *cavea*. To see Alexandria, to understand its pervasive influences on Paphos and the connections to those other great Hellenistic cities, Ephesos, Pergamon, and Alexander's capital in Macedonia, Vergina, is the point of this trek by myself around the Mediterranean coast. Hellenism – the Greek language and culture first unleashed by Alexander – miraculously continued in this region into the Byzantine Empire, gaining a new impetus under Christianity. The latest moments of the Paphos theatre, in the fourth century, are reflected in the haunting monuments of early Constantinople.

In the ancient world there were entities called 'psychopomps', who conducted the soul to the place of the dead. As I travel alone I meet people who seem to give clues to the point of the journey, who guide me to a different sensibility, offering glimpses of another, vanished perception. As in fairy stories, it is people met in the street or along the way whose actions or words seem curiously significant. The long taxi journey this morning from Paphos to Larnaca stopped in tiny towns and remote suburbs to pick up eight people to fill the limousine. At one point, while waiting for a passenger the driver jumped out and pulled down a bunch of ripe loquats from a tree overhanging the street, and shared them with me, wordlessly.

'There are many small cities in this big one,' I was told by Ihab, the man from Sun Tours who met me, very impressively. (I had organised hotels in Egypt before leaving Australia, fearing it would be difficult late at night.) In that drive from the airport, in a van padded with carpets, the immense city was exotic and deeply unfamiliar. Small groups of long-robed men waited – for what? – on the corners of the night streets, in the mild warm air. The hotel was in an older part of the city, near a main road with the endless hoots of taxis and rumble of traffic. At the door there were three men in white uniforms, and a porter took my luggage, as if I were a nineteenth-century aristocrat and had arrived in a different time, as well as a different place.

18 April

Waking up in Cairo, even vivid dreams seemed faint in the realisation of finding myself in such a city. I looked out the tall window at the clustering concrete buildings all around, their yellowish grey monotony broken by one elongated palm with a curving trunk, dusty but perfectly entire, the only organic form to be seen. Far below my room on the fourth floor was an abandoned open-air terrace with heaps of junk from the hotel: old porcelain baths and toilets, even crates of drink bottles that seemed unopened. All these objects were encrusted with thick grey dust – they could have been from an excavation. Later, walking around the Cairo Museum, I saw objects thousands of years old that might have come from the waste in that old bar. The dryness of the atmosphere is transfixing and covers new and old things indiscriminately with powdery dust.

The hotel was cavernous, but the dining room pleasing in its decor, with that distinctive turquoise blue-green which flashes everywhere in Cairo among the dominant grey tones. I tentatively ate a boiled egg and some bread. In this city, 'concrete jungle' has a sudden pungent meaning; the jumbled sizes and infinite number of apartment buildings are baffling, without a clear point of focus. Here is a vast celebration of concrete architecture for millions of people, elaborated on a giant scale. The grey harshness of the concrete is occasionally contrasted with softer yellow ochre areas of mud brick and red stone. And in the streets, innumerable throngs of people.

It's not possible to fly directly from Larnaca to Alexandria, so I planned to spend a little time in Cairo to look mainly at the Greco-Roman antiquities, and particularly to catch a glimpse of Coptic textiles and art. I had always wanted to see the famous collection of early textiles in the Coptic Museum, as it was the pleasure of Coptic textiles that first directed me to tapestry.

The word 'Copt' comes from the Arabic assimilation of the Greek word *Aigyptios* into *kipt*[1] and present day Copts retain a distinct identity as a sizeable minority in Egypt. They have been Christian since the first century when the apostle St Mark is supposed to have brought Christianity to Egypt. In art history 'Coptic' stands for a diversity of styles in the later Roman empire. From the first excavation of Egyptian tombs in the time of Napoleon, vast quantities of textiles were found preserved. In the Hellenistic and Roman period Egypt was the centre of linen and even silk production, and

Alexandria exported textiles across the known world. The Roman army was clothed by Egyptian workshops, formed into weaving guilds. Since I first came across Coptic art in the British Museum I had wondered at the marvellous colours and vibrancy of Coptic pattern, as well as the intricate textile techniques, which included tapestry, embroidery, inlay, pile techniques and resist dyeing.

After consulting an impenetrable map of Cairo I decided to get a taxi to the Coptic Museum. The doorman hailed a cab and I got in, but the driver, in a long striped garment and an anxious expression, knew no English and in fact had never been to the Coptic Museum before. He drove uncertainly through a very poor part of the city heaped with mounds of rubbish like archaeological spoil heaps. The narrow streets were streaming with people, half in European clothes, but all the women with headscarves at least, except for the young girls who got away with short skirts and close-fitting trousers. Very dark faces flashed by, with brilliant costumes – I saw in an instant, a balcony of emerald and purple, a black woman standing in the door in a long red dress.

A very strange relationship to traffic emerged as people flowed over the road in a remorseless tide, not put off even by the multi-lane highways; and cars, donkeys and horses wove between them. There was the constant hooting of horns. People leaned out of cars too and shouted to one another; someone opened the door of our slow moving taxi and got in to direct the driver. A sort of symbiosis seemed to exist between pedestrians and cars – no rules, no traffic lights, vehicles just wove in and out in a mysterious pattern. I made the driver stop when we finally came to the great and generous Nile, deep and strongly flowing, with palm trees along a promenade. People fished, and men stood in clusters, waiting and smoking. I felt such emotion to see this river, the source of Egyptian culture, and the driver smiled at me and said a few words in Arabic. We were able to share something. The Greek historian Herodotus (born 484 BC) famously commented that Egypt is a gift of the Nile, but that no one knows why the river floods so prodigiously every year, or where the source of the Nile might be. He tells a story he heard from a priest in Sais of an unfathomable and prodigious fountain, the actual source, set between two hills with conical tops.[2] To represent the astonishing fertility of the great river, sculptors in Greco-Roman times carved the reclining figure of the river god of the Nile, a vast cornucopia of abundance on one arm. Climbing over the benevolent deity were many babies, each representing a cubit of water in the Nile flood.

'Welcome! How are you?' There's very little English – why should there be? I felt very conspicuous but people seemed friendly and courteous despite the few tourists. Security police were everywhere especially at museums such as the Coptic Museum, which was in a Christian enclave entirely surrounded by barriers. Guides attached themselves to people entering – I had been told that all the archaeology graduates, thousands every year, have to be employed, even at a pittance, so these well-informed graduates offer themselves as paid guides.

One introduced himself to me as a Christian, and immediately launched into a detailed and scholarly account of Coptic iconography, in English (although all his dates seemed very early). The imagery is an animated interpretation of Greco-Roman mythology of river gods, Dionysos, Ariadne and bacchantes, horsemen, fantastic flying *erotes* or little cupids, twining vines, flowers and birds with encrusted ornament and woven portrait busts. Many of these are crypto-Christian emblems – the cross and ankh entwined. I moved slowly through the rooms of figured textiles, dense intricate carvings and painted heads reminiscent of those same faces seen in the street. Amazingly, the ancient dyes in the dim Coptic Museum were still vibrant, and the images intensely formed out of the characteristics of the weaving process itself. Curving wefts outlined vigorous gestures – Heracles grappling a lion, a Nereid waving from a shell, with an economy of line that is almost cartoon-like. Richly detailed tapestry panels were sewn onto linen tunics, and sometimes kept and re-stitched onto new linen. Contemporary weavers I knew would have loved the 'mark' of the unravelling, disintegrating fabrics. The swift, spontaneous style of the figures and plant motifs reminded me of the fresco motifs of the Paphos theatre in their bold simplicity, probably made about the same time, in the third or fourth century. I did some rough drawings, and was permitted to turn on lights and photograph.

The Christian aspect was pervasive, especially in the early books and papyrus, yet with mixtures of myths from Egyptian and Greco-Roman worlds. It was breathtaking to see a Christian gospel of the fourth century in a round clear Greek script, with traces of burning. The book, said the museum label, was found in a shallow grave under a young girl's head in the large poor cemetery of El Mudil. The manuscript was made up of thirty-one quires stitched together and is the oldest book that preserves its original polished covers. It was written in the Coptic dialect of Oxyrhynchos. Egypt was the source of all the papyrus of ancient literacy, until parchment was invented in Pergamon, and is one place where the power of a text, continuing in the tradition of the Pharaonic *Book of the Dead*, was seen as emblematic of divine powers.

The earliest travel story must be the *Book of the Dead*, with its detailed instructions and diagrams for the dead man to negotiate the underworld. Is the need to put a gospel with the dead girl a faint echo of that more ancient practice, of sending the dead away with instructions for the journey written in a sacred text? I remembered how Sigmund Freud had kept on his desk a statuette of Thoth, the baboon-headed Egyptian god of intellect and writing. Thoth had charge of the 'weighing of the heart' ceremony that took place in the underworld after death to judge the goodness and truthfulness of the dead person. For Freud the underworld was like the dark passages of the unconscious mind.[3]

I caught the clean bright metro coming back from the Coptic Museum into central Cairo, for a fraction of the cost of the taxi.

Some women sitting opposite were brightly dressed in the latest clunky shoes with contrasting patterns in scarves and dresses, dark and vital faces, very handsome, with some exquisite children on their knees. Their expressive eyes seemed to echo that compelling Coptic gaze.

A great deal of the Greco-Roman material I had come to see was in the Cairo Museum, where what looks like old piles of laundry are just heaped up anyhow in ancient museum cases not touched, it seemed, for fifty years: it's a museum of a museum. Casually piled in shelves were abundant textiles, especially linen, which must have been woven in vast quantities, to judge from the amount remaining in museum cases. Sometimes the fabric was as coarse as hessian, at other times as fine as the old Victorian linen sheets that I have at home. I saw great rolls and swathes of plain linen, including one twenty metres long from a tomb. The textiles were slowly turning to dust behind the glass of the heavy old cupboards. Again I sensed the once primary importance of cloth, invisible to us in a society where industrial textile manufacture has so changed the arduous processes of making fabric. The afterlife required a sufficiency of cloth to allow the dead person to achieve a satisfactory place in eternity.

The Coptic tradition of textile expertise is descended from the Hellenistic love of rich cloths associated with the good life, far from tombs. Here is the Roman poet Propertius, who was very influenced by Alexandrian styles, talking about his lover's preference for a luxurious life symbolized by glorious cloths and the green-gold gems called 'chrysolites':

> The life she led was a model for anyone who is greedy
> For chrysolites from the eastern shores, for fancy
> Purple Tyrian dyes and Coan silks, for expensive
> Patchwork quilts with insets of cloth of gold,
> Or Egyptian bric-a-brac from palmy Thebes.[4]

The mummy portraits lined up and staring out from the walls had a great presence, as if in some indefinable way the individual character of these long-dead people had indeed been captured to survive in the afterlife. Sadly and solemnly the mostly young faces gaze out at you, as if urging awareness of the moment. Just at that instant, as I was thinking this, a crowd of vivacious Egyptian children, perhaps twelve years old, thronged through the room, kin to the people in the portraits to judge by their glowing eyes. They crowded around me with a few English phrases – 'Hullo! How are you? What is your name?' And when I told them they laughed and fluttered their hands and said 'Diana, Lady Diana! We love you very much!', touching me, laughing, moving on.

I sat amongst the massive Old Kingdom sculptures on the ground floor, figures of seated kings or standing gods three or four times human scale, in glittering hard stone. This seemed to be a place for couples to meet, in a city that has few public parks or private spaces outside the home. Sitting looking into each other's eyes, they were surrounded and seemingly protected by heavy figures full of authority and gravitas. The statues of the pharoahs were certain of the power of those fearful gods evoked in signs on each of the mummies ranked in shelves in another room. Stacked one above the other, they were carefully painted with the winged goddess Hathor, with eyes and cobras. Bird-headed, dog-headed, animal and human worlds were not quite separate, instinct and intellect merged. Perhaps this was what appealed to Freud.

Wandering through Cairo in the late afternoon was absorbing. I went into the Nile Hilton where I could be anonymous and international, and had a delicious meal of spiced chicken and rice from one of the small restaurants. It was a very fine hotel, with large plaster casts of bas reliefs from Karnak in the busy foyer, somehow looking right in that polished and ornate setting, put back amongst the crowds. The great river streamed on, an earthy green, just beyond the doors.

I got lost in Ramses Square in the thronging crowds; all roads looked the same, and I couldn't find the hotel after emerging from the Metro. The giant statue of Ramses striding above us seemed to show that the ancient deities were still moving around in the dense crowds of the city. A man in flowing garments and a white hat, selling hoops of bread covered with sesame seeds, very politely asked if he could help, took my arm and guided me through chaotic traffic around a swarm of little buses. I tried to give him some money; he refused with pride and said it was his pleasure. Very formally he came out with his last English phrase, to my astonishment, just as the children had proclaimed earlier: 'I love you very much!' We shook hands on this, and parted. I went up that street and it was a market – a mass of everyday valuable small things, a pile of red apples, children's shoes, batteries, socks, string bags; each with a seller crouched patiently beside. I stopped a passing taxi at last, totally lost, and he too was a pleasant man. We renegotiated a price to the bus station for Alexandria, via the hotel to pick up my luggage. After some fuss – the porters at the hotel did not want the taxi driver to take their fee – we set out through the city.

This brown city, covered with dust, where it rains perhaps once a year, had a quality of intense desiccation that must affect the character of the inhabitants. Packed populations existed in this moulded, dust-coloured, fantastic world – mosques and minarets projected from narrow streets. Worlds within worlds, just as Ihab had told me. Suddenly we were moving through a cemetery of imitation houses for the dead, terracotta houses with no roofs, open to the skies, stretching in a long perspective as far as I could see. Children were playing in those unreal streets in the dusk with no lights, a make-believe town. Cairo is a city unlike any other; a compilation of cities built one above the other. The past is implicit in the present, in the bread in baskets at all the street corners, exactly like the three-cornered shapes of bread laid in tombs three thousand years ago, and in the same coarse baskets.

The bus to Alexandria was a lavish, new, high vehicle with a video and air conditioning. We left at 6.30 in the evening and did not arrive until nearly five hours later because of the density of traffic. The married women on the bus mostly had head scarves, combined with western clothes, and their little babies and children were very well behaved. The well groomed woman next to me – perhaps my age – gave me a biscuit, smiled. How courteous people are, despite my foreignness. (I dress to be as anonymous as possible). It took two hours just to get out of Cairo, which has the same population as the whole of Australia.

At last the video came on; there was a stir of anticipation – a film in Arabic about two women who share the same man. The role of women was clearly prescribed, to look glamorous and to be endlessly seductive. The large bosomy heroines in glowing make-up sparkled voluptuously with jewels, satin dresses, and long hair, attributes suited to their melodramatic lives. The passengers loved the video, and laughed until they cried at the perils of the lover caught between two such women – their sympathy seemed to be entirely with the women. The film reaffirmed the intensity of those domestic worlds hidden behind the decorum of the street, behind clothes and veils.

Alexandria appeared as lights along a stretch of water, and an easing of the dry atmosphere – a sense of being again on the moist edge of the Mediterranean. A second intention in visiting Alexandria was to evoke my father's journey here as a young Australian soldier in 1941. His regiment had travelled by train from Cairo, and had been left beside the railway track in the pitch dark at midnight. They had marched through the desert to the camp nine miles away at a place called Ikingi Maryut. Arriving in Alexandria about the same time at night, I couldn't imagine having to march such a distance, with my pack. Instead I negotiated a taxi at an extravagant rate to take me to my hotel, rather out of town along the eastern edge of the sea. The hotel, built in the 1960s, was a bit chunky and too big with vast numbers of storeys and rooms, and an army of doormen and porters, waiters and clerks. Situated in a congested suburb, it was close to the above-ground metro. Beneath the window of my sixth-floor room was a chaotic scene – old buildings demolished to make way for more concrete, with piles of earth and a stalled bulldozer stark under the yellow street lights. In my fatigue the endless concrete towers pierced with apartments seemed like fragile shells, like fantastic coral structures on the edge of the reef, teeming with unknown creatures.

2. CITY OF MEMORY: ALEXANDRIA

18 April 1999

When I first found myself in the mixed heart of this extraordinary city, the life of the narrow, crowded streets was mesmerising. Alexandria has been the 'city of memory' for European writers, who have drawn on its stories since the time of Shakespeare. The imaginary world of the Greek poet Constantine Cavafy, which draws the past into the fateful present, was suddenly crystallised. In the crowds a heart-stopping face is glimpsed, such as Cavafy might have noted, and then vanishes into an alley. I carried my slim book of *Four Greek Poets*, which I'd read since I was a girl, and found this, *One of Their Gods*:

> When one of them passed through the market
> Of Seleukeia, at about the hour of dusk,
> Like a tall youth of perfect beauty,
> With the joy of the inviolate in his eyes,
> With his black and perfumed hair,
> The passers-by would gaze at him.[5]

In Alexandria I felt this piercing gaze of the passers-by, as if I were the only blond woman in the street, or the only tourist; children giggle at me, boys yell, men wave, policemen wink and smile, despite my long dark blue clothing. (Security guards are outside every building of note, on every street corner.) I negotiated the tram, full of schoolgirls, some elaborately layered in coats and scarves, but some bare-headed and in jeans. It took ages, twenty-three stops to the centre, through decayed and dusty buildings seemingly awaiting demolition. The tram though, was efficient, clean and very cheap.

When finally I reached the centre I caught my breath at the famous curve of the corniche, the curve of the seawall and concourse that divides the city from the sea, dimpled and rippling in the morning light. I could see why Lawrence Durrell had called it 'the shining city of the disinherited' on the edge of Europe, filled in both ancient and modern times with people from Asia, Africa and Europe.[6] The arc of the city against the sea was edged by stocky palms, while in the distance were minarets and the point where the lighthouse, the Pharos of antiquity, must have stood. The many worn down and crumbling European buildings had the tall elegance of another era – out of context, I was told, in contemporary Egypt. A family leaned against the wall, looking out to sea. The pale waters of the bay hide water-worn statues and fragments of carved marbles, revealed by French archaeologists in remarkable underwater photographs that are like surrealist paintings. A stone sphinx crouches in the blue depths, like an image in a dream, and a monumental torso in finely pleated robes lies on the sand in a liquid space of darting fishes. The divers report that there is a chaos of fragments from thousands of years scattered over the sea floor, and amongst these, possibly, are the architectural blocks of the lighthouse, one of the wonders of the ancient world.[7]

The city of Alexandria was founded in 332 BC by Alexander himself, who believed that he had a special connection to Egypt. He had dreamt that he was the son of the god Amun and travelled across the desert to the oasis at Siwah where his divinity, it is said, was confirmed by the oracle at Amun's temple. After he died in Babylon in 323 his general Ptolemy carried his body to Alexandria for burial. The hunt for the tomb of Alexander is still very active today: in Roman times it was said, his body lay in a glass coffin at the central crossroads of the elegant grid of his city, designed by the famous architects Dinocrates and Sostratus.

In Cyprus, Nea or New Paphos, with its harbour, was established shortly after Alexandria, because old Paphos, fifteen kilometres inland, lacked a viable port. The theatre of Paphos was built, it is judged by the style of lettering on the tiered seats, in the late fourth century BC, at the same time that Alexandria's monuments must have been coming into existence. Paphos was also ruled by the dynasty of Ptolemy, one of Alexander's energetic generals who divided up his empire. In this time of expansion, art changed too, the understanding of space in architecture and painting became charged with a new dynamism and expression. Delicate artefacts in pottery, jewellery and metalwork showed a new preoccupation with individual and intimate life. Much has been written about the elusive Hellenistic painting, only to be dimly perceived, it was said by scholars, in poor Roman copies, imitations and reproductions. I wanted to understand this common Greek tongue, this *koine* of images that was found throughout the eastern Mediterranean, and which persisted in Roman art into the fourth century AD (and some say even down to the end of the Byzantine Empire in 1453).

The Greco-Roman Museum was a central focus in my search to understand the relationship between Paphos and Alexandria. Not far away from this modest neo-classical building the ancient museum must have stood, which was like a great university with a library of nearly half a million books, or scrolls. Literary critics and editors chased after first editions of renowned authors – meticulous scholarship in Alexandria favoured an elegiac brevity in poetry. Leaning in the columned portico at the entrance to the museum was a round, smooth man who greeted me warmly, to my surprise, and introduced himself as the curator of coins. He had studied in England at the University of London in 1984, and would, please, like to come to Australia. He wrote his name and address in sprawling letters across a whole page of my address book. There seemed to be many officials, possibly underpaid archaeologists, just sitting around. The curator, Hassan, insisted on giving me a rapid guided tour of the frescoes, textiles and coins. He told me he was thinking of doing a huge publication of the coins, more than a million of them, for the University of Frankfurt. He pleasantly but firmly insisted I buy merchandise at the museum shop in return for the guided tour – I meekly complied to this reasonable request and acquired a large, gorgeous turquoise hessian bag printed with hieroglyphs, a very useful guidebook of the museum, and some wonderful fold-out postcards of the almost alive mummy portraits.

The museum was spell-binding, full of strange contrasts and overlaps between Greek, Coptic, Roman and pharaonic Egypt. Each high room had unexpected treasures as I wandered, entranced. I was drawn to a carved sarcophagus with a scene of Ariadne lying rather awkwardly on the ground against a column, abandoned by Theseus (you could see the prow of his ship leaving) and about to be rescued by Dionysos with his satyrs and maenads. The rooms had some natural light, and electricity that clicked on for short periods. These museums are journeys of discovery because so much can be seen in such a detailed and subtle way, just by eye, a viewing entirely unlike all mimetic forms of reproduction, even photography. The eye can see tiny degrees of difference, can scan surfaces and textures and make sense of them in a way that can then direct sensitive photography and allow it to reveal what the thinking eye can discern. But photography, or even digital scans, cannot replace the informed eye. This is the wonder for me in watching archaeologists at work, this infinitely precise looking.

Near the Ariadne sarcophagus, hovering on a shadowy wall was mounted a piece of mosaic with an optical pattern of cubes in perspective, which I had been longing to see, part of a Hellenistic floor from Thmuis near Alexandria.

The mosaic shimmered with different ways of reading the oblique lines of cubes in perspective, a pattern said by some to indicate the presence of a sacred enclosure. About sixty-seven centimetres high and two and a half metres long, its colours, made up of tiny stone *tesserae*, were muted but beautiful – a buffed white, ochre red, black and sienna yellow. Around the edge was a pink and white 'turreted' border, with alternate towers and crenellations, an architectural motif that again plays with positive and negative space. Both these ambivalent patterns impelled me to think of textiles, as they were so like carpet motifs. This vital patterning formed the grammar of the articulate decorative language of early Christian (Coptic) as well as Islamic ornament.

The same turreted border occurred around one of the famous female heads in an exquisite mosaic also from Thmuis ('a casual discovery in 1918'), framed in rich ornamentation. The protean Polish archaeologist Viktor Daszewski (whom I had met in Paphos, where he had been excavating Roman houses) has identified the passionate female figures in the two mosaics as Ptolemaic queens. The women's heads in these two exceptional mosaics were strangely crowned by the prow of a ship, their eyes wide open and shining with longing or *pothos*. This quality was a sign of Alexander's heritage, a sort of passionate intensity to conquer the unknown that persisted in his generals, founders of the Hellenistic kingdoms, who had been part of his empire building. The remarkable representation was signed, 'Sophilos made me', and may well be a portrait of the powerful queen Berenike who ruled Alexandria when her husband Ptolemy II was at war in Syria in the late third century BC. This is exactly the time that the Hellenistic form of the Paphos theatre would have been at a highpoint, in the same spate of feverish activity of the ruling Hellenistic princes.

I was pleased to note the floating fillet or ribbon, adding another emphasis of celebration, twining around the queen's head. It is fascinating that the idea of a symbolic portrait may have come from woven examples rather than painted portraits. Plutarch tells the story of the Hellenistic princes Demetrios Poliorcetes and Antigonos. They rashly had their portraits woven into the ritual *peplos* or garment annually given to the goddess Athena on the acropolis of Athens; 'an exhibition of arrogance that moved the goddess to send a violent wind which tore the garment to pieces as it was carried through the Agora.'[8] The implacable place that painting has had in the twentieth century as a high art form compared to textiles is subtly challenged in these commanding mosaics. The intricate complexity of textiles and all their allegorical associations were a powerful sign in Greco-Roman times and may well have been the source for painting, rather than the other way around. These Alexandrian mosaics of Berenike are outstanding exhibits in the museum, and made me thoughtful about the role of art and theatre in the sister-city of Paphos. Athenaeus wrote of the lavish interior, defined by textiles, in the pavilion of the Ptolemy Philadelphus: 'Over this [capital] was spread in the middle a scarlet veil with a white fringe, like a canopy; and on each side it had beams covered over with turreted veils with white centres, on which canopies embroidered all over the centre, were placed... And under the golden couches were strewn purple carpets of the finest wool.'[9]

Berenike must have been a compelling character. She is supposed to have introduced the cult of Aphrodite to Alexandria and became herself identified as Aphrodite in Cyprus, where her portrait has been found in Kition. Her daughter, Arsinoe, was also a vital cult figure in Cyprus, thought of as a constant companion, even a kind of surrogate Aphrodite.[10] The Hellenistic figures of the third and second centuries BC have a living gesture to them compared to the Egyptian sculptures. A battered limestone statue of Berenike in the museum had this vibrant quality, as well as a wonderful fragment of a seated draped figure, a child at her knee, modelled with an abstract power.

The number of votive terracotta figurines of the grotesque figure of the dwarf-god Bes indicated an affection for this pudgy, stump-legged deity. His ugliness was seen as apotropaic, a protection against evil; he was particularly the protector of women in childbirth, and was thought to bring good luck and prosperity to marriage, so you can see Bes all around the Mediterranean, even in Cyprus at Amathus and Kition. The Romans took on Bes with enthusiasm, and dressed him as a legionary. In Roman mosaics dwarfs, often grotesquely formed, were a powerful deterrent against ill-luck.

Many small figurines of Aphrodite in marble and terracotta, some very beautiful, had that slender quality familiar from Paphos examples. Aphrodite 'crouching at her bath' appeared in many variations and particularly the gesture of holding out her hair with both hands as she kneels on one knee, repeated constantly until Coptic times. A Coptic Leda and the Swan had a sensual emphasis and liveliness. The exquisitely painted Hellenistic Tanagra figurines, sadly from the tombs of girls who died before marriage, were entirely lovely in their delicacy and handling of layers of drapery, with a shivering gesture as they clasped their shawls. The nubbly, fine cloth, the 'woven wind' of silk scarves has vanished. I remembered that Strabo, writing in the first century BC, had said that the very shape of the city itself, laid out like a parallelogram between the sea and Lake Mareotis, was like the shape of the *chlamys*, the oblong mantle or scarf worn over the shoulders, the long sides washed by the two waters.[11]

It's evident how layered, how hybrid, the culture of Alexandria was, borrowed and appropriated from past eras. A remarkable giant stone eagle, transported from the Aegean island of Thasos in the fifth century BC, had a late archaic rigidity influenced by Egypt. Many eighteenth-dynasty Egyptian statues were brought to Alexandria by the Greeks, presumably to add by their ancient monumentality and grandeur to the credibility of the Ptolemaic rulers. They would have been 1,200 years old in the Hellenistic period. Some of these Hellenistic thefts (such as the obelisk called Cleopatra's Needle) ended up in London or Istanbul, and are now an intrinsic part of the fabric of those cities.

A small crocodile temple had been reconstructed in the central garden courtyard of the museum, a much loved deity apparently, but for some reason I found it repellent, the mummified crocodile black and leathery in its painted shrine. Sobek was an ancient Egyptian crocodile god, admired for his royal ability to snatch and destroy, and strangely taken on by the Greeks, who must have encountered him in the swamps of the Nile estuary. A powerful image, but not quite comprehensible to me. I know crocodiles are revered by my Aboriginal friends in Yirrkala and seen as benevolent, but I didn't understand my almost fearful reaction. There was much magic and superstition in the pharaonic religion that was continued in the Greco-Roman period. The Ptolemies seemed to want the same power as the pharaohs — their gigantic portraits were carved in granite with rigid expressions and empty eye sockets, with the same aura as that of Egyptian king statues, though more naturalistically modelled.

A fresco painting of a mural scene with oxen pulling water was vividly drawn, in what seemed like the famous pastoral 'Alexandrian' style. The drawing of the ox and the landscape was effortlessly impressionistic. So much has been lost, so these were glimpses. A painted limestone gravestone of a Greek horseman in red, a cavalry man who must have died in Egypt, showed the same understanding of movement in space, with the horse rearing. Pattern is subtly everywhere, as compulsive as figuration but more invisible.

I emerged from the museum and walked through the city to the crowded crossroads where the great ancient Museum of Alexandria is supposed to have stood, and the Great Library. They may still be there, deep underneath the unprobed layers of the present city. Tattered nineteenth-century buildings, concrete apartments, an old decaying Piccadilly Hotel and a patisserie conceal any hint of such grandeur. (The foremost European language of Alexandria is French rather than English.) Huge old doorways six metres high were elaborated with festoons, palmettes and columns, leading to cavernous dark entrance halls drifting with rubbish and cats. These five-storey apartment buildings with tall shuttered windows and balconies must have been quite sumptuous, and some restored ones on the waterfront still resonate with overtones of a rich literary and social life.

I saw only one other tourist in all my wanderings in the city – a fair man sitting in an Egyptian coffee shop reading, like a character from a Durrell novel. It is tiring being so noticeable, even though people are polite and helpful. Despite my visibility I felt safe in this old cosmopolitan city, and of course there are those guards with guns everywhere, guarding mosques and even the locked up Orthodox Church.

I got lost again near a looming nineteenth-century building in which many people were thronging, in a vast square – what was it? Not one sign in Latin characters, only Arabic. Finally I realised, feeling stupid, that it was the railway station, El Masr (shades of my father again.) Some handsome boys helped me, and I took a horse cab that had been following me relentlessly. The horse was extraordinary, moving fearlessly in the stream of hooting small cars. A whip with bells and fodder lay on the floor beneath my feet. The vehicle was really not unlike the chariots in the Cairo Museum, the wheels identically made of a simple iron frame. Except one could sit down, and there was a hood.

It is such a luxury pleasing myself. I had a late lunch at 4 p.m. in the Hotel Cecil, a place of historic meetings. Most notably, generals of the Allied forces met there, it is said, to plan the battle of El Alamein, while my father was having officer training in Cairo in 1941.

I sat in a peaceful and elegant old dining room and ate Egyptian rice with sauce and delicious bread, even a glass of wine, and looked out along the corniche to the old fort on the point where the lighthouse once was, and thought of the treasures below that sea. I drew the curving wall, with boys running along it, while enjoying the unobtrusive service, heavy cutlery, white linen, the impeccable waiter, a bubble of tradition surviving, like the old days of the cosmopolitan European city.

Later, driving along the corniche in another horse cab, I sank back into the darkness of the seat, into the sensations of the city at dusk, overflowing with people out for the evening stroll, men arm in arm, girls in gaggles, families, older women. I saw men selling tea in glasses, boiling water in old kettles balanced precariously on gas jets. Images flashed past: great baskets filled with bread, wonderful fruit shops with bananas hanging up in bunches, mounds of strawberries. The palm trees along the waterfront were still in their winter wrappings of straw matting, which seemed such an affectionate gesture. The still water of the bay was deep ultramarine under the street lights. The spacious sea contrasts to the seething activity of the city, the deteriorating buildings, piles of debris, the trams rattling up and down. *I polis* was the name for Constantinople, just 'the city', and this is another such city, an organic, mutiplicitous entity without much reference to modernity, a different species of city to those I know in Australia.

19 April

In this crowded and overwhelming day I spoke every fragmentary language that I possess – Greek, French and Italian.

In the morning early I took the tram to the centre, through many lost, dirty and decaying suburbs. Peeling concrete, long abandoned shops, debris everywhere. I walked to the Greco-Roman area of Alexandria, where a large site was still being excavated. I found the excavations and introduced myself to the young woman in a cheerful headscarf selling tickets, saying I had been working on an excavation in Cyprus. Five others were sitting with her, drinking tea, with round rosy faces. She said, 'We are also archaeologists. I studied at the University of Alexandria. But after we get jobs, we are not interested in archaeology any more.' When I asked her about the theatre she directed me to a dusty glass noticeboard with some photocopied pages in English, from a Polish report about 1960 I should think. 'You could go and talk to some of the archaeologists from the Polish Mission, who are busy, but somewhere around.' She shrugged and turned back to her friends, and for the two hours I was on the site they sat there without moving.

The small theatre of creamy marble was architecturally almost complete, and captivating in its detailed passageways and carved ornaments – egg and dart, intertwining palmettes, mosaic floors, spiral columns in the *orchestra*. It was used for political assemblies as much as performances in the fourth century AD, but was built from a larger second-century AD theatre. Made from scraps of other buildings, including some magnificent marble architraves, it had the charm of resourceful recycling, a stylish quality of making something new out of old materials. The *parodos* or entrance to the stage was almost square, and most intriguing were the small rooms, barrel-vaulted, perhaps dressing rooms off the *parodos*, which would seem a likely place for frescoes. But if there had ever been any painting, there was now no sign.

It seemed an essentially sophisticated building, made for rhetoric, debate and poetry, at a time when all these were rapidly diminishing in the face of fanatical Christian monasticism. I was shocked to find out that it was Christians who had finally burnt the Great Library, the repository of so much ancient knowledge, because it was associated with the Temple of Serapis. The Christian Patriarch Theophilos and his 'army of wild black monks' lynched and killed Hypatia, a notable woman scholar of the neo-Platonic school, in AD 415 as she was going to a lecture. E.M. Forster in his 1920s' guidebook writes simply, 'She is not a great figure. But with her the Greece that is a spirit expired, the Greece that tried to discover truth and create beauty, and that had created Alexandria.'[12]

When Amrou Ibn El Ass conquered Alexandria for Muhammad in the seventh century he wrote, 'I have conquered the great city of the West and I find it difficult to list all its riches and its beauties. Let me say only that it contains four thousand palaces, four thousand public baths, four hundred theatres ... and twelve thousand fruit shops.'[13] (I was pleased that the jewel-like fruit shops still seem to be flourishing.) So this small theatre would have been one of hundreds in a city where theatrical life, and the power of Dionysos (or Bacchus), was profound.

Plutarch tells of a haunting episode in the last days of Mark Antony, an omen of his defeat, 'when the whole city was in deep silence... On a sudden was heard the sounds of instruments and voices singing in tune, and the cry of a crowd of people shouting and dancing, like a troop of bacchanals on its way. This tumultuous procession seemed to take its course right through the middle of the city to the gate ... and suddenly passed.' People believed, Plutarch goes on, that this meant that Bacchus the god, to whom Antony had been devoted, had now forsaken him.[14] And Cavafy of course wrote his poem *The God Abandons Antony* on the same theme, in the ancient elegiac tradition:

> Do not lament your luck that now gives out, your work
> That has failed, schemes of your life
> All proved to be false.[15]

Around the theatre were the rough hillocks of a huge site under excavation, with repeated mounds of brown dust, and labourers slowly carrying rubber baskets of earth to empty on one of the heaps, cleaning a previously dug trench of loose earth fill. They worked at a fraction of the speed of our strapping, well-fed Australian students. I found out later that they earned 10 Egyptian pounds a day (about $3), 'good casual rates' and more than the tea-drinking archaeologists, though the educated ones have some security of employment.

I spoke at length to the Polish archaeologists, Gregory and Renata. Gregory had been working on the site for eighteen years. They'd both done student digs with Professor Daszewski (now digging at Marina, on the coast near Alexandria) and had indeed met at one of his excavations and had visited his excavations at Paphos. They showed me some fragments of lovely mosaics – the workmen lifted the canvas covers for me to see – a panel of birds with interlacing, a large rosette of the second century AD and a panther. Some of these were discovered in the 1970s, some only a few months ago.

Above the mosaics, covered by a roof, towered eleven metres of earth and rubble. Each layer of the town had been built on the destruction of the previous layer. They had removed a whole Turkish necropolis in order to excavate the Roman layers, but Hellenistic levels had only been reached in a few places. In the cold north wind, massive walls of a gigantic Roman brick bathhouse stood out clearly in the harsh light. In the summer the unshadowed site must be like a furnace. Gregory stood beside a large tripod and pulley, perhaps four metres high, which was used to move blocks of stone without damaging the site.

'It's just the same equipment as the Romans used to build with,' he explained. 'It's exactly what we need.'

Renata had made a clean and pleasant place for herself near the pottery shed, with a bit of garden cleared of rubbish, and was sitting there mending glass. The fragility of those fragments contrasted with the chaotic nature of the site. Bringing us tea, she told me stories about Alexandria, speaking of the city almost as a living character, and described how conditions had deteriorated for Europeans over the last few years. 'They really do not want us here, they want us out.' It was no longer permitted to drink wine at an outside café table, the dress codes had become more severe, shorts were no longer allowed. But often, she said, Egypt is 'easy'. The Poles could not see themselves fitting into any bigger picture. The authorities, she thought, were eradicating the beauty of old Alexandria as fast as they could, pulling down old hotels, pouring sewage into the Mediterranean, not clearing rubbish. They had built villas all along the coast to Libya to attract rich Saudis. But the Saudi Arabs were not interested in puritan fundamentalism and a view of the sea, they wanted the pleasures of life in Cairo. So, she said, the villas stand empty, and the sea is polluted.

'The city has changed so much,' she went on. 'Yet it still has an almost numinous effect on the lives of those who live here.' An artist she knew who had had an apartment here for years said, 'When I walk along the corniche, one side has not changed, still true to Alexandria, but I never turn my eyes to the other side that is no longer Alexandria.' The sea remains constant, calm, stretching away. Despite all the changes, 'You meet everyone in Alexandria,' Renata told me. 'Odd people from your past.' She said the Egyptians had no understanding of the city as a port, it was hardly used as such any more. People from Cairo, middle-class people, were not attracted any longer for holidays, preferring rich villas on other coasts, as the beaches around Alexandria were now too dirty. Such sadness in her story, an Alexandrian lament it seemed. Perhaps the government will change the city irreversibly, so that the nineteenth-century town becomes another city of memory, like so many of the layers of Alexandria. I thought of Cavafy's insistence on the indelible character of the city despite all efforts to leave it:

> You will not find new lands, nor find another sea,
> The city will follow you. You'll wander down
> These very streets, age in these same quarters of the town,
> Among the same houses finally turn grey.[16]

3. IKINGI MARYUT

19-20 April

I parted rather sadly from the Poles, feeling a kinship with their strain, their anxiety to explore this remarkable site despite such difficulties with policies and the changing mood of Islam. But I thought I could also see the viewpoint of the Egyptians, who might wish to be in control of their own idea of the past, and might feel constrained by funding that came from countries sometimes inimical to an Arab position. There are many approaches to municipal organisation, and the Polish excavation is funded by an American foundation.

On Renata's advice I had lunch in the Greek café Élite, not far from the excavation. I was greeted by a striking woman with blue eyes, perhaps eighty years old, her thin neck weighed down by an immense amber necklace. She introduced herself as Kyria Christina. The low room could have been any provincial Greek restaurant, but faded posters of Matisse paintings, French art from the 1960s, and old wall paintings gave the place a different air. It was a relief to be able to communicate in Greek after my complete ignorance of Arabic; suddenly the cadences of Greek seemed like home. She'd been born in Alexandria but her parents were from Paphos, it had been so lovely in Alex once, the sea, the climate. No, she hardly spoke Arabic, went to a Greek school, the church was nearby and this café was her business. The young waiters treated her gently, and as we spoke, brought dishes for her to inspect before taking them to the tables. The food had the pleasure of familiarity, kalamari with chips, cucumber and tomato.

There was a photo on the wall of a middle-aged man who looked vaguely familiar. 'Matisse,' she said. 'I studied art and he came here once.' She didn't have much family left now, only two sisters in Athens. All had changed since what she called the 'catastrophe', in

1952, when Alexandria became Egyptian rather than being a cosmopolitan port. I took her photo, sitting in a chair outside the door, and she seemed pleased, posed carefully and did not smile. 'Goodbye, *kori mou*, my girl.' So many goodbyes. In every old Greek woman I saw a glimpse of my first Greek landlady in Athens, Irene, who had worked in the Greek court as a seamstress before the abdication of the king; the same sadness and dignified acceptance of inevitable loss. The 'black ladies' I used to call them. Kyria Christina no doubt had had a varied and interesting life in that busy street, built on top of the heart of ancient Alexandria, in the region where it is suspected the Library once stood; but the Greek community was now tiny, and fading.

After lunch I was determined somehow to reach Ikingi Maryut, the place where my father had camped in 1941 when his regiment trained in Alexandria. As I walked uncertainly in the direction of a bus station, I was pursued by a handsome horse-cab driver with an immaculate horse and carriage, who persuaded me with his forceful enthusiasm to go with him to the catacombs and Pompey's pillar. He agreed to drive me to the bus stop to Ikingi Maryut. He referred to his horse as Number One, glossy and well looked after, with little brass hands and blue beads on his bridle. Most Egyptians seemed to use horse cabs rather than taxis, I noticed, and the animals were astonishing in the way they mingled with dense traffic and were really as quick as cars in that narrow warren of streets.

The two sites I wanted to see were in the souk, the poorest part of the city. I found the poverty quite confronting, and reflected that in different circumstances I might be like the people there, just sitting and squatting in the street with such lassitude and carelessness. Later, talking to the young lift boy in the hotel, I realised just what effort is needed to escape from those implacable conditions. The atmosphere was a little like Aboriginal settlements I'd seen as a child around Walgett in New South Wales. Piles of rubbish had hens scratching, and people crouched on the dusty roadside selling anything; I noted some loofah sponges, bananas, a few car parts, and even some elaborately carved chairs placed out in the road among the crowds of people. We passed a bazaar, a man cooking sweet potatoes on a portable brazier, hoops and cushions of bread, and a Turkish-looking tea seller with his kettle and tea glasses, wearing the red *vraka*, baggy trousers which you still see occasionally in Cyprus.

At the site of 'Pompey's Pillar', two guides, probably those underemployed archaeologists again, attached themselves to me, there being few other tourists, offering tentative English, wide smiles and, irresistibly, a red geranium. This enormous column made of a single piece of granite twenty-two metres high is the only ancient landmark still standing in Alexandria, and was raised in honour of Diocletian, rather than the general Pompey, to commemorate the fact that he had saved the city from famine, in AD 291. The misnomer 'Pompey's Pillar' came about through travellers from the time of Napoleon imagining that the column was erected by Julius Caesar to mark the tomb of his enemy Pompey, who was beheaded by Ptolemy XIII, brother of Cleopatra in the first century BC.[17]

They took me down below the hill of ruins with its spectacular column into what had been tunnels below the vanished Temple of Serapis, that strange mixed religion that so successfully brought together Greek and Egyptian cults.

Here were niches in the cut-rock passages where papyrus documents were supposed to have been stored for the Serapeum Library – long empty tunnels, eerily quiet after the hum of the city above. Full of ghosts. At the far end of the tunnel a figure appeared, another foreigner, and as he approached me in the dim light, to my great astonishment he greeted me by my name, in English. 'You are Diana!' (As if to reassure me). His name was Stephen, and he had worked as an excavator at Paphos in 1996, a rather reticent boy with dreadlocks I had observed then, but now he seemed focused and adult, speaking basic Arabic and travelling around sites. It rather unnerved me to have Renata's rule about always meeting someone you know in Alexandria so quickly confirmed; it seemed so unlikely in this pulsing city, deep under the ground to meet a known compatriot. But of course humans are like birds and animals, keeping to their own niche in the environment and performing a regular pattern of predictable actions.

Serapis, by coincidence, was a deity combined from Egyptian and Hellenistic gods, invented about the time of the establishment of Nea Paphos in Ptolemaic times. His name contains 'Apis', the sacred bull of Memphis. Serapis had aspects of Zeus, Dionysos and Aesculapius, so was linked most satisfactorily to fertility, healing, and an afterlife. These useful attributes travelled well: there's a wonderful coiling limestone serpent in the Cyprus Museum, scaled and feathered, from the Temple of Serapis in Soli in Cyprus.

I continued in the friendly horse cab to the Kom El Shawqafah catacombs and here I had an older guide, a thin, almost cadaverous man with excellent English and a true passion for the site. He gave a very clear and coherent description of the weird amalgam of styles in the complex paintings and sculptures of the tombs and catacombs. Here were Egyptian gods in Greek mode, wearing Roman armour, with Medusa, 'goddess of evil,' said the guide, on the roof. Thoth, Anubis, Horus were all there looking after the dead, and the terrible crocodile god I had met in the museum, Sobek. The painted tomb discovered in Tigranes Pasha Street of the late first or second century AD was fascinating for its unexpected analogies to the Paphos fresco fragments. I saw this likeness in the fillets suspended by the winged sun disk above the mummy of Osiris on the bier, and in the plant patterns on the ceiling of the low-arched roof. So, I thought, theatrical and funereal motifs have more in common than theatre has with genre scenes. Theatre, because of Dionysos, has the same iconography as tomb painting, which is to assert the continuance of fertility and abundance despite death. 'The function of art,' said Aristotle, 'is to purify the soul through pity and terror.'[18]

Then deep, deep, we went, into a round shaft with a spiral staircase descending into the catacombs, like a ritual descent into the underworld. The impressive organisation and structure of these complex tombs looks in plan like the diagram of a space ship, a vessel perhaps to negotiate the vast underworld which had always been a main preoccupation of Egyptian culture. A traveller from Bangkok unexpectedly joined the descent, listening with serious attentiveness to the guide. Here first was an underground cavern with an elaborate carved tomb for a rich couple, perhaps Romans in government in the second century AD. The man and woman had Roman portrait heads attached to standard Egyptian bodies with one leg forward. (It's supposed to be right leg forward for a man, left leg for a woman, but both had their right legs forward, 'to be symmetrical,' said the guide.) Human-sized snakes coiled on either side, like the chthonic serpents carved on the thrones of important seats in the Theatre of Dionysos in Athens. 'The snake,' said our psychopomp, 'is the deity of Alexandria.' (As we descended into this underworld the intense quality of the guide became more than a little uncanny.) More Medusas and garlands appeared on other tombs, all carved in low relief out of the sandstone, with lotus columns topped by ionic scrolls. Faint indications of painting, a narrative mythological scene of funerary gods, showed how rich the imagery had been.

It was like a 'mix and match' book, where you turn the pages to make unpredictable combinations of animals, people and ornament. For postmodern eyes that have recently found the notion of hybridity so significant these figures are intriguing, although the guidebook describes the images as a 'very unhappy marriage between Egyptian and Greek canons'. The lower levels of the catacombs were flooded, and water was still half way up the figures of the second level; water unmoving like glass, and dark. A 'banqueting hall' with stone seats had access to the tombs, so that families could bring food down to dine, mingling the dead and the living in a place between worlds. They must have feasted, or at least made offerings to the dead, because the place was known as Mound of Sherds, Kom El Shawqafah, from the thousands of remains of pottery dishes from funeral feasts.

My cab, now seeming an almost magical transport, set off for the bus station to Ikingi Maryut. 'Not far,' said the driver, Ali, but time became suspended, across a devastated landscape, along a putrid canal, with abandoned concrete shells of old factories, full of building rubbish. Though spiky with rushes, the canal stank. The sky was pale, the landscape as if washed with grey. People had set up forges beside the road, mending car parts, using old car bodies as improvised workshops. A truck dumped more rubble beside the road. Four older men sat in chairs amongst all of this, talking and drinking tea. Everyone stared at me in the horse-drawn cab so far from the tourist route. Fumes, smoke and haze made for a depressing and barren scene. There was a cotton mill, a refinery, and all their waste went straight into the canal. Where were we?

At last a crowd of buses and people appeared on the flat plain, the bus station. I felt exhausted by strangeness, by not being able to speak or read, by not knowing the price of anything. To reach Ikingi Maryut, that place only 20 kilometres from Alexandria, seemed an almost impossible task. Eventually I found the right taxi bus and gave Ali what he felt was too little but which I knew to be more than a day's wages. I said goodbye regretfully to the faithful Number One. The bearded driver in a long robe demanded ten pounds as I got in, I said five pounds – I found out later the price was 75 piastres for Egyptians, but I was helpless, with glaring men shouting at me in Arabic. I must have seemed like all the stereotypes of a tourist, immensely rich, and dumb (literally) as well.

I sat next to a very pretty girl, soft and rosy, without a headscarf, who helped me with money and introduced herself as Shaymaa. She was eighteen, a student, and lived in Ikingi Maryut, now an outer rather wealthy suburb of Alexandria. Her few words of careful English were a blessing. She asked me why I wanted to go to this out-of-the-way place, and I carefully explained that my father had been encamped there with thousands of soldiers in 1941 and as he was now an old man, I had wanted to visit the place when I was in Alexandria. This story was translated to the whole bus; everyone wanted to find out more about me. The bus went on and on through more industrial landscapes and passed a huge expressway on mushroom concrete supports almost as high as Pompey's Pillar. The air was full of chemicals, with refineries for oil from the western desert. Now the road to Ikingi Maryut, where my father's regiment had marched through the empty desert, is lined with half-finished buildings, no made roads, only dusty tracks. A few trees had been planted along the road, but most had died.

After half an hour the bus set Shaymaa and myself down, and she walked with me along a wide track of dusty sand between rows of high-walled villas, some very rich looking, even with glimpses of bougainvillea flowers. Fragments of glass were set into the top of the walls. The road was piled with uncollected rubbish, blowing with plastic.

'Where do you want to go?' she asked me, as if she might wave a wand.

'I don't know where the old camp was, is there a café?' I thought I might sit and reflect, walk around, before returning to Alexandria. My father had said that there must be much war refuse, old guns and trucks, but I thought it more likely everything had been recycled. 'I'll take you to the motel,' she decided. I took her photo as the sun suddenly seemed to be setting into beiges and gold, touching her serene face. She told me I'd been ripped off by the blue-robed van driver with the loud voice. (It seemed that all my movements had been circumscribed by money haggling. I tried to be fair and give more than the lowest price. Knowing what the daily wage was, huge performances of rage were hard to deal with, when clearly it was all a performance. But tourist prices are in another league, and this is the golden opportunity to escape from remorseless poverty. It is understandable, but stressful.)

After ten minutes more the motel improbably appeared, where I thought I could have a tea, and telephone for a taxi. How sweet

Shaymaa was, like an apparition sent for my personal fairy story, kissing me before leaving me at the motel. Two dark, fine-looking men at the reception desk were curt, and charged eight pounds for me to sit down for a minute with a glass of hot water with a teabag on a dirty tray, no smile. But I sat thankfully by the unlikely oasis of the blue swimming pool, which was heaped around with up-ended chairs and tables, waiting for summer. I drew the palms, the pool, and the cats, a drawing for my father of the transformation of his desert camp. The cats were the most charming surprise, five spotted and striped cats walking around and around the pool, as if to engage me with some ancient cat ritual. Finally I collected some of the sand that was blowing through the garden and put it in a film canister for my dad.

The night descended abruptly. That Ikingi Maryut of nearly sixty years ago was lost and gone, as so many Alexandrias are, only recalled in the memory of old men. Who knows where the dump of armaments from the War has gone? (It may be under the sand, awaiting future archaeologists.) I thought of those young, fresh soldiers, about to fight the battle of El Alamein, who were the same age, twenty-three, as my own son is now. I thought how pointless war is in a general sense, and yet that battle did hold Rommel back. Alexandria was a neutral city, watching while Europe fought, so perhaps even the memory of this twentieth-century war seems unimportant to the present population, in the general melee of such a past.

Suddenly, there I was in a very strange place at nightfall. I went into the reception with the unfriendly young men in their white hotel jackets, to pay my exorbitant bill and find out about buses or taxis back to Alexandria. They were offhand and hostile, not prepared to ring a taxi for me, and advised me to go down to the corner of the dark, unlit road and just hail a bus. It was all too much, tears flowed from my eyes and I felt deeply upset.

'Why do you treat tourists like this?' I said. 'Why are you so inhospitable and unfriendly? My requests are simple, I am prepared to pay reasonably – why do you make every transaction so difficult and charge five times the ordinary price for everything?'

I wept, and they were truly astonished, as if they were seeing me for the first time. 'What is the matter?' the older one said. 'What has happened?' (Their English was good, but I suspect they just suffered from straightforward indifference, so common in Australia too.) I told the story of trying to find the place where my father had been stationed in a war that had killed so many, how hard it was to get any information from officials. I sat down and tried to be calm as a great wave of fatigue rolled over me. Westerners come from a different world, and I had been naïve.

Their expressions changed, the masks became human, I became perhaps the kind of woman they understood, a tearful woman in need of help. Now they refused money for my lukewarm teabag, insisted on giving me the correct fare back to Alexandria – a mere 75 piastres compared to the 50 pounds they had told me. Escorting me along the dark street to the main road, they hailed a hurtling van, and it took me to another van going to 'Iskandriya'. Before leaving Ikingi Maryut the bus stopped again beside the motel, and my three white-coated receptionists looked in to enquire if I was there and alright. Somehow my tears had made me human, just a middle-aged woman with an old father. Before I must have been an invisible stereotype, a tourist of great wealth. They had not liked criticism of hospitality – no person from the eastern Mediterranean would.

This time a robust man about forty years old got in beside me and started to talk, in Italian. Somehow I dredged up some words – a language I was once easy in. He had studied in Rome, and was now an engineer building that new freeway to Cairo. He spoke of his wife and two children in an apartment in Cairo and seemed Western and middle class. The atmosphere was entirely changed in that night van, rocketing back into Alexandria; fate took another turn. The engineer insisted on paying my fare, and the driver was kind and got me a taxi to my hotel, telling me the exact price I should pay. This too, was as confusing as the indifference had been – no middle way seemed possible. The driver of this taxi was a big brown man with a huge smile, again working two jobs. He had only a few words of English, but pointed to the murky Lake Maryut dimly on our left, and said 'boat', like a hieroglyph.

On arrival at the hotel there was a fuss because I had had an apple for breakfast instead of cold meat, and therefore should pay extra (the usual ten pounds). I refused very cheerfully, and went upstairs to my high room. The young lift boy insisted on escorting me, and told me he was learning English, he had a day job as well as this night job to support his parents, but more than anything he wanted an education, and it was so difficult. All I did was listen, encourage him, played my part by giving him a tip. All these men in hotels and taxis had two jobs – 'We want to come to Australia, we want a visa.'

Early the next morning I spent a cold mosquito-ridden dawn waiting in the small airport to fly to Athens. The passengers were mostly businessmen, except for several older Greek women and two Egyptian mothers heavily swathed in cloth, with two doll-like children. One of the Greek women had a poodle which she treated like a child. I of course was assigned the seat next to the poodle, and although it was undoubtedly a pleasant if neurotic animal, I asked to change because of an allergy to dogs. I sat next to a Polish engineer who had been at a seminar in Alexandria with a big German oil refinery in the western desert. He thought the future for Egypt looked rosy.

What did I observe in Egypt? Its past is all-encompassing, still littering the present. Nothing rots, only dries, withers, and makes dust. So many buildings and statues are on a great scale, like the column rising from the Temple of Serapis. To the people of Paphos, who were so closely associated with Alexandria, the country and its monuments must have seemed huge. The pharaonic scale and heaviness, the multitude of deities, the force of the Nile, this was nature beyond the human measure of the Greeks. The sight of the vast mound in the Polish excavations, entirely composed of the pounded remains of habitation demonstrated the layering of the city, generations of many languages and peoples.

Egypt underlined for me the astonishing fact that Greek naturalism existed at all, with its pleasure in the ephemeral present. The hand clutching a veil, the graceful turning hips of those pink and blue Tanagra figurines seemed frivolous but necessary in face of the weight of the granite bull of Serapis and the monstrous heads of the Ptolemies. Reason, humour, and tolerance seem fragile and easily dispensed with. The Romans understood the power of the state, and the cruelty of that power, like the Egyptians did. The painted tombs of Alexandria with their hybrid images were a revelation to me, and their funerary customs must have profoundly influenced Paphos, where painted tombs are beginning to be found in numbers. I could start to understand the longstanding relationship between Paphos and Alexandria.

All through my stay, the call to prayer boomed out five times a day, from before dawn to after dark with a compulsive rhythm, so that when I left the country, the passing hours of the day seemed unstructured and oddly private.

4. ATHENS

22 April

A celestial blue morning flying over the Aegean from Alexandria. Umber-coloured islands scattered over the still sea, with intricate curved coastlines and tiny towns. From so high up it looked like a dream of peace and simplicity. After all, sometimes all I want is to have a plain ordered house, a few lovely objects and quietness; after the seething crowds of Egypt one can perhaps understand the growth of monasticism, the retreat to the desert.

I first arrived in Athens after a long sea voyage from Australia in the 1960s, docking at Piraeus on a milky winter's day. Arriving by ship is a slow arrival, pervaded by smells and sounds of the sea and the port. Ever since then, coming back to Athens has had a sense of homecoming, perhaps because I wandered the crowded noisy city as a student, understanding for the first time how a city can have so many layers which are not clearly presented in a linear sequence, but confront you all at once. A tiny brick Byzantine church is built near a shrine to the nymphs in the old Agora, overlooked by the rhythmic columns of the Parthenon, which is almost suspended above the city on its high rock. New and old apartment blocks form canyons in long streets that divide the city into distinctive suburbs.

The Australian Institute of Archaeology just below the Acropolis is welcoming, with a few rooms to accommodate scholars. I ate a familiar lunch of fetta, olives and tomatoes on the balcony of the Institute, watching the light on the Parthenon and tiny figures moving amongst its scaffolding. Later, I walked on the hill of Philopappou nearby in the cloudless evening, with women walking dogs, lovers entwined on a ruined wall among the pines, and watched the sunset over the vast city spread between the luminous mountains, the three humps of Hymettos, Pendeli and Parnitha. Once I had searched for a cave of Pan on Parnitha and got lost among the rocks and thyme. The hills still rise intact, mottled only with the shadows of clouds above the encroaching blocks of houses on the lower slopes.

That night a professor from the University of Athens gave a lecture on the iconography of Macedonian grave reliefs of the fourth century BC, and their complex relationship to known genealogies of prominent families. I realised that any discussion of Macedonian art is of intense interest as it is at the heart of contemporary Greek identity. The audience was highly educated and multilingual, from every archaeological school in Athens, which includes British, American, French, German, Italian and Scandinavian.

I spoke to Richard Anderson, an architect at the Agora, working on a reconstruction of architectural monuments for the American School, and a friend and associate of Peter Megaw in Cyprus. He had been completing the drawings of the ecclesiastical buildings at Kourion, and has worked in Cyprus for years, excavating with Peter. Mary Sturgeon, an American scholar working on sculptures in Corinth, was intrigued by the presence of painted fresco in the theatre in Paphos, as there are also some traces of painting in the Roman theatre of Corinth. There does seem to be a gap in knowledge about Roman painting in the eastern Mediterranean after the eruption of Vesuvius in AD 79, so all clues have to be scrutinised. Whether any painting that was discovered had been conserved too is crucial, as so many Greek theatres were excavated in the nineteenth century when methods of storage and conservation were often dubious. So the search must take me to the remarkable discoveries at Vergina near Thessaloniki in northern Greece, where exquisite examples of Hellenistic painting were discovered in tombs in 1977. But first, a few days in Athens.

23 April

The Agora, with its reconstructed Stoa of Attalus just below the Acropolis, holds an extraordinary collection of pottery and figurines, artefacts of everyday life, and monumental sculpture from every layer of Athens, from the Mycenaean to Byzantine periods. Today, the extensive site was transformed by a glowing, glittering carpet of silky red poppies; an evocation of the colour the white marbles must once have had when they were painted. People were coming from far away just to look at the sea of red flowers.

I was taken over the drawing studios by the architect and Anne Hooton, an Australian archaeological illustrator, and was impressed with the fastidious drawing techniques. The skill in reconstructing a whole capital from a worn fragment of marble makes a precise view of the early buildings of the site possible. The orders in Greek architecture, Doric, Ionic and Corinthian, were the basis of European architecture until the twentieth century. Even today, echoes of columns and pediments appear in malls or apartment buildings. Slight variations in the evolution of Doric or Ionic capitals cause great excitement, and are comparable to the discovery of a new species in science. Anne took me on a tour through the immense storerooms of the Agora, lined with shelves of material that would have pride of place in the main exhibition rooms in most museums.

The detail required in archaeology is exhaustive. In one dim corner, seated at a small wooden table with a light, was a young scholar from Canada, studying amphorae in order to make a comprehensive catalogue of the types of vessels. He seemed like a man on a quest to accomplish an almost impossible task, his head bent over a magnifying glass in the circle of light. Surrounded by looming shelves of heavy fragments, he will be in that timeless basement, in that stony silence, for many weeks. Eventually, the work will flesh out historical realities of storage and trade, as amphorae were the essential containers of antiquity. There was something about his devoted work, measuring and writing at the bottom of the building, that seemed like the process of an alchemist transforming base metals to gold, the gold of more knowledge.

Anne told me a story of transformation concerning the marvellous classical sculptures standing in the porch of the Stoa. The marble philosophers, gods and nymphs had all become encrusted over the years with deposits of lead and pollutants from the city. The conservators have discovered that a very expensive cosmetic mud beauty pack from Paris is the best way to gently clean the marble surface and allow the creamy texture of stone to shine again.

The civilised ancient world existed through the protection of the sword, and if that failed, death and destruction followed. Athens was destroyed by the Persians in 480 BC, and this devastation allowed a complete re-thinking and re-building. A different kind of city rose in the ruins, and the archaic monsters were hidden in the new sculptures of the fifth-century Parthenon. War remained a constant and pervasive theme – between gods and giants, between Lapiths and Centaurs. There was no choice about this. Some of the early sculptures in the Acropolis Museum had an impression of joyful violence – almost a glorification in the savagery of animals – so that any idea of pacifism would have been incomprehensible. There were wonderful lions like those from Tamassos in Cyprus, full of power and snarling energy to protect the sanctuary of Athena from terrible forces. Two carved snakes from the pediment, with open toothed mouths, have thick bodies twenty-five centimetres in diameter.

But beside these monsters, beside the warriors with their bulging muscles and lunging swords, are other figures. The statues of women dedicated to the goddess were called *korai*, girls; the same name, Kore or Maiden, was given to Persephone the daughter of Demeter.

One head of a *kore*, delicately carved in Parian marble, has almond eyes and curving lips with a glimmer of an 'archaic smile'. The wall text proclaimed that this sculpture was 'the most sublime expression of refined vitality'. Clothing in the *korai* is a complete means of expression – it is looped, folded, pouched, crinkled, patterned, and columnar. When the human forms turn naturalistic, they become somehow more vulnerable; I caught my breath at the nuances of the transition. The gesture of the Nike, or Victory, adjusting her sandal is acutely perceived and must have been actually observed, a fleeting moment defined and made memorable by drapery. Each of the caryatids, I noticed, though worn and corroded, is subtly different.

A short walk below the Acropolis leads to Ermou (Hermes) Street and another world. Screeching with traffic, it is plastered with ferocious graffitti, and contains a market for all kinds of clothes and domestic objects. Here was an astonishing assortment of objects laid out on the pavement by people swarming to Athens from eastern and central Europe, from Romania, Russia, and Albania. The Athenians I spoke to in the taverna nearby regarded this influx with distaste. The garden of the Kerameikos, the ancient potters' quarter, with an entrance on Ermou is a respite from the noise and desperation of the refugees.

The tumult of the street drops away as you go into the site of the potters, full of sweet smelling flowers and myrtle, the urns and tall gravestones making it appear almost like a Victorian garden cemetery, a picturesque scene with an enchanting view of the Acropolis. The Kerameikos seemed to me unchanged after decades, as if museums really are in a kind of time warp. This museum was full of little treasures, spindle whorls, loom weights, lovely funerary vases, the curvacious tall *loutrophoroi* and white *lekythoi*, as well as tiny objects from graves, figurines, beads, and toys.

The inscription from the grave monument of Anaxilas of Naxos refers to ancient immigration. Naxos may have seemed as far away as Albania to the ancient world: 'Here I stand, stone monument of Anaxilas, fraught with grief, sorrow and lamentation, a Naxian immigrant whom the Athenians esteemed for his prudence.'

The prudence of the contemporary emigrants laying out their poor objects on the pavements in Ermou Street may not save them.

24 April

The paintings of Theophilos, the early-twentieth-century 'primitive' painter, have been restored and beautifully mounted in a room in the Popular Art Museum. His painting had the pure colour of my fresco fragments, red, blue, gold, roughly painted with a vigorous hand. Here was the longing for the heroic life – Alexander the Great appeared like a nineteenth-century brigand, a folk hero, with a voracious black moustache and long boots. The quality of the images reminded me of travelling in buses in central Greece, where the driver played the anguished music of Epirus, or hovering laments sung by an unaccompanied contralto voice. The brushy 'mark' of Theophilos is not unlike the rapid brushstrokes of the Paphos frescoes I have been examining, and the small active figures with their large eyes had a 'Coptic' vitality of gesture. He was an intuitive painter, who still strikes the heart.

In my favourite bread shop I met an old friend, Jonas Eiring, about to complete a complex study on Hellenistic pottery in Crete and very knowledgeable about the intricate activities of all the archaeological institutes in Athens. We bought cheese pies and an almond pastry and sat and had coffee on Makriyanni Street. Hearing about my chase after second-century Roman fresco, he advised me to contact the Austrian Institute because they would be working in Ephesos at the same time as I planned to pass through. This was another useful lead.

I searched in the Nordic Library unsuccessfully all afternoon for more information on Roman painting in Greece, and finally went back to the Institute. I sat on the balcony drinking ouzo with Con, an Australian of Greek descent who specialises in Byzantine history. The Parthenon slowly faded into dusk, and then became floodlit, and the great mound of Hymettos that rises beyond all the suburbs gradually darkened. Con told me the monasteries had had an entirely functional attitude to manuscripts, which were often burnt as fuel if the monks saw in them no relevance to their own life. Even as late as the sixteenth century, the tenets of Byzantium were firmly in place in Greece, although it was just a small part of the vast reach of Byzantium through Asia Minor, Armenia and the Balkans. And the manuscripts were written in classical Greek, just as the Islamic tradition kept classical Arabic, despite the existence of many local dialects.

25 April

A long morning in the National Museum reminded me how pervasive and long-lasting motifs in painting could be. The same images appear in the Roman frescoes as were used in the fifth century BC, more than five hundred years earlier. The white funerary vessels, the *lekythoi*, are decorated with a remarkable restraint, with a taut intention to convey grief with minimal means. Here was Charon, black-robed ferryman for the dead, the mourning woman with hands above her head in a pose almost parodying the ecstasy of the maenad, the young warrior seated at his tomb with his head bent. Such a sensitive line; Picasso emulated these line drawings in his neo-classical works. These images of loss – the bent head, the raised arm, the fallen youth – are like scenes from the inner narrative of dreams.

Clothing, loops of fabric that swirl, cling and trail into the air, is a main element in indicating the mood, together with garlands, fillets, festoons, swags, and baskets – all these textile artefacts are associated with funerary ceremony and the theatre. Women are represented with much sympathy; the images do not show the legal constraints on their activities that we know existed.

I walked on the bruised rocks of the hill of the Areopagos at dusk with crowds of people speaking every language. The ancient place of discussion and assembly has steep slopes made dangerous because they have been polished smooth by a million feet, burnishing the marble steps to a high gloss. I looked carefully too at the high Roman arches of the nearby Theatre of Herodus Atticus, and particularly at the vaulted entrances to the stage building, but could see few analogies to the Paphos theatre, and no signs of plastered surfaces.

Earlier I spent many hours walking up and around the scattered stones of the celebrated Theatre of Dionysos, a step away below the cliffs of the Acropolis. Until recently a wonderful carved cylindrical altar rested under the pine trees, with heavy garlands of myrtle, laurel and olive twined with ribbons, interspersed with staring satyric masks. (It has now been moved away from the site to the museum, rather sadly.) The huge span of seats, the *cavea*, which must have held twice as many people as the Paphos theatre, fades into grass at the upper levels near the cliff face. The circle of the *orchestra* is still paved with a fine diamond inset of delicately coloured marble tiles, and ringed by upright slabs of marble. Here, there is a row of carved thrones for important officials, some with the scaly snake of Dionysos in vigorous relief. A young man knelt in the middle of the *orchestra* as if at some ritual – he was weeding spring flowers from the stones. His kneeling stance uncannily echoed the pose of a giant crouching silenus just behind him, part of a carved balustrade or rostrum with scenes of the life of Dionysos from the Roman period.

The theatre was the place where people gathered in an emergency, a place where a message could be voiced clearly, where a political drama could be played out as succinctly as a theatrical one. Diodorus Siculus described the scene just before Philip of Macedon conquered the city:

> The news spread into every household and the city was tense with terror, and at dawn the whole people flocked to the theatre even before the archons had made their customary proclamation. When the generals came and introduced the messenger and he had told his story, silence and terror gripped the assembly.[19]

The acropolis of Athens is an island surrounded by the muted roar of the modern city. I have crawled around the sites at all ages of my life and they transform themselves as I get older, revealing different aspects of their construction in the changing light of each season, and in the changing tenor of my thought. In the twenty-first century the layering of histories takes on a fresh significance. (After all, as the scholar Andrew Stewart has pointed out, one of the laws of archaeology is that 'only the future is immutable, the past is always changing'.)[20] Once I saw only archaic Athens with its exuberant monsters and ornament, the marvellous marble girls and boys with their secret smiles. Now I notice the Roman structures and the complexity of the later empire. Why did I never see that there was a little brick vaulted house perched on top of the temple architrave, supported by the huge columns of the Temple of Olympian Zeus? Because I did not find the second century as significant as I do now, and I did not scrutinise this extraordinary building. The little building, like a swallow's nest in the megalomania of imperial Rome, was a retreat for a stylite, a monk who became holy by living on a column like St Simeon the Stylite. No one now finds such an original use for the fragment of a standing temple dedicated to glory, a hermitage for the renunciation of the world. (St Simeon, born about 390, converted many to Christianity, it is said, because of his 'kindness and sympathy and freedom from fanaticism'.)[21] It must have seemed a small sign of hope and order, at a time when Athens had been devastated and laid waste in a wave of invasions, beginning in 267, by the Heruli, the Visigoths, and the Vandals from the north.

26 April

Antiquity and more recent wars are also interconnected. With Jan Casson Medhurst from the Australian Institute, and following my experiences tracking Australian regiments in Egypt, I decided to go to the Anzac Day ceremony at the War Cemetery in Piraeus (ANZAC stands for Australia New Zealand Army Corps.) The cemetery at Kalamaiki holds the bodies of Commonwealth troops who died in Greece in 1941, especially in the terrible rout of Crete. On a cool wet day, veiled with misty rain, the landscaping of the cemetery was classical and ordered, designed elegantly by Louis de Soissons, with neat rows of inscribed marble headstones among clipped bushes and luxuriant flowers. Many of the soldiers had been very young when they died, only eighteen or nineteen years old. All the ambassadors from Commonwealth countries and the representatives of veterans' groups laid wreaths – of bay, of olive – against a marble altar very similar to one I'd seen in the National Museum.

The Australian ambassador, holding an umbrella, read in English and Greek from Pericles' funerary oration: 'For the whole earth is the sepulchre of famous men; and their story is graven not only in stone over their native earth, but lives on far away, without visible symbol, woven into the stuff of other men's lives.' I appreciated the pattern and organisation of the ceremony in the gentle rain. When cemeteries are abandoned like that Turkish graveyard in Alexandria, which was removed in order to explore deeper levels of the city, that past is truly desolated and forgotten.

Women were not mentioned in the ceremony, and all the dignitaries were men, but the textile metaphors were in place. I'm aware of almost palpable presences hanging around the sites, 'woven into the stuff' of my experiences. The past here seems such a gift. Perhaps this is because I come from another kind of country, *terra australis*, on the other foot of the world, Antipodean, where the Aboriginal past is unimaginably old, expressed in geological time frames such as 'before the last ice age'. Living with Aboriginal people who have a matter-of-fact relationship to such aeons of time taught me another kind of tentative kinship to the Greek past I studied as a young woman. People in Yirrkala or on Bathurst Island in northern Australia have an intersecting relationship with a mythical period that allows them to move in and out of the present, and to perceive the past as a kind of doubling of the present, a faint shadow or mirrored gleam in the most ordinary activities.

As I journey there's no longer such a clear-cut line between the ancient past and the present, but a blurring of boundaries, so that the layered seams of Athens seem surprisingly connected to the stitching of my own thought patterns and language.

5. VERGINA

27 April, Hotel Macedonia, Veria

I took a flight to Thessaloniki very early this morning. The people on the plane were dressed for business, in sophisticated suits, computer bags over their shoulders, expensive sunglasses, like the executive commuters on similar early morning flights between Sydney and Melbourne. The view from the plane was engrossing, as every dimple of the landscape was clear in shades of indigo, outlining that familiar map of Greece – I saw Euboea, Velos, even Mt Olympos – and some ominous warships sailing north. Because of the war to the north, on the edge of Macedonia, Thessaloniki is at present a meeting place for NATO. From every kiosk in the airport newspapers had displayed photographs of huddled bodies at bombsites, collapsed buildings with refugees holding traumatised children.

I wanted to look at Hellenistic art, that phase in art that emerged after the conquests of Alexander, an art enhancing naturalism and intimacy just as democracy became increasingly fragile. Hellenistic imagery finds a place for the poignant individuality of persons – a drunk woman, a boxer with his damaged face, a baby sleeping or a dog scratching, as well as the first female nudes – and flowers with twining leaves and insects. The great museum of Thessaloniki allowed some insights into that compelling Hellenistic imagery, with rich tomb finds from Sindos and Derveni. What did they believe, putting such golden treasures in tombs? As in Egypt, the dead had to be provided with objects that indicated their status in life. The cremated bones were put in boxes, and then into sarcophagi. One sarcophagus of a woman and her newborn baby was delicately painted with flowering spirals and heads, and personal ornaments hanging on nails (painted naturalistically) – a trailing red fillet or ribbon, a perfume vessel, a mirror, or a bird. This naturalistic delicacy of expression and subtle use of space and colour existed in what must have been a milieu of constant war-making and harsh competition for power.

It's now 9 p.m. and I am in a pleasant hotel room in Veria, about seventy kilometres from Thessaloniki, overlooking a mountain and the edge of the town against the great plain stretching away to the sea. The country is open and spacious, and feels European, with chestnut and plane trees in first leaf. Veria is just near the ancient capital Aiglae, now known as Vergina, where the 'royal' tombs of the Alexandrian dynasties were discovered and excavated in the 1970s.

As the bus had journeyed here across the fertile plain I saw beehives and people attending to them, and espaliered peach trees. Outside the hotel come the sounds of birds, among traffic and voices from the street – '*Ela!* Come here! *Pame!* Let's go.' The hotel was nearly empty, and the solid houses and ordered town with its nineteenth-century civility felt like Epirus or Ioannina. Once, there was a flourishing Jewish community here which was entirely deported during the German occupation. The outward façade of the pleasant streets conceals many layers. I saw some instances of really violent anger: coming into Veria a man roared at the bus driver, pulled him out of the bus, and pushed him hard while all the passengers gaped. People look preoccupied, and there were graffitti against the war everywhere in Thessaloniki. 'No to NATO! NATO is fascist!' People spoke of their long hatred of the Americans, the way they had propped up the Colonels' oppressive regime and now supported Muslims. The tension of the conflict so close to the Greek border was just below the surface. The twelve-pointed star, symbol of ancient Macedonian glory, indicates a golden moment for this northern province of Greece.

There seem to be no tourists at all in Veria – if I didn't speak some Greek, I would be lost here. I walked for an hour in this charming and rather secret town, with its forgotten Ottoman streets, before finding a hotel open, the only one I saw. The sad-faced man at reception brightened when he saw my Australian passport. 'Ah, so you're not involved in the war, eh?' He had thought I was American, and was gruff when I first came in. All those horrors are just on the other side of the northern mountains.

Alexander's mythological aura is about individual greatness, about the immortality deserved by the hero who performs awe-inspiring deeds. He is the prototype traveller into the unknown, and was the model for future Roman leaders with imperial ambitions. His face must be the best known face of antiquity, and his features became like a visual vocabulary of power, to be re-cast in all portraits of subsequent kings and generals. At the same time there is in his expression an undercurrent of feminine delicacy, an almost androgynous leaning. He is represented with deep brows, far-seeing eyes as if longing for the impossible, and he did achieve impossible conquests across Asia. Brought up by his mother to believe he was the son of a god, he identified with Achilles, who died young and glorious.

28 April

I woke early and looked out at Veria as dawn came up over the plain, the plain where those horse-riding aristocrats grew up, plotted and fought, training their strengths for the phenomenal expansion of Macedonia in the fourth century BC.

The bus to Vergina followed the line of the hills, with the plain on the left. The road crossed a rushing river of cold green water pouring down from the mountains. The bus was full of friendly women. One was off to see the doctor; she told me sadly that she was alone, all her children were far away. Another woman in violently coloured clothes and a headscarf, perhaps a gypsy by her brown and weathered face, came onto the bus with two bulging plastic bags of green leaves, *horta*, the wild greens, dandelions, collected in the fields and boiled to eat with oil and lemon. I was dropped in the small square at Vergina, no one in sight, no sign, and when I asked the way to the antiquities from three old men sitting on a bench they all answered simultaneously, and differently. I set out in the general direction, with much goodwill.

It was such a perfect morning, not a soul around as I headed into the hills to the old palace site. Passing one of the tombs as the road curled upwards I was astonished at the elegant classical columns and pediment of the tomb entrance, solidly built like a temple, with remains of red and blue colour in the metopes and pediment. Thousands of flowers, 'millefiori', like a medieval tapestry, carpeted the hills and the verge beside the road, which had been planted with bay trees and oleanders. A goat shed sprawled down a steep hill and the brown shiny goats spilled out, bells honking in the quiet air, like a pastoral memory.

In his booth beside the tomb site looking far over the plain, an attendant sat quietly reading the classics and books on engineering, between infrequent visitors. What a lonely task it is for the site officials many of whom are qualified people. Often they seem melancholy, perhaps with boredom.

Over the palace site, a deep silence. A spring ran into a basin at the entrance, set around with plane and oak trees, a forest which continued thickly in the hills above. Water could be heard continuously from an unseen stream in a gorge. The earthy smell of oak trees is a scent from childhood, when I spent much time climbing a giant oak tree in my grandparents' garden. The site is dominated by one spreading oak tree, which arches over scattered, lichen-covered column drums. The architectural fragments had a geometric precision, sometimes carved with ornament, contrasting with the wildness around. In the distance, snow-covered mountains, and in the encroaching woodland, twining single roses.

The theatre site below the palace is now just a horseshoe curve set into the hill, overlooking the spreading plain below. This is supposedly where Philip the Great, father of Alexander, was killed in a palace conspiracy, as he walked into the theatre. The *orchestra* space was clear, a few stones of the stage building and several rows of seating were all covered by grass and flowers. I found small purple grape hyacinths and yellow euphorbia, a few anemones. There was still a freshness and mystery to this place, the scene of such turbulent events.

Diodorus Siculus, the Roman historian, gave this account of Philip's death:

> While it was still dark, the multitude of spectators hastened into the theatre and at sunrise the parade was formed. Along with lavish displays of every sort, Philip included in the procession statues of the twelve gods wrought with great artistry and adorned with a dazzling show of wealth to strike awe into the beholder, and along with these was conducted a thirteenth statue, suitable for a god, that of Philip himself, so that the king exhibited himself enthroned among the twelve gods. Every seat in the theatre was taken when Philip appeared, wearing a white cloak, and by his express orders his bodyguard held away from him and followed only at a distance, since he wanted to show publicly that he was protected by the goodwill of the Greeks, and had no need of a guard or spearman. Such was the pinnacle of success that he had attained, but as the praises and congratulations of all rang in his ears, suddenly without warning the plot against the king was revealed, as death struck... While the guards kept their distance Pausanias saw the king left alone, rushed at him, pierced him through the ribs and stretched him out dead; then ran for the gates and the horses he had prepared for his flight.[22]

Perhaps after such a description of glory and pride, the immensity, and spectacular presentation of the Royal Tombs should not have been surprising. You actually go into the great tumulus, threaded with individual tombs, into a dim light, with black walls and the very delicate objects lit up separately, almost like icons. Here there were crowds of school children, listening to the history of their country loudly declaimed by guides, as this is a sacred site for the origin of the Greek spirit. The workmanship of the remarkable objects is of extraordinary quality – exquisite ivory carvings of the royal family, metal vessels of classic simplicity, with a head of a satyr, a Dionysian scene in golden metal on the Derveni *krater*, with a dancing maenad of breathtaking poise. Beliefs about the afterlife must have been profound to justify burying such treasured objects – were some of them just made for the tomb? Despite their almost mythological aura the richly decorated weapons and armour must have belonged to individuals. Thinking of the ornate tombs of the descendants of Alexander in Alexandria, I could now understand their affinity with the Egyptian obsession with the afterlife.

I was entranced by a gold and purple cloth from the fourth century, of almost unbelievable fineness, that had been a shroud for the bones of a high-born person, and which had survived by being enclosed in a *larnaka*, a small marble coffin. Peering as close as I could, I was not able to discern whether it was indeed silk and whether the imagery was woven or embroidered in gold thread. The pattern showed a central vase sprouting fantastic spirals and acanthus leaves, with floral ornaments and tiny birds, such as were found in south Italian and Pompeian painting (and went on flourishing in the Grotesque and Rococo decoration of much later European tapestries). What an inspired invention, a kind of narrative in labyrinthine plant forms.

The tomb paintings were a revelation, particularly the Tomb of Persephone, the tomb of a young woman with a child. Could it have been a woman like Alexander's sister, Cleopatra, whose wedding celebrations Philip had been attending before he was killed? According to the ancient historians, she died suddenly soon after, with her baby, possibly killed because she was too close to the line of descent (always a dangerous position in Macedonia). Archaeology discourages speculation, but the tomb must have belonged to a high-born woman. On one wall were the three seated Fates, Clotho the spinner, Lacheso, the caster of lots, and Atropo, the unbending, who gave out the destined portion of life. For the owner of the tomb it must have been that moment when as the Alexandrian poet Theocritus said, 'All the thread of the Fates is run'.[23]

On the other wall, an energetic Hades carried off the girl Persephone, Kore, daughter of Demeter, in his chariot, down into the dark underworld, while her companion, left behind, crouched on the ground and raised her arm in a stricken gesture, the upraised arm of mourning. Pinks and golds, and a pale intense green-blue appeared to float off the wall.

The facing wall with its faint image caught at my heart and I stood motionless. Above a band of lovely ornament one mounded figure was painted in the centre of the wall, surrounded by empty space. This was the draped figure of the mourning Demeter seated on the 'mirthless' stone at Eleusis, drawn with understated authority in muted reds and pinks. Demeter sat on the stone and mourned for Kore, so that the earth withered, growth stopped. It was the Fates, sent by Zeus, who persuaded her to restore the natural order.

The concept and composition of all the figures was of great sophistication, with the representation of drapery, the three-quarter turn of the head, the diagonal gesture of the girl showing an incomparable understanding of movement in space drawn on a flat surface. This was the same living gesture that I glimpsed in the Hellenistic sculptures of Berenike in Alexandria, who lived a generation after the period of the Royal Tombs. This was a level of naturalism rare even in Pompeian painting, which was profoundly influenced by Hellenistic art. The Paphos frescoes, four hundred and fifty years later, continued the themes of floral ornament, and the red tied fillet, seen on the marble grave *stelae* from Vergina. The crinkly red ribbons on the Paphos wall still belonged to this same vocabulary of mythological narrative, even if in a very different world.

The technique of the fresco seemed very fresh, and the colour painted on the translucent marble also had a rare quality. I especially noticed a painted grave *stela* of two women taking leave of each other, with shadowy layers of chiaroscuro, light and dark tones.

What I came away with was a sense of restrained passion, of fervour, of grief and violence, joy in the transient natural world, and no inkling of romantic love. The idea of the funeral pyre is hard to understand. I copied this from an explanatory plaque on the wall: 'The fire purified the mortal flesh... The gifts of the living, his garments, his weapons, his ornaments, everything he had loved and needed in his earthly life, followed him on to the pyre. The fire had a transformative power. By being consumed in the inferno, the material objects could be made useful once more to their owner, who had passed on to the other side. The mourning experienced by all proved a catharsis... The dead man became a re-unifying force.'

Something of this same dire elegance in seen in the portraits from the cenotaph of Nikokreon, the last king of Salamis in Cyprus, defeated by Ptolemy. The cracked and disturbing terracotta heads had astonished me in the Cyprus Museum in Nicosia. It seems that at least four leading members of the royal family all committed suicide in 310 BC to avoid capture, and the unfired masks were burnt on their pyre. These haunting images capture the extremes of violence and beauty that make up the qualities of *pothos*, longing, across the vast Hellenistic world.

Long and complex funeral ceremonies as the culmination of a life are what I have experienced in Aboriginal communities, and these ceremonies, like the ancient Macedonian ones, also cement together the living members of the clan, and reaffirm beliefs in natural forces.

29 April

Glimpses are, perhaps, all that is possible in comprehending the past, and to view the past, to find the key objects in museums and among ruins you have to negotiate the present. Travelling alone there are odd encounters and insights that seem to arise from the very stress of such travel. The tension of the journey can sometimes be paralysing. Such a moment occurred in Thessaloniki: arriving from the airport in the square of an entirely unknown city full of great activity, traffic roaring past, high buildings, ships in the distance – I felt for an instant entirely unknown and almost invisible. I had mislaid my map of the city.

Taking a deep breath, I approached an older woman sitting at a bus stop, one still figure in all the flowing crowds, and asked 'Can you tell me the name of this street?' She looked at me intently and was kind, directing me to the known central square, so I could become orientated to the grid of the city, to the churches, to the great seafront. The pattern fell into place again, order was resumed, her courtesy calmed that strange panic that can come 'out of the blue'. The word 'panic' is derived from the goat-faced god Pan, after the sudden emotion that can send a flock of sheep or goats racing madly over the mountains. It is said that the Persians heard his cry at Marathon, and screamed with fear, dispersing panic-stricken.

I realised freshly an obvious aspect of Greek art; the fundamental inclusion of violence in Greek life. Animal savagery in the hunt, hand-to-hand conflict in battle, are as vital to the balance of life as peace. I thought, tentatively, that I had rediscovered for myself the notion of the 'mainstream' – the central idea of 'greatness' reverberating down European art from Aristotle's first study of art making, *The Poetics*. Aristotle, of course, was the tutor to the young Alexander the Great, here in Macedonia. *Poesis*, or 'making', he thought, must arouse emotion in the viewers, as the funeral did for the mourners. The art of representation was in the narrative, and the metre or rhythm. 'The story must be constructed as in tragedy, dramatically around a single piece of action, whole and complete in itself, with a beginning, a middle and an end, so that like a single living organism it may produce its own peculiar form of pleasure.'[24]

Such an idea of a central wholeness in art has been scattered, diminished, and has become almost incomprehensible now, where the peripheral, the marginal, the fragment and the hybrid pervade the imagination of the 'post-humanist' West. The vocabulary set in place in Hellenistic art became the language of Roman and Byzantine art, able to encompass not only the brutality and power of great empires, but fragile moments of beauty and transience.

6. THE HELLESPONT

4 May, Çanakkale, Turkey, 10 p.m.

I'm propped up in bed in a lovely room in the Bakir Hotel. Çanakkale is built near the site of the ancient city of Abydos, overlooking the straits of the Hellespont to the Dardanelles on the European side. Below me is the promenade, still lit up, with people walking up and down beside the sea, looking at the fishing boats; bits of music and voices rise up. The car ferry to ancient Sestos, on the other side, goes back and forth every hour. The sea is clear and transparent close up, a sheet of blue-grey in the distance as the light fades – people sitting and talking in a café, children playing, a pack of dogs wandering past, a pregnant cat stretched out on the still-warm stone of the sea wall. Ice-cream carts, a man selling balloons. A little further on an old mine-layer, a metal ship, the *Nusrat*, was set up as a memorial to the First World War.

I sat beside it in the late evening and drew the little town on the opposite shore, with its white minarets and old heart-shaped fort (the story was that the architect was in love, and the shape he built was to persuade his beloved.) That Greek idealist Lord Byron, fully aware of the poetic connotations of this place, swam the Hellespont successfully, a channel notorious for rips and bad weather. The monuments of the drastic conflict of powers in the 1914 War were all around; even in the Tourist Office where I went to find a hotel, there were bits of shrapnel and metal fragments from Gallipoli.

After sleeping on the bus coming here, I had woken suddenly

to see the rolling hills of Thrace in the most intense shades of green, a hill of young grain, mustard and rocket rose before me, blue-green, yellow-green in the pale light, like a painted tile. Purple irises grew beside the bus stop where we got tea and toast. (I became very admiring of the excellent comforts of the Turkish buses, which move so quickly across every available road to each village and town.) I remembered the wild Thracians in Greek art, with their distinctive peaked caps, always having to be subdued, always rising up again on their fierce horses. So close to the Greek border, the country looked the same as Greece, with its folded bays, coves and peaceful distances. How unlikely it seemed that one of the most bloody battles of the twentieth century was fought here at Gallipoli, where both sea and land became filled with explosive devices, on the crackling border between Europe and Asia.

5 May

I began the day with breakfast in the pleasant hotel dining room overlooking the port; with tea, delectable fresh bread and apricot jam. The waiter forgot the bread, and as I did not know the Turkish word, and as he spoke no English, I drew a picture. He looked at the long roll I'd drawn with its pattern of diagonal slashes and returned in a moment, smiling, with a bread roll, an exact replica of the drawing, like a magic trick. Now I know: bread is *ekmet*. Two Greeks next to me slurped their tea and talked loudly into a mobile phone, a Turkish kind of Greek which I didn't recognise at first.

I watched the straits of the Dardanelles as I drank tea; powerful freighters, liners, oil carriers, fishing boats, ferries, boats of all kinds constantly streamed, quietly and steadily, to and from Istanbul and the Black Sea, three hundred and fifty kilometres away. I could just see the enormous white soldier carved into the hill on the opposite side of the strait: DUR YOLCU it begins. 'Traveller stop, this earth you tread unawares is where a generation sank. Listen to this quiet mound, the heart of the country beats here.' The red Turkish flag with its crescent and star flies everywhere, very pretty against all the blues. Mustafa Kemal Atatürk is remembered like a saint and a great hero. His portrait was in the restaurant where I ate, as it is everywhere. Not only Australians have their myths of national identity tethered to Gallipoli.

Before joining the Gallipoli tour at midday, very early in the morning I took a taxi to Troy, or Truva. A large man without English, Mehmet, all of a piece with his forceful if dilapidated Mercedes, drove me the thirty kilometres, and waited an hour or so drinking coffee while I wandered the site, before driving me back. (It was quite complicated negotiating the trip to Troy and finding a car, but I remembered how getting to and from Troy had always been difficult, material for poetic epics in fact.)

On a pale blue spring morning, the countryside was verdant, orchards of peach, grain fields, and vegetables. Shepherds with goats and sheep were dotted on the uplands, men ploughed fields with small tractors and even with a horse. Small villages were clustered intermittently along the edge of the strait; a dreaming landscape like a nineteenth-century watercolour.

In modern terms the acropolis is tiny for a city of such influence. It has been the scene of extensive excavation campaigns for more than a hundred and fifty years, and was now overgrown after the winter with wildflowers and grasses. A jumble of masonry of many periods was dominated by sloping Mycenaean walls of grey cut stone forming narrow passages with occasional views of the plain. The 'settlement mound' consisted of continuous cities layered to a depth of thirteen metres, with much evidence of destruction. The particular level of the Bronze Age 'Homeric' sack of Troy has not been conclusively identified archaeologically.

Troy was legendary through the poetry of Homer, and the archaeology of the site has from the beginning had a close relationship with the poetry of the *Iliad* and the *Odyssey*, fraught with tension and argument between poetic myth and the analysis of the material culture.

Poetry incited and inflamed archaeology in the case of Heinrich Schliemann. Under the influence of an unshakeable faith in Homer he succeeded in making a fortune in order to begin an archaeological career excavating Troy from 1870 to 1890, unearthing evidence of an unknown and possibly mythical society. The romantic influence of Homer still gives a particular aura to the stones, ceramics and artefacts from the site, even though 'Homer' remains elusive. The violent emotions of the characters in Homer became fixed in the European imagination as examples of heroic action.

Emphasising the Homeric episode of the Trojan Horse (when the Greeks' gift to the Trojans was a trick to get their troops into the citadel) a great wooden sculpture of the horse by the Turkish artist Izzet Senemoglu was set up in 1975, just outside the entrance to the site. Coincidentally this was a moment when contemporary Greek and Turkish relations were at a very low point.

Archaeologists have made inventories of the marvellous objects described in Homer. Most evocatively there are references to 'shining and fragrant' cloth made from both linen and wool. Apparently the fabric was made to shine from a perfumed oil treatment, and this poetic description has been given a basis in fact by Mycenaean and Minoan inscriptions. 'Fragrance' and 'radiance' are usually ascribed to gods (the fragrance came from their ambrosia and nectar) but occasionally heroes in poetry can also wear shining perfumed clothes. Both textiles and smells, like sound, are lost to us, except in poetry.

More than eight hundred spindle whorls were found at Troy, so it is evident that the processes of spinning and weaving wool were fundamental activities. The bone spindles and whorls I saw in the museum had incised patterns, very similar to the Roman whorls I had described in Paphos from a thousand years later. The craft of spinning thread, like language, changed only in small matters of idiom and emphasis, but remained as a constant technique, a common tongue or *koine*, into our era.

Cyprus was part of the Homeric sagas, and the lovely chalky Cypriot white slip pottery of the late Bronze Age (thirteenth century BC) has been found in Troy. What did the pots contain? Maybe opium, and probably the bowls were used for drinking milk or wine. Possibly they were filled with yoghurt or fetta, and may have been covered with a cloth, transported in wide-ranging ships from Cyprus, which also traded with Crete, Athens, and Rhodes.

To me, it's the journeying Odysseus, homeward bound, wandering through perilous seas for ten years after the fall of Troy, who resonates with the migrations and turbulent displacements of our own time. Most interestingly Vitruvius, that Roman historian of the second century, described 'the wanderings of Odysseus through landscapes' as favourite subjects for wall painting. Some of the earliest landscapes that survive (from the Esquiline in Rome) showed Odysseus and his sailors as tiny figures in the land of the Laestrygonians, amongst craggy towering rocks, with distant views of the sea, or in the palace of Circe. One of the most compelling sequences in the *Odyssey*, and in the Esquiline paintings, was the hero's descent into the underworld to meet the souls of the dead, who clustered palely beneath a vast arch of rock.

Troy gave Odysseus the ten-year journey back to his home in Ithaka in western Greece. The idea of home impelled him on his way, giving an aim to his endless journey, as Constantine Cavafy pointed out in his memorable poem: 'Have Ithaka always in your mind. Your destination is to arrive there but do not hurry your journey in the least.'[25]

Penelope's domestic realm was also threatened by the men's departure for Troy, and perhaps this balance between the harmony of a peaceful *oikos* ('house' or 'home') and the chaos of the end of Troy, is really what gives the *Iliad* and *Odyssey* their great power. Agamemnon sacrificed his daughter Iphigeneia against the will of her mother Clytemnestra at the beginning of the epic, setting in train a whole sequence of tragic events, taken up and elaborated by later playwrights, Aeschylus, Sophocles, and Euripides. Children were pitilessly sacrificed in the name of honour; Astyanax, the youngest son of Hector, prince of Troy, was thrown from the walls, or was sometimes shown as beheaded by the sword of the Greeks. After the dreadful fall of the city, and its destruction by fire, many women of Troy were killed or became slaves, speaking bitterly in the chorus of Euripides' play *Hecuba*: 'Breeze, ocean breeze, who carry sea-faring ships swiftly over the singing waters, where will you take me in my misery? Whose house shall I come to, a purchased slave?'[26]

The extravagance and outrage of the collision of human and divine fate in Homer went on reverberating. Aristotle commented, in the time of Alexander, that Homer is great poetry because of the dramatic characterisation and the inimitable plots. The importance of Troy to the Roman Empire was immense, because Aeneas, the mythical founder of Rome, had come from Troy, and the emperors Augustus, Caracalla and Constantine all visited the city and supported it with special decrees. A statue of Hadrian, and fragmented marble inscriptions in authoritative Latin lettering lay on the ground beneath the trees near a lovely small theatre from Roman times, an Odeon just outside the walls. The influence of Homer persisted throughout the Late Roman period in this welter of myth/history.

The plain stretched away to the sea with lines of poplars, fertile fields, the glimmer of water just visible. How strange that a populous and long inhabited site like this is now abandoned, while the once unpopular and dangerous ancient places by the sea are overcrowded and developed. Centre and periphery are so relative – this central plain in the European imagination is now utterly peripheral in physical terms, even though enshrined in literature. Giant asphodel and the butterfly flower, *gaura*, blew in the intermittent wind among eroded trenches of stratified walls and fallen buildings. The site seemed very small to be at the centre, to be the referral point of so much European history. The great stone road, trodden by myth, sloped upward, lined with fig trees and oaks. You notice small things, red beetles, and crested birds calling in the silence. A young cat followed me along the path, and I gave her some bread and filled my water bottle from a spring.

I rested at the site of the temple of Athena, on one of the highest points, with small oak trees shadowing the altar and the remains of a marble floor. Alexander came here and sacrificed his armour to this shrine. His biographer Arrian wrote:

> The ferrying of the army took place from Sestos to Abydos, and according to the prevalent story Alexander steered the Admiral's boat himself when he crossed, sacrificing a bull to Poseidon and the Nereids in the midst of the Hellespont strait, and pouring into the sea a drink from a golden bowl. He then went up to Troy, and sacrificed to the Trojan Athena, dedicated his full armour in the temple, and took down in its place some of the dedicated arms, swords and shields still remaining from the Trojan War, which were later carried before him into battle.[27]

The story from Diodorus Siculus is that Alexander flung his spear from his fighting ship after crossing the Hellespont and fixed it to the ground, and then leapt ashore himself, the first of the Macedonians. This meant that he had received Asia from the gods as a spear-won prize. He also visited the tomb of the hero Achilles, on whose life he modelled his own, and honoured him with offerings.[28]

A waning moon hung white in the midday sky just above the horizon throughout the journey back to Çanakkale.

About ten assorted travellers had joined the group for Gallipoli, mostly from Australia and New Zealand. The crossing over the Narrows (1.3 km between ancient Sestos and Abydos) to the peninsula of Gallipoli was choppy, with strong currents moving the ferry diagonally to the other side. (I couldn't help thinking that sacrificing a bull to Poseidon would have been quite tricky.)

It is remarkable to think that the Hellespont has not been bridged since the fifth century BC. Harpalus, a Greek mathematician from

Samos, devised an extraordinary combination of a suspension and pontoon bridge for Xerxes the Persian king in 480 BC, as he prepared to invade Greece. The construction of the two bridges was dependent on woven cables, one and a half kilometres long, of flax and papyrus. Six of these woven cables were suspended from strong land posts over warships anchored in the fast current, and twisted taut. Over the cables a roadway of planks, brushwood and earth was laid above the warships – more than six hundred of them. Although the exact number of Xerxes' forces is not known, hundreds of thousands of men and supplies from all over Asia crossed the Hellespont – Herodotus proposed five million.[29]

Later, after the Persians had been defeated on land and sea, the Greek general Xanthippus found the great cables of linen and papyrus that had suspended the bridge and carried them off as marvels to be dedicated in temples at Delphi and Athens. In fact, I thought, if cast into bronze, those thick cables would have looked very similar to the bronze serpent column in Istanbul, which stands, a vertical bronze of twisted spiral ropes, the bodies of three entwined serpents. The serpent column was dedicated at Delphi in the fifth century BC, made as a thank offering for the defeat of Xerxes, and the three heads were later broken off, although they survived until the eighteenth century. The spiral column was taken from Delphi by the emperor Constantine to his new city Constantinople about 330. Perhaps, I thought, there was a faint textile memory in that powerful spiral, the bridging rope that brought the Persians so miraculously across the Hellespont. Brought back to Constantinople, this truncated bronze, worn with memory, seemed an unconscious sign of joining, of the broken ties and irresistible attraction between Europe and Asia.

The guide to the sites of Gallipoli, Ali, was a retired submarine commander who had joined British merchant ships and sailed all over the world, with a particular love of India. He spoke excellent English and had made the sites of Gallipoli a life study, producing a guidebook to all the memorials. He must have been in his late sixties, a small spry man with a thoughtful face and very bright brown eyes. His impressive information and rhetoric were directed at Australians and New Zealanders, who flock here in increasing numbers, despite the fact that hardly any veterans survive from that distant war. As a guide he showed an exceptional passion for the history, and knowledge of stories. He was studying Japanese at the University of Çanakkale and was planning to teach Japanese there when he graduated.

A minibus met us, to drive around the many sites of the peninsula. Anzac Cove was particularly memorable, and has become a contemporary 'sacred site' for people from the Antipodes. We sat around the stone plaque set up by Kemal Atatürk in 1936: 'You the mothers who sent your sons from far away countries, wipe away your tears, your sons are now lying in our breast ... having lost their lives on this land they have become our sons as well.' One older man moved away from the group and sat by the water's edge, holding his head in his hands. I noticed, with constricting heart, the name of a boy of seventeen, the same age as my son, inscribed on one of the innumerable white gravestones.

'Dear visitors,' Ali said rhetorically, 'the ANZAC spirit was a golden gate for two young nations to pass through for independence, and this has been more important than military victory. We gained Mustafa Kemal Atatürk, the Father of the Turks; we became a Republic. We were local men fighting for our own land and families. Today's modern Turkey is our victory of the campaign and that is why we don't feel any bitter spirit to you, dear visitors. My grandfather wrote, "I give my life to defend my family". He died at the age of twenty-one; his younger son, my father, was one month old. He was a fisherman living near Çanakkale and I live in his house still.' He went on, 'There are two teachings for the grandchildren, first, that we are not enemies any more, and secondly, after having lost their lives, all these soldiers have become sons of mother Turkey.'

High on the central ridge of the peninsula was a museum, near a bronze sculpture showing a dead soldier, with the new Turkey, symbolised by the flag, rising from his body. In the museum were actual bits of bodies looking very ancient – a skull with a bullet stuck in it, rib bones, leg bones, false teeth. They were scattered amongst tobacco tins, fragments of tools, bits of leather. I was transfixed by the crumpled letters of the soldiers from both sides, neatly laid out in glass cases. Here was a letter translated from the Arabic script of Hasan Ethem, who died April 19, 1915, as a 'holy martyr'. Writing to his mother, he had described a green plain, the corn waving by a stream, and the orderly who had just given him fresh milk, bought from a herdsman with his mother's money. He said he thought of her and her wise advice, and the world was very beautiful. He was killed two days after writing the letter.

I also found a photograph taken at Kuring-gai Chase in Sydney of 'Gallipoli and WWI veterans, war widows, junior legatees, medical and military support staff at the Sphinx Memorial before departure to Gallipoli, April 1990.' This was a photograph of a childhood picnic spot, a Sphinx carved out of the sandstone rock in forest near the edge of Sydney, by a veteran of the trenches, Mr W.T. Shirley, who suffered from tuberculosis. He had seen the Sphinx in Egypt before serving in France. The projecting rock above Anzac Cove was known as 'the Sphinx' by the soldiers battling beneath it. In antiquity the Sphinx was often a creature of death, particularly fond of devouring young and beautiful men. How moving that an image of the Sphinx was translated into stone in Sydney and eventually found its way back to Gallipoli.

We drove around the sites of famous encounters fought over tiny stretches of land as the allies tried to reach the heights at Chunuk Bair and the Turks drove them back. Ali told us, 'Half a million men were killed, equal numbers on both sides. The Turkish soldiers were men from the local areas – first the isthmus, and then villages on the other side of the strait around Çanakkale. They often could not read but believed they were fighting for their own land and families and had the unswerving dedication that is so hard to withstand. And, unlike the Australians, they were led by an ingenious commander, Mustafa Kemal, who went on to lead Turkey to a republic after his experiences on Gallipoli. By contrast, the British commanders did not know the terrain and did not come near the firing line, whereas Mustafa Kemal was always in the forefront.'

'I am impartial,' said Ali. 'I just tell you the facts of the military historians. From my reading, the Australians were literally used as cannon fodder.' Such readings are mired in the history of war, and in national interest.

After the initial disastrous landing the Australian general, Birdwood, wrote to the British commander-in-chief, Sir Ian Hamilton, safely watching the battle from his warship, suggesting an immediate evacuation of troops. Sir Ian Hamilton, classically educated in Greek battle strategy, advised him to dig in and hold on, and later wrote in his diary: 'Better to die like heroes on the enemy's ground than be butchered like sheep on the beaches like the runaway Persians at Marathon.' This 'heroic death' was a direct descendant of Homeric values, as idealistic – and as indifferent to the individual – as the Islamic soldier's martyred death and arrival in Paradise.

Another bronze sculpture that emerged out of the rocky heath showed a staggering Turk holding in his arms a wounded British soldier, with the story inscribed of how, by raising white underwear on a stick as a truce (textiles again, I thought), he came over and laid the wounded man gently on the Allied side. All the piercing stories of war are about individuals, just as in the *Iliad* the accounts of Menelaus and Agamemnon, Achilles and Patroclus are memorable because of their distinct characters. Stuck in the trenches for the long months of the summer of 1915 the two sides had to live only ten metres apart. I saw the trenches, now in a pine forest, looking like the neolithic fortifications of pre-Roman Britain, deeply curved hollows in the ground, with mere traces of planking, reverting to just a natural declivity. The steeper gullies were still pitted and eroded by channels and trenches.

The Turks and Australians got to know each other in this particular stretch of the trenches, according to Ali, exchanging names and presents: fresh fruit and tomatoes from the Turks in exchange for chocolate; local tobacco in exchange for tobacco paper, which was often old newspapers or magazines. Smoking time was at 3.30 every day, and the officers couldn't get soldiers to fight then – elements of a gentleman's war of another era. Both Turkish villagers and rural Australians, in a strange affinity, were caught up in a conflict between the imperial powers of Europe.

Gallipoli in May was an austerely beautiful place; the steep forested hills were full of wild flowers growing to the edge of the glassy sea. The island of Imbros faintly appeared in the distance (from 'ambrosia', which the gods drank there, Ali told us, that same ambrosia that made fragrant the shining clothing of the Homeric heroes). The vegetation had long grown back over the scarred earth and the burials in gentle masses of colour and delicacy – poppies, irises, wild rock roses, herbs, small oaks and pine trees. Lone Pine and Poppy Valley were the names of battlefields.

In the mid-afternoon it was very hot and still at the cemetery of Lone Pine, where five thousand men had died in the space of sixty metres in 1915. 'They died embraced – the Australians had tunnelled into the Turkish trenches and in hand-to-hand fighting they died with bayonets entwined together,' said our guide, emphasising the bond between enemies. 'Really,' he said, 'the Turks had no quarrel with the Anzacs, they were fighting the British, who had offered Russia parts of Turkey if Russia came in on the Allies' side, and Russia was an ancient enemy. The Turks were defending their motherland.' (It is interesting how Greeks have a fatherland, *patrida*, by contrast to the Turks.)

Because the battle took place in the heat of August the trench at Lone Pine became a mass grave, as they filled the earth in above the bodies. Nobody really knew who died where. The Turks did not put up a name on a stone unless there was an identified body, and they regarded their dead as martyrs fighting a jihad or holy war. Both sides died in huge numbers, often knowing they would die in the next sortie. Ali told stories of how soldiers on both sides saw the implacable situation – Australians took off rings and watches, and gave them to friends to be sent home. Atatürk himself was supposed to have been saved by the watch he wore around his neck, which broke the force of a bullet. Objects matter, when so much else has gone. The trenches were still full of the litter of war, our guide told us, showing us a little box, with a Turkish iron bullet, an Australian 303 cartridge, and some shrapnel.

Finally, after a long stalemate, the Gallipoli peninsula was evacuated. Not one soldier was lost in the process; the Allies said because of clever ruses (these are stories I had heard since I was a child – odd guns left to shoot randomly, tins banging, lights showing, in the hope of covering the evacuation); while Ali told us it was because the Turks did not shoot their enemies in the back. 'Every soldier,' he said, 'in his secret heart longs to return to his home and to those waiting, and knows that those enemy soldiers have the same hope.' 'Safe from both war and sea,' said Homer, of the soldiers who escaped destruction and returned home. Gallipoli was a great victory for Turkey.

Gallipoli was an extreme place, despite the calm beauty of the panoramic vista of sea and cliffs. The aura of human dread, a miasma of memory, still hung over the Gallipoli peninsula as it did not over Troy, but the battles were fought over the same vital stretch of sea, the Hellespont. This fast moving strait symbolised the division between Europe and Asia.

I felt deeply shaken and upset in the ferry back across the narrow stretch of water, torn with currents. I wept. Ali put his hand on my shoulder as we sat in the evening breeze on the ferry and said, 'Each day brings a new day, fresh changes.' We crossed the swift flowing strait, leaving that peninsula of battlefields and memorials. In the War Memorial Museum in Canberra, I remembered, was a plaster cast of an inscription set up by Greeks after 480 BC. Brought back to Australia by soldiers returning after the 1914-18 War, the inscription recorded, 'These by the Hellespont lost their glorious lives in battle ... The air received the spirits and the earth the bodies of these men.' War memorials all say the same thing whether ancient or modern.

In the museum of Çanakkale there had been some exquisite objects, and thinking of the waste of young men from both sides of the straits, my attention had been caught by the life-size torso of a marble *kouros*, or youth, from Lampsakos, the region east of ancient Abydos. With broad shoulders and slim hips delicately modelled, the torso conveyed a vibrant intention towards action, its muscular strength softened by skilful plasticity, a characteristic of Ionian art of the late sixth century. Unlike the realistically sculptured war memorials of soldiers, in bronze or stone, on Gallipoli, there was no story, no event, the figure was headless and mute, with no inscription to enlighten the viewer. Like the girls or *korai* from the Acropolis, the *kouros* figures were either gifts to the gods, or markers over tombs. In present-day as well as ancient art, the experience of loss, especially the outrageous loss of young men, has been formative in structuring revolutionary gestures.

The passing ordinariness of everyday life can be illuminated by small gestures. As if to emphasise the significance of the day, Filis or Phyllis (so many ancient Greek names), the slender and charming assistant in the Tourist Office of Çanakkale, helped me organise a bus to Bergama (Pergamon). She came to the bus station to see me off into the night, bringing me a red rose and kissing me warmly.

7. PERGAMON

6 May, Acroteria Pension, Bergama

I woke, struck by a dream, in an unknown room. In the dream I had been convinced that the particular circumstances of climate, season, and the fertility of the soil had allowed the dry bones of the boy who was buried in the grave to come alive again – I watched the bones swell, grow, flesh and fibre reappear. Even a web of cloth began to cover him. Shaken, I opened my eyes, just before his transformation was complete.

The room I found myself in was very simple but clean, really just a bed and a table, with a door and window onto an upstairs veranda facing a courtyard. I arrived here last night at one o'clock in the morning, after the three-hundred-kilometre ride from Çanakkale. I had not realised that Bergama, the old city of Pergamon, is six kilometres from the main highway, so the bus full of sleeping passengers stopped after midnight on a quiet road, in all-encompassing darkness – dim shapes of trees, or mountains perhaps? 'Bergama,' called the driver. I got out, the bus roared off. For a moment I stood dazed in the dark silence, but there was an old, comfortable taxi on the empty road waiting for me, with a cheerful young driver. The Tourist Office in Çanakkale had phoned ahead to my modest pension, and they had organised the taxi. This was very impressive.

The courtyard of the pension had almond trees and pigeons, next to the disintegrating dome of an old bathhouse or *hamam*, with a grassy tiled roof and a minaret close by. Geraniums and herbs planted in rows of painted kerosene and olive-oil tins under the almonds were homely on this cold grey day. I could see from the breakfast room that the modern town was dominated by the spiky crenellations of a ruined basilica, while high above the town the ancient acropolis loomed against a cloudy sky.

I shared a taxi up to the acropolis with two young New Zealanders (more wandering Antipodeans). The fierce wind emphasised the spectacular situation and the wildness of the position. I felt a keen emotion on entering the deserted and ruined city, especially a city that had once controlled nearly all of Asia Minor. The Attalid kings of Pergamon in the second century BC had had high ambitions of making a new Athens in the grandeur and extent of their public monuments and major cults. We walked up an old stone road rutted with wheel marks, with vestiges of past glory visible in the massive foundations of the library (once as famous as that of Alexandria) and signs of the temple to Athena, now just stumps of columns in the long green grass. An occasional exquisite marble fragment of an acanthus capital, palmettes or scrolls on a piece of architrave, even the carved marble cuirass of an emperor near the pediment of a temple to Trajan, lay in pieces on the ground. As I walked through the absorbing and fragmented maze of great buildings, streets and houses, the question in the back of my mind was, could our cities ever become like this? The recent ruin of a renowned European city, Sarajevo, came to mind. As I feel secure in contemporary technologies and resources of food and energy, so might have felt the people of Pergamon in that other world, looking around at the wonders of their prosperity. But perhaps those constant encounters with the Gauls, the wild destructive 'barbarians' from the north, had kept them aware of the fragility of civilisation.

Such a question is unanswerable. I had come to Pergamon because it was here that an extraordinary art emerged in the Hellenistic period of the second century BC, also the time when the Paphos theatre was prospering in that same burgeoning world. A group of artists from Pergamon and Athens had invented a 'baroque' style of sculpture for the great altar of Zeus set up on this acropolis. Diagonal lunging forms of arm or sword, bodies twisting in space, eyes cast up, mouths open in an expression of longing or pain were enhanced by rippling, curving, flickering folds of drapery. The sculptures of the battle between the gods and the giants on the long frieze of the altar were exceptional in conveying emotion. The site was excavated by the Germans and the sculptured friezes are now displayed in Berlin as a high point of classicism. What I wanted to know was whether the place itself, the *genius loci*, could have had something to do with this leap of invention.

Looking out from the city to the space all around, there did seem to be an almost formal connection. From the heights of the acropolis a mountain landscape lay spread out like a wrinkled cloth under the windy clouds, in layers and curtains of steep hills, textured with forest, billowing into the blue distance, seamed with rivers pouring into deeply folded gorges. In antiquity the images of the cult statues of different cities served to crystallise a local personality, almost a local geography. The cult of Zeus in Pergamon entirely matched the situation, as he was the god of the heights, of the sky and weather, and was symbolised by the great bird of the sky, the eagle. Thunder and lightning, the *diosemi* or signs of Zeus, were interpreted as omens. Homer referred to Zeus as the cloud-gatherer, the thunderer on high, the hurler of thunderbolts. In Istanbul there is a colossal cult statue from Pergamon, of Zeus, headless but very impressive with a torso as rocky as a mountain range emerging from the emphatic pleated hills and valleys of his robe. Above all, Zeus stood for sovereignty and power.

As I travel, I remember other journeys as a much younger woman, so that the vivid experience of one place is enfolded and transposed onto other places, like a series of transparent images laid one on top of the other. The perception of sites changes with each traveller, and the sites themselves, emblematic of long, jumbled periods of time, only reveal fragments to the individuality of visitors, through what they are in the present moment. A small epiphany can take place through an instant of light or shadow on an object, or through the fleeting relationship with local people, the guides, shopkeepers and hotel staff. I had brought with me notes from a letter I'd written to my mother on visiting the mythical birthplace of Zeus in Crete, more than thirty years before this visit to Pergamon. The geographical character of Zeus was similar in Crete to that of Pergamon, numinous, high and airy, and the visit had had a momentous character.

Crete, 28 February 1967

It was a wonderful drive in the bus to Psychro in the Lasithi plateau, through spectacular mountains and tiny villages. It became colder and colder, there were no more flowers, even the almond blossom was not out. And then Mt Dicti was visible, all humped and glinting white above the Lasithi plateau. This plateau is very remarkable, about eight kilometres long and perfectly oval and flat, with mountains ringing it. It's very fertile, so all the villages are built on the foothills not on the plain – and it's covered with thousands and thousands of windmills. The village of Psychro was very delightful, it was built on exactly the same principle as a Minoan town, with steps going up to the second storey on the outside of the house and all the animals, cows, pigs, hens, goats, and sheep on the bottom floor. I went to sleep early because the village is without electricity and the lamp wasn't strong. The stars seemed almost to be resting on the mountains, they were so big and near.

Next morning it was bitterly cold and the whole place was smothered in a thick white mist, all the plants crystallised in frost as well as the cobble stones of the road, which had frosty patterns on them. It was uncanny. I had arranged a guide, a very hairy man with large boots and a soft white dog, and we all set off up the mountain to find the cave where Zeus was said to have been born, the cave of Dicti. It was my birthday. Suddenly as the path got steeper we emerged from the white mist into brilliant sunshine – it was still only about eight o'clock, and there was all the plateau before us, like a white ocean exactly with streams and curlers of mist rising slowly up. And all the mountains of the far side sharply profiled against a vast sky. It really felt as though the whole self-contained plain was miles above the earth and that if one got beyond the mountains there would be sheer bottomless precipices descending into space. The cave was huge, in the side of a hill with two great openings going steeply down into darkness for two hundred feet. There were fig trees and pomegranates growing over the entrance, all glittering in the sun with newly melted frost. And no sound except the irregular dripping of water from the stalactites.

The guide and I ate some almonds (he was a nice man) and he got some candles and we started down until the light was all greenish, and then the candles were lit. The story is that Zeus' father Cronos swallowed all the children that his wife the giantess Rhea bore him, because his son was destined to be greater than he was. So she hid in this cave, and hid the baby Zeus too and gave his father a stone to swallow. To go into the darkness of the inner chambers, with the immense roofs covered with a tracery of pillars and melted rock was very overpowering. It is the sort of cave that would make legends by itself. And there was a pool too, very dark, and full of votive offerings from Neolithic times.

I stayed on the hill drawing until all the mist had risen, and went down into the village to eat. It was very enjoyable to sit in the square eating an omelette and a great hunk of brown bread in the sun, and watch the women come to the fountain with buckets and amphorae, and wild men on donkeys and horses go by, with other people leading all kinds of animals. Everyone moved very slowly, the women talked together, leaning against the wall spinning, and the men sat motionless in the sun.

And back in Pergamon, as well as the heights, Zeus was also the god of the house enclosure, the security of home and the preservation of order against those dark forces of his origin. *Deus*, god, *dies*, day, both came from his name.

Designed to show the battle between the giant forces of chaos and the civilising order of the Olympians, the action in the frieze of the altar of Zeus moved rapidly between clamorous figures in every aspect of battle. The Pergamenes had a passion for literature, and this sculptured frenzy was a profound dramatic narrative with rich iconography: dogs, eagles, horses, sea centaurs, a fish, a bull-headed giant, and a giant with a lion's head mingled among the combatants. Such complex scenarios must have been played out in the nearby theatre.

Pergamon had an inimitable theatrical ambience because of its dramatic situation. I walked across the city in gusts of wind and rain, longing to see the theatre hanging on its precipitous, impossible slope. There it was, breathtaking, looking almost like some primeval stony shell, like a fossil perhaps, a natural form, with the steep steps and seats of the tiered *cavea* covered with grass and flowers. The stone is cut from the mountain itself, a grey-blue andesite. As I sat on a pitted and pockmarked stone in the tiers of seats amongst flowering thyme, the sheer descending rows focused my eyes on the *orchestra* and stage area far below, with the great vista of country beyond. Any performance here would have been extravagantly dramatic.

How could one have heard the actors? The tiered seats were related to the pitch of the voice according to Vitruvius, who wrote that 'the ancient architects, following in the footsteps of nature, perfected the ascending rows of seats in the theatre from their investigation of the ascending voice.'[30] An acoustic specialist once told me that he thought the ancient world was extremely quiet compared to ours, which is full of the residual noises of air and road traffic, of industry and emergency sirens, just as the sky at night over cities is never quite dark. Electronic music and voices murmur incessantly in the dense webs of communication; and electric lights and computers have an almost imperceptible sound. We have forgotten this, living in a hum of low noise so familiar that it is unheard. The oral skills of classical actors in such a theatre as this would have emphasised the power of gesture through hand and body language. A formal, measured delivery, even the exaggerated mask, must have added to the actual sound of the voice. The stage building has vanished down the cliff, and the stones of the theatre have been scoured by the weather. No trace of painted plaster was to be found; but in such a rich city sculptured friezes would no doubt have decorated the theatre, as in the theatres of Perge or Aspendos to the south.

I remembered one figure in the tangled story of the altar frieze: a goddess with an intense fixity of expression who rushed to hurl a pot twined with snakes at a giant. The movement of her pose was defined by the swirling torrents of drapery, diagonally swinging from her shoulder and between her running legs. The lines of the deeply sculptured folds captured the flying impetus of her movement. The language of cloth in these marvellous Hellenistic figures continued to entrance me.

Contemporary thinkers have put forward the idea that if language is the most characteristic human invention, other aspects of human culture, such as sculpture or textiles can also be 'read' as a language, with intricate metaphor and layers of association that relate to social and political circumstances. Although we have so few actual textiles from this vibrant Hellenistic period, the language of drapery reflected the common Greek tongue itself, the Attic Greek dialect or *koíne*. Spoken across the vast expanse of Alexander's empire, as well as that of his successors, the Hellenistic kings and the Roman emperors, the Greek *koíne* united vastly different geographical regions in a common vocabulary of image and text.

Around the altar of Zeus once stood remarkable draped sculptures of women, Muses, nymphs, or allegorical figures like Sophia, Knowledge, or Nike, Victory. Similar female sculptures were found in niches and pediments on many buildings in the Hellenistic world. The delicate quality of the carved marble, with its translucent surface (once brilliantly coloured), made these authoritative sculptured figures of women very arresting in the museums of the wide arc of the eastern Mediterranean – not only in Athens, but also in Rhodes, Cyprus, Alexandria, Thessaloniki, and Istanbul. Often drapery completely defined these life-size sculptures, many of them headless, with no unclothed skin except a hand or a foot. What we have is a character entirely composed of cloth. As if it were a dummy in a fashionable shop window, we must read and understand the figure through the 'designer label' codes of the period. The subtleties and abstractions of mantles, thick tunics, girdles caught beneath the swell of the breasts, fine pleats in multitudinous folds indicating the curve of shoulder, buttock or a clenched arm, must have sent out particular signals and had many readings. Women cared deeply about how they dressed as we know from the Hellenistic poet Theocritus:

> 'That dress with the deep pleats suits you very well, Praxinoa. Tell me, what did the material cost you?'
> 'Don't remind me of that, Gorgo; more than two minas of good money, and as for the work! I put my very life into it.'[31]

Each female sculpture could be subtly varied; the diagonal roll of cloth could be obliquely arranged in a slightly different way, the transparent mantle over the thicker undergarment showed the twist of the hip in a variety of gestures. Sometimes fine silk was represented stretched over thicker wool in a marvel of abstract surface, almost like carving water in stone. Other signals could be given through the precise arrangement of drapery, indicative of age, marriage status or availability, even a priestly or divine status. The thin mantles that were used to such erotic effect were expensively made of fine Egyptian linen, or silk from the island of Kos, just to the south of Pergamon. Like paisley shawls in the nineteenth century, these mantles proclaimed the sophistication of imperial trade as well as the dignity of the wearer. Rippled and crushed silk might also represent the innocence of a child, in the series of sculptures of young girls holding birds or fruit, or might accentuate the active limbs of a running Artemis or a dancing nymph.

Like the nuanced carving of marble, the Hellenistic poets were renowned for their polished and elegant style. Love poems expressed *pothos*, longing, seen in those creased brows and fiery glances, and in the frisson of drapery in the sculpture. Apollonios of Rhodes imagined an early meeting of Jason and Medea, before disaster struck their lives, filled with those gleaming glances which seemed so emblematic of Hellenistic art:

> And her heart grew warm within, melting away as the dew melts around roses when warmed by the morning light. And at one moment both were fixing their eyes on the ground in embarrassment, and then again they were casting glances at each other, smiling with the light of love under their radiant brows.[32]

Seeing the city of Pergamon perched on its lofty crag, a place of alarming vertigo and rushing winds, underlined and extended for me the understanding of its art. What aspirations to glory – a Byronic site of grand emotion where ideas of romanticism seemed almost foreshadowed, except of course the landscape was understood through the figurative metaphors of deities and monsters, not through any imitation in art of mountainous distances and space. Just being in the place makes the idea of Alexandrian longing become comprehensible. In a lyric of love lost, Theocritus described the anguish of Simaetha in a phrase that could be a caption to so many images from Pergamon: 'And I will bear my longing as I have endured it till now.'

As I slowly walked down the steep road back to the town, gusts of rain and wind blew intermittently. A winding track through rough grass and fallen stones led to a lower terrace of the city, where there was an inconspicuous rocky hill, with elegant steps leading only to a small pine tree. This was where the great altar of Zeus had once stood, excavated by the Germans in 1871, and transported stone by stone to Berlin, far away from this wild landscape, its perfect context and background. New meanings, new trajectories of allegory emerged out of such transported artworks, just as I had observed the Roman emperors had re-erected trophies from Delphi and from ancient Egypt in the hippodrome of Constantinople. The Gigantomachy frieze, the battle between the gods and the giants more than twenty metres long on the altar of Zeus commemorated the victory over the barbarian Gauls by Attalos I of Pergamon. It's ironic to think that the altar of Zeus had been moved by remote descendants of those same Gauls to new cities of civilisation in the north.

8. EPHESOS

8 May

It was quite tricky to organise a meeting with the Austrian archaeologists. After many faxes, the fresco expert at the Austrian Institute in Selçuk near Ephesos had invited me to meet him outside the Selçuk museum at seven in the morning. I had never been to the place and had no idea where it might be, or even how big the town was or whether I would find a convenient hotel. But I located the museum the night before the meeting, after finding a very pleasant hotel room down the street, below the old crusader castle. Rising early, I hurried through the early morning streets to the silent square in front of the museum, a square which had all the usual comforting features – a sweeper, a little park, and the necessary monument to Atatürk.

In Australia I had discovered a rare book with coloured images on the excavation of painted Roman houses in Ephesos, written in 1977 by V.M. Strocka, an Austrian archaeologist.[33] The paintings had seemed to me to be curiously similar in subject matter and style to the frescoes in the Paphos theatre. I had been delighted to hear in Athens that the Austrians would be digging at the same time that I planned to be in Turkey.

No one in the Austrian team seemed at all surprised to see me there when I was picked up in their minibus and taken to the ancient site of Ephesos about three kilometres away. Once, the city had been close to the sea, but now that the port had long silted up, the sea had retreated to a line in the distance. I sat in the bus next to the museum official who was doing a catalogue of inscriptions. He asked me where I had been working and when I said Cyprus he sighed, knowingly. Mortal enemies, but so alike, we agreed – so deeply known to each other. When we came to the site, in a valley between high rocky hills, the first rays of the sun were just touching the extensive ruined buildings. A long marble-paved street gleamed, the theatre seemed carved into the hill. Sheep and goats grazed, with their attendant shepherd on the rocky summit above the old city. Faint sheep bells were just audible in the stillness. To one side of the main marble road was a hill of ruined houses, once occupied by aristocratic Romans; it was these that I had come to see.

The Austrians have slowly excavated this great city over a period of a hundred years, and are spending millions to enclose the whole slope of magnificent Roman houses, called the Hanghäusen or 'hanging houses' in a kind of giant transparent aircraft hangar. Construction of the supports for this enclosure had begun, and the house sites were closed to the public. There must be almost a hundred rooms still existing in the two- and three-storey houses.

The young Austrian academic and fresco specialist, Norbert, led me to the top house high on the hill. We walked along precarious planks, and down ancient staircases until we arrived in the courtyard or *atrium* of one of these houses, which were built all together in *insulae*, rather like modern apartments. The first impression was how little light there was; the houses had been re-roofed for their protection – it was eery, quiet, and cold. Norbert shone his torch into rooms and it was breathtaking to catch a whole painted wall – suddenly some garlands, cupids or *erotes*, an actor in a flowing garment; glowing patches of deep red and purple. It was a shock to realise that as the main light came from the courtyard, the rooms would have been nearly dark at the time they were inhabited in the first and second centuries. Our contemporary compulsion to have works of art brilliantly lit was of little account in the ancient world. What seemed to have been important was that the appropriate subject matter was in place, even if it was not seen all at once but partially lit by oil lamps, or perceived gradually in the dimness of a room lit by filtered daylight. Like icons, ancient painting could be apprehended not only visually, but also symbolically, in all tones of lightness and darkness.

I was mesmerised by the complete painted *cubicula* or small rooms, probably used for sleeping, with fillets flying among flower sprigs held by birds. The sprigs and fillets were similar to the Paphos examples, but here they covered a whole wall. These *cubicula* had doors into a larger room with theatre scenes and masks, and the whole apartment of rooms was decorated with brushy paintings full of verve, surprisingly close in style to the Paphos fragments. It was particularly interesting to see the same iconography as that of the theatre – plant motifs and celebratory ribbons were associated with Dionysos, the god of luxury and pleasure, and as well, the god responsible for the release of emotion through the theatre. The fertility and abundance of the natural world were Dionysos' domain, which perhaps explains why his images and attributes were found not only as propitious signs in houses, but also in the theatre and in tombs. I had a sense of an intense and sophisticated life lived in these intricate rooms. Their inhabitants must have attended the great public buildings of nearby Ephesos, the temples, the library, the theatre, the gymnasium, and the baths.

Norbert took me through the whole slope or honeycomb of houses, from the top houses right down to the houses on the level of the central road, leaping ahead over obstacles, talking, enthusiastically pointing to a multitude of wonders. A beautiful green and purple fish excavated on one layer swam among flower sprigs of another layer, possibly fifty years earlier. As we walked quickly through I would catch a glimpse of an enticingly beautiful image – an emerald bird on a deep red wall, cherubs flirting in a creamy space, a fluttering garland on powder blue.

The area of the lower 'hanging' houses had been dug continuously since 1983, and because of the complexity of the archaeological stratigraphy, it was still in the process of being published. For this reason, of course, I was not permitted to take photographs. The colour of the paintings was clearly comparable to Paphos pigments, a pale greeny-blue turquoise, a grey-blue, a Venetian red, creamy yellow and black. In a slightly burnt room black soot and evidence of burning also changed the colours, turning yellow ochre into red ochre.

I stood among several archaeologists painstakingly excavating the floor for contextual pottery, artefacts and clues to dating. They crouched on the floor in the low light, while on the white plastered wall behind them, elegant figures of servers hovered, carrying laden plates for visitors, and also fillets to tie around their heads, looking directly out of the panel at the guests. In that half-light these figures seemed as real as the dark forms scraping the ground.

Hospitality was an important function of the Roman house, and it was vital to make guests feel at home with appropriate food and decorations. Sometimes the plaster had been picked out in little holes to take a new layer, sometimes not. Why were there so many changes and renovations? The archaeologists thought it could have been because of a changing function – from guest room to dining room, to audience room. Possibly every twenty years or so a new young wife or husband might have wanted to redecorate and put her or his own more fashionable taste in view, as the role of the various rooms changed. 'Not those rosebuds and nymphs! That's really impossible. We must have a Nile scene with fish! And what about some landscapes or philosophers in the loo?'

Fascinating graffitti appeared in one of the larger rooms, scratched into the paint of the architectural panels. Many of these rooms would have been used as semi-public spaces, where clients of important officials would have waited to see the influential owner of the house. Roman bureaucrats and businessmen did not go to the office, but received clients formally at home, and these people might also be poorer or younger members of his extended family who were dependent on his largesse. A special publication is being written dealing with the varied and lively graffitti – naïve drawings of acrobats about a metre above the floor may have been the drawings of a bored child. ('Sit still and keep quiet! He won't be long!') Near a pleasant dining room, or *triclinium*, was a lavish toilet with three seats of marble and sketches of philosphers looking at sundials – Plato and Aristotle – and an inscription scratched on the wall: 'There's three places, but nine came to dinner, have to be quick.'

In the rooms around the courtyard and in its peristyle, 'fake' marbling was painted on the lower panels, often copying the actual marble nearby. Marble was extraordinarily important in the Roman hierarchy of materials, a substance that added glamour and mystery to a room, and it was imported by emperors from quarries all over the empire. Lucan, a Roman historian writing in the first century at about the time of these houses, described the splendour of the (Hellenistic) palace of Alexandria:

> The walls shone with marble; nor were they merely overlaid with a thin surface of it; and agate stood there, and porphyry. Alabaster was laid all over the hall to tread on; and the ebony of Meroe. The sofas were bright with coverlets of divers colours, most had long been steeped in Tyrian dyes and took their hue from repeated soakings, while others were embroidered with bright gold, and others blazed scarlet.[34]

I was excited to see parallels to the Paphos patterns in the imitation marble patterns – streaks, wavy lines, irregular blobs and dragged brush marks were familiar devices. Norbert agreed that there was a close likeness, when I showed him my gouache documentation of the frescoes.

Wall painting in substantial houses like these in Ephesos could imitate and refer to the luxurious stones and textiles described by Lucan in a less costly setting. Each room, instead of a woven carpet had a mosaic carpet set on the floor, exactly like a rug, with elaborate geometric patterns – diamonds with rosettes, interlacing, triangles in complex and optical designs. Even runners appeared in corridor areas, with petalled rosettes on a dark ground. To offset the geometric patterns, emblem panels of very fine *tesserae* were chosen, with figurative subjects, and these were treated almost like paintings, often signed by the artist, and were sometimes moved around. Here was a lovely red-gowned sea goddess, Amphitrite, seated casually on a coiling, looping seahorse with her veil fluttering about her head. A muscular Triton with two waving serpent tails for legs held the reins, and brilliant colour in small touches like a Fauve painting appeared in his blue hair and in the gold drapery slung over his arm.

Textiles must have existed which showed just such scenes in embroidery or weaving; they were so influential on the wall paintings that there was a 'tapestry style' in Pompeian houses, which copied the elaborate filigree borders of carpets with their central medallions of mythological scenes. Athenaeus described 'cloaks with portraits of kings' and 'counterpanes embroidered with exquisite art.'[35] Conversation between the lively women, Gorgo and Praxinoa, brought this to life in a poem of Theocritus.

> GORGO: 'Praxinoa, do come here. Before you do anything else I insist upon your looking at the embroideries. How delicate they are! And in such good taste. They're really hardly human are they?'
> PRAXINOA: 'By Athena! The weavers that made that material and

the embroiderers who did that close detailed work are simply marvels. How realistically the things all stand and move about it! They are living! It's wonderful what people can do. And then the Holy Boy, how perfectly beautiful he looks lying on his silver couch, with the down of manhood just showing on his cheeks, thrice beloved Adonis!'[36]

At the lower levels of the 'hanging' houses was a spacious basilica, an audience room for an important Roman official whose sons had become consuls in Rome.

Each room was carefully organised into visual zones through painted panels, and sometimes with relief panels in stucco and actual marble facings. The painted columns that divided up the walls were carefully rendered in perspective in these public rooms, whereas in private areas of the houses they could be simplified into a stripe or band. Walking through these immense silent rooms in the shadowy light with my guide, I thought that life in those spaces must have been very different to contemporary apartment life, yet with familiar elements, probably because so many of the architectural conventions that the Romans invented continued so long and are still part of domestic architecture in the eastern Mediterranean.

The pervasive rituals of everyday Roman life are hidden from us, but they were implicitly associated with architecture, and even shaped it. The *domus* had an ideal character, a formal arrangement of parts, according to Vitruvius, and in the first hall of the house, just beyond the 'jaws' of the entrance way, there was always a shrine to the Lares and Penates, the gods of the household. (English got 'economy' from the Greek word for house, *oîkos* – originally 'running the home; and from the Latin equivalent, *domus*, came 'domestic'.) We paused by another niche in the wall with a small painting of a female figure, an altar, and a stag that might have been the representation of a sacrifice to Artemis and could have formed a shrine. Perhaps an important member of the family, or the family itself, had had a particular connection to this deity whose great temple was so close by.

I spoke to Norbert all morning, as we examined fifty or so rooms, moving up and down planks, sometimes suspended five metres above lower rooms. I exclaimed and pondered, and he answered my questions. The houses made an extraordinary impression of a rich order, of a witty and well read imagery. That whole hill, excavated only in part over the last hundred years, must still be full of treasure. Norbert pointed to some brick that was protruding from unexcavated rubble nearby and said, 'In another hundred years!' Under the mound were large houses that must wait to be unearthed. Excavation in distant and exotic sites in Turkey, he told me, is so expensive that many archaeological departments now prefer to do topographical surveys for Roman ruins in Austria itself. Here in Turkey the ground is so tilted and distorted by earthquakes that such surveys are not possible. After frescoed walls are revealed they must be conserved, as they disintegrate rapidly without treatment. Many paintings known in the nineteenth or early twentieth centuries have vanished from Pompeii and Ostia in Italy, with only drawings and perhaps a few black and white photographs to indicate what might have been there. Once excavated, the houses do not remain in a static condition, but have a new set of relationships in another context of scholarship and tourism. Like all houses, they need maintenance, which is why the overarching enclosure with a transparent roof of cockpit glass, and computer controlled openings, was being built by the Austrian engineers.

We agreed that archaeologists often found painted plaster problematic on excavations, compared to the well-known sequences of pottery. Pottery is the language of digging, and practical archaeologists can sometimes regard finds of painted fresco as marginal, just as art historians may perilously ignore the archaeological record. Archaeological techniques are crucial in dating fresco, but there must also be some knowledge of the style and iconography of art and social history. These are very old tensions in the field of archaeology – really the interpretation of evidence from a site needs experts of every persuasion. I have loved the fact that I can visit

Athens, Alexandria or Ephesos and immediately communicate with archaeologists from other countries about a common obsession with, for example, Roman theatres and painting. They know a different aspect of the same ancient landscape that I am interested in: small differences and strange analogies between sites are exclaimed over, and references exchanged.

Many questions emerged in my hunt to understand the Paphos frescoes through conversations about this vibrant series of painted rooms in Ephesos. Could Paphos, further to the south and to the east, have been on the same trade routes as Ephesos? Both cities enjoyed the great Pax Romana of the second century AD, when ships and people could travel safely to all the many ports of the eastern Mediterranean. Were patrons in touch with each other, recommending certain painters? The artists might have travelled also, with their partners the plasterers, bringing their repertoire with them. One can imagine the artists saying to the patron, 'This Narcissus theme went down very well in Paphos in the governor's house – why don't you think of a Narcissus theme at the entrance to the *triclinium*, or possibly some Muses?' (The layering of lime plaster and the mixing of colours were skilled crafts, and needed a team of at least two artisans, quite apart from the drawing and measuring of decoration and figures.) The close connection in image and style between Paphos and Ephesos could be explained by such contacts.

Seeing the complete layout of the houses, and the relationship between architecture and decoration, I wanted to know more about the audience for painting in Paphos and to understand the architectural function of the *parodos*, the entrance to the theatre. These questions would be central to the continuing work on the Paphos frescoes. Just as in Ephesos, there were palatial houses in the Paphos of the second and third centuries belonging to Roman officials, who would have attended the theatre. Both cities had early contact with Christianity through Paul and Barnabas, just as both cities had outraged Christian sensibilities through devotion to Artemis and Aphrodite.

How intriguing it was to see the ancient houses now occupied by the archaeologists themselves, the last in a long succession of inhabitants, setting up their own rigorous rituals of brushing, sifting, scrutinising with magnifying glasses and cameras, drawing and measuring, like some obscure form of housekeeping. I thought the Lares and Penates, possibly still around, must have been touched by this great care and dedication to the reconstruction, and I hoped the ancient guardians would reward the archaeologists with flashes of insight.

As a marvellous finale to the morning, and with complete unselfconsciousness, improvised tables had been set up in one of the larger rooms, and we were called at midday to a simple but delicious lunch for about ten people, including the engineers. Fresh bread, yoghurt, salad, goat's cheese – it could have been the second century. The archaeologists were using the house as it was intended, for dedicated work, for dining and conversation. This was the only time I had ever eaten surrounded by such red walls, in such a complex of remarkable rooms. I almost imagined I might have heard a chuckling echo in the dark corners from previous inhabitants, and perhaps a few out-of-work deities.

9. MUSES

9 May

After the exhilarating morning exploring the Roman houses, I sat quite stunned on a warm marble seat in the famous theatre of Ephesos, looking out at what must have been the harbour before the sea moved away to its present position. The contrast between the almost cold interiors of the dark houses, and the bright light and view over the plain was uplifting. The sun was hot and high in a blue bowl of sky; a few tourists stood transfixed in the *orchestra*. Ancient theatres are good places for thinking I've noticed, something about the form focuses the mind. This theatre was where Paul had preached to the Ephesians against their beloved Artemis, and he had been briefly detained for causing such a disturbance. To those urbane Romans (no doubt some of them had just come from lunch in one of those painted dining rooms, as I had) he must have seemed like a fanatic of a little known cult rather than someone who could influence the invincible course of the Roman Empire.

A tumble of red brick in the distance was the ruined Mouseion of Ephesos, the temple of the Muses, the nine daughters of Zeus and Mnemosyne (Memory), who had lain together for nine consecutive nights. Zeus, as the sovereign god of the Olympians, had a prodigious number of children, many of whom were also deities. For the first time I realised the obvious fact that a museum was indeed the home of the nine Muses, and this was where inspiration and intuition met with scholarship. In the hanging houses I had seen an elegant painting of seven Muses (two were missing) represented as slender figures on a pale gold background, each with their attributes and their name in Greek. The wall painting had shown Thalia with her mask (responsible for comedy and pastoral poetry), Euterpe (music, lyric poetry), Kleio holding a book (Muse of history), Polyhymnia (heroic hymns), Erato with a lyre or a viol (lyric and love poetry), Terpsichore also with a lyre (dancing and song), and Kalliope with a stylus for writing (epic poetry). Instead of Melpomene, Muse of tragedy, and Urania, Muse of astronomy, Apollo, god of inspiration, and Sappho the lyric poet appeared in the painting. Sappho was the only human, and the only historical figure in this painted group; living in the sixth century BC not far away in Lesbos, she was regarded with intense admiration in the second century. (There is a colossal head of Sappho in Istanbul, almost a metre high, with huge 'pothotic' eyes.) How interesting that writing and sound are predominant in this list of art forms, and visual arts are not mentioned. Lyric, dramatic and epic poetry was allied to history, and stringed and vocal music to mathematics and science. The whole area of visual arts was seen as belonging to physical skills; ceramics, sculpture, painting, textiles, metalwork and architecture, although immensely important, with individual 'great artists', were in another category.

The uncertain nature of artistic creativity was comforted and helped by the presence of a Muse, who could sometimes be found near particular rivers, or on high mountains, rather like nymphs. A well-known writer in Australia revealed that he had found Muses in the oddest places, sometimes in the kitchen, occasionally in bed. Oliver Sachs, the famous neuro-scientist who was intrigued by the sudden flash of inspiration that can solve a longstanding problem, met a Muse while getting on a bus. By the end of the journey, he had the answer to the problem.[37]

If poetry and drama were of primary importance in the ancient imagination, all the paintings and sculpture I had seen in Pergamon and Ephesos from this vibrant Hellenistic and Roman time could be understood best through ideas from these texts. Unlike our own time, where the emphasis has been on the materiality of the artwork, without 'literary' overtones, Greco-Roman art was structured by the central *poesis* of the time, emphasising poetic dramatisation, character and plot. So much of the literature has completely vanished. The great collection of the Library in Pergamon was transported to Alexandria in Roman times, and lasted there until the seventh century; it was burnt in the fifth century by radical Christians and finished off at the time of the Arab invasions. Just down the road from the Ephesos theatre was the captivating Library of Celsius, which had been richly endowed. The two-storey building flickered with a wonderful play of light and shade over projecting columns with draped female figures of the Virtues (Wisdom, Knowledge, Valour and Thought) and coffered ceilings were still in place inside, with exuberant vine friezes. Although no texts have survived, it is likely that contemporary dramas and certainly mimes were still being written for the theatre until the fourth century AD. As St Augustine attests, theatres remained a passionate concern far into the Christian era, and actors could attain a cult status, as they can today.

An ancient city is not simple; all periods are juxtaposed and overlap each other. The early Christian history of Ephesos was really what we might call post-pagan, with style and imagery related to the Hellenistic past. I had returned exhausted from negotiating the cavernous houses and had slept for an hour in my lovely room overlooking the fortified hill of Ayasuluk. Later in the evening in the long twilight I walked to St John's basilica, on the same hill. Roses flowered wildly and abundantly among date palms in the soft light. A man sitting beside two sheep rose as I approached the great gate and said he was a guide at the ruins during the day, would I like to buy an ancient coin? He opened his palm; a haughty Hellenistic profile could be glimpsed. Dangerous work; illicit selling has been a problem across the eastern Mediterranean, when treasure is accessible, and people are so poor. He guided me to the entrance so I gave him some change; he smiled rather sadly at my refusal to buy the tantalising coin and rejoined his sheep.

From up high the small town with its minarets looked a model of peace – children were playing on the roofs of houses, flying kites high above the town, skipping ropes. There was a smell of grilling meat from small barbecues. Looking towards the sunset, the rich plain stretched out towards the sea, dotted with poplars.

The guard at St John's offered to take me around even though the gate was closed at that hour. The large expanse of the basilica, originally built by the same Justinian who had conceived of Ayia Sophia in Constantinople, had been beautifully reconstructed by American and Turkish archaeologists – a long nave looked directly west from the marble slab marking St John's grave. This was the beloved John, the *theologos*, the writer of the gospel: 'In the beginning was the word.' In the old bishopric in Paphos I had seen an icon of St John with his pen poised, words appearing on the page as a great beam of inspiration swept down from heaven. He was reputed to have written his gospel here in Ephesos, where he came with the aging Virgin Mary (taking up residence just when that other virgin, Artemis, was in serious decline). The guide, an old weathered man, kept picking flowers and giving them to me, red roses, hyacinths, clustered together like an Ottoman embroidery.

I saw the fresco that Norbert had mentioned in a small chapel: Mary, John, and James, draped, standing figures on a plain ground of red or indigo, hardly visible in the dusky light – all the faces scraped away, but colour and technique identical to 'pagan' work of the same time. I could see here how Christian and pagan merged seamlessly in this sixth century. I laid the flowers on St John's grave, always one of my favourite apostles.

Not far from St John's is the stately mosque of Isa Bey, with a broken brick minaret and massive stalactite gate. The minaret had a head of shaggy hair; it was crowned with storks' nests, and the great birds sat perched above the town looking serenely in control. I passed a woman wearing a scarf and baggy trousers, helping three young goats find soft grass. A man came trotting past on a donkey, leading a fine white pony – he was withered but spry, in jacket and cap. This was another world, an older layer of Turkey, like the Greece I knew in the 1960s.

This small town had so many resonances, and had always been a place for intense cults, from Artemis to the Virgin and St John, and then to Islam. The greatest material contribution of Islam was pattern and textiles, perhaps beginning in the scattered sprigged walls and the optical carpet mosaics of the Roman buildings in the ancient town.

Coming down the road from St John's I passed one of the enchanting carpet shops, where the weavings were of high quality, from all over Turkey. There were no other customers around, and the vivacious owner offered apple tea, seeing me pause to look. Easily falling under the spell, I stepped into that familiar smell of wool, linen and dyes, that magical world of pattern and colour in carpets stacked and folded, piled to the ceiling. The owner was Osman from Cappadocia, and his partner was Mehmet. Apprentice boys of fourteen or fifteen years were quick, smiling, efficiently making tea, dusting, rolling and unrolling carpets. Osman had started in the same way at the same age, mending kilims in his village, and had then moved to a carpet shop in Istanbul, where he had studied English. He said he was always searching for older carpets, from thirty or forty years ago at least, and these older carpets were superb, with glowing colours and intricate designs. Carpets were a solid currency, always retaining a clear value despite the variability of the Turkish lira. They talked about the rugs in detail and were not in a hurry. 'Does this one speak to you? Does this one?', rolling and unrolling carpets from every region, kilims, dense pile rugs, silk soumaks. After six cups of apple tea, one of the silk soumaks from the region around Ararat in central east Turkey did speak to me, very clearly. Three central hooked motifs were surrounded by a myriad of tiny geometric animals, lions, sheep, goats, cattle, snakes, all kinds of birds, scattered like flowers on a cream silk ground. Knowing how time-intensive soumak was to weave, the carpet seemed to me like the physical expression of a dense web of time. It was a 'Noah's ark' soumak from east Cappadocia, demonstrating how Old Testament figures have been incorporated into Islam, appearing in the Qur'an as important prophets. I remembered Athanasius describing the carpets from Persia in the palace of Ptolemy in Alexandria: 'Smooth Persian carpets had beautiful designs of figures woven in them with minute skill'.[38] My carpet, being mainly of silk, was wrapped up quite small in brown paper and tied with string.

The carpet, with its Islamic and biblical theme was like a talisman of intermingled threads and images, the perpetuation of distant traditions and other ways of life. The story of Noah, his family and animals, had been about surviving a great disaster and beginning settled life all over again. The dream of the dead youth coming alive that had haunted me in the ancient cities of Ionia, since visiting Gallipoli, seemed to be laid to rest on this carpet.

INTERLUDE

Art Works

My work at the Paphos theatre excavation and my travels in Cyprus and the region have inspired me to produce a very large number of pieces of art, from archaeological drawings to watercolours and tapestries. A small selection follows.

Fresco fragment with blue spots, from the Paphos theatre *parodos* (No. 2234). Gouache, 26.5 x 15 cm, 2001.

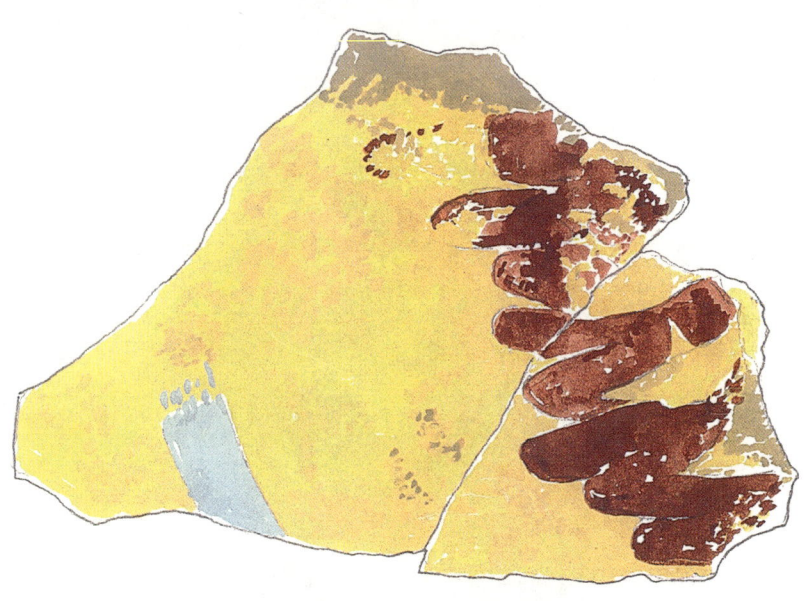

Fresco fragment of fillet and tendril on stone block, from Paphos theatre *parodos* (No. 2315). Gouache, 14 x 10.5 cm, 1997.

Pebble mosaic of dolphins, serpent and figure. From a Hellenistic floor, Fabrika Hill, Paphos. Pencil and watercolour, 15 x 20 cm, 1998.

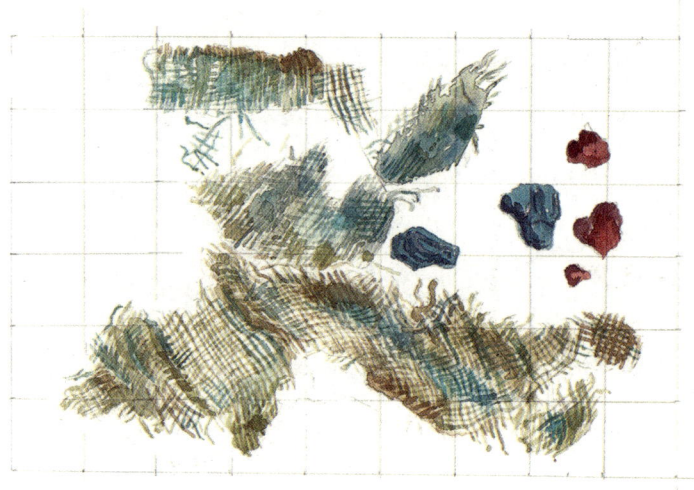

Fragment of linen cloth, 7.5 cm in length, from the House of Dionysos. Second century AD, Paphos Museum. Pencil and watercolour, 1998.

Kilim rug, possibly Anatolian, now in the Cyprus American Archaeological Research Institute, Nicosia. Pen and watercolour, 19 x 15 cm, 2002.

These by the Hellespont lost their glorious youth in battle. Detail. Inscription taken from the plaster cast of a memorial to those lost in the Persian Wars, 480 BC, Australian War Memorial Museum, Canberra. Woven wool tapestry on canvas with acrylic and gouache, 50 cm x 1.8 m, 1997.

Alexandria. Detail. The original has the inscription in my father's handwriting 'At midnight the regiment marched to a camp at Ikingi Maryut nine miles from Alexandria.' Tapestry, linen and wool, 65 x 200 cm, 1999-2000.

Net. Woven tapestry, wool and silk weft on linen warp, 22.5 x 29 cm, 2002.

Unwritten country with fragment of a Roman mosaic. Detail. Woven tapestry fragment, in linen and silk, on canvas with acrylic and gouache. 1 m x 2.5 m, 1998. The 'cube in perspective' motif is from a mosaic at Kourion.

Katabasis/going down: fragment with grapes and a roundel. Woven wool tapestry with gouache, graphite and ink on paper, 55 x 120 cm, 1995.

Shellal Mosaic. Detail. Woven wool tapestry fragment with drawing on paper, 230 x 230 cm, 1992.

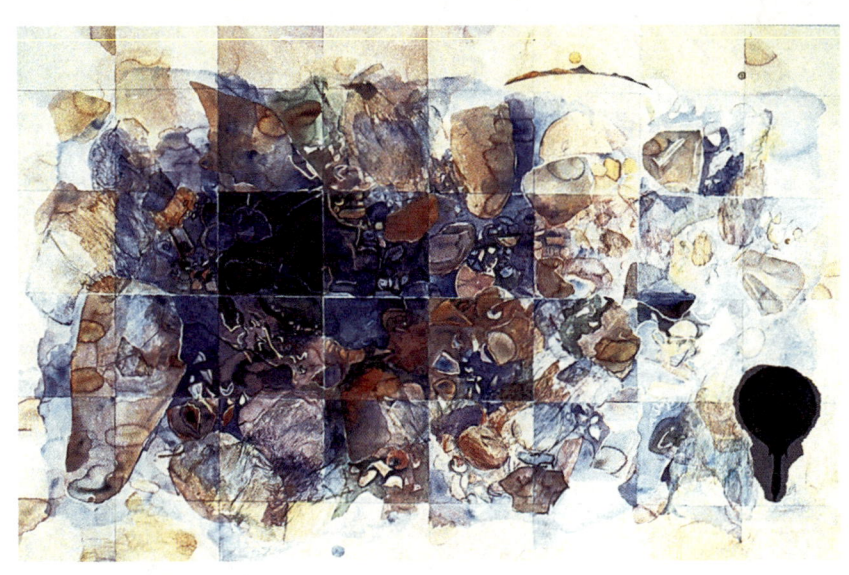

Site map with flawed mirror. Tapestry fragment with gouache, pencil and collage on Canzon paper, 110 x 170 cm, 1993.

Anemones, February. 12 x 15 cm. Watercolour and pencil, 1996.

PART III

The Theatres of Southern Turkey, 2000

Head of Tyche, from Arsos, Cyprus. Larnaca Museum.

1. IN SOUTHERN TURKEY: THEATRES OF PAMPHYLIA, LYCIA AND PISIDIA

8 June 2000, Falez Hotel Antalya, 8 p.m.

The sun is just setting, turning the looming Taurus mountains pink. They rear up from the depths of an indigo sea into snowy, extravagant peaks and shadowed ravines, impossibly romantic. I feel as if I am flying still, because I'm on the ninth floor of a tower hotel looking down at the swinging arc of the bay surrounded by that wall of mountains. Here Alexander the Great once brought his army, walking around a coast so steep that his men were forced to walk half in the sea. 'Mountains like tents,' observed Freya Stark when she stayed in Antalya.

The land called Pamphylia surrounding Antalya derives from *pan philia*, 'all the allies'. The plains of Pamphylia do not extend far from the coast, and great cities (Perge, Sillyon, Aspendos and Side are their ancient names) were established by Greek colonists who are supposed to have come as refugees from the Trojan War in the time of Homer, the seventh and eighth centuries BC. So many overlords: Croesus of Lydia and Xerxes of Persia preceded Alexander the Great, who conquered the area around 333 BC. After being ruled by the nearby Seleucid dynasty in Antioch, the province was ceded to King Attalos II of Pergamon in 190 BC (when it was known as Attaleia), and finally came under full Roman control in 140 BC. It is a parallel history to that of Paphos, although Paphos was ruled by the Ptolemaic dynasty from Egypt, rather than by the Seleucids and Attalids. Similarly to Paphos, after a long and prosperous period of seven hundred years under the rule of Rome, Pamphylia experienced an early Christian fervour of conversion that is well documented in the texts of the New Testament. The region remained Christian under the Byzantine Empire. Pamphylia, like Cyprus, was invaded by Muslim Arabs in the seventh century. Later still came the Selçuk Turks in the eleventh century and, of course, crusaders.

The new part of Antalya is a city of towers, so that from this height I look down on a labyrinth of gardens, with jacarandas in flower among bougainvillea and palms. Swallows dip and swoop at a level with my eyes against a cloudless sky. It's like being a deity, being able to look out so far in the suffused gold light. This was a pirate coast, lost to history at various times through its remoteness and the constant violations of raiders, an abode of escapees and refugees from official empires. The extraordinary geography may have imposed a kind of extremism on historical events.

Yesterday at Marmara University in Istanbul I parted from the cordiality and warmth of the artists at the Faculty of Fine Arts where I had been attending an International Student Triennial and conference, mounting an exhibition of student work with five of my students. There had been a loving, slightly tearful, departure from them, from Sarah, Melissa, Libby, Emma and Daniel, who went off on their own adventures before returning to Australia. When he heard I was travelling to the far south of Turkey, to Antalya, Professor Hüsamettin Koçan insisted that I stay with a 'dear friend' of his who owned a five-star hotel. His bushy eyebrows leapt above his dark eyes and smiling mouth, and like some vital Anatolian genie he declared, 'This hotel room is a gift to you for three days. The faculty exhibits in its gallery and it is free for faculty artists.'

I left Istanbul airport on a grey morning when the city was dimmed and overcast, in a daze of fatigue. Flying in to land at Antalya nearly two hours later, I was astonished to see from high up, from space saturated with brilliant light, a white glittering gash falling into the sea from the cliff near the town: a waterfall. It was like arriving in a mythical place. And there outside the small airport was a white Mercedes hotel limousine to meet me in the forty-degree midday heat; the driver taciturn, not speaking English. He took me to the imposing Falez hotel, and from the great lobby I was taken to the 'executive floor', the ninth floor, and given an elegant room with a marble bath and the incomparable view. It seemed like a fairytale after the modest electricity workers' hostel where we had stayed in Istanbul. Weariness descended in huge waves and I sank onto the quiet bed and slept. On waking I bathed luxuriously, putting on the thick white towelling robe, and poured a raki from the bar – the fatigue begins to lift – what other wonders will appear? Anything seems possible.

The purpose of this journey is to consider that very prosperous time from the second century AD when nearly every town in the regions of Pamphylia, Lycia and Pisidia along the Mediterranean coast had theatres. Their history is similar to that of the theatre in Paphos – most were constructed first in the Hellenistic period in the wake of Alexander's conquests, and then re-modelled extensively during Roman times. It is like the passion for bird watching, to view another theatre site – each distinctive and often magnificently ruined in this spectacular, hard country. My idea was to visit as many as possible and to compare them to the theatre in Paphos, only three hours by boat to the south-east.

The ancient theatres in sites around Antalya, although diverse in style, size and in building materials, do relate directly to the theatre in Paphos in their architecture. All of these towns and cities must once have been in constant contact by sea with this stretch of coast, so accessible to Cyprus. Most famously, as told in the *Acts of the Apostles*, St Paul and St Barnabas travelled this route from Cyprus to Pamphylia in the first century. Specifically, I wanted to find out if there was evidence of painted decoration in the theatres. From research done prior to setting out this does not seem likely, but perhaps I would find some of my motifs from the frescoes – imitation marble, tendrils, flower sprigs or swags of drapery. At least I would have some intimation of whether painting may have been placed in a vaulted and closed-in *parodos* or entranceway.

A smaller subtext in visiting Antalya was a fascination with Alexander the Great's journey to this land as a vital move in his conquest of Asia. Establishing theatres was a primary step in Hellenising the East – no one could resist Greek entertainment. (This is comparable to America's conquest of world entertainment in the twentieth century.) The grand visions of Alexander predated and set in motion the idea of *koine*, a common civilisation across Europe and Asia held together by the Greek language, just as 'English' in all its permutations is spoken across our contemporary Asia. Under the Pax Romana of the second century these countries prospered again – Pamphylia, Pisidia, and Lycia seem to have had a kind of renaissance vigour in building great cities with impressive theatres.

I took with me Freya Stark's *Alexander's Path: from Caria to Cilicia*. In 1954, in the tradition of archaeological travellers since the eighteenth century, she tried to follow Alexander's route through these inaccessible mountains. Greece, she thought, was the supreme civilisation, which in spite of cruelties and errors can never be superceded, since even the merest trifles it has left us, the siting of its buildings, the stray stones of its walls, the fragments of its marbles hold 'that strong thread of immortality we are in danger of forgetting, our only home and native country in the world'.[1]

Like earlier travellers she believed that the Greek spirit of enquiry was at the foundation of western life, and I suspect she accepted the implications of colonisation and empire. The inevitable assimilation of small-scale societies, like those of these mountain provinces, into the complex Greco-Roman culture of sophisticated concepts and commodities was for her a civilising assimilation of the lesser culture to the greater. The original tribespeople of the region may have had other perceptions of the overwhelming power of Greece and Rome. They may have seen that fitting in with their overlords' demands could well be a creative strategy, allowing access to superior technologies while quietly retaining traditional beliefs, customs and even language. Such strategies are understood in the postcolonial British societies of the Pacific.

I am not sure if I too may be unconsciously 'orientalising' this singular land, denying its present voice in order to listen to the distant and exotic past, like so many scholars and artists before me trailing from western Europe.

Later

The hotel is a palace, with palms and lattice screens, and polished marble floors. I walked in the night gardens, the radiant pools floating in darkness, the date palms like metal totems, and grids of precise zinnias in flower beds edged with volcanic pumice. Tanned people with gold jewellery gleaming were dressed in casual sophistication – they wandered around a buffet, looking at the vast array of food, and sat down to eat outside as the moon rose in a deep blue sky. I heard fragments of English conversation, a few American accents, but this hotel caters mostly for Turks from the great cities of Istanbul and Ankara. A small band playing traditional music sounded mournful and fatalistic.

My head is full of images – listening to the music I suddenly remembered being in a crowded bus stop in Istanbul and seeing a large soft woman sitting on the ground, crouched over, stroking something. A tiny baby, a few weeks old, was feeding at her breast, one arm raised to hold the fabric of her dress, fingers moving in a rhythm to the sucking. The baby was oblivious to the fumes and noise, unaware of the shifting throngs of people in the heart of Kadiköy, ancient Chalkidike.

2. PERGE AND SIDE

9 June

The cheeps of awakening birds float up to the ninth floor and they sound like they have in any other year of my life. But a tower removes you to the skies. Descending to earth, I found that the hotel in its garden was near the spreading buildings of the Antalya Museum, signalled by one of the strange Gothic sarcophagi with a peaked roof from ancient Lycia, raised high beside the gate.

    I am part of a history of travellers with an archaeological preoccupation. Interest in the material remains of the ancient world increased at the same time as a scientific categorisation of the natural world became a passion in the eighteenth century. In 1764 the Society of Dilettanti in England instructed three young men led by Mr Richard Chandler to go to Ionia and 'some parts of the East'. They were told to 'make excursions ... to the remains of antiquity' and from information collected on the spot 'procure the exactest plans and measures possible of the buildings you shall find, making accurate drawings of the bas-reliefs and ornaments', taking views, copying all inscriptions, and noticing everything 'which can give the best idea of the ancient and present state of those places.'[2] Their observations and drawings in that long and dangerous journey did lay the groundwork for later archaeological study, especially as many of the details of inscriptions and carvings later became lost. Ruins seem changeless, but in fact they are fragile – what I see today may have crumbled and fallen in a few years. The very interest in the material remains of the past often contributes to its demise. The archaeological wealth of this southern province of Turkey has survived because of the profound disinterest, the benign neglect, of Islamic and Ottoman rulers.

    Amongst the rich collections of the museum I was particularly drawn to the wealth of theatrical sculptures from the stage building of the Perge theatre. Perge was a great city on a rich plain about seventeen kilometres to the north-east of Antalya, and still has an impressively intact theatre, a stadium, an agora, baths and fortifications. The city, it is related, welcomed the conquering Alexander and flourished under the Romans.

    The Perge school of sculpture was remarkable, as impressive as the earlier sculpture from Pergamon much further to the north and to the east. I gasped at the great statues of Herakles, of Alexander – they were only discovered in the ruins of the theatre at Perge in the late 1980s and have not yet been published. Professor Jalne Inan from Istanbul has been excavating this complex city site over many years, and more than a hundred complete statues have been found, even before the excavation of the theatre stage building. (How much we have lost in Paphos.) A fleshy, sensual Dionysos seemed to seethe with emotion, with *erotes* at his feet playing with a panther and a serpent. One of the largest figures was that of Hermes, more than three metres high with wings on his feet and a *caduceus* in his hand, and a ram beside him. His impressive eyes, deeply drilled, stared out above the subtlety of a body formed and proportioned according to classical models.

This school of sculpture seemed to prefigure the grandiosity and confidence of Michelangelo, yet the references to these discoveries in German and Turkish journal publications have eluded English-speaking scholars. I did not know these sculptures existed. Such power is evident in the gestures, in the monumental heads, and shadowed eyes. The figures were designed for the intense light and shade of this southern climate, to maximise effects of chiaroscuro, so that each deity and hero could be identified even from the top gallery of the theatre by stance and attribute. The naked male body was triumphant, with torsos like armour or like the rocky mountains veined with minerals all around. Here were Hermes, Marsyas, Dionysos, Herakles, Alexander and the emperor Trajan.

Because the sculptures have not been fully published, I was unable to photograph them, merely drawing the heroic head of Alexander, turned to a god five hundred years after his conquest of Pamphylia in the fourth century BC. When I was studying Roman sculpture it had been a truism that Rome added nothing original to the Greek canon; but here I felt was a group of theatrical sculptures that had unerringly caught the astonishing brilliance and power of this second century. This is the time that Edward Gibbon in his vast chronicle of *The Decline and Fall of the Roman Empire* described as 'the period in the history of the world during which the human race was most happy and prosperous'.

As Antalya had been ruled by Pergamon in the second century BC it is conceivable that there were still long established cultural ties that allowed an echo of the Pergamene baroque even three hundred years later. The common Anatolian syllables in the names of the two cities suggest possible affinities. In antiquity Perge was on a main road that actually began in Pergamon hundreds of kilometres to the north-west and ended in Side, a Pamphylian city a little further to the east. The theatre at Perge has particular resonances for the theatre in Paphos because of very ancient connections to Cyprus. St Paul and St Barnabas came from Paphos by ship, sailing up the then navigable Cestros River directly to Perge, probably around AD 50, in order to convert the city to Christianity. As at Ephesos, they may have preached in the theatre itself, long before these dramatic statues were installed in the theatre building. Paul seemed to find a particular challenge in confronting the devotion of cities such as Paphos, Ephesos, Perge and Corinth to the great goddesses Artemis and Aphrodite.

The language of Pamphylia may have been connected to the early language of Cyprus, as well as that of Anatolia, and both Cyprus and Pamphylia are thought to have been influenced by the Dorian Greek tongue of the Arcadians. Both were colonised by the Homeric Achaeans. There are many overlapping comparisons, made difficult by the current political situation.

During my prolonged study in the sarcophagus room at the Antalya Museum the museum curator was talking to an assistant about the exact colour of dusky pink to paint the walls. He suddenly turned to me and asked in English, 'Which shade do you like?' I preferred the deeper tone, to set off the translucent creamy marble of the carvings. He introduced himself as Mr Edip Ösgür – a vigorous grey-haired archaeologist who looked as if he would enjoy the strenuous fieldwork of Pamphylian sites.

Later, I had a tea with him, to ask about the existence of any Roman frescoes in the region. Edip was full of admiration for Professor Jalne Inan from Istanbul, who had excavated Perge over many years. Now the excavation was in the charge of Professor Haluf Sacioglu. Edip told me that there had always been a special reverence for women in this Mediterranean part of Turkey, which was after all home to Artemis and Aphrodite. It was appropriate that Jalne Inan, a woman, had been excavating Perge, some of whose major monuments had been commissioned by Plancia Magna, priestess of Artemis Pergaia. Some fragments of painting had been found in the great baths in Perge and also in houses there. In the excavation of the library at the other hill town of Sagalossos there was evidence of painted walls in conjunction with mosaics. But he knew of no painting in theatres, apart from the Selçuk frescoes of the eleventh century painted on the stage building at the theatre of Aspendos. He spoke about the high quality of ancient marble in sculptures and architecture in southern Turkey. It came from three main sites, from Proconnessos in the sea of Marmara, from Afyon, a site four hours north of Antalya, and some even from Paros and Naxos in the Aegean. Trade was highly developed across large distances.

The full force of the afternoon sun was on the theatre when I arrived by car, and the temperature more than forty degrees. The tarmac road runs right beside the Perge theatre, making the great masonry wall that abruptly appears from the side of the hill seem curiously modern, because of its conjunction to everyday traffic. The theatre is on the south-west of the ancient city on the eastern slope of the stony hill, Koca Belen, looking over the substantial ruined amphitheatre, the agora, and baths. The redoubtable and wealthy Plancia Magna endowed the building of the theatre about AD 110-20. The giant figures from the Perge theatre stood in niches in two tiers of the stage building which was completed about 190. The theatre was altered again in the third century. Remarkably, there is evidence that the building was still in use in the times of the emperor Justinian between 527 and 565, long after Christianity had become the official religion of the eastern Roman Empire, and nearly two hundred years beyond the long life of the Paphos theatre. The constant changes to the structure show how vital this great gathering space was to the identity of the city, and how many times a theatre would re-invent itself after earthquakes or hard times.

The site was closed for renovation, and astonishingly well preserved. As I walked around the outside of the building through the prickly bushes and withering flowers to the gallery at the top of the theatre, the great structure reminded me of Florentine architecture in its heavily bossed stones and arched entrances. The arches of the top gallery still loop almost half way around the curve of the seats, like vertebrae beside a ribcage. I looked down onto the tumble of the stage building from which had come the astonishing figures in the Antalya Museum, which had lain there unregarded, and easily accessible for so many centuries. I wondered why the Turks did not use ruins as the Greeks did, as a source of material for the lime-kiln, or for rebuilding newer walls and cities. Ranged in a fenced field opposite the theatre was a remarkable grid of exuberant architectural carvings – palmettes, egg and dart and acanthus – in a profusion of variations lying amongst lavender and white hollyhocks for about two hundred and fifty metres. The collection of marbles was like a spreading stony carpet of fragmentary motifs that might conceivably be re-woven.

The entrances to the theatre had vaulted *parodoi* sloping from a five-metre-high entrance on the outside, to a three-metre arch into the *orchestra*. The beautifully laid large stones of grey travertine in the wall of the entrance had no trace of the plaster I was looking for, or any carved or painted decoration. The semicircle of the *orchestra*, as at Paphos, had been railed off with a higher stone wall in the third century to allow for gladiatorial shows with wild beasts. In this large theatre about 14,000 people could be seated. The stage building has been reconstructed in drawings and must have been one of the richest in Anatolia with its three levels of the heroic and divine sculptures I had admired in the museum. A frieze now in Antalya showed the birth of Dionysos, the founder of theatre, from the thigh of his father Zeus, as well as his childhood in the care of nymphs, and his triumphant travels with his retinue of satyrs, maenads and wild beasts. His very strange birth prefigured his identification with intense and transformative realms of emotion.

Late afternoon, 9 June

When I arrived at Side, the ancient port eighty kilometres to the east of Antalya, set on a jutting neck of land and surrounded by sea, it was again the hottest time of the afternoon, fainting hot. 'Side' is an Anatolian word that means 'pomegranate'; with Greek colonisation in Homeric times, the citizens retained their original language while adopting the Greek alphabet. The theatre, closed to visitors and crumbling, was a fascinating and ornate building. Constructed at the same time as the Perge theatre, in the prosperous second century, it had Hellenistic foundations, and was built up on a double row of arches from the flat land. This gave the structure a fragile look, as if the stone had been crocheted like lace. A lovely row of shallow arches supported the second tier of seats in the *cavea*. Side theatre was the first Pamphylian theatre I had seen with no rocky supports or attachment to steep mountains. Even larger than Perge, it could hold maybe 17,000 people. It was just possible to discern the arches of the entrances, the *parodoi*, almost hidden under a mound of rubble.[3] I thought of the sculptures lying in the mound, if the excavation of Perge is any guide. I could see no plaster on any of the walls, but there was waterproof pink plaster on the high walls put around the *orchestra* in the third century or later to allow it to be flooded with water for re-enactments of naval battles. This was intriguing in the light of the prevalence of waterproof plaster in the Paphos theatre. From the viewing point up one of the vaulted staircases, I saw that the stage building was heaped with fallen stones, and the complexity of the ruins, arches and columns pierced by vaulted dark entrances gave it the look of a seventeenth-century Piranesi engraving.

An exquisite columned fountain stood nearby the theatre. How welcome the Islamic fountain houses are which continue the ancient tradition of public fountains – I am continually filling my water bottle from their flowing basins. The columns and pediment of the Temple of Apollo in beautiful creamy marble were part of another dramatic building, set oddly within a vast Byzantine basilica beside the sea. Christian Side became the 'bishopric of eastern Pamphylia', and like Paphos, also close to the sea, its rich basilicas fell to the Arabs in the mid-seventh century. A layer of ash in excavation showed the complete destruction of the city.

Now the town has a new prosperity as a destination for travellers – the centre was swamped by tourist shops and brown, scantily clad people from all over the world, perhaps not unlike the swarming Roman crowds of the second century. My guide from Antalya told me he had worked in Side one summer but he still lost his way coming into town because all the streets he knew had been pulled down to build a tower suburb of apartments. He knew some people running an orange-juice bar, so we sat and had refreshing juice. The old man who owned the shop was seventy, unshaven and grumpy, and he didn't smile. He'd been a farmer who owned a house and land in the original village.

'So now he just sits and earns money without doing anything. They all pay him rent.'

He asked a high price for the orange juice – I couldn't help thinking how the ancient people of Side had had a reputation for greed, selling even their neighbours as slaves it was said, and tolerating pirates who paid them a dividend.

Side Museum was converted from Roman bathhouses and it exhibited relief carvings on altars and sarcophagi, and fragmentary sculptures in the blinding sun of open courtyards that were once the closed-in bathchambers. An abundance of lavishly decorated sarcophagus reliefs and dedicatory statues with inscriptions were mounted against the stone walls – Side was a sophisticated, literate society in Roman times. All the stones and images with their rows of words seemed to be speaking, but I couldn't understand or even hear their voices properly, while sensing an engrossing world, still undeciphered. Softly modelled heads of Apollo and Hermes from the second century held a touch of Greek vitality, of *pothos*, a longing for something beyond the present.

The museum garden reminded me evocatively of my childhood archetype of the Mediterranean 'villa garden'. A courtyard of red geraniums and rows of mulberries and cypresses was set around with sculptures along a terrace above the turquoise sea. Clouds of sparrows settled in the date palms. A headless marble Nike on a plinth tried to fly in a stream of drapery, halted by the loss of her stony wings, which lay in fine pleated feathers on the pavement on either side of her, grounding her.

3. ANTALYA MUSEUM

10 June

This morning, a little overwhelmed by strangeness and solitary travel, I walked slowly from the hotel to sit in another enticing garden, the Antalya Museum garden, to collect my thoughts, and perhaps call up any resident Muses. The wonderfully idiosyncratic sculpture garden was dotted with marble fragments under pines, oleanders and date palms. Here was a standing leg, there a male torso and a headless draped woman, while many intricately carved altars, heavy with marble wreaths or carved ivy, stood near a sundial and column capitals among pink rosebushes and cascading bougainvillea. Many of the trees had been shaped into topiary patterns, as if vegetation too should sympathise with sculpture. A man and a woman held hands, sitting close on an old stone bench. Rather than leading to domesticity and harmony, *eros* in the Greco-Roman understanding could be a sign of metamorphosis, transforming a lover into a daphne bush, a cow, a sea monster or a mulberry tree.

In the formal halls of the museum, the grandiloquence of the Pamphylians, not only in the theatre but also in death, was extraordinary. Marble sarcophagi of translucent stone from Perge, the size of small rooms, were deeply carved in relief, or with freestanding figures between spiral columns, hung with swaying carved garlands and Medusa heads. The garlands were detailed and heavy with a variety of leaves and flowers hung between curling ribbons.

One of these sarcophagi was inscribed:

> I, Marcus Aurelius Hermas of Termessos, have ordained that while still alive, this cenotaph is for my wife Aurelia Agaraste and myself only. None else shall be granted permission for burying another corpse inside, otherwise a fine of 50,000 denarii to be paid to the imperial treasury shall be imposed on this person.

What confidence in bureaucracy – and in the continuance of culture. I seemed to recognise this voice from my own time. Here's another imperious statement on another immense sarcophagus from second century Perge:

> I, Aurelia Botlare Demetria, commissioned this sarcophagus for my own self. I believe that my corpse only shall be buried in it, and sealed with iron and lead by my heirs immediately after my death.

But poor Aurelia's wonderful sarcophagus was re-used two centuries later, and a much later sculpture added of a reclining couple, with the man's face unfinished. The sarcophagus was only discovered in 1997, dug up by smugglers in the western necropolis of Perge and then retrieved by security forces. Her splendour in death had led to an unquiet but eventful afterlife.

I paused before a solemn marble statue on an inscribed pedestal of a heavily draped woman, Plancia Magna herself, the benefactress of Perge who commissioned many buildings and statues for the city. She was considered a demi-goddess, a priestess of Artemis Pergaia, lifetime priestess of the mother of the gods, priestess-in-chief of the imperial cult.

Marble slabs with inscriptions were stacked up in the courtyard. I looked closely at a lovely text with boldly serifed letters, in a local dialect of Greek. The dense surfaces of stone were inscribed all over, as if stone was as easy to write on as paper.

One figure was quite breathtaking, a more than life-size dancer in two colours of marble, her white marble face and arms, smooth as flesh, contrasting with her drapery of dark stone floating against gravity as she twisted through the air, her graceful head slightly tilted to one side. She was found in the extensive baths of Perge in 1981. The haunting Hellenistic figures of Pergamon were still in the mind's eye of the sculptor, and this figure may be a direct copy from a sculpture of the fourth or third centuries BC, now lost.

I read on a wall text in the museum, 'The ancient ports of Attaleia and Side were important Mediterranean commercial centres, trading grain, olive oil, wine, timber, wild boar, horses, fish, salt, textiles and furniture'. Alexander took the cities of Perge, Sillyon, Aspendos and Side in 333 BC and then, after his death, they belonged to the Hellenistic dynasty of the Attalids at Pergamon. The golden age of peace and wealth so celebrated by Edward Gibbon began in the second and third centuries, under the Antonine emperors.

Pamphylia was bounded on the west by the province of Lycia, a steep coast fissured by rivers and rich valleys full of astonishing sites such as Myra and Olympos. To the north was Pisidia, a very mountainous district, bounded to the east and north by Phrygia. Although these places are now almost unpopulated and for that reason are isolated and difficult of access, once there were more than fifty Hellenistic and Roman sites, some perched in perilous high locations such as Selge and Sagalossos. Reading the sonorous lists of unknown but once famous cities – Antiphellus, Aperlae, Arykanda, Balbura, Kalynda, Khoma, Korydalla, Limyra, Olympos, Oenanda, Patara, Phaselis, Rhodiapolis, Telmessus, Tlos, Trebenna, Xanthus – few of them completely excavated or even surveyed, is like discovering a litany of little known and fabulous countries.

After leaving the museum I walked in the intense heat of the day through the substantial old town of Antalya at Kaleiçi, once a Roman port. It is very like old Rhodes, with Ottoman houses, graceful and well proportioned. The empty and collapsing ones are slowly being restored into charming small hotels or restaurants along narrow streets. I found some formidable Selçuk buildings in the jumble of architecture; suddenly a glimpse of order and power in the great gate built by the Selçuk grand vizier Cemaleddin Karatay in 1250. A small Fiat car was parked neatly in the pointed archway. I leaned against the wall in the deserted street and drew the intricate interlaced carving in the pale gold stone almost obscured by abundant caper bushes. Some people drinking tea in another doorway smiled and waved.

Walking around the exquisite little harbour at dusk I remembered those lost and vanished textiles once traded across the Hellenistic Mediterranean, those 'tapestries woven of gold and silver' referred to in the wall texts of the Antalya museum. As consolation, I came across a carpet shop above the marina with a wonderful reproduction of the ancient Pazyryk carpet in muted reds, greens and cream, about two and a half metres square, hung against a stone wall. The owner found it easy to draw me in, as always, even without the promise of apple tea. The original carpet was found encased in ice in the Altai Mountains of Siberia in 1949, and is dated to the third century BC. Most likely it was commissioned by Persian rulers from the renowned Armenian weavers described by Herodotus, as it shows men riding stallions in an outer border, with reindeer or elk in an inner border around a grid of star-shaped floral patterns. The composition woven here of the Pazyryk carpet has had to be re-drawn from that original embedded in ice, but the Turkish knot in which it was woven is still in use. A textile, like oral poetry and music, reproduces itself through entrenched skills and a pattern remembered through mnemonic devices of sound and pattern. Sometimes the sequence of patterns is chanted in carpet workshops. In another shop I saw reproductions of Picasso and Kandinsky, minutely woven in fine silk knots, as if they were as distant in time, or as close, as the Pazyryk carpet.[4]

I feel much more foreign here than I do in Cyprus or Greece. Many Turks look at me in silence, with sad eyes. The expensive Falez Hotel is full of Turks, but few even glance at me to say good morning, as if I were invisible, which perhaps I am – a woman travelling alone. Even the women in the hotel, if we are all standing in a lift, look anxiously at their reflections in the mirror, and avert their eyes from me. All the varied and lovely greetings so familiar in Greek are absent in this setting, because I am dumb not only in the Turkish language but also in the mores, the etiquette of this society. This is not 'home' yet, and although the ancient part of it is recognisable it is so much richer, more substantial and extravagantly fashioned than the Greco-Roman world of Cyprus that I feel I've entered another region of experiencing the past. I move carefully, almost holding my breath, through both ancient and contemporary spaces.

The tremulous evening sea stretches to the horizon, and the triangular purple mountains are like stage sets, as Freya Stark observed. She would find it hard to believe the city of towers that has appeared along the coast like another stage prop. The clusters of immense white and glassy buildings catch the light – accentuating sculptured and geometrical forms completely unrelated to the old historical town at their foot. The towering hotels are set down on the beach side to the west of the old town like giant stranded liners, a universe of concerns set apart, self sufficient, away from the ordinary life of the town. 'The hotels are full but the people don't come into town,' said Ithan, the tour operator.

In my own fantasy hotel room high in the night sky I watched a Turkish fashion show on TV. Amazingly slender girls wore almost unusable clothes – glittering gold shreds hung from a nipple, tiny wisps curled from an arm or thigh – clothes for extreme desires. Sometimes, I imagined, there was a faint allusion to the ancient metamorphosis of desire into animal or plant, in sparkling fake fur or stamen-like fronds. By comparison how robust those Roman bodies were, imbued with physical power and *dignitas*.

4. ASPENDOS

11 June

On a very hot night I caught a bus to the famous, almost complete theatre of Aspendos, with hundreds of other people, to attend a performance of Beethoven's Ninth Symphony. It's about forty-five kilometres east of Antalya across a plain bordered by flat-topped hills and tomato houses, with the jagged peaks of the Taurus Mountains always in view. The sudden appearance of the fortress-like building looming beside the road was a shock to me. I'd never seen an ancient theatre with an intact auditorium, galleries and stage building. The impressive scale of the great stone box of the Aspendos theatre reminded me again, like the Perge theatre, of sombre Florentine Renaissance palaces with their heavily 'rusticated' stone walls and fortified arched gateways.

Great throngs of people arrived noisily by bus and car, greeted by water sellers, women kneading *pide* bread and cooking kebabs, boys selling cushions made out of plastic from fertiliser bags, all lined up around the public fountain and calling out to passers-by. People moved slowly in through the vaulted *parodos* entrance, in an orderly way – this was the only entrance. You could take inner flights of stairs (*vomitoria*) to the top seating, or you could walk directly into the *orchestra* and proceed up the stairs of the curving stone steps. It was memorable seeing how the theatre functioned, at last, after working in the ruins of Paphos. All those people went into the high arched entrance beneath inscriptions in Greek and Latin stating that 'two brothers, Curtius Crispinus and Curtius Auspicatus, commissioned the building and dedicated it to the gods and the imperial family' during the time of the emperor Marcus Aurelius, AD 161-80. In under an hour the procession of the audience moved steadily through the dim-arched tunnel of the *parodos* – lower at its entrance, and rising to a higher arched doorway into the *orchestra*. The walls of the entrance were of heavy corrugated stone, rough but still showing concrete-like patches of plaster.

What struck me was how the towering stage building cut off all views outward to the surrounding country, although some spiky mountains could just be seen against the darkening sky. It was like being in a huge cage, open to the cloudless blue-green sky, with a few stars and half a moon. People carried children, and cushions to soften the hard stone benches, bought bottles of water and little snacks, waved to friends, and having decided on a place, walked around taking photos. Gradually the tiers of seats filled up with thousands of people. The orchestra filed in from their own front entrance into the *skene* (and actually set up in the *orchestra*) and began tuning up in a hum and throb of discordant sounds. Above them a temporary wooden stage had been constructed for the singers, decorated with a Chinese dragon, as an opera by Verdi was to follow. The dragon did not seem out of place in that overwhelming space. I tried to estimate the crowd – a hundred people to a row, twenty rows in each tier of seating, and few empty spaces. It might have been eight or ten thousand people, to hear Beethoven at night in the middle of Turkey.

Around the top of the tiered seats was a marvellously theatrical arched colonnade, also plastered, though I could not see any paint in that night light. (I was stopped from walking here by a soldier, who said it was dangerous.) Such a breathlessly hot night, with not a cloud – a faint wind was refreshing about 10.30. The weather was a stereotype of holiday weather, with unremitting sun in the day and the moon at night, in cloudless skies.

Individual sounds were outlined, hung in the air – a baby crying, a bottle falling. I sat high up beneath the arches of the gallery, which, I found later, was the traditional area for women. No one in my section of the crowd spoke English – they spoke German, and Turkish. A boy moved around the stairs selling bottles of water from a plastic basket. Children got settled on cushions. The enormous choir brought from all over Turkey filed in – the State Opera and Ballet Chorus, with the Mersin Opera and Ballet Orchestra.

I remembered the story in *The Golden Ass* by Apuleius, that lively second-century storyteller, about a time when he was given a mock trial. Very often, vital judicial and political decisions were made in the theatre, just because of the intense communication possible between speaker and audience through the design of the architecture. Apuleius wrote:

> Since the trial was of such unusual interest the magistrates agreed to a change of venue; and the crowd emptied itself into the theatre with remarkable speed. Every single seat was occupied, every entrance blocked; even the roof was alive with people. Some balanced on the pediments of columns, some clung to statues, some squeezed themselves in at the windows or straddled the rafters; nobody seemed to pay the least attention to his own safety in the general desire to witness my trial. The constables led me across the stage and placed me right in front, close to the orchestra.[5]

The way the tiered seats focused vision was unexpected: I could see the faces of the singers and the gestures of the conductor with great clarity, as if normal vision were enhanced and dramatised. The smiling Minister for Culture, opening the festival, welcomed us in English and Turkish to 'the only Roman theatre that survives after 2,000 years in such a solid and enduring state'. The concentrated attention by thousands of viewers enhances the intense response by the performers. For an hour or so ordinary life recedes, and perception is enlarged and extended.

The stage building must once have had a baroque magnificence. One of the marble plinths for a statue was carved in an elliptical series of curves, with faint inscriptions. Acanthus reliefs in jungle varieties were just visible on the top level, while the first story had *bucrania*, ox's horns, and garlands. Although the stage building is now very battered, the underlying structure is intact, with three levels and two tiers of niches for statues of gods, heroes and emperors, a backdrop that offered a dramatic cosmology for the actors. Deeply coloured frescoes and carvings would have added to the effect. Five doors led onto the stage above the *orchestra*. In the triangular pediment at the centre of the upper level I could just see the relief of Dionysos, the god of theatre, its founder and patron looking rubbed and blurred with age and exposure.

Dionysos was the masked god, a god of many identities, who appeared and disappeared at will in many guises, sometimes even in a form that is neither man nor woman but with attributes of both. The god of theatre could engineer apparitions, could suddenly appear (the meaning of 'epiphany')[6]. I understood, watching the orchestra, how exaggerated masks and costumes, wigs and platform shoes would give a vivid sense of fantastic drama and engender imaginative spaces where the psyche could escape the everyday through both tragedy and farcical humour.

The architect of the Aspendos theatre was Zeno, who is supposed to have won the competition to build the theatre because of his skill with acoustics. Even a whisper, it was said, could be heard in all parts of the auditorium.

I couldn't imagine how an awning could be stretched over such a huge extent of the seating and *orchestra*, yet some sort of shade would have been necessary. In antiquity plays were held during the day, not at night. Even late at night, the lichened stone seats were still warm from the great heat of the sun poured onto them all day. I could see some sort of zigzag painted decoration high up on the *skene*, and resolved to return in daylight.

There was absolute silence before the orchestra played those first notes, low and clear, making me feel that electronic sound must be slightly fuzzy compared to this absolute clarity. I thought Beethoven would have been pleased with the glorious resonance of sound; the curved stone shell did seem to amplify it, transforming the Ninth Symphony into something different from the composition known almost too well since childhood. Many recordings of the Ninth Symphony may be more perfect than that performance but the occasion in the ancient theatre of Aspendos made it a transcendent experience, momentarily. It was sung with a slightly idiosyncratic timing, but the solo voices were true and piercing, allowing me to hear the music as if for the first time.

'Classical' music is constructed on the same principles as classical architecture: mathematical formulae to evoke shapes of order. The rhythm of the high narrow arches in the upper gallery seemed to echo the patterns of the music. I was unprepared for the encompassing and breathtaking sound. Like colour and fabric, taste and smell, the loudness and softness of the sounds of the past has vanished. I had remembered in the precipitous Pergamon theatre Vitruvius' description of architects who 'had perfected the ascending rows of seats in the theatre from their investigation of the ascending voice'. Now I was able to hear the singing lifting up and reverberating in the stone shell of the building, as if it were itself a musical instrument designed to enhance and focus sound.

The response of the audience was ecstatic at the end of the performance. They wanted more, but the conductor, a large man with a bushy grey head, would have none of it. Then surprisingly, a complete choir started singing from the *cavea*, a group in the audience obviously from Germany. They stood clustered together, high up in the auditorium and sang a Bach chorale that sounded piercing and uncanny in the dusky theatre under the ultramarine sky. The rhythms echoed the repetitive arches and curve of the seats. The singing was greeted with more enthusiasm, and then with a kind of collective sigh the massive crowd moved slowly out through the tunnelled stairs and the one open entrance, emptying the theatre in twenty minutes. (The ancient theatre structure was very efficient in controlling the crowd, but in the parking area there was complete chaos as hundreds of vehicles jammed the exits.)

I went back to Aspendos a few days later and in the solid heat of midday examined the plastered surfaces. There were traces of fresco on the *skene* wall to the left of the stage, with rows of zigzags in a deep red – from the Selçuk time when the theatre was used as a caravanserai (an originally Persian word for a travellers' inn) and embellished with tiles and fresco. How strange that the theatre in fact fits the needs of an inn, a place where a company of merchants could put up for the night, travelling together for the sake of security – the caravanserai is typically a large quadrangular building enclosing a spacious court. Another set of customs, different kinds of food, stories from further east must have inhabited the theatre for several hundred years. Perhaps the merchants slept in the many rooms of the stage building, or in the capacious arched gallery above the seats, while animals were tethered in the *orchestra*. The small entrances could have been easily defended. One should not look at one time in history without considering all the overlapping events.

I scrutinised the patches of plaster in the upper gallery and there were traces of painting, but just stains and splotches now – perhaps a faint group of black parallel lines? The many layers of plaster could have been from all periods. I was fascinated to see that the theatre was made of a coarse conglomerate stone, coarse like the sandy limestone of the Paphos theatre. This roughness made the use of smooth plaster comprehensible, to brighten and enrich the surface so that it could look more like shining marble, the most prestigious building material.

As I walked around the building in the saturated sunlight the stage machinery from the previous night's Verdi was being taken down and put into trucks – much noise and shouts from workers moving sets amongst groups of tourists. It seemed a lovely irony that Chinese dragons were carved on the sets; this theatre has seen every kind of hybridity from East and West. A babel of language could be heard all around; French, German, Russian proclaimed the new visitors, and emphasised the vigorous life of the theatre as part of a popular tourist festival of arts. The building continues to evolve and transform itself as if the original conception of its architecture had an innate flexibility to all kinds of performances.

I climbed up the top of the hill behind the theatre, situated like the Paphos theatre facing a south-east direction, but much bigger. The view was awe-inspiring, crops of yellow grain glowed under the sun, and in the distance were the white Taurus Mountains. A river wound through the valley, crossed by an ancient arched bridge, while other arches of an extensive aqueduct that once supplied the city marched across fields dotted with tomato houses. Perhaps this panorama would still be recognisable to a viewer from the second century. The hardly excavated city of Aspendos waits on the acropolis above the theatre, marked by the crenellated, ruined basilica towering above humps and mounds. What aspirations those people had – the magnitude of the city planning and a sense of possibility in the grandeur and scope of the architecture was astonishing.

Evening

High latticed windows in the old town of Antalya allowed a glimpse of the bay beyond the jumble of roofs and houses, in various stages of repair. 'It costs more to restore than to build a new one,' said Naci the carpet seller, when I lingered in his shop. I bought an exquisite old and faded kilim in reds, greys and a touch of gold, and cushion covers made from fragments of soumaks and Uzbekistan embroidery, for friends and family.

In the jumbled heart of Kaleiçi I came across a wild and complex ruin, abandoned rather than nicely set out for display to tourists. An interlude for reflection in the centre of a square; the ruin called the Korcut Mosque stood fenced off, full of rubbish, overgrown with giant asphodel. Bushy outgrowths hung from the remnants of tall piers and arches, almost covering an exquisite marble door frame carved with egg and dart ornament of the second century. A Byzantine marble column had a capital of woven stone, and other bits of classical marble were inserted in a Byzantine wall. Once it had been a great Byzantine Church of the Virgin. Some arches were formed by the clean-cut Selçuk style, when the building was converted into a mosque, yet there were echoes still of the basilica, signs of an apse. Cats crouched quietly in the shadows. In the hot afternoon time seemed suspended as I walked around the square observing all the facets of the ruin. A thin and friendly carpet seller followed me, some remarkable silk carpets (Kurdish, he said) over his arm. Other carpets had been spread in the thick shade of a mulberry tree and a heavy man slept there as if he would never awaken.

Outside the small shops people sat quietly drinking tea, the violently romantic ruin invisible to them because of its familiarity – the whole scene glimpsed and held in the mind as if mimicking a nineteenth-century watercolour where peasants go about their ordinary life amongst the ruins of the past. But, I realised, the sense of space in this town is quite different to that picturesque perspective with its foreground, middle ground and deep distance.

It is odd that I can never find the sea when I am in Kaleiçi, the roads curve and block the view of it with buildings. It is the art of pattern that is dominant, rather than the way through, rather than the deep perspective of more western cities that pulls you into the distance, into the future. The houses look inwards, as the Turks excel at the inner garden behind high walls, small but satisfying arrangements with detailed colour and texture of gleaming pools, herbs, flowers and fruit trees. But there is no view dragging you away, no vista or perspective to tantalise with longing.

5. LYCIA: OLYMPOS

12 June

Yesterday while reading about Termessos and feeling tired, with pains in the joints and back, I decided to find a guide to take me to the remote theatre sites around Antalya. Many of these are situated at the end of long mountainous dirt roads. I went to hire not only a car but a driver as well, one who spoke a little English. After asking in three or four places, I settled for what seemed a reasonable fee. The old white Toyota Corolla arrived at 7.30 in the morning with Mehmet driving impeccably. There was no air conditioning but his gentle courtesy made me feel very luxurious – to have a guide and a chauffeur allowed me to concentrate on the inner narrative that must accompany the outer journey.

My guidebook said that the province of Lycia on the coast west of Antalya had a 'thoroughly original civilisation' and thirty-six mountainous settlements forming a 'mysterious world' known for a fierce love of freedom and independence. The guidebooks for all the sites in this area, written by Turkish archaeologists in a mild and scholarly style have illuminated my journeys with instructions for 'pleasant options'. Most of these extraordinary sites are slowly being excavated, with modest funding and the limited capacities of small museums. The buried wealth of the ancient cities is like a natural resource, and it seems wise not to excavate without full resources of equipment and personnel. With such riches lying around, looting of sites and illegal smuggling out of Turkey is a continual problem.

The tiny theatre at Olympos on the coast of Lycia was an enchanted place (Olympos is a favourite ancient name). The Hellenistic city was built along a narrow valley beside a river, with crags and steep forest towering above the track that meandered through the valley, scattered with ruins. The strangeness of the place was accentuated by tree houses of the Solym nomads who come here every summer, houses and tents nearly hidden in the forest. The buildings had almost returned to nature, the rocks so lichened and overgrown that the precise cut surface, the relief carving of ornament was not immediately apparent. No archaeologist, no earth-moving equipment had ever disturbed the soil, which must be dense with treasures.

Mehmet seemed lit up by the thrill of finding theatres and set off along tracks and paths like a man inspired. I realised he felt proud of the unconsidered past, pleased to be able to find and display these places for me, who had come from Australia with this fixed idea of looking at theatres. As my personal chauffeur and guide, he approached people to find exact locations, explaining what we were doing, even organising where to eat, and through his translation my presence became comprehensible and interesting. It was a great relief to me to have our roles so clearly set out; I think it was a comfort to both of us. It was a marvel to him that I had come from so far. To be a guide to curious travellers and scholars has been an important and dignified task here since the eighteenth century. Freya Stark makes it clear that without such guides her travel to the same remote sites would have been impossible. In mythology Hermes was the guide, the psychopomp who led souls to the underworld through trackless terrain to the fearful river of Lethe, river of Forgetfulness. The Greek word for truth is still *alithia*, a word meaning 'not forgetting'. To remember a little of what had been forgotten, to find the scumbled forms of structures almost dissolved, to perceive the forgotten cities struck by Lethe became for me a most absorbing task. Mehmet became my guide for this 'unforgetting'.

Near the centre of Olympos, lost and silent among rocks and

trees, I followed a brown goat through dense pines and came suddenly across a small theatre. The goat trotted around the site very knowingly, like a reincarnation of some satyric presence, as I stumbled over roots and dense pine needles. The arched *parodos* leading to the *orchestra* was still intact although leaves and earth almost choked the entrance. I bent over and made my way through it to see the theatre seats sunk and overgrown, but with remnants of a balustrade from the stage building still in place. The large stones of the *cavea* wall were heavily bossed. It may have held three thousand people – small compared to the immense theatres of Aspendos or Perge but comparable in size to the theatre I had visited in Alexandria. The enclosing forest has made the theatre part of some natural world, part of a different kind of species – I thought a 'wild' theatre, as one might say a 'wild' rose. As I sat in the theatre, caught in the strangeness and wonder of the place – sweet resin of pine needles in the heat, cicadas in cypresses, a yellow butterfly – the goat hurried into the theatre through the arched *parodos*. She maa'd at me, looking confused, and went straight through to the other entrance; like a ghost of some memory, her gestures were like a woman distracted and anxious who had lost something. Watching her, the boundary between animal and human became less certain.

Wandering in the forest by the sea, I came across a substantial curved wall of finely cut white marble with trees arched over as if to complete the form. There was an arch in the wall almost hidden behind bushes, and there on the other side a tall tower with small windows. Was it a watchtower, to look out to sea? Then further on, a wall of grey 'Cyclopean' stones, honeycombed together, and a rhythm of arches entangled in vines, half smothered by dense oak and holly. High-roofed graves stood under pines. Looking at a plan later I found these architectural fragments belonged to the baths, the agora and the great wharves which once stood by the river.

With Mehmet (he seemed as enthralled as I in discovering the ruins in the forest) I walked down to the beach beside the deep transparency of the green river which blended across a sand bar into the cerulean sea. The river, with the ruined town on each bank, flowed between steep rocky crags jutting into the sea. The sea was the main highway in antiquity, and its ineffable blue looked calm and heavenly at this moment in early June. Against one of the rocky overhangs appeared two tall Lycian sarcophagi carved of pale yellow marble with peaked roofs. Beneath a pediment with a Medusa head was inscribed the shallow relief of a curved boat without sails, with the figure of a woman, Aphrodite, engraved on the prow, one slender arm outstretched as if swimming. She was, of course, always the goddess of sailors, because born from foam. Here is a glimpse from Lucretius:

> Sweet Venus, who under the wheeling signs of heaven
> Rouse the ship-shouldering sea and the fruitful earth
> And make them teem – for through you all that breathe
> Are begotten, and rise to see the light of the sun;
> From you goddess, the winds flee, from you and your coming
> Flee the storms of heaven; for you the artful earth
> Sends up sweet flowers, for you the ocean laughs
> And the calm skies shimmer in a bath of light.[7]

These were the graves of Marcus Aurelius Zosimas, and his uncle Captain Eudemos, who had sailed as far as the Sea of Marmara and the Black Sea. (He must surely have sailed to Paphos, only a few days away in summer weather.) The faint Greek inscription was roughly translated on a plaque nearby, in Turkish and English:

> The ship sailed into the last horizon and anchored to leave no more
> There was no longer any hope from the wind or daylight
> After the light carried by the dawn had left Captain Eudemos
> There they buried him and his ship, with a life as short as a day,
> Like a broken wave.

There were a multitude of small ancient ports like Olympos all around the coasts, lining the highway of the Mediterranean, so that modest ships like that of Captain Eudemos could make their way to far countries, keeping close to the coast. Like the same little ports today, there would be a muddle of trade, arrivals and departures. Here is a vivid fragment of St Augustine in the late fourth century when Olympos was still a flourishing town. He is remembering his mother Monica in Carthage on the Mediterranean coast of Africa, when he left her to sail to Rome: 'The wind rose and filled our sails, the shore slipped from our sight and on that shore, in the morning light she stood in a frenzy of grief.'[8]

It is recorded that Olympos was a great and notable city when the emperor Hadrian stayed here for some time in the second century. Now it is a favourite place for backpackers, who come not for the scattered ruins but for the white pebble beach set among rocky headlands and most of all, for the luminous sea. Walking out from the shadowy pines the liquid blue looked breathtaking in the white light. Out in the open the heat felt almost dangerous in its intensity. I sat for a while near some salt-stained English speakers who were discussing travel plans and scratching vaguely at tattoos that patterned their young lithe bodies, staring at the sea. It was the proximity of the city to the edge of the Mediterranean that eventually led to its abandonment – its riches were too vulnerable to the pirates who successfully hid out along this intricate coastline.

Mehmet and I walked back up from the beach along the ancient path beside the river. Young Turkish men walked ahead of us, slim and brown. In the shade of the forest a spring trickled into a clear cold pool, damned with old architectural stones, and one by one they immersed themselves in the fresh cool water, washing off the heat and salt. Mehmet spoke to the older man who accompanied them – he was a retired university teacher, a well-known artist. The boys bending to wash themselves were as beautiful as an ancient frieze.

6. LYCIA: MYRA

13 June

Along the coastal road for another forty kilometres or so from Olympos we came to Demre, the ancient Lycian city of Myra. Mehmet found other drivers that he knew, and sat down at a deeply shaded outside table to have some tea and catch up on the news, while I set out to explore.

Beneath a high acropolis, against a soaring rocky outcrop, appeared the sweeping curve of the theatre of Myra. All through Lycia the importance of grave monuments is noticeable – the little tomb dwellings and large memorials are set close to the places of the living. The clamour of the dead reached a climax in the Myra theatre, set below a sheer cliff honeycombed with a network of tombs. Dated to the fourth century BC, they were already nearly five hundred years old when the Roman theatre was built. Each was carved like the façade of a house, with elaborate windows and doors topped by pediments resting on the round sections of roof beams, interspersed with fragments of sculptured relief. Squinting into the glare of the sun, I saw two running figures and a blurred inscription, while higher up in the cliff face was a carving of a nude soldier holding a shield. The audience must have sat with their backs to this elaborate necropolis where their ancestors lived – in fact the dead could look right down into the theatre, and, peering through their windows, appreciate the performance in the *orchestra* far below. Further around the cliff was a deep cave above the theatre with figs and pomegranates growing at the entrance – the glowing red flowers of the pomegranate hovering against the darkness.

If Dionysos was the god of shifting identities and inchoate emotions amongst the living, he was also notable for blurring the boundaries between the living and the dead. Carved sarcophagi show the heavy garlands laden with fruit and flowers carried in the Dionysian procession of bacchantes and satyrs, playing music and enraptured by the dance. The mystery religion of Eleusis near Athens famously revealed to its initiates the secret of life, not to be revealed on pain of death. The mysteries were closely associated not only with Hades, god of the underworld, but also with Dionysos, the god of epiphanies. (The secret, the central mystery of life was never fully revealed, but there are intimations that an ear of wheat, a poppy, and a covered basket held the clues.) In nearly every theatre I visited on this Mediterranean coast there were long narrative relief sculptures associated with Dionysos and his life, just as, a little later, the lives of the saints would become the theme of the theatre of the church. The theatre itself, the performance space where the everyday world gave way to an imaginative drama played by masked actors, was on the boundary between the known and the unknown, and usually situated a little away from the central activities of the marketplace and the town.

The Myra theatre was another confident second-century Roman structure, built up and into the rock with an intriguing structure of arches and two concentric passageways (*vomitoria*) that twisted around and under the theatre as curved and stepped tunnels leading to the highest seats. I was reminded of the temporary theatres that were erected in Sydney for the Olympic Games. Made of reinforced steel the supporting structure for the tiered seats (identical in function to the ancient theatres) was locked together in an elaborate vertical and horizontal scaffolding carrying the weight of the seats and the audience, just like the engineering marvel of the Roman arched vault.

Above the central walkway of the Myra theatre (the *diazoma*) there was a niche with the battered form of a draped woman, with a cornucopia on her left arm, the figure of Tyche, with an inscription to her: 'Fortune of the city be ever victorious, with good luck.'

I had found a similar dedication to Tyche in Perge and on an inscription above the theatre of Dionysos in Athens. Tyche was the goddess of fate, of luck, of chance, liable to afflict and strike down even a good and prosperous person. Tragic theatre detailed the trials of fate, the sufferings of a reasonable human being who may find himself or herself in an impossible situation, through the agency of Tyche. For example, Oedipus imagined himself the 'fortunate son of Tyche', blessed at finding himself king of Thebes, but in fact he finds out Fortune has played a cruel trick on him, allowing him through mistaken identities to kill his father and marry his mother.

At a more ordinary level, Apuleius' story of Roman life, *The Golden Ass*, makes it clear that ill luck is catching. To be free but abjectly poor is a sign of bad luck and people of better class should carefully avoid all personal contact with ill luck.

In the transfixing heat of the afternoon I set out to examine the spectacular theatre. The *parodos* entrance into the theatre from the south was open to the skies while the one to the north was arched over, very high up, like that of Perge. The walls had never been plastered, but the stones were bossed — each one with a smooth edge and left rough in the centre. An English traveller, Fellows, in the 1840s observed life-size painted figures in red, blue, yellow and purple in the Painted Tomb cut into the cliff. No sign of any painted surfaces remained in the theatre itself. Wandering high up in the seating I found holes in the parapet which might have held up the awnings so necessary in this radiant heat. Here is Lucretius, a contemporary of the Myra theatre, writing about the vivid colour of the spectacle:

> Awnings, saffron-yellow or iron-blue
> Or russet, stretched taut over wide theatres,
> Ripple above the beams and the poles and the people.
> Beneath from the bleachers down to the boxes and all
> The stage itself and the senators in their regalia
> They dye it all and make it ripple with colour;
> And the closer the walls are huddled around the theatre
> Catching the sunshine, the more will all within
> Laugh in a wash of colourful delight.[9]

A high balustrade stretched around the floor of the *orchestra*, which was still heaped with a pile of exquisitely carved architectural stones that must have come from the stage building. Special marble seats with griffins' bodies lay on the heap, once used for senior officials and priests. Nearby on the ground a relief carving of masks and rosettes formed a frieze, the black void of the masked mouths open in a silent shout.

Alluring fragments of marble columns and sculptures lay scattered around, fragments that would have been prized in most museums. Most strangely, staring up from the dirt, I nearly stumbled on a riveting head of Medusa, her hair twined with snakes, blindly gazing at the sun as if to halt its movement across the sky. Her dreadful gaze was another image that might stop fate and turn your luck around, expelling any malevolent eye that might blight or maim you. She too is carved on tombs and sarcophagi (as I saw in Alexandria) as an apotropaic emblem to turn away evil.

Myra was another ancient city linked to Paphos through the travels of St Paul – his ship stopped in the port of Myra on the way to Rome about AD 60. And early Christian Myra was renowned for being the home of St Nicholas, the miracle-working saint who was kind to children, and who became a primary saint in Greek Orthodoxy, and a protective icon for seamen. The fragmentary church of St Nicholas at Demre (built on the site of a sixth-century basilica, like Kourion or Paphos in Cyprus) was familiar, with its barrel-vaulted aisles and remnants of domes. The sarcophagus of St Nicholas once held his body, before it was abducted to southern Italy. The building is a museum now, an arched and reflective space, somewhere between a mosque and a church and remarkable for its jewel- like *opus sectile* floor of coloured marbles polished by centuries of feet coming to see the shrine of the great saint, patron of Russia, Father Christmas.

A guide leaned on the chipped and ancient altar (so like the pagan ones – it could easily have been one.) 'Why would pirates from Bari take the bones of the saint?' (All stories of prosperity seem to end in pirates on this coast.) He answered the question himself. 'Because such relics were great and precious treasure, equal to gold and jewels, or even a powerful laptop computer. They gave the owner influence and authority, and the possibility of miracles.' It occurred to me that archaeologists are the relic hunters today, seeking another kind of revelation. The faded paintings of rows of saints in the dome of St Nicholas were a dim echo of the storytelling friezes in the theatres, placating and personifying mysterious deities who might control our lives.

7. PISIDIA: TERMESSOS

14 June

A few days ago I moved from the lavish Falez Hotel, where Hüsamettin had arranged to pay for everything (even the raki and room service meals). Very few people had spoken to me in that wonderful palatial hotel. On leaving I went to the receptionist who had looked at me blankly during my stay, and gave him a letter of thanks to give to the manager. Momentarily his indifferent politeness changed to something much warmer. 'Thank you, I will take it to him myself,' he said, and actually smiled.

I was now able to sit outside at breakfast near a fountain, in the lovely courtyard of the comfortable Dogon Hotel. I had discovered the air-conditioned hotel, a restored Ottoman house, in the old part of town close to the harbour. Orange trees with trunks painted white stood in the courtyard, enclosed by the soft ochre walls. I watched a small man sweeping leaves from the stone pavement. His shirt proclaimed in large English letters JOY AND FUN, a good sign for the day. An entrancing deep swimming pool lay in an adjacent courtyard, lined with small mosaic tiles in many shades of blue, with a waterfall at one end. In the blindingly hot days to come, climbing over stony baking sites, I would think of the clear cobalt depths of this pool with intense pleasure, and return from exhausting hikes to sink into its coolness.

In the freshly cleaned Toyota, Mehmet arrived, smiling in anticipation as we left Antalya behind, heading north-west into the foothills for the mountain site of Termessos. Short in stature and contained in presence, Mehmet was an experienced driver. Even though the car kept stalling, he coaxed it along. He was patient and helpful – an intelligent man who had not had many opportunities. Once he had played the cello, but he had worked for Avis cars since 1980. He was 48 years old and had two children. Mehmet had never left Turkey. He preferred to play classical western music on the car radio, rather than Turkish music.

We passed pink oleanders on dry riverbeds, a farm truck unravelling hay along the road, a rose garden beside a crumbling village, steep foothills with wild hollyhocks. Above in the rocky heights, were tiers of fortifications, almost blending with the tissue of the mountain itself.

Mehmet parked under some pines and pointed out the ancient paved road winding steeply into the mountains to the city of Termessos. A few distant figures, tourists with backpacks, gave scale to the extensive ruins that I could just discern spread over the spectacular hills and stony ravines. I walked upwards alone, among minty herbs; oregano, tall yellow spikes of rocket, pink pea, convolvulus, hollyhocks, broom and some last rock roses flickering with butterflies of all colours. Shy birds darted after grasshoppers. Pine, oak and holly grew in the thick forests that nearly consumed the site, and many other trees I did not name.

As I walked up the long path alone towards the mountain towering before me, Mount Güllük (Mt Rose Garden, Mehmet told me) glittered in the unshadowed light, sprinkled with small pines like a Chinese painting. I felt very alone suddenly, and yet imagined

I was not quite solitary, sensing a step, a rhythm beside me up the steep track. The thrusting scrubby forest nearly obscured great sculptured and chiselled stones, walls, whole buildings, suspended in the great quiet of the high mountain. The silence was so intense it was like a sound, numinous, as though you could reach back and hear the past – I strained to hear voices, and imagined I heard goat bells and distant cries. (In the hypnotic repetition of the Australian bush this apparition of sound can happen in the ringing silence of a particular place. Living in a lonely eucalyptus forest I used to hear at night the persistent crying of a baby among the pinpricks of crickets and the hoots of mopoke owls.)

The heat rang down in almost blinding light, every stone revealed like a Miro painting where each object creates its own world. As I looked and gradually focused on the tumble of stones I suddenly saw a carved relief of a torso of a soldier, and the *spolia*, the armour of war in relief. I was moving towards almost complete buildings densely shrouded in trees and vines. Here was a carved metope from a pediment, there a shadowy inscription. A spiral tendril on a lintel lay among columns precisely engraved and fluted. Inscriptions were scattered among the large architectural stones as if about to speak – written in Greek letters, but using the local language of the Anatolian Solyms who first built the city, probably in Homeric times. I could see that the lie of the fallen stones made sense – as if the structure had just been knocked over, and could easily be put together like a child's set of building blocks, even though it had lain like that for centuries.

It was awe-inspiring to move unhindered into a town abandoned in antiquity, but still so much in place. I imagined myself like the romantic travellers discovering the ruins of Greece in the early nineteenth century, when all lay entwined and untouched by the present. In fact, Termessos had been rediscovered in 1841, and visited by the English travellers T. Spratt and G. Forbes in 1842. Graf Lanckoronski studied in detail the monuments above ground and published two volumes of descriptions and drawings in Vienna in 1890-2. He managed to construe genealogies of Solym and Greek names going back eight generations from the extensive necropolis of carved tombs. His exquisite drawings were still being used in the little Termessos guidebook I had bought in Antalya.[10]

Reaching a high plateau I turned along a wide path bordered by fragments of walls and found myself looking down from the top of the seating into a small theatre, its familiar geometry just discernible under bushes and fallen stones. 'The most beautifully situated of all Pamphylian theatres,' Freya Stark had declared. 'Her children must have loved a city so high so strong, so beautiful and remote.'[11]

It was a breathtaking small theatre, probably holding about 4,000 people. Built first as a horseshoe-shaped Hellenistic theatre, the stage building and vaulted entrances linking the stage to the seats were added in Roman times, when the horseshoe curve was straightened to make a half circle. The *orchestra*, bounded by a low wall, was nearly circular in front of the small stage and was roughly sixteen metres in diameter. Three doorways were set in the stage wall, entrances that framed sky and rocky cliffs, as if this might be a stage building for flying deities who would emerge from the chasm below. The view was immense – I looked out down a canyon of mountains to the distant sea.

I clambered with difficulty over the litter of stones in the *orchestra* and noticed traces of a stage building with a tumble of beautiful spiral columns, and bits of an egg and dart architrave. I found an altar leaning in a heap of marbles at the top of the seating, where one of the main entrances to the theatre was situated. The cylindrical stone was inscribed to Artemis in Greek lettering, slightly uneven, with the pointed serifs catching the letters, dating them to the second century or later. The Greek deities of Termessos were linked to more ancient cults – Zeus Solymeus was a principal god – and as at Perge, Artemis may also have had another more eastern name.

As I stood and gazed, some Americans came up the path, easy and well dressed, overflowing with confidence. A tall man went to the edge of the stage building and peered through the empty doorway into the ravine beneath, and yelled as loudly as he could 'Budweiser!' The echo was quite shocking, mythological in its power, as if indeed there was an entity responding from the mountain. You call out your instinctive culture – this shout, the man said, laughing and pleased, was such a good ad on TV. The culture that created such a theatre is really beyond imagining – I wondered what sounds rocketed up into the tiered seats in those days. The Solyms were famous as a warlike people; evident from many stone gates and watchtowers (still almost workable) that were built into an impeccable masonry of large stones in the high city walls. Alexander tried, but he could not defeat this impregnable fortress city in 333 BC. He passed by on his way further east, merely cutting down all the city's groves of olives. But it is because Arrian mentioned Termessos in his history of Alexander that nineteenth-century travellers set out to find it again, lost to memory after being abandoned more than a thousand years before.

The little theatre is much smaller than the Paphos one, but comparable in its Hellenistic origins and in its Roman re-modelling. When the Americans had gone I spent hours clambering over rocks, drawing and measuring the *parodos*, completely absorbed in this treasure of a theatre hidden in the mountains. The vaulted *parodos* was exciting in being similar in scale to the Paphos theatre: it was about six metres long, nearly four metres wide and possibly four metres in height. I stood in the dimness of the *parodos* vault and peered through into the theatre, noticing that if there had been paintings they would have been easily visible in the strong reflected light. But there was no trace of plaster on that grey white stone scoured clean by extreme mountain weather.

I lost all sense of time while exploring the theatre and it was past midday when I returned to the car. Mehmet had been worried when

I didn't reappear after an hour or so, and had gone all over the site looking for me. He had become concerned with all the possibilities of falls and slips in that wild ruin. I felt I had been thoughtless of the dangers of the hidden cisterns, passages and tombs. After many explanations we sat companionably on a rock not far from some steps leading up to a cluster of elegant columns and ate the food I had brought – fetta, olives, tomatoes, and cucumbers, with the usual delicious bread, and the local orange juice like nectar.

8. SELGE

15 June

Another remote and distinctive Pisidian theatre was in the ruined city of Selge, another warlike mountain fortress and the traditional enemy of Termessos. We drove up into the Taurus Mountains, on a road going north from Aspendos through looping hairpin bends and vistas of chaotic tumbled rocks fringed with pines, sometimes heaped up in a parody of building. The forest changed from tall cypresses to lower scrubby trees. A great rushing river, the Köprüçay, hurtled down the steep valley with wonderful freshness. We stopped briefly at a canyon arched over by a Roman bridge, which Mehmet took very slowly, easing and coaxing the Corolla. Two young men were sitting by the bridge waiting for a lift up to the village of Zerk. Mehmet looked at me with raised eyebrows, I nodded, and they got in, just like Australia – a car going to a remote town along a dirt road will always pick up locals. The thin young man worked guiding tourists down the river canyon on rafts. They both looked tired and rather worn.

We crept up the dirt road, higher and higher, arriving onto a kind of plateau with four hills (I begin to recognise a Pisidian site), scattered with low village houses. The intricate terraces were cleared of stones and crops of vegetables and grain grew everywhere in tiny irregular plots. Old houses had vine-covered wooden verandas. Our arrival caused a stir, and three girls, led by the oldest, Rukiyir, enthusiastically came forward to accompany us, with Mehmet translating.

They brought hand-crocheted doilies and carved wooden spoons to sell to me. Mehmet told me that there was only primary schooling and no running water – it made him angry that the government ignored the need for basic amenities in these remote villages. We walked to the fountain near the mosque, where women were collecting water in plastic containers. Wiry barefoot children were climbing in a great cherry tree nearby, trying to reach the few cherries that still remained, very high up. Again I felt the centuries shift – the poet Sappho observed the same last unreached fruit and there is a fragment that has been rewritten and rephrased over many centuries:

> As the apple ripening on the bough, the furthermost
> Bough of all the tree, is never noticed by the gatherers,
> Or, being out of reach, is never plucked at all.[12]

Only a thousand people now live here, in a city that once had an army of twenty thousand men. Those fertile valleys between the hills must have been very richly farmed to sustain such a population. The founders of the city are connected to the Trojan War, and to the Spartans, and its history is one of fierce independence, even within the Roman rule. They spoke a Pisidian language written in Greek letters, related to an Indo-European language, Luvian. They were still strong enough at the end of the fourth century to fight the invasions of the Goths, who devastated much larger cities.

At 5 p.m. on this hot clear day the light was piercing and crystal, and being so high in the mountains lessened the oppressive heat of the plains. As we walked along the narrow road, accompanied by a cluster of children I did not at first recognise the theatre for what it was. I thought it was just another rocky hill, part of the landscape – it rose up exactly like a natural formation, supporting its own garden of cascading caper bushes and myriad wild plants not known to me. Great walnut trees grew beside inconspicuous houses set in gardens of intense blue-flowered thistles and artichokes. An encompassing quiet lay underneath the small village sounds of sheep bells, children's high voices, a woman calling and the all-pervasive sound of flowing water, streaming down the slopes from the immense snow fields of the Taurus Mountains. The village wove itself around the towering theatre exactly as if it had been a natural hill. Its old function as a human performance space seemed to be invisible to the people around, who used the structure simply as a useful rock formation.

One of the vaulted entrances had become a goat pen, and part of the seating also held an animal pen. The low houses of Zerk looked like temporary and transient huts, compared to the immensity of the theatre. The imagination needed to make and use such a structure seemed breathtaking, part of a larger conception of human possibility. I climbed up and up into the topmost seats and marvelled at its preservation. The children moved lightly up and down the seating – they had favourite places. It was a similar size to the Paphos theatre, with a seating capacity of about 9,000, but built in a horseshoe shape. I walked all around to see the *parodoi*, almost concealed and blocked by vegetation (one sealed for goats). They were low, vaulted and dark and had been added in the Roman period. There was not a trace of plaster or paint.

The little boy, Emrah, about ten years old, who accompanied me all over the theatre had an open, wondering face and kept looking at me with some sort of longing. 'Schreiben,' he whispered, making writing motions with his hand. I had a green pen, which I gave to him. I hoped he would write about himself and the place he lived, and those hybrid classical ancestors who had made so much out of this difficult land.

Sitting in the topmost row of seating I could see more ruins on a hill to the west, fragments of the temples to Zeus, as a mountain god the chief deity, and to Artemis. Other parts of the city, the agora, nymphaeum and cisterns, lie to the south-east – and nothing has been excavated of this city which existed and flourished here for possibly fifteen hundred years. I gazed at the view over the serene intimacy of the little farms to the folded drapes of the formidable mountains, still snow covered in the far distance. Below me was the stone heap of the Roman stage building, once with five doors and a colonnaded façade which could just be picked out amongst the tilting blocks. I was struck again that these beautiful cut stones lay there untouched – in Greece or Cyprus they would have been re-used a thousand years ago. It looked as if it would be perfectly possible to reconstruct the stage building, if anyone wanted to.

The artist and the archaeologist are related in their love for the material culture of the past, but each has a different way of looking. The Australian artist John Wolseley put it clearly to me. 'The artist's journey has no end, we don't know what we are looking for, while the scientist (the botanist, geologist and archaeologist) moves within a framework.' For an artist, the marvellous fragments of sites like Selge are evocative and promising in their lack of completion, in the possibilities they offer for fresh insights and an imaginative re-visioning of the past. The archaeologist's task, by contrast, is to reconstruct the fragments into a whole through the analysis of existing material evidence.

9. ISPARTA AND SAGALOSSOS

16 June

The bus north from Antalya to the inland city of Isparta came through blistering heat rising from great stony outcrops. The hills bordered fertile plains of oranges and crops, unpeopled in the heat of the day. A little boy almost five years old sat next to me on the bus, clutching a piece of bread. His father gave him a drink of water (we all carry water, continually necessary in the dry heat) and he sat there quietly until he fell deeply asleep.

I read a copy of *The Pilgrim's Progress* I'd found in the Dogon hotel, leaving one of my paperbacks in exchange. I had loved the book when I got it as a prize as a child. The language of John Bunyan is another kind of English, almost without any of the common assumptions of today, but full of acute observations of people and situations. This journey is a kind of pilgrimage – will my own 'theatre' emerge from all these observations? Bunyan believed in revelation backed up by reason. He suggested how effortlessly the story came to him once he started – 'I did it my own self to gratify.' We pass poplars and cherry trees in orderly groves, against vistas of ragged mountains, and a glimpse of a minaret in a village hidden by trees. The mountains can be seen in the clear air even over a great distance. How surprised Bunyan would have been to know that his book would be read while travelling through this biblical landscape.

When we arrived towards evening Isparta felt like a large and pleasant provincial city, four square and plain with tree-lined streets thronged with people in the dusk. Authoritative government administration buildings had been put up in the time of Atatürk, that now almost mythical time when Turkey was transformed into a European secular state.

My friend Enis found me somehow in the turmoil of the bus station. He had arranged a large and pleasant suite of rooms for me in the shining clean university hostel where he was also living. A life-size statue of Atatürk watched over the entrance. I sat in the evening drinking tea with Enis' friends and colleagues who, like him, all obtained their doctorates and master's degrees outside of Turkey, in the USA or Australia, paid by the Turkish government. Now they have to work many years in provincial universities like Isparta to pay off the debt. His friend Brucke was desperate to return to Los Angeles, where he had been offered jobs, but because of visa problems he was still in Turkey. A shy boy of nineteen or so, Ibrahim, joined us with many brochures from universities around the world: he wants to study abroad.

The Faculty of Fine Arts was set up in an old high school, and there were few resources – no computers, old wooden tables and chairs, but 'excellent students,' I was told by Professor Asmah. I was shown painted gouache designs derived from, once again, that pervasive Pazyryk rug, in vivid colours. I met the dean, elderly, pale and upright behind a padded leather desk with a Turkish flag. Atatürk beamed down from a painting on the wall, and his figure was also woven into the carpet. I was treated with great courtesy as Enis' former teacher. The highly trained staff – all able to speak other languages beside Turkish – were frustrated by lack of equipment.

Enis and his close friend Mehmet did not believe me when I told them there was a famous ancient town on a mountain near Isparta. No one had ever been there that they had heard of or had ever mentioned it at the university. Mehmet had been born in this region 'so I should know about it'. But there it was on the map, Aglasun, the ancient Greek town of Sagalossos, a mere thirty kilometres away. I hired a car (I paid, Enis negotiated and drove) and the three of us set off on a radiant day on a road curling through soft hills, higher and higher on a precarious track. I had an impression of immense space and light, as though we could look directly into the heart of Asia, hills and mountains like an ocean rippling into the far distance with extreme clarity. After winding our way up the narrow road, a precipice on one side, Enis said, 'Why on earth did they live here?' Because of course, as at Termessos and Selge, they could defend it. On arrival, we were the only figures in that high landscape, apart from the cheerful watchman who lived near the gate in a small house. The ruins of the town extended for a kilometre or so, on a plateau up to 1,700 metres in altitude, beneath the grey white cliffs of Mt Akdag. The sheer rock was pierced with the façades of tombs.

As at Termessos and Selge, Sagalossos was recorded in history through its relationship to war – especially to Alexander, who managed to conquer the city in 333 BC. A long period of prosperity, of elaborate buildings and a sophisticated urban life followed. Sagalossos was finally abandoned in the seventh century, due to a combination of earthquakes and Arab raids, a common pattern across the eastern Mediterranean, as at Paphos. It lay buried under landslides until visited in 1706 by a French traveller, Paul Lucas, who called it 'a city of enchantment'. Unlike Termessos and Selge, much of the town of Sagalossos had been carefully excavated since 1990 by the Belgian archaeologist Professor Marc Waelkens, supported by the Leuven Catholic University.

Near at hand I began to discern carved stones, with a detail of acanthus covered in lichen, or egg and dart moulding – the now familiar litter of these high sites. A Greek inscription lay in the flowers. The springy heath vegetation formed an intricate and abundant rock garden around the ruins – great furry-leaved bluish plants like lamb's tongues, forget-me-knots, clouds of a purple pea, a button daisy and yellow chamomile, sage, thyme, oregano, and little gold-brown wall flowers. Mehmet, who had been brought up in a village, said that a spreading yellow-red euphorbia was very poisonous. He pointed to a vivid yellow yarrow that was an antidote to snake venom. I walked mesmerised up and down through the ruins of the agora, the extensive baths, past an enchanting group of standing Ionic columns of a temple near a gated wall, shimmering in the heat. We were the only visitors, and I felt we were being observed. Suddenly in the silence there was the sound of running water – we had reached a fountain house.

The beautiful nymphaeum had been miraculously restored to its original function by the Belgian excavators – a colonnaded court, with water gushing out into a deep channel on three sides, rather like a stage building. Deep grooves still showed on the ledge, where water jars, the *hydrias*, had been set to fill from the fountain, as is still done in remote villages like Selge, where I had seen the animated group of women and children. My two companions became very joyful – shouting and laughing and dipping their heads in the cold water, filling our bottles, those blue-lidded clear plastic bottles that are the water containers of our time, everywhere. We all drank deeply, washed our hot faces, sank wrists into the cold – what bliss water is. I left a small bunch of the unbelievably blue-purple forget-me-knots as a thank offering to the nymph. The humming quiet of the site, accentuated by mountain bees, was interrupted by our noise.

The library of Flavius Severanus – a library! Up here? – was restored on the hill above the fountain. A marble wall carved with eight arched niches, elegant with Greek inscriptions dedicated by the *demos*, the town council, looked down on a beautiful mosaic floor of interlocking shields and rosettes. Once there had been wall paintings, I had been told by Edip Ösgür in Antalya. The museum in Burdur held all the extensive finds including any fresco fragments and statuary from the site, but it was closed on the days I was in Isparta.

Looking around the main layout of the city I at last saw the theatre built up into the hill and on a series of arches. It lay considerably above the main area of the town, unexcavated, sunken into the great bare hillside beneath the grey crags like a hollow navel open to the sky.

Walking into the theatre, said to be the highest theatre in existence, clambering over great blocks of fallen masonry was an extraordinary experience. The double-arched passages of the *vomitoria* that supported the seating were intact in places, wide open as if waiting for a new audience. Enis and Mehmet climbed precariously up and over the broken arches and tilting stones of the vaults and stage buildings. The horseshoe-shaped theatre seemed roughly the same size as the Paphos theatre (the *orchestra* is 18-20 metres in diameter), and held about 9,000 people, but with the scene building separate, not joined to the tiers of seats. There was certainly no painted entrance way here. The three doors of the stage could still be seen in the tumble, lintel stones just balancing to form the rectangle of the doorway. Enis pointed out the earthquake line, shivering across the rows of stone seats.

I thought how I had not found any evidence of frescoes remaining in any of the theatres of southern Turkey except that of Aspendos, which was built of a conglomerate stone that had a rough surface. All the other theatres were made of good hard stone, marble, or grey travertine. Carved relief was the preferred form of decoration, and good quality stone is abundant in Turkey. In Cyprus the porous sandy limestone required surfaces to be plastered. The very absence of fresco theatre decoration in southern Turkey makes the painted fragments from the Paphos theatre particularly interesting.

Sitting in the Sagalossos theatre, you could look out across the low green valleys to layers of mountains splintered with snow. The flooding intensity of the light seemed to contain the etched detail of a carved acanthus frond with as much clarity as the distant sweep of the Taurus mountains. It appeared as if space had become truncated in the shining transparency of the sun. I wished I knew what performances had taken place here, what political gatherings. The backdrop of such a vista must have given a certain severity to even a comic drama. The study of the rich archaeological finds and the inscriptions may reveal something of this complexity.

Coming from the margins of European culture myself, it is poignant to see how the ancient peoples of Pamphylia, Lycia and Pisidia adopted the classical idea of civic government, with its ordered architecture of agora, temples, theatre and necropolis. Greek culture was absorbed and stitched onto the languages and beliefs of indigenous Anatolian tribes over a period of a thousand years (approximately 600 BC to AD 400). The combination of such alignments gave a fierce intellectual and physical energy to the cities. I could understand how Freya Stark could uphold the idea of the essential, inevitable 'good' of Greek culture colonising tribal communities like the Solyms of Termessos. At the same time, I realise that fragmentary history does not record the feelings of the dispossessed. The Pisidian cities are extreme sites, spare and aesthetic in their impact. The places have a presence, and I thought how in Aboriginal terms the viewing experience would go both ways. Not only do I observe, but also I am observed by the country; I look, but I am also looked at by the land and all that it holds.

One of my first passions in Greek art concerned the sculptures of *kouroi*, or youths, torsos taut with action, dedicated to gods. The American poet May Sarton aptly quoted from a poem by Rainer Maria Rilke called *Archaic Torso of Apollo*: 'Here there is nothing that does not see you, You must change your life.'[13]

Walking down slowly and breathlessly from the theatre (noticing carved architectural ornaments and inscriptions at almost every step) we met a Turkish archaeology student and two friends, but no one else, except the guardian at the entrance. The drive back from Sagalossos was very beautiful in the deep blue afternoon. People on the road wore timeless clothing, like the woman carrying a huge load of sticks followed by two black goats. Here was a small river winding through a narrow valley, a stone animal pen, and small fields of wheat, barley and sugar beet. The road was lined for a brief distance with laden cherry trees, people leaping up to grab the fruit. Again the sight pulled me back into ancient lyric poetry, as if that past world still existed just below the surface, a feeling perhaps like an Aboriginal sense of ancestors constantly re-invoked through the places and patterns of the present. Here is Propertius, from the first century:

> But once, in the youth of the world,
> We must have been like that, too,
> Happy, at peace, content with the earth's riches
> Of fields and orchards in which one could shake a tree and receive
> The delicious gift of quinces, or walk in the woods
> And come back home with baskets brimming with crimson berries.[14]

10. WATER

17 June

This is a land of many kinds of water. Last night at dusk I visited the waterfall, the gush of white that I had seen from the plane on arriving in Antalya, not understanding what it could be. ('Remember,' said Mehmet, my driver, speaking with the confidence of an ancient precept, 'Happiness is the sound of water, the sound of a woman's voice – and the sound of money.') The great waterfall swept over a cliff face with urgent momentum into the sea two hundred feet below. Its opaque green surface was smooth and silky, flowing with the force of a flood, the last moment of the melting snows of the Taurus Mountains. I couldn't help thinking of Cyprus, parched and drought-stricken to the south, and remembered a story about transporting fresh water to the island in a great plastic bubble at least ten metres in diameter that could be dragged through the sea by a ship. There was a pearly light on the sea far below. A small boat and two swimmers moved towards the churning foam where the two bodies of water merged.

The mingling of salt water and fresh water is a metaphor in Aboriginal philosophy and art for reconciliation and for states of being. Toni Morrison wrote about the site of memory in relation to water, and relates the flow to an idea of archaeology. The dryness of the site can become flooded with imagination.

> How I gain access to the interior life is what drives me – it's a kind of literary archaeology: on the basis of some information and a little bit of guesswork you journey to a site to see what remains were left behind and to reconstruct the world that these remains imply...
>
> All water has a perfect memory and is forever trying to get back where it was. Writers are like that: remembering where we were, the route back to our original place. The rush of imagination is our 'flooding'.[15]

The suburbs behind the waterfall cliff were in a state of transformation, with concrete towers rising out of a mud-brick village. The roads were crowded with stalls and shops, filled with people moving between displays of abundant figs, mulberries, and guavas. We passed the community of houses where Mehmet lived, an island of order, with painted doors and windows shining among balcony gardens.

Perched on the cliff above the waterfall was a simple park with wooden walkways along the rushing river. Two solid older men were sitting on a wooden bench facing the pale sea, softly singing a kind of lament or possibly a love song. I looked out over the sea and saw that they were watching the moon rise.

PART IV

Theatre and Tomb:
Cyprus, 2001-2002

Relief carving of a stone head amongst vegetation, Ayia Khrysaliniotissa, Nicosia, c. 1450. Ink and wash, 2002.

I. DIONYSOS AND ARIADNE IN CYPRUS

8 April 2001

The pale ochre stones of Fabrika Hill are almost hidden in the bursting tourist town. Coming back to Paphos after two years, after seeing the marvellous theatres of southern Turkey, is like a homecoming. The site is a tumbled piece of empty land with a question mark over it, a gap in the fabric of the village, full of holes and incomprehensible foundations of walls and stairs. The ruins reflect the glancing light from clouds flowing across the spring sky.

The young archaeologists appear there like a sudden epiphany, a Dionysian procession carrying spades, picks, buckets and sieves, filling the space with voices and activity. They had cleared the covering of yellow daisies and poppies that hid the site by the time I arrived, and were working in focused teams on specific areas of the theatre, particularly the western entrance way and stage building. The tattered theatre is just an echo of those in Perge, Myra, or Aspendos, and yet its echoes have tones of many layers and sequences in the life of the theatre, Ottoman and medieval, as well as the classical period. The careful archaeology is showing how the theatre was embedded in daily life as well as in the grandiosity of public ceremony.

I went first to look at the long painted wall of the western *parodos* with a new respect for its distinctiveness. The ruined wall is like an enigma to be solved. No other painted theatre entrance exists that I can find, after all my travels. After much research I can see that our painted wall, and the whole elusive architecture of the Paphos theatre is exceptional. Unearthed slowly over five years, the long wall that supported the auditorium is still hidden in the ground at both ends, towards the *orchestra*, and towards the outside perimeter of the theatre, concealed by the tarmac road.

I sat on a column drum near a carob tree opposite the wall and reflected that the clue to understanding the painted wall is in the idea of ancient architecture as a space built around rituals, designed for the flow of people and events. Interiors were defined by the shell of colour made up of paintings, mosaics and marble facings. These decorations formed an architecture designed for movement, crowds moving through the coloured spaces, glimpsing colours and ornament as a sensuous enrichment of the performance. The richly coloured ornamental panels that I can dimly see on the walls may have formed a background to the ritual procession required by theatrical performance and by the masked god of theatre, Dionysos. Performances re-enacted the divine edginess of taking on another persona, away from your normal self, becoming a masked entity that mimicked the gods. The mask was the sign of this dangerous 'other' realm, and masks were dedicated in temples, sometimes as small votive terracottas or carved in friezes. Gilles Deleuze summarised the elusiveness of images of the masked god, always about to appear: 'Art invokes Dionysos as the god of places of passage, and things of forgetting.'[1]

The place for those glittering dramatic processions is now cluttered with fallen stones, dusty with collapsed plaster. I'm looking at the 'through-way', the *parodos*, sometimes a low dark tunnel in theatres I have seen, sometimes open and high. The shape of the Paphos entrance is not clear yet. The *parodos* was a transitional passage, a corridor between everyday life outside the theatre and the drama within.

Ariadne, the consort of Dionysos, the feminine side of theatre, has a strange history in Cyprus. All through my travels I was drawn to her images, in that mysterious way that an image will capture and disturb you. Her myth is like a kaleidoscope, shifting according to the needs of the time. 'Fair Ariadne, daughter of cruel-hearted Minos,' says Homer. She helped Theseus, the prince of Athens, to kill the Minotaur, her brother, to prevent the sacrifices of Athenian young men and women ordered by Minos, King of Crete. The Minotaur was the monstrous progeny of Pasiphaë, Ariadne's mother who Zeus enflamed with lust for a divine bull. She was helped by the craftsman Daedalus to conceive the bull-headed Minotaur. The canny Daedalus also built a great labyrinth, and in its centre the Minotaur lay concealed. Ariadne gave Theseus a ball of thread to lead him into and out of the dark passages of the labyrinth. They fled to Athens in Theseus' ship, after she had betrayed her monstrous family. On Naxos, while Ariadne was sleeping, Theseus 'forgot her' (Homer says), slipped away and sailed to Athens with her sister Phaedra, leaving her abandoned on the island.

But then Dionysos and his retinue find her, and she becomes his closest companion, coupled for life in many versions of the story. In another account, she dies in childbirth at Amathus in Cyprus, where a grove was dedicated to Ariadne-Aphrodite. Sometimes she hangs herself. Plutarch says that Theseus commemorated her death by establishing an animal sacrifice at Amathus, and erecting two images of her in bronze and silver which demonstrated human nature (bronze) united with the divine (silver).[2] This story reminded me of the poignant marble figurines in the Paphos Museum, joined at the base; two draped standing women, one in black stone engraved with rosettes, and one in white.

Many images of Ariadne that became archetypal in the Renaissance show that moment of vulnerability before the god discovers her. Ariadne lies on the ground with one arm curled over her head, her head thrown back, in the gesture of the maenad who has fallen into a divine trance. Her robe is slipping down to her thighs as she sleeps.

I saw such an Ariadne figure on a dim wall decorated with flowering sprigs in Ephesos, in a series of rooms painted with scenes from the theatre. In the Khania Museum in Crete I found a mosaic of a beautiful Ariadne reclining on a leopard skin, with Dionysos approaching her, and another slumbering and melancholy Ariadne in the Thessaloniki Museum, also a mosaic.

Propertius wrote of the emotional edge of sleep:

We have seen those paintings: Ariadne fallen in a swoon
On Knossos' shore as Theseus' ship disappears,
Dwindles, a dot in the distance; or Andromeda,
Loosed from her cliff,
Resting exhausted; or else some Thracian bacchant
Utterly spent from her frenzied dance,
Collapsed on the greeny bank of the Apidanus.
And Cynthia too, seemed asleep, her breathing barely perceptible,
Head pillowed on her bent arm, as I staggered home.[3]

Intricate sarcophagus reliefs constantly represented Ariadne waking to a better life after her discovery by Dionysos. The owner of the sarcophagus might find immortal life and happiness in the loving arms of the divine, as Ariadne had. The same images tie together the theatre and the tomb – twining flowers, the vine, wreaths and ribbons. Dionysos was the god who had died (he was eaten by Titans) and returned, promising a new life after death. Together Dionysos and Ariadne on their chariot promised eternal happiness after death and disintegration. I had found a lovely carved Dionysian sarcophagus in Alexandria, with a satyr pulling aside a curtain to reveal Ariadne asleep, until the noisy arrival of Dionysos and his troupe.

Ariadne was famous for dancing: examples are those formal dances shown in Mycenaean and Archaic art, or the dance to waken a sleeping goddess known from Naxos. I was captivated by early images of Ariadne on the Archaic black figure Kleitias vase, in the Museo Archeologico in Florence where I worked for a time. On its delicate painted bands, Athenian young men and women sent as offerings to the Minotaur danced with a regal Theseus and Ariadne at their head. Each period interpreted Ariadne's story differently, and in this Archaic era she was a kind of *potnia theroun*, Mistress of

Wild Beasts, a confident and tightly clothed woman in embroidered robes, facing Theseus eye to eye, on the same level, not prone on the ground.

Dance was fundamental to theatrical performance at all times, and Apuleius described complicated 'dancing mazes' that read like a mosaic pattern:

> By way of prelude a number of beautiful boys and girls in rich costumes were moving with dignity through the graceful mazes of the Greek pyrrhic dance. Sometimes different streams of dancers would weave in and out of the same circle; sometimes all would join hands and dance sideways across the stage, then separate into four wedge-shaped groups with the blunt ends enclosing a square space; sometimes there would be a sudden divorce of the sexes, the boys and girls separating from each other.[4]

Three islands, Crete, Naxos and Cyprus, are all associated with Ariadne – these are the islands where I have lived and worked. All have remarkable textile traditions, sumptuous embroidery and weaving. The Cypriot cult of Ariadne and Aphrodite at Amathus had one strange custom reported by Plutarch – a young man would imitate the sounds and struggle of a woman going through childbirth. It seems Ariadne was not only the dancing woman with the ball of thread, but was also tied to childbirth, and to Aphrodite, goddess of procreation.[5]

I keep returning to the key moment in the Ariadne story, repeated again and again in images of all periods. She wakes abandoned in the rocky landscape – to heartbreak, the common experience of a primal stab of loss, waking to a terrible realisation. She may have waited, hoping for someone to arrive. She may have even attended to those small tasks that keep the mind steady, that even in her ancient world might have needed attention, such as the mending of wreaths and drapery no doubt torn and covered with stains after a flight in a tarry boat. There were probably some slaves who were abandoned with her, invisible in the public record, who watched over and served the princess on the rock, finding nuts, honey, wild olives, managing to make life bearable. No doubt they comforted her – 'Someone will find you' – and gave her sound advice – 'Perhaps this will teach you to be more cautious, not to run off with heroes from an enemy country. Work hard and consolidate, don't expect much. Who could love you after this has happened? You must have had something badly wrong about you if such a promising man left you here on this rock.' And they were surprisingly wrong. She was caught up into the shining pageant of Dionysos, who was nothing to do with order and calm reason. The god arrived on his chariot drawn by leopards, sweeping from the heavens, trailing ivy leaves, musicians, centaurs, suffusing the whole animal world of instinctive life with momentary glory.

Looking at the plan of our theatre with its concentric semicircular rows I imagined that the ruined theatre was like half of Ariadne's circular labyrinth. Vaulted passages and circuitous levels for seating, tunnels curving around and underneath the building in semi-darkness evoke a similar mystery. The great ruins in southern Turkey, covered in Dionysian vegetation hold secrets in their labyrinthine and unexcavated depths. The paintings in the passageway of the Paphos theatre, that passage between inside and outside, like the transition between sleeping and waking, might lead towards the heart of the matter.

2. THE LABYRINTHINE THEATRE

12 April

I went off in the early afternoon to visit the Roman mosaics nearby and think about their connection to the theatre. The World Heritage site has now been enclosed by a two-metre fence, so that it's no longer possible to walk from the theatre to the House of Dionysos, through meandering tracks, old peasant houses, or come across the shepherd and his sheep. It is now an 'archaeological park' – somehow this redefines the space and sets it apart from the town, with a formal entrance only through the port. Access to the wonderful mosaics of the House of Theseus was immensely improved through high walkways placed over them. Open to the weather, the mosaics are clean and windswept in the full sun. Streams of English, German and French tourists moved over the wooden walkways, like pilgrims, looking down at the mosaic carpets which define the architecture of the palatial houses. All that is left are these stony sparkling patterns – evidence for the nineteenth-century idea that pattern and textiles might be the beginning of enclosed spaces, at the root of architecture.

It was breathtaking to see the labyrinth mosaic again, miraculous in its tight form and in its delicate and precise technique. The circular labyrinth is more than six metres in diameter, formed by a twisted guilloche or spiral thread, in soft red, blue and gold with a diamond design to represent walls. At the centre of the concentric and turning meanders is a rocky grotto, with Theseus raising his club against the fallen Minotaur, while an older man, named as Labyrinthos, looks on. Above are the busts of two crowned women, Ariadne and Crete, both named. Theseus' gaze looks out far beyond and away from the slain Minotaur struggling at his feet.

The ancient world saw landscapes personified in a human form – Crete in the labyrinth mosaic is a regal woman observing the action, again with that slight distance in her expression, as though considering her inner life. Ariadne is in pink – elegantly coiffured and crowned, one hand raised, the owner of the thread that is the clue to the labyrinth. The representation of the story is intriguing – the way the figures seem to be self reflective, as well as reflecting on the action. Some say that Theseus destroyed the old matriarchal emphasis when he killed the Minotaur, turning Greek culture towards masculine intellectuality and causing the invisibility of feminine creativity. The Theseus story in this Late Roman period was understood as a defining and crucial episode in the history of Greece and Rome.[6]

I had seen in Alexandria the dynamic mosaics of Queen Berenike, wife of Ptolemy, with her 'shining, radiant, lustrous and terrifying glance', which showed divine inspiration, made five hundred years earlier. The artist who made the labyrinth mosaic had made Theseus almost womanly, beardless with long curly hair and large dreamy eyes which appeared to look inwards as well as outwards in a way that cannot compare with the gleaming ferocity in the eyes of Berenike.[7] By the end of the fourth century, when the mosaic of Theseus' head had been restored after an earthquake to its present form, pagan beliefs were in competition with Christian ideas.[8]

The labyrinth (according to Professor Daszewski, who excavated the mosaic in the 1960s) had become an allegory, a symbol of the difficulty of life, of the long and painful road to truth, a symbolic place of transformation, of initiation, final victory and the end of desire. The victory of the hero over the monster foreshadows St George and the dragon, where spirit triumphs over material values. By this time, after the great earthquake of 360, it is likely that the theatre was at the end of its life, despite the prosperity evident in the luxurious houses and their costly mosaics. To the early Christians the theatre was an infernal labyrinth, almost a metaphor for Hell, exciting passion and arousing sinful desires. St Augustine loved the theatre in his youth, and then preached against it.

In two corners of the mosaic labyrinth floor are sinuous curving fronds that seemed to me in their exuberant abundance to be a hidden sign of Dionysos, the god of vegetation. The subterranean world of Hades, the underworld, was also thought of as a labyrinth, a place for monsters such as the Minotaur. The puzzle of the labyrinth with all its associations may well have been apotropaic and prophylactic to those who commissioned it, turning away evil, and protecting the house.[9]

Set in the earth the faceted mosaics seem to be rooted, growing from the soil like flowers. Surrounded by a vivid meadow of purple statice and white anemones, pink mallows and convolvulus, the images are like a natural truth, as if their message had become absorbed into the seasonal cycle of plants.

3. THE PROCESSION: THE POMPE

13 April

The evening of Good Friday was still and overcast as I walked with Ian and Bob up to Ktima, the upper town of Paphos. (Both these Australians were volunteers on the excavation, with longstanding professional lives, as an artist and an engineer.) The streets were silent and shut until we neared the cathedral, where dark clothed people were hurrying into the church and assembling in the square.

The *mitropoleo* or cathedral church is near the ridge of a steep hill looking over the whole of Paphos. Below we could see the town and port spread out like a map. The theatre site was hidden behind Fabrika Hill, where the three tall crosses had been put up for Easter. Swarming concrete buildings only emphasised the fact that Paphos still had the character of a village. We walked the quiet streets as the sun sank into the sea in a grey haze, and said good evening to two older women musing on their porch behind geraniums.

Inside the cathedral every surface was teeming with modern wall paintings on a blue ground, painted in the Orthodox Byzantine style. The holiest scenes from the life of Christ were at the highest level of the walls towards heaven. Below them were angels and apostles, and at the lowest level familiar Cypriot saints stood in rows gazing out just above the congregation. (This hierarchy reflects the ancient order of the theatre stage, with gods at the top, semi-divine heroes and human emperors lower down.)

I wanted to see how the paintings merged with the rituals of the intense Easter ceremony. Ian and I stood in a crowded aisle near the image of Ayia Paraskevi, carrying a plate with two eyes, and Ayia Helena, mother of the Emperor Constantine, who travelled to Cyprus bringing relics of the Cross. Both these early saints were shown as very calm. These perfect new paintings are correct in every detail, but my guidebook described them as 'lacking spiritual force' – an elusive aesthetic quality for any artist to achieve. The importance of the icons is to provide a 'window into eternal life'. Later Ian told me he had seen a famous icon of the Virgin in the museum at the Kykko Monastery that he felt did have a forceful power, not quite comprehensible.

The church was packed, and people moved slowly down the aisle to the bier covered with white flowers; lilies, roses, and gypsophila, baby's breath. These were the spring flowers of Dionysos and Adonis, both gods of vegetation – I thought of the Feast of Roses in Hellenistic Alexandria, which was associated with remembering the dead. The choir sang from the gallery, picking up the underlying theme of the priests' chanting. The bishop's mitre shone below the chandeliers as the crowd individually kissed the bier, moving constantly, greeting others, changing seats. I remembered that Paphos has had a bishop since the fourth century, because of its connection to the apostolic tradition. Men, women, children – a little girl sat wide-eyed on her grandmother's broad blue lap. A woman of about forty seated near where I was standing asked if I wanted to sit for a while – she was strangely like Kyria Anna, my landlady's sister many years ago in Athens, even dressed with the same short dark skirt and jacket, bouffant hair and scarf. The congregation seemed intent and restless at the same time; people shuffled, murmured, and went out for a smoke through the long ceremony with its Byzantine chants and clouds of incense. (I looked for Dr Theophilos, a chanter in this cathedral, but the crowd was too dense.)

There is a connection, I decided, between the attributes of ancient theatre and an ancient festival like the Good Friday ceremony: processions of priests waving censers, the mesmerising sound of chanting and singing, the vivid and scented space lit up by glittering lights and iconic paintings. The congregation in its best clothes was a cross section of the population: everyone was here.

I had been reading St Augustine, who experienced the overlap between pagan and Christian in melancholy detail:

> The man who enters a church is bound to see drunkards, misers, tricksters, gamblers, adulterers, fornicators, people wearing amulets, assiduous clients of sorcerers, astrologers ... the same crowds that press into the churches on Christian festivals also fill the theatres on pagan holidays.[10]

By ten o'clock the square outside the church was a crowded mass of people, waiting for the procession, the highpoint of the ceremony. The night was now black and cold, with a tearing wind, as the ornate bier carried by young soldiers slowly processed through the dark streets. It was accompanied by a band of woodwinds played by young boys, repeating the same hauntingly sad refrain heard in the church, and taken up by the choir in the main square. Their conductor, his long black robes wrapping around him in the wind, walked backwards in front of them, urging them on. At the head of the procession was a young man carrying the cross, with the priests and bishop swaying forward in embroidered vestments. Caught in the surging crowd we were merged into the throng, gathered up and swept along to the centre of the town. Flickering torchlight in the darkness, flowers and rich fabrics glinting among fragments of piercing sound; this is the *pompe*. Being in that crowd, following the procession, was like sinking back to another age.

14 April

Thinking about the elusive figure of Dionysos and his part in theatrical performance, I walked across the town in the late afternoon to gaze again at the Bacchic procession on the mosaic floor of the great dining hall of the House of Dionysos.

Leaning over the wooden viewing platform I could see, enclosed in a border of twined ribbons, the long mosaic frieze of the Bacchic procession. The naked god arrives in a chariot from India drawn by panthers, led by Silenus (the head satyr, with goat's feet). He is accompanied by satyrs and maenads playing trumpets and cymbals with bacchantes carrying libation bowls and baskets. Ariadne is not with him. One satyr stumbles under a huge blue wine jar, dragging an animal skin. Three dark Indian slaves move in the procession, their hands bound, and all the gesticulating figures are silhouetted against a cream background. Dionysos was known as Bromios, 'The Roarer', because his appearance was always accompanied by pandemonium, shrieking wildness, an incredible noise – and then suddenly, the opposite, deathly hush. Maenads are characterised by a rigid stare, a melancholy quiet, a deep inner preoccupation, even while surrounded by clanging and shattering sound. The edge between clamour and silence is shown in the unsettling images of masks with black stretched mouths below empty eye sockets.

The *pompe*, the procession, was the essential part of drama, sacrifice and festivity. In Alexandria, sister city to Paphos and ruled by the same Ptolemaic dynasty, Dionysian pageants are recorded where people carrying baskets, offerings and wineskins paraded down the street to the theatre accompanied by extraordinary mythological 'tableaux vivants', on floats. Traditionally in the main Dionysia festival in Athens large models of phalluses were carried (sometimes wheeled because of their size) and dedicated to the god. The sight of the monstrous phallus was said to be liberating in its comic and grotesque effect, provoking laughter, underlined by overtones of 'sacred terror' of the phallus in the mystery religions.[11] The performances and their attendant rituals began in the centre of town, and then paraded into the theatre as a prelude to the performance, reminding me of the dancing girls and music before a major football game in Australia.[12]

Similar processions must have filled the streets of Paphos. In Euripides' play *The Bacchae*, the punishment for not giving Dionysos his due in ceremony and offerings is madness and death.

In this story there are disturbing images of the power of Dionysos, a seemingly vindictive and unforgiving force to those who assert logic over desire. In the tragedy the rational King Pentheus of Thebes denied the divinity of Dionysos, and was punished with a fearful death, torn apart by his own deranged mother. Together with other housewives who had kept weaving at their looms despite the appearance of the god amongst them, Dionysos transformed her into a maenad, a 'maddened one'. They were sent, raving and wild, transfixed with a divine spirit, into the high forests to wander 'on the roofless rocks, beneath the pale pines', where they suckled wild beasts.

> There's not a woman of old Cadmus' race,
> But I have maddened from her quiet house.
>
> Even housewifely weavers tore apart living flesh with their mouths:.
>
> From the distaff, from the loom,
> Raging with the god they come.[13]

Dionysos was a terrible god: the implication is, sacrifice to him when he and his strange retinue dance into your land, or tremble at the possibilities of destruction.

There's another very fragmentary mosaic of the Triumphal Procession of the Baby Dionysos a few hundred metres away from the

House of Dionysos, in the House of Aion. Disjointed fragments show what must have been a captivating rhythmical composition, with the young Dionysos – only his feet survive – in a chariot led by two centaurs, one playing the lyre. Most evocative is a hand holding a flaring torch with the rest of the figure destroyed. A maenad bears a covered basket (supposed to hold the sacred phallus in the Dionysian mysteries) and a baby satyr lifts a plate with a pomegranate and grapes. I found the whole narrative full of warmth and grace, the participants affectionately bound to each other. Made in the early fourth century, it is a hundred years later than the much starker procession in the House of Dionysos. The suffused tenderness towards the baby Dionysos, nursed by Hermes and nymphs in another late mosaic in the House of Theseus, prefigures the loving nativity scenes of Christian art. The Procession of the Baby Dionysos is a long way from the terror of the Dionysian epiphany – and by this time, the Paphos theatre would have been a disintegrating ruin.[14] The emotions surrounding Dionysos become transformed and the shape-changer shifts into another guise.

4. LAYERS

15 April

Scrutinising the tiny details of encrustations on the wall at the theatre reveals that there are still clues to the patterns – vertical lines in black and red. The painted section is much longer than I thought – the plaster extending in patches and traces for nine metres. I spent many hours drawing the wall on a scale of one to ten on a long sheet of graph paper, with tape measures, rods and a magnifying glass.

The mayor and district officials came on a theatre tour today and peered down at me two metres below ground level on the *parodos* floor, drawing and measuring amongst the tumbled rocks. 'This was the main entrance to the theatre,' said Richard. 'Actors, audiences all came through here.'

Later, everyone was talking about frescoes in the Paphos Museum. Dr Eustathios Raptou, the director, took Richard and myself to the storeroom to see the spectacular new frescoes that had come out of a large tomb discovered just a few weeks ago in March, when sewerage pipes were laid down in the area of Ktima, not far from the cathedral. Newspapers have been describing the find as 'very rare'.

At the moment the mysterious figure of a woman, painted on a stone slab, appears shrouded because of the gauze laid across her to protect the surface. After looking serenely into the breathless dark of the tomb since the first or second century, she was brought into the light to be gazed at, rather than to be the guardian who watches over the dead. I felt shaken to look at this freshly excavated image, as I did in that other tomb when the painted fragment ΜΗΤΗΡ, mother, came to light — like finding a glimpse of something hidden, some intimation of new and significant knowledge. The woman stands large-eyed with a steadfast expression between garlands or trees and possibly holds a cornucopia, a basket overflowing with fruit and flowers. These Dionysian motifs are associated with both the theatre and funerary art. The colours are warm reds, turquoise and ochres, similar to the palette of the theatre frescoes. She wears earrings, and on her forehead is a distinctive jewel. She has a pomegranate or apple at her feet, and some grapes. There is a partial inscription, undeciphered.

'So beautiful. Yes, certainly a goddess,' said Eustathios. 'And what is the inscription?'

With enthusiasm he showed me different fragments from separate areas of the large tomb. Encrusted with crystals, the plaster was sharp and white but with fine, clear floral decoration. He drew the plan of the tomb in my notebook clearly and slowly — it's right in the centre of the town, near the little pavilion with the fountain and the park dedicated to Grivas Digheni. I wondered at these fragile images, drawn with verve and appreciation of the curve of a leaf, the softness of a pink flower, the wiggle of a red ribbon. They have been underneath the ground, sealed in a dark tomb since the second century, seen only on occasional visits by the grieving survivors, who might have come to bury another member of the family. Perhaps the existence of the painted images show a belief in a parallel reality – the exuberant gush of flowers and leaves from the garland, the ribbon twisting in the breeze may have brought life, light and air to counter the stillness and darkness of the tomb.

As the tomb appears to be intact, and not plundered, there are the remains of many individuals in its chambers, or *loculi*. Our forensic archaeologist Estelle has been laying out tiny fragments of half burnt bone in the museum storeroom and analysing them. The bones indicate a high proportion of children and babies, though the reason is not clear. The adults seem to have been short people with distinctive skull structures. Vivid and enticing fragments of painted floral and geometric ornament from the walls of other sections of the tomb were spread out on trays in the storeroom and I longed to examine them. The connection between art and archaeology is engrossing in this discovery.

Driving back to the site from the museum after viewing the newly discovered tomb frescoes, Richard said, 'It seems that there may have been a major fresco school in Paphos – all the material is emerging here.'

19 April

Some rare seventh-century coins were found in the rich trench near the stage building and the diggers hope this is a secure Byzantine deposit (seventh to eleventh centuries). The well in Kerrie's trench is now five metres deep, with its ancient footholds reaching all the way down and it is a challenge to go down and excavate the wonderful deposits. Here Holly was delighted to find some beautiful glazed stemmed bowls, in green, brown and gold, apparently all from Paphos workshops.

It is impossible to attend only to one chronological period, when the site is multi-layered and artefacts emerge without respect to 'proper' sequence. A book on medieval food and containers is planned, reflecting the unexpected variety of the finds. I listened to Richard talking to Crystalla about the French who came from Provence to Cyprus in the fifteenth century bringing *flaones*, the extraordinary Easter breads, baked with cheese, herbs and spices. (She shrugged, looking incredulous.) In the Theoskepasti church on Easter Sunday I saw another medieval still life, a table set with a white embroidered cloth with a small bottle of wine, oil and bread. The round and heavy loaves had crosses, and the table stood in front of an icon of the Virgin.

Lying on rocks to give birth is the Virgin Mary's pose in the early icons. She has a comparable vulnerability, out in the wild, to Ariadne on her rocks, and the attendants hover over basins of water and hold long-necked jars as if they had recently escaped from the Late Antique. The sixteenth-century icon of the Virgin giving birth, from Klonari in Cyprus, shows her lying on the ground, legs crossed, with dense and concealing clothing and her arms tightly folded around her body. Her hand flies to her face, turning away from the infant as if she foresaw only grief. But there is the rocky landscape with the intense, distorted trees, and a heavenly host of angels appearing like well-mannered maenads who'd been to finishing school. The little infant is so swaddled he looks like a miniature Lazarus, and his cradle a tiny sarcophagus, a prophetic birth foretelling death. A tiny satyr from the mosaic scenes becomes a small angel or cherub leaning from the sky in the Byzantine icon.

Our visiting professor Pascale Ballet is a French 'proto-Byzantinist', here to examine the Late Roman pottery from Egypt. Her experience is far-reaching, after ten years in Cairo and Alexandria. We visited the Byzantine Museum in Paphos together, exclaiming over entrancing details of everyday life to be seen in the icons. Like a true archaeologist she knows how to look, how to see the revealing detail in each icon. The narrative friezes that border the main image show vivid scenes from the lives of saints and apostles, almost like cartoon strips – a woman pouring water to wash the baby (a Nativity), two friends greeting each other (Elizabeth and Mary), people standing around a bed (the death of the Virgin). In the desert landscape of Egypt stands a gaunt and hairy St Janoufrios, a desert father. St Marina, in her red cloak, shoos away small demons, and St Mamas, riding a lion, holds an alert but fragile lamb. St John the Divine receives a line of text beamed down from heaven into his large head, frowning slightly. The Last Supper shows platters and bowls straight from our excavation. Icons of the Virgin indicate how pre-eminent she was in times of oppression – she was called the Virgin of Tenderness, or Consoler of the Afflicted and Wronged. That steep hillside shown in the icons, with a few jutting trees visible behind the shoulder of a saint, still exists in the shadowed forests of the Troodos.

It was refreshing to be out of the town and high in the mountains a few days ago, after driving up one of the long valleys from the coast into the Byzantine landscape of rocks and pines. Four people in a little hired car, eating Cyprus Delight, on the free day. We stopped to photograph, I scribbled drawings – a little mosque at Kidasi with its crescent and star all bent, but delicate wrought iron on its high railing, and a pointed witch's hat for a roof. The Venetian bridges in the Troodos were the endpoint of the journey, set over streams in the high pine and fir forests. Sycamores grew on the banks, gentle deciduous trees in new sharp-pointed leaves. The milky water rushed over its shallow bed, over grey rocks and under the pointed bridge which rose in a hump. Once camel trains used these bridges, bringing copper ore down from the Troodos to Paphos.

The remote rocky valleys and heights still seem possible sites for the Bacchae of Euripides – I thought of the 'wild women crouching in the ferns like birds'. The stones on the bridge supported a garden of thyme and oregano, and on the banks, grape hyacinth and rock roses bunched on the steep slopes with orange moss and twisted pines, exactly like the birth scenes in the icons. Here the monks and priests retreated in times of persecution by Arabs and Lusignans, by Venetians and Ottomans, to practise the ancient Orthodoxy protected by fortress-like ravines. In the mountains, even in the time of Euripides, travellers and devotees of Dionysos had experienced extreme states of mind. Building precious churches in every high village, the Orthodox Church was secured by inaccessibility.

5. FRAGMENTS

21 April

The wall is my focus – it is one of the dominant architectural features on site, after the quarried remains of the seating. Closely scrutinising the traces of colour on the wall reveals a pattern of vertical red and black bands, with a curve of grey-indigo swung between them that I imagine as a curtain, a swag of drapery. Above the curve the field is yellow cream, with traces of terracotta red, which may indicate ribbons or flowers. The wall must have been deeply coloured, divided into vibrant panels but without evidence of figures.

Every day I go to examine the wall as the disordered rocks and layered dirt slowly decrease through Jenny's excavation. A few clean lines reveal at last that the *parodos* wall on the east stretches straight towards the stage. The earthquake tumble is clear, with perhaps lighter stones indicating a fallen arch. Each great block is 1.2 metres long, cut with beautiful precision, a wall that exudes confidence and strength. Once it would have been at least five metres high, and even when half ruined in the seventh century it would have towered. By then squatters had moved in, building little rooms in the passageway of the *parodos*, tethering donkeys in the *orchestra*, digging a storage pit in the ancient and elegant plaster floor.

20 April

The wind has gone; it's a still morning with the pale light seeming to come from within the battered stones. Each warm day the spring daisies become more withered, but the small asphodel is still in flower with its delicate stars.

Christina, the Danish archaeologist of Roman amphorae, brought me some sprigs of purple blue statice, with tiny white trumpets inside – what a warm, enthusiastic woman she is. She gave a talk on her work in the late afternoon – each expert speaks to the whole team, clustered around the outside eating table for an hour at this time. She spoke about fragments from the theatre site, of transport amphorae from all over the Mediterranean. Amphorae come in many shapes and can hold as much as eighty litres – they are bag shaped from the Levant, but with high necks and sharp contours from Greece. Some of the fragments showed how the handles had been manually twisted in wet clay, still with finger prints. The fabric of the clay had to be made strong and flexible in the firing because these vessels carried everything – but particularly oil, wine and *garum*, the fish sauce which was a staple of Roman cooking. The 'cardboard box of antiquity' was recycled and used prolifically, criss-crossing the trade routes, and because shapes changed slightly every thirty years or so, amphorae can be 'read' as a key to dating. 'The eighth hill of Rome is a hill of amphorae fragments,' said Christina.

Sometimes the long day seems like a succession of isolated moments, each stretching out and overlapping with the next. It is a pleasure to have my son Rowan, now a student at the University of Sydney, working in the drawing office. As well as drawing, he has taken on the task of providing excellent coffee, always welcome after the early morning start.

I had coffee briefly with Richard under the palm tree beside the drawing area. Most of us work outside, with the partial shelter of a veranda on the old farmhouse that is the study area. Swallows and sparrows swoop among people busy at many essential tasks, standing at sorting tables, washing and mending pottery, photographing outside with improvised lights and props.

Brush, the retired geologist, was seated today as usual on a stool beside an old iron bedstead, loaded with fragments of architectural marble: fluted column drums, bits of architraves, marble in every tone from dark grey to pure white. He writes lists extremely neatly in a school exercise book, momentarily in control of the unruly fragments. The old bed reminded me of the lists of blankets written out in copperplate by the early administrators of the Illawarra, blankets designating particular Aboriginal people, their names and tribe. The dispossessed Aboriginal people were lined up and given basic foodstuffs and coverings by the British government officials, who noted every item and the name of the recipient. Lists to cover disintegration and trauma, something small and orderly, which turned out to be the only documentation of the loss of a whole way of life.

The marble from all over the Mediterranean had intricate affinities to place, Brush told me. 'This striated peach colour is Breccia di Settebasi, from Skyros off Euboea in Greece. This is Verde Antico, an expensive thin facing which came into fashion in Hadrian's time. The marble called Africano is variable, sometimes grey, sometimes honey-coloured with streaks of white. A conglomerate of grey-white may be from Libya, or even Numidia. The distinctive spiral columns are of a blue-grey dark Breccia, and the columns are worked both right-handed and left-handed.'

Brush's deduction that many of the theatre's architectural marbles may have been re-used in the basilica of Ayia Khrysopolitissa, not far from the site, has been very significant. He was from Liverpool, and after being demobbed in the war he went to Cyprus as a geological engineer/surveyor, long before the 1974 division. (Smiling, he tells me stories about the time of the British colonial government: 'Turks in Paphos were richer than Greeks, and for a Greek girl to marry a Turk was to be upwardly mobile.') His discovery of the recycled stones gives a date for the end of the theatre at the same time as the building of the great church, probably after the major earthquake of AD 353. Looking at all the Roman columns on the basilica site suggests to Richard and Geoff the restoration of the stage building with more certainty – plain columns on the bottom storey, spiral ones on the top.

I sorted and labelled all the less crucial, 'non-diagnostic' plaster, anxious to get to the major pieces which wait under the olive tree, with tantalising clues to the painted wall. Estelle worked beside me brushing and sorting piles of animal bones excavated over many years across the theatre site – chickens, donkeys, goats for the most part, often with signs of butchering. Bone dust floats in the heat. She is small and intense, with clouds of hair above her large eyes, and is susceptible to breathlessness. For someone whose task is bone, dust is inevitable. Holding up a tiny jawbone – 'This is the smallest lamb I've ever seen.'

The endless talk around me sometimes drains my attention. We all work in cramped situations, open to weather and wind, dust or sun. Today there was an erratic conversation to lighten the concentrated work – an endless game imagining which film star might play each member of the team in a dramatic film of the dig. The theatre in Roman times must have catered for just such an appetite for the beautiful, the quirky, or the idiosyncratic. (The cast included Judy Davis, Helena Bonham Carter, and Woody Allen.)

6. THE FIFTH CENTURY

23 April

The arc of the sea from the top of the site this morning was an almost indigo blue. Augustine at the end of *The City of God* observed death and destruction were all around him as the Gauls moved in on his city. He wrote of the consolation of the sea, 'the grandeur of the spectacle of the sea itself as it slips on and off its many colours like robes ... shades of green, now purple, now sky blue.'[15]

Richard came in with a tall thin woman, Charlotte Roueché, a very experienced archaeologist and epigrapher from the University of London who works in Aphrodisias in Turkey. This is another Greco-Roman site with a complicated theatre of many periods. She looked at my tentative reconstruction of the painted wall, with its animated and even garish patterns, and thought it was plausible. Her alert and charming interest in the problems of the *parodos* warmed me, as well as her respect for the later mosaics in the House of Theseus and the House of Dionysos. 'My period, fifth century, so interesting.' She had come to Paphos just to think about the mosaics. We talked of how the entrance to the theatre must have been a public space, with the Dionysian motifs of ribbons, flowering sprigs and swags of drapery forming a backdrop to the people entering in rich clothes, and perhaps actors carrying masks. She also mentioned an elusive painted wall in the theatre of Ephesos, of which I had found no trace. It had once shown seated figures in fifth-century clothes but had gone black and encrusted after exposure to the light, and had never been published. She reminded me that the theatre was a political entity, a place for the display of power and status.

The presence of a theatre in Late Roman towns defined the status of the society. Libanius, an intellectual in Antioch, a city in close contact with Paphos, wrote to the apostate emperor Julian (who resuscitated the ideals of paganism) in the late fourth century. He described how the emperor's statues had been attacked by the crowd, 'dragged along, either whole or smashed to bits'. When the emperor punished Antioch with a military attack for this outrage Libanius wrote poignantly:

> Our city has changed entirely – to be more accurate it is not a city at all. The theatre there is shut: so is the racecourse... No bridegroom takes his bride back home, no torch is lit for the marriage, no marriage song is sung. All the flutes and pipes and songs have left us. There is no jest, no witticism, no drinking party. Absolutely nothing can be seen here that is conducive to pleasure and enjoyment.
>
> There are to be no horse races: no one is to go to the theatre, either to give or partake of enjoyment. The great city is to have the title of a petty town, and it is to keep away from the luxury of the baths.[16]

Libanius makes it clear that to be denied the civic and public life of the agora, the theatre, the baths, the racetrack or amphitheatre, was to be outside a civilised life, a life of stimulation and enjoyment.

Deciphering rubbed and fragmentary inscriptions in dialects of ancient Greek and Latin is a formidable sphere of knowledge that is increasingly rare and gives scholars an air of singular dedication and sometimes eccentricity. Estelle, a forensic archaeologist who studies human bones, told us she was always served first in the shops of Pompeii and people tended to cross themselves as she went past.

Because of the conversation with Charlotte I went to look again at the astonishing fifth-century mosaic of the the First Bath of Achilles in the main audience room of the House of Theseus. A nurse kneels, holding the baby Achilles in front of a large basin of water, while a servant girl, Ambrosia, brings more water in a jug. His mother Thetis lies on a couch, with a curtain swung behind in rigid folds. (Charlotte was particularly interested in this curtain as a theatrical device.) The three Fates stand near Peleus, Thetis' husband (but not father to Achilles), and have come to pronounce the future of the child: Clotho carries a spindle and a distaff to spin the thread of his life, Lachesis has a wooden panel and a stylus to write his history, and Atropos an open scroll to record his destiny. Their wide eyes and stiff postures foreshadow Byzantine compositions in style as well as content. Once the mosaic would have been in a dim if spacious room but now only traces of walls remain. The figures look strange set in the ground among meadow flowers under the open sky. They gaze up at us, travellers from another hemisphere, unknown to their world.

It is intriguing that there are two scenes focusing on children in the Late Roman houses of Aion and Theseus – the Procession of the Baby Dionysos, and the the First Bath of Achilles. The western Roman Empire was in turmoil by the fifth century, and the great city itself was sacked by invading Goths in 410, about the same time as this mosaic was made. Augustine reported on how Pelagius, a monk from Britain who was in Rome at the time, experienced the inconceivable event:

> Rome, the mistress of the world, shivered, crushed with fear, at the sound of the blaring trumpets and the howling of the Goths... Everyone was mingled together and shaken with fear; every household had its grief and an all-pervading terror gripped us. Slave and noble were one. The same spectre of death stalked before us all.[17]

Although the eastern Roman Empire, including Cyprus and the provinces of southern Turkey, remained secure for a few more centuries, there must have been great anxiety. The terror of the Goths had replaced the terror of Dionysos. At such times, the birth of a child might have seemed a potent symbol for survival.

7. THE PAINTED WALL UNCOVERED

24 April

Today was the very significant day. Geoff, examining newly excavated stones, said we had found the keystone for the arch of the barrel vault of the theatre entrance. I caught my breath as the curved stone was carried over from the trench in a wheelbarrow and placed under the olive tree (the study area for painted stones) and I could see, from Geoff's measurements, that indeed it must have been in the centre of a shallow arch. Even encrusted with earth I could see a curve of a red stroke against a grey background – could it be the ribbon again? The plaster is fragile and liable to damage from light and atmosphere. Bob is one of the excavators from this trench and is helping me clean the stones in the afternoon after digging all morning, delicately scraping the encrustations with a dental pick, under the supervision of the conservator, Jo. I cannot look at the plaster properly until it has been cleaned.

Many more pieces of painted plaster and plastered stones are being lifted out of the earth from the *parodos* trench – the fragments are passed up by the shovellers to the top of the baulk, half a metre above their shoulders. I keep darting over to the excavation to see what else has been found. The entrance is now clearly defined on both sides, with clear evidence of a barrel vault in the shaped ceiling stones from the tumble on the floor.

Later I walked with Rowan across Fabrika. A cloud of white and tortoiseshell butterflies floated among the withering flowers of the site and – what Rowan calls the minaret flower – high stalks of wild garlic with tight purple clusters in a circle. These are just opening now, in the intense dry heat and hot winds. Rowan showed me the rock where he sometimes sits to draw, near the cliffs of the north-east gate, just beside the theatre. Here the pilgrims used to leave to walk to Palaepaphos and it's still an evocative entrance set among fallen rocks, with small terebinth trees and dessicated flowers. The dusty ground is littered with potsherds and fragments of plaster, ancient and modern.

30 April

The sky was grey, booming with thunder, and a hot dusty wind made conditions difficult all day. I worked at precisely documenting the main pieces, which showed several layers of paint, with new plaster applied over an older layer. The minute observation under the magnifying glass does give new insights. I think I've identified a coarse painted pattern in red on white as Late Roman. The odd scumbled pieces with what Bob calls 'smears' of red paint are illuminating and oddly remind me of the wild strokes and patterns done on bark by Aboriginal women in Bathurst Island in north Australia.

The soil around the stone tumble of the entrance included not only fragments of painted wall plaster, but also plaster that once covered the seats of the *cavea*, and another kind of coarser plaster, unpainted, which may possibly be medieval. I collected small samples painted with different pigments, to be analysed in Sydney, after permission is given for them to travel out of Cyprus.

Grit constantly blown by the hot wind on to my notebook has to be ignored.

I began to make drawings and descriptions of the painted stones from the arch of the *parodos*, which the architect Geoff calls one of the most important discoveries to date. The spontaneity of the fresco artist's hand in placing the sprigs and curls of vegetation — this is still fresh. Surprisingly, more can sometimes be shown in the drawing of the fragments than in photography — the photograph, subject to the vagaries of light, does not easily show hints of a form of a leaf or a flower.

Mostly, the painted stones show flowers — a scattering of turquoise tendrils and red buds across a creamy yellow ground, with no discernible repeat pattern. The field of floral ornament and crinkled ribbons seem to be bordered by deep red bands. The looping red ribbon on the grey-cream background could have formed part of a central design of the vaulted ceiling.

Finding the curving red ribbon or fillet painted on the block was an exhilarating confirmation of my reading in theatrical and funerary images. The word comes from *filum*, a thread, and refers to the ties which adorned sacrificial animals, as well as to headbands. Roberto Calasso has described the invisibility and ubiquity of these fillets or ties in his layered book on Greek mythology:

> Whenever the dullness of the profane was left behind, whenever life grew more intense in whatever way, through honour or death, victory or sacrifice, marriage or prayer, purification or mourning ... the Greeks would celebrate with fluttering strips of wool, which they tied around their heads, or arms, or to a statue... The modern eye encounters these woollen strips everywhere in the fragments that have come down to us but doesn't see them, removes them from the centre of attention as insignificant. To the Greek eye the opposite was the case: it was those light fluttering strips of wool that generated meaning, gave it boundaries.[18]

The same twining, floating ribbons are found in the Hellenistic garland tomb down the road, and around the Dionysian mosaics in the Roman houses. Wreaths and garlands had a double meaning – victories achieved in life, and also a sign of passing away. For an actor, the highest award in the dramatic festivals was the 'crown', the wreath, when the acclaimed actor was *stephanites*, garlanded. There's a fine gravestone of an actor in the Pierides Museum in Nicosia showing two round wreaths and proclaiming 'Agathocles, son of Mopsos, an excellent actor and writer of mimes'. From the Hellenistic history of Paphos, four hundred years before Agathocles, inscriptions show the existence of a vigorous Guild of Dionysiac

Artists. They may well have paraded into the theatre through the *parodos*, and held meetings there.

Flowers and leaves are at the heart of the ephemeral, their beauty lasting a few days, and this sentiment pervades ancient poetry. Marcus Aurelius, the philosopher emperor, in whose time Paphos and its theatre had status and prosperity quoted this passage of Homer in his *Meditations*:

> Men in their generations are like the leaves of the trees. The wind blows and one year's leaves are scattered on the ground; but the trees burst into bud and put on fresh ones when the spring comes around.[19]

With stoic fortitude he warned that the multitudes of voices around him shouting praises or curses were transient:

> One and all they flower in the season of springtime... Impermanence is the badge of each and every one; and yet you chase after them, or flee from them as though they were to endure for all eternity. A short time, and your eyes will close.[20]

Buds and tendrils are scattered in the frescoes on the entrance to the theatre, just as they sprinkle the ground around Ariadne on the painted wall in the theatrical rooms in Ephesos. Ribbons, garlands, trailing vines or just a few red buds trace the passage of Dionysos, a diaspora of flowers.

Making the indispensable garlands and wreaths for public and private festivities was a fulltime occupation. 'Garland-weaver' has been found on tomb inscriptions. Because garlands were an intrinsic part of life, people dreamt about them and Artemidorus in his renowned dream book categorised the meanings of a great variety of different leaves and flowers. He was writing in the second century, about the same time as Marcus Aurelius:

Garlands of narcissus are unlucky... Violets in season are a sign of good luck, but garlands of dark blue violets signify death – for the colour dark blue has a certain affinity with death. Garlands of roses in season indicate good luck for all except those who are sick or trying to conceal themselves. They symbolise death for the sick because they wither quickly.[21]

As the seasons change I notice the persistent flowers growing in the crevices of the site; cyclamen, asphodel, anemone and spring poppy are like a memory of ancient ceremonies. An emotion of perilous fragility hovers over the fragmentary flowers of the frescoes.

8. EMERGING COLOUR AND SPECTACLE

26 April

A beautiful clear day with no wind as I sorted and cleaned the new plaster excavated yesterday, and found some unforeseen designs. Slowly, tremulously, I brushed off the dusty earth of a thousand years and saw that spontaneous painted mark emerging – spots of brilliant blue, softer green 'celadon', Indian yellow, strokes of red oxides like blood stains on the cream plaster.

With his refined expertise in colour, Ian is mixing exact reproductions of the fresco colours in gouache, so that we can use a colour template in photographs. When the plaster is damp it is bright and deep in hue, and then dries to a much paler tone. The Romans polished their painted walls, burnishing the plaster smooth and shining to deepen the colour.

Tone, lightness and darkness, was a most important aspect of colour. It was the brilliance of colour, rather than its hue, that held meaning. Light was life, 'the light of the sun', and darkness was the shadowy afterlife. In Athens I had copied an inscription from a memorable Attic gravestone from the Sacred Way. A woman, Ampharete, with bent head, holds a baby above the fine rippling folds in her lap: 'I am holding here the beloved child of my daughter, whom I held on my lap when alive we beheld the light of the sun; and now I am holding it dead, as I am myself dead.'[22] When the fifth-century BC gravestone was first excavated there were still touches of colour on the smooth marble.[23]

Although the rich terracotta red that is on nearly every fragment is dark in tone, in ancient times red was the colour of the sun and of fire, the colour of light. Purple was considered the most beautiful colour because it held tones of red in its lustrous surface. Some of the patterns I am describing on the painted plaster imitate red and gold veined marble. The dense purple-red marble, porphyry, seen in the scintillating marbles of Ayia Sophia in Istanbul is imitated in fresco. Purple was the imperial colour – you could be prosecuted for dressing in a purple robe if you were not of the imperial class. I try to draw the fragments with their drifts of colour exactly, to the last millimetre. This requires absolute concentration, and the pleasure of documentation, of making sense of the traces, is obsessive.

Mixing the right purple-red is difficult, as it is a shifting colour, sometimes aubergine, sometimes more a Venetian red. The table is heaped with my boxes of plaster in different stages – some still to be sorted and labelled. I can't understand how so many patterns could fit in a five-metre-long vaulted corridor. The essential task of marking the inventory numbers and location on the fragments is a job I dislike because of the smell of the acetone varnish and the rough, difficult surface of the back of the plaster fragments.

The colours are composed of about ten distinct hues, and I recognise the colours in all the fresco I have seen in Cyprus, as if the pigments had a common origin. Red and yellow earth colour with black and white were the classical palette from earliest examples. Added to these is a turquoise green, a cerulean blue (probably from Egyptian blue frit, called *caeruleum*), an indigo, and purple grey. We know that colours were not often mixed together to make shades, but were used as unmixed pigment, each with its own distinct character. Colours may have been mixed on the painting itself, through cross-hatching or layering, because of the philosophical aversion to mixing. There's a strange comment in Plutarch about mixing colours:

> Mixing produces conflict, conflict produces change, and putrefaction is a kind of change. That is why painters call a blending of colours a deflowering.[24]

It's the architectural function of colour in the painted ceiling that is compelling, as well as the motifs themselves. It seems as if the ceiling may have been a creamy tint with red flowers and green tendrils, within a geometric figure. The yellow colour may have lightened the dimness of the arched corridor. I had noticed in the Roman houses in Ephesos the low level of light in the windowless rooms or even in the shadowed peristyles of courtyards. Unlike the bright white walls usual in looking at contemporary art, the viewer must have seen paintings in a faint light, as is still common in churches. The painted decoration added to, and perhaps mysteriously extended, the sense of space and volume in low luminosity.[25]

I have intimations, suddenly, poring over these fragments, of a different kind of sensibility that might be relevant for makers of contemporary decorative arts. Mark Rothko, the American colour-field painter, was influenced by Roman murals when he visited Pompeii in 1959. He commented that the great sheets of intense colour made an architectonic environment controlled by colour, lifting the mind to a place beyond the reach of logic. He felt his work was linked to remote antiquity through the use of emotive colour. 'I have been painting Greek temples all my life without knowing it.'[26]

There are often hurrying clouds in Paphos. We were called to the top of the site to look at a great grey water spout in the early afternoon, a long twisting funnel like a tornado reaching down into the sea out of a massive nimbus cloud of indigo.

5 May

I'm writing this on a hot night after a day when the heat dried and shrivelled the last green touches – now the grass is a rustling orange yellow in the evening light.

Plaster is coming up from many places: a pattern of decorative designs across the theatre is emerging, from Mel's uppermost trench on the western perimeter, to Craig's orchestral trench with its actors' tunnel. I'm involved in working out the conundrum of many motifs, dreaming of the former richness of the theatre that must have been, as Lucretius described, 'a wash of colourful delight'.[27] The variety and diversity of patterns within a relatively small area emphasises for me the importance of making a brilliant and extravagant spectacle. Richard has often talked of how the theatre was converted for aquatic spectacles by the addition of waterproof plaster and a balustrade around the orchestral area, allowing imitation naval battles and possibly gladiatorial events to take place.

Apuleius describes the irresistible attraction of mimes and elaborate scenery using water in the second century:

> The scene was an artificial wooden mountain, supposed to represent Homer's famous Mt Ida, an imposing piece of stage architecture, quite high, turfed all over and planted with scores of trees. The designer had contrived that a stream should break out at the top of the mountain and tumble down the side. A herd of she-goats was cropping the grass, and a young man strolled about supposedly in charge of them, dressed in flowing Asiatic robes with a gold tiara on his head. He represented Paris the Phrygian shepherd.

After Paris gave the golden apple to the ever popular Venus more marvels took place:

> Then a fountain of wine, mixed with saffron broke out from a con-

cealed pipe at the mountain top and its many jets sprinkled the pasturing goats with a scented shower, so that their white hair was stained a rich yellow traditionally associated with the flocks that feed on Mt Ida. The scent filled the whole theatre, and then the stage machinery was set in motion, the earth seemed to gape and the mountain disappeared from view.[28]

Another kind of spectacle is absorbing me at the moment, a spectacle for the small screen. The computer allows moving images to be made from a sequence of still photographs. Late in the afternoon when it was cooler and without direct sun I went on site to help Patrick the photographer set up the shots for me of the wall to use in such a 'virtual reality' reconstruction. A postgraduate scholar, Hilary Rhodes, is constructing lost and imaginary landscapes digitally, with reference to geo-scientific data, through an amalgam of software programs. She will construct a moving version of the wall, on which I can place a possible reconstruction of the paintings.

Washes of pale light at dusk brought up every detail in the surface of the wall – the cracking plaster, the tiny caper bushes, occasional glistening beetles and a few intrepid snails. First Patrick organised a series of overlapping 'texture' pictures, on a 50 lens, then another series using a 28 wide angle lens, turning the camera on the tripod for nearly 360 degrees. Patrick is thin and totally concentrated on whatever he is doing. Half of his face and shirt was covered with dust through lying on the ground to photograph, like some scholarly jester. It is a constant challenge to produce excellent results in fieldwork conditions, needing an ability to focus on the problem itself rather than the discomfort.

The setting sun reflected a particular luminosity on the eroded stones, as I made notes. I felt happy, crouching on the *parodos* floor again, looking up at the light sky of evening soaring with swallows and one small pointy-winged hawk high above the summer foliage of the terebinth tree. As I stared at the ruined wall I seemed to see a procession, the *pompe*, of actors and dignitaries passing endlessly in the flickering shadows.

9. THE DIVIDED CITY: NICOSIA

2 January 2002

In this winter season I've set off alone from Australia for a month of focused work. The best place to do research in Cyprus is the capital, Nicosia, or Lefkosia, home of the Cyprus Museum, the University, and the Cyprus American Archaeological Research Institute. It is such a political and edgy city, which tends to define priorities clearly.

Viewed from the jet highway thousands of metres in the air the star shape of the old fortified city of Nicosia is astonishing, embedded like a mosaic of scattered *tesserae* in a brown plain drenched with light, not far from the folded shadows of the Kyrenia mountains. Height and distance hide the bitter conflicts of the divided town, where the Green Line has been patrolled since 1974 by the United Nations, with Greek and Turkish soldiers confronting each other across a no-man's land that is sometimes twenty metres wide sometimes much more. From high in the air the city is detached from its history, like an archaeological map of a site. The closer one gets the more the city is like a palimpsest of histories inscribed one above the other in a series of textured and disintegrating layers. The Paphos theatre site, although more than a hundred kilometres to the west, with all its broken walls and fragments of many periods has a kind of resemblance to the contemporary archaeology of the derelict streets dividing the centre of the Cypriot capital.

The process of travelling to the city on the ground can also be momentous. Once I drove into Nicosia late in the afternoon with the last light raking low over an almost medieval landscape, such as you might see in the background of an icon. Among white crusty hills, a few twisted black trees grew from rock in hills terraced like an exercise in geometry. Black clouds hung over rippling fields of grain, rows of ragged olive trees and eroding stone walls. A few villages crouched in the softer valleys, and then the high pointed peak of Stavrovouni, the Mountain of the Cross, appeared, a mark of extreme piety up against the sky.

This almost empty bit of country so near the border with Turkish occupied Cyprus seems to be in a different time zone from the present. If one could stop the car and move away from all responsibilities one might move into another time and place, vanish into that country where I once picked wild purple lavender growing profusely in the rocky ground. And suddenly, from a rise, there are the Kyrenia Mountains, with an improbable and enormous image of the Turkish Cypriot flag drawn in stones suspended on the slopes above the city, Nicosia.

On another occasion during the tensions of the Balkan wars the taxi driver who took me from Larnaca airport to Nicosia was a heavy youngish man with great dark eyes. The car radio was playing patriotic music – I caught fragmentary phrases '*Ellas, patrida, emaste Ellenes.* Greece, fatherland, we are Greeks.' It was the anniversary of the day the British left in 1960. We spoke in Greek and I managed to understand his Cypriot accent that sometimes seems almost another language, with its low 'sshh' sound recurring. He was born in Kyrenia and now lives in Nicosia with his mother. His father was killed in fighting the Turks, whom he spoke of with a tribal hate, like the traditional ferocity so apparent in the countries of the former Yugoslavia, an emotion which refuses to recognise that the mirroring of hatred on each side could go on forever. His manner was cool to me, I felt, as an English-speaking westerner, though he was perfectly polite.

The Cyprus American Archaeological Research Institute (CAARI) when we arrived was quiet with the public holiday. So often this lovely, capacious house has been a destination and a sanctuary when staying in Nicosia, with its simple but comfortable accommodation for a few scholars or students and its great reference library of Cypriot culture. Dr Nancy Serwint, the director, told me there had been many demonstrations against the American embassy here and in Athens, because of the bombing of the Orthodox Serbs by NATO. 'You should lie low,' she said, even though I'm Australian. The colonial past was also difficult; the British had been clumsy in their handling of desires for independence. The name Nicosia, used by occupiers of Cyprus since the Crusades – Lusignans, Venetians, Ottomans and British – is now replaced in all signs with Lefkosia, the ancient name.

I walked early the next morning down Byron Avenue. A few domains of nineteenth-century family houses in gardens of bougainvillea, geraniums and wisteria remained, but many of the houses were empty shells awaiting removal or possibly restoration. People were preoccupied and unusually, nobody greeted me in the streets. When I asked the way, an older man almost snarled directions at me. Of course, yesterday was the celebration of the overthrow of the British and I saw graffitti in Greek – 'No to the Americans!' 'Death to fascists!' The Greek Orthodox Church identified with the Orthodox Church in Serbia against NATO. It was perhaps logical, if simplistic, to identify every blonde foreigner with the bombing.

At the Paphos Gate, near the Green Line watched over by Turkish soldiers, is a bronze statue of a Markos Drakos, an EOKA fighter, throwing a grenade. A group of young soldiers in camouflage gear was shuffling across the road in front of this monument, with their black automatic rifles slung over their shoulders, or hanging rather randomly. I walked through the gate where old sand-bags were sandwiched with rough concrete and brick gun towers built over the sixteenth-century fortifications. These massive Venetian walls which form the eleven-pointed star of the city plan still give a shape to the present conflict. Nearby was the Spitfire Café, long empty, shrouded in dust.

The Roman Catholic Church alongside the Spitfire Café is technically in the dead zone and the altar end of the church actually abuts on to Turkish-occupied territory, so one entrance is permanently closed. I went in hesitantly: and was struck by the calm spaciousness of the neo-classical interior, with white and grey trompe l'œil marble, and a roof with clerestorey windows. Very realistic statues of feminised saints stood in side chapels, standing firm against the menace all around. Christ was bloody and dead, rather too graphically, I thought, at the foot of the cross. An old man walked up and down the aisle, reading. An English woman came in, and smiled at me as she hurried to the sacristy. A small Sri Lankan woman crept in near St Francis' altar and knelt. At least, a place of order and sanctuary for some. But if one reads a place through glance, gesture and fleeting impressions in the street, Nicosia at that moment was not welcoming, although its melting layers and juxtapositions of old and new make it a fascinating and thought-provoking city, its wounds laying bare what other cities have concealed.

This time, two years later, Nicosia felt different. Arriving on a Sunday morning I found the key to my room in an envelope pasted on the outside door, and let myself in to the familiar, peaceful rooms, decorated with traditional Cypriot artefacts. Remembering the past tensions of the streets accentuated my need to rest. I thought I would lie down for a little before starting work in the library, but a great tide of sleep washed over me. Months of dense work, nights shortened in order to read the next thesis, must have caught up with me. I slept for twelve hours, and then lay awake, moving thoughts around in the luxury of solitude and unstructured, reflective time.

10 January

I wake every morning in my calm room, sun coming in onto the tiled floor, making moving patterns of curly wrought iron through the white curtain, illuminating the thick-skinned Cypriot oranges on a plate on my table. The balcony overlooks a garden beneath, with an old palm tree, a carob, lemons, and a towering pink bougainvillea. After the day's work investigating nuances of Roman painting, I often go outside. While the limpid evening sky is spotted with birds, I hear the distant muezzin of a mosque on the other side of the city. Sounds can't be shut out, even with the armed barrier of the Green Line.

I search the library for clues to the frescoes and to understand the place of theatre. The mosaic of research is punctuated with individual stories that cross over disciplines, and weave together past and present. CAARI is a place where streams of scholars pass through, each defined by some passion or concern – a young American making forensic studies of Neolithic skulls, a geologist examining rock strata for evidence of earthquakes, a sculptor working with 'objects of memory' from refugee villages. Robert, a linguist in ancient languages from Edinburgh University, showed me a photocopy of the painted patterns from a Bronze Age dish that illustrated the attributes of the goddess Astarte. The tree with its cross-hatched trunk, the birds on either side, were all signs of fertility, indicating a 'readiness for love'. Waving the paper around, he said excitedly, 'You can read this like writing, the images function like a text.' His work in languages, in cuneiform and Hebrew is extraordinary. People come to archaeology through strange routes – Robert had turned to ancient languages after a career as a rock star, and brought the same passionate momentum to the decipherment of inscriptions.

'What do your Mesopotamian and Phoenician texts talk about?' I asked him. 'Well, essentially, the importance of having children, and of passing something on.'

10. THE STREET

17 January

Half way along the strange, short road called Odos Andreas Demetrios is the old house and garden of CAARI. Every day I walk down the road, which sometimes seems like a series of stage sets belonging to entirely different dramas. At one end of the road is a substantial marble war memorial, with life-size bronze figures of heroes, a memorial to those lost in the troubles leading up to the establishment of the republic in 1960, and in the confrontation with the Turks in 1974. The heroes look out at gleaming government buildings that have just opened in the next block, while Andreas Demetrios Street still waits to be re-developed. Nearby, taking up several city blocks, is a vast empty stadium with fading soccer advertisements, also due for demolition. Cafés are built into its long walls, some still functioning.

Opposite the war memorial is a boarded up taverna, about to be demolished, and an old open-air cinema, long empty. On the footpath outside the entrance are two concrete containers for plants. No one tends them, and yet the spiky cactuses and aloes persist in living. The ticket windows and painted surfaces are encrusted with soft shades of ochre and purple, textured with flaking fragments of old posters and rusty, faded lettering. Inside the cinema the worn concrete and the tiered stairs look almost ancient in abandonment, even though the structure only dates from the 1950s. A dry and empty fountain sits improbably on the empty concrete floor below a string of washing (sheets, dishcloths). Empty plastic containers roll around in the wind. I imagined that this is how the Paphos theatre must have looked at the end of the fourth century when pagan theatre became unfashionable, and an earthquake had left it severely damaged. Strings of washing would have appeared, as the attention of the town focused away from the old ruin onto the shining new basilicas.

The street has occasional large eucalyptus trees. A curving set of marble stairs, drifting with leaves, leads up from the road only to end in a deep hole cut in the ground. Here are extensive excavations of ancient Nicosia or Ledra, and remains of an early church. Perched on the edge of the trench, looking down at the old basilica, is a tiny white chapel to St George. A strange assortment of offerings hangs from the dense bindings of warp threads wound around the small building, like the old church at Kouklia. A green and black sneaker, a baby's slipper, a white sandal, and a pair of school shoes are tied to the threads, with a shirt and more shoes in a plastic bag. The saint intercedes for children at risk. Steps lead up to the chapel from the small wayside shrine beside the road. The size of a letterbox, it is tilting and unlit, nearly obscured by long grass. But the chapel is well tended – there is a sturdy woman guardian who sits in a white plastic chair, and keeps the candles alight. She places flowers before the innumerable small icons and sweeps the dusty ground around, making an island of order amongst the disintegrating mounds of the excavation. St George, Ayios Yiorgos, is said to cure the sick at the time of the new moon and the full moon. Occasionally he helps children who are late in learning to walk, as well as relieving lunacy, and finding husbands for unmarried girls.

Further down the road, opposite CAARI, a group of colonial barracks built by the British has been bulldozed and the site is a temporary parking area. Early every morning cars pour into it and elegantly dressed people rush away into the nearby city. Substantial family houses are succeeded by gift shops, and a doctor's surgery painted pink. At the farthest end of the street from the war memorial are elite boutiques with designer clothes from Italy and Paris. The impossibly thin mannequins in the window wear filmy dresses of silk organza with detachable sleeves. They are bizarre yet intriguing and beautiful, promising sophistication.

The road is a passageway of emotions, a throughway showing the spasmodic layering of the town. I feel I'm looking at a series of fragmentary tableaux from the distant past into the present. It takes less than ten minutes to walk its entire length. Discarding old buildings and putting up others the city continues to re-invent itself, so that the streets have an unfinished quality of constant readjustment to some ideal, which is not quite clear.

II. WITHIN THE WALLS

19 January

The city centre within the Venetian walls continually draws me back, as a contrast to the prosperous and contemporary city of glass, concrete and metal architecture growing up all around. Every time I walk in the old city I find signs of a hidden and idiosyncratic world. Behind the piled Venetian walls is a maze of small streets and irregular squares from another time, that might have been painted by de Chirico in a surreal moment. I wander and allow myself to become lost.

Glimpses of other lives: here was a woman ironing a red silk shirt in a cavernous workshop. I paused at the sound of music coming from a bicycle repair shop where a large man was bent over, mending an umbrella. I realised that the mesmerising repetitive sounds were a piece by Philip Glass being played on a CD. Nearby in the window of a tailor's shop were two sad, unclothed dummies, while a figure immersed in cloth leaned over a sewing machine. There's an untidy space of tin shacks and crates piled around the old Turkish baths where hairy grass grew out of the low domes. (Perhaps they were still functioning: a sign, 'Women on Tuesdays and Thursdays', was still nailed to the door.) In a quiet street a wooden door weathered with delicate sprays of peeling paint opened on to the narrow road, while a fig tree grew beside it out of a crack in the pavement. Turning a corner, there was an unexpected view of a walled courtyard with blowing palms.

Disconsolate men stood on corners, waiting, or sat at tables in cafés. Older men played backgammon in a shadowed café near the mosque with its surprising Gothic arches – it used to be the Lusignan cathedral and monastery. An exquisite arched doorway with carved quatrefoil reliefs now leads to a car mechanic's yard. This mosque, once the church, was the scene of the terrible sacking by the Turks in 1570, when they defeated the Venetians. I sat in the café across the square and ate goat's cheese soup, its strong flavour leaving an aftertaste like the taste of history. I went into the white painted mosque past carved stone capitals of clustering leaves and saw the lines of string diagonally across the stone floor giving the true orientation to Mecca. Being originally Christian the building had not been properly aligned for the Islamic faith. (I thought of the pervasive history of ritual lines of string.)

Not far away old mud-brick houses were collapsing through neglect and wear – a whole floor had tumbled and prickly pear was growing vigorously from the rubble. Wooden lathes protruded from underneath the melting mud brick with its outer coating of plaster or cement, while an upstairs balcony tilted at a crazy angle. A notice proclaimed in Greek and Turkish, 'Danger: House Collapsing', as if the process might be allowed to continue like a slow motion study. Further up the street a woman was crooning to a baby in a patch of bright sun. Looking over the Green Line into the frozen streets immediately beyond the barrier I saw empty houses with wooden balconies inhabited only by pigeons, grass growing in the street, an old sign saying 'Dentist', flapping. Such desolation seemed much older than a mere twenty-five years or so, and evoked for me the traumatised cities of the seventh century, where the living must have sheltered in whatever they could find, next to ruined areas like this. There was a dead pigeon on the road, a hardly feathered nestling. Perhaps because of the silent emptiness of the area, young men on scooters made as much noise as possible, echoing in the stone streets.

Rising from the centre of the city in Ledra Street is an improbable modern tower from which you can see the whole of Nicosia. I gazed out at the city in crystal winter light, from brown and gold older buildings to the light white and grey concrete of today. The distinctive skeleton of old Ayia Sophia towered above smaller buildings in the Turkish-occupied section of the city. Fairy-tale pointed mountains above Kyrenia made the city a zone of romantic fantasy. In the Leventis Museum nearby I drew a delicate embroidered textile of rioting plant forms in silk on cream linen, and admired a sixteenth-century tapestry of a grandiloquent coat of arms with curvacious ornament, flowers and drapery. A room adjoining was full of spoons and knives (the unexpected joys of small museums) with an astonishing pair of Ottoman spoons which seemed emblematic of stories of the Arabian Nights. They were to serve pilaf, and the bowls were of transparent and beautifully blotched tortoiseshell, while the long handles were of creamy ivory with tips of deep pink coral.

21 January

I found the kind of house that might own tortoiseshell spoons in the Ottoman House of the Dragoman built in 1793. The dragoman's task was to be an intermediary between the Christian subject population and their Turkish rulers, between the Church and the pasha, a difficult job though one where financial acumen could result in great wealth. Set right on the street, the house of Hadjigeorgakis Kornesios had more than thirty-eight rooms and was evocative of an intense family and communal life. It had echoes of large Roman houses, also built with austere unbroken outer walls right on to the road. Inside, there are surprising courtyards and arcades around a garden with a carved fountain and a *hamam*, a small Turkish bath.

Public and private worlds must have intermingled. The two-storey house was spacious and spreading with lofty verandahs and inner rooms somehow poised between inside and outside – in its time it was flexibly furnished with rugs, cushions and mattresses so that rooms could be used as dining rooms or for sleeping. Above the great entrance-way where carriages would have driven in over the cobbles, was a latticed window in the 'kiosk' projecting over the street, where women could sit and look out, without being seen. The present division of Nicosia between Greek Cypriot and Turkish Cypriot is a more hostile version of that ancient and pervasive divide that was in place for nearly four hundred years. The house showed a gracious melding of two points of view tentatively coming together in the patterns of everyday life.

I was the only visitor one winter day, the vast rooms, so sensitively restored to their original colours seemed almost haunted in the spectral light. I caught my reflection in a smoky old mirror, nearly black with age so that the image itself was blurred and softened. I looked like a reflection of the younger travelling woman, a past self I've been so aware of tracking. The indistinct tall blonde looked out of place, the wrong reflection in that mirror which might have held the vivid face of Maroudia Pavlidou, the wife of Hadjigeorgakis. Some friends I had met recently, brought up in Nicosia in the 1950s, remembered the eccentric and forceful character of the last descendant of the family, who lived in the house until her death in 1979, Ioulia Piki. A portrait of Iouliani (died 1894) showed a graceful and restrained woman in a flowing Turkish dress, with her hands curiously placed in her lap, as if in a gesture of resignation.[29] Redolent of cushions and coffee, the house was a focus for family, church and business and was inhabited all day long by many layers of people, who still seem to have an intense presence, like a faint buzz in the air in the empty rooms.

One room was painted an all-encompassing ultramarine blue, and in the main reception area the walls and ceiling were decorated in soft rich colours. A bunch of lilies, narcissus and roses floated on an indigo ground, amongst imitation marble panelling similar to that of the Paphos theatre fifteen hundred years earlier. In another room fragments of all the different colours that had been painted on the plaster one above the other were carefully retained, looking like a small abstract painting of great subtlety. Blue-grey, turquoise, cream, rose-red, and ochre were the same basic vocabulary of technique and colour as ancient frescoes. This fragment of painted wall is an apt metaphor for the city; tears and shreds of colour showing through other faint hues.

Rose Macaulay quoted the nineteenth-century traveller W.H. Mallock in describing the ruins of medieval Nicosia as one of 'confused sadness'. Traces existed of a great Lusignan palace, where one of the kings, Henry II, described by a contemporary, Benvenuto da Imola, lived like a beast 'in superfluity of luxury, gluttony, effeminacy and every kind of pleasure.'[30] The difficulty of the Ottoman period is underlined in Hadjigeorgakis' turbulent life. Despite his attempt to match past grandeur, or even because his riches incited the hatred of his enemies, Hadjigeorgakis Kornesios was beheaded in Constantinople in 1809.

I left the great house and went out into grey rain. I passed an animated market lit up by brilliant piles of oranges, lemons and apples among great baskets of potatoes. Pink and white cyclamens in pots glimmered nearby. I bought some scented narcissus and went to have a fresh orange juice and spinach pie at a small café in the square. 'Ah,' said the woman who brought my food, 'my favourite flowers. They grow up in the hills around my village.'

I walked behind a heavily clothed figure, bent double by plastic shopping bags, who suddenly disappeared into the maze of the city. I looked around for her, but the light fell on empty streets, just one old man stretching on a balcony and two children playing on a roof terrace. People make the streets come alive. The carpenters' yards were thriving, a smell of sawdust drifting out, with little kiosks open for the workmen, for coffee and souvlaki. Two old men sat with a table of oranges, while women served coffee, and opposite the church of St Anthony, stacks of rush-bottomed chairs leaned unsteadily by a carpenter's shop. Deeply weathered surfaces were offset by substantial carved doorways and shuttered windows. I glanced into a narrow alleyway, and saw a date palm flaring at the end.

22 January

I loved walking during my winter month in the cold streets at night under the yellow lights, and the new moon. This protean city is full of gaps, continually being razed and rebuilt. And surprises: walking home late from a concert, there was the floodlit garden of the museum, with sculptured lions, emperors and deities illuminated amongst tapestry trees. Miraculously, even at the late hour, the fountain was playing. The falling water rippled across the pool in the quiet of the night.

12. WINTER PAPHOS

25 January

At the University of Cyprus a few days ago I had a thought-provoking conversation with Professor Demetrios Michaelides, whose wide expertise encompasses knowledge in mosaics and paintings in Hellenistic and Roman sites across Cyprus. The archaeology department is in a beautifully restored house in Gladstone Avenue, near the Anglican Church, revitalising the heart of British colonial Nicosia. We spoke about the tombs in Paphos, where he had taken students last month to see the painted garlands and representations of alabaster. Then he surprised me by mentioning their astonishing ceilings, painted like carpets or the memory of a tent canopy, with fringes and a central panel bordered by decorative panels with kilim-like steps. The connection between painted walls and textiles has been well documented. I was very excited to think there might be a direct connection in Paphos between frescoes and textiles. Generously Professor Michaelides gave me an unpublished study of his to read.

Later, I asked permission from the Department of Antiquities to visit and photograph the two painted tombs in Paphos, and arranged with the director of the Paphos Museum to have the tombs unlocked.

This morning I drove to Paphos through fresh winter landscapes and was warmly greeted at the museum. Then, with the director, Eustathios, and museum staff Neoptolemos and Pambos, we drove to the Greco-Hellenic tombs first explored by Dr Nicolaou in the 1960s. (This is the 'garland' tomb I first saw in 1996.)

I felt a sense of mounting excitement and pleasure in newly exploring the site that I have walked over so constantly, but never in January. We parked the car near the lighthouse and walked, along the old city walls in the late morning, beside the deep blue sea. Brown goats were tethered nearby and the low winter grass was tossing with anemones in white, pink, and blue. A few cyclamens were emerging from under stones at the edge of the wall. I paused beside a spectacular plant with purplish green crinkled leaves spread out in a great rosette on the ground with clusters of small purple bell-shaped flowers rising up from the centre.

'Could it possibly be a mandrake?' I asked Neoptolemos. He was casual – 'Yes, it's a *mandragore*, they always flower here in winter.' This almost mythical plant has deep roots forked like the body of a man and has been used since ancient times for its strong narcotic and poisonous qualities, and even more for its aphrodisiac and amorous properties. As a 'love apple' it was given to sterile women to make them fertile. The plant guide describes its habitat as 'common on roadsides, abandoned fields and stony places'.[31]

Inside, the tombs were damp from the winter rains. Eustathios came inside the 'garland' tomb with me and as I lay on my back on the dirty floor to take overlapping pictures of the ceiling 'carpet' he talked about the significance of the images. He pointed out that the myrtle wreaths were chthonic, of funerary significance in Alexander the Great's Macedonia. The story is that Dionysos had taken a sprig of myrtle to give to Hades when he went to rescue his mother Semele from the underworld and set her amongst the stars. I made some quick notes about the carpet pattern on the roof, getting completely covered in the deep soft dust. Blue green bands surround a deep red central panel, with faint indications of a tracery of leaves and twigs. The outer borders contained stepped patterns, and on two sides (just as in a real woven carpet) long thin triangles of the fringe hung above the myrtle garlands on the walls.

Through detailed scrutiny in the second tomb I discovering a grid pattern for marking out the design incised into the plaster. A meander pattern and a border of spirals surrounded a faint alluring pattern of green leaves in the centre. In the theatre too, the ceiling is painted with leaves, tendrils and flowers. The tombs need much deeper study and detailed drawings, but I was able to mark similarities in the organisation of space and colour to the theatre frescoes.

I asked Eustathios, as I had asked Demetrios Michaelides, 'Do you know why the tombs are painted so beautifully and then locked away? Could it be an Egyptian influence?' There is no clear answer yet to this question until there is much more evidence. Certainly, the painted ceiling might be a lovely visual device to comfort the dead, with a good view from the arched niches where the bodies were laid.

As we emerged from the second tomb, Neoptolemos was waiting outside, smoking and staring at the moist earth at the entrance. Suddenly he leaned forward and picked up an ancient earring, tiny but intact; a very delicate hoop of a gold circlet emerged gleaming from the earth. We all laughed with delight, and the director scrutinised it through his glasses. 'Possibly first century,' he said. At last I thought, there is a shred of truth in the folk story of the 'gold of Aphrodite', buried in tombs. The blue winter day had been propitious, lavish with signs – a mandrake in flower, painted tomb carpets, and a chance find of gold.

Back at the museum I looked at another remarkable find. Sitting in the courtyard under plastic was the heavy marble sarcophagus (sarcophagus I had just realised means 'flesh eater'). Sewerage excavators had unearthed it from a shaft grave two metres deep in the main road in Kato Paphos. I had seen the fragments of the lid with its scales lying in the earth last May, the hole half filled with water. The relief carvings were wonderful, with *erotes* or cupids at games, fighting and wrestling each other on the main side. Medusa heads with garlands filled the other side, and on the ends there were vases with two cupids drinking with little tails like satyrs. The artist understood how to render the gesture of bodies, that living Hellenistic gesture I have found throughout my travels. The sarcophagus was imported and not quite finished, with many figures just roughed out, and is a rare find in Cyprus. Any treasures it might have contained had been looted in antiquity.

26 January

Crystalla taught me two new words today – *traumaturgoi*, for terrorists, and *diabolos*, for the little devil at the foot of Ayia Marina's robe. I am staying in the Crystalla Apartments, run by George and Crystalla, old friends. It's more spacious than the Pyramos and very close to the theatre site. Paphos is home, *to spiti mou*, despite the ferocious development spreading around the town. My room here looks over the little chapel of Ayia Marina with its tiny belfry and barrel vaulted roof. At dusk while I was having tea on the balcony, two slender girls in tight jeans carrying a baby went in – when I went to visit the chapel after dark they'd lit all the floating candles, and the icon lamp. It is homely – an old wooden table in front of the iconostasis, with a white cloth. The icon of Ayia Marina had been half covered by a lace curtain. Her hand, which sometimes holds a hammer, was encased in metal, and the painting around it very worn, probably through kisses, so that half the image of the devil that she was expelling was rubbed out.

It is astonishing to see metal and encaustic paint worn away through the pressure of lips. Lucretius wrote about the slow wear of metal and stone through the touch of water and flesh:

> And with the returning sums of many years
> A ring will wear away on the inside,
> Waterdrops gouge out stone; the hooked plowshare,
> Iron though it is, when worked in the fields will secretly
> Grow thin; we see stone pavement trodden and worn
> By the trample of crowds, bronze guardians of the gates
> Show right hands thinned away under the touch of people
> Greeting them as they stroll by.[32]

Crystalla told me people call in to the chapel briefly whenever they go past, as she does herself. Because Ayia Marina is such an early saint, possibly sixth century, and the chapel is very close to the theatre – less than fifty feet from the eastern entrance – the site of the chapel may well have been a shrine in ancient times.

I woke this morning to a beautiful clear day after anxious dreams. There I was, at home in Paphos, Ayia Marina softly outlined in the early sun, and the pervasive twittering of sparrows – that chattering which is the sound of Cyprus. When I walked down to the theatre I felt as though the site was pleased to see me. (Aboriginal friends would say 'the country recognised me'.) This bit of land is deeply known, yet always changing. After the rains it was covered with lush green meadow plants and sprouting tobacco bushes. Already the sharp cut lines of the trenches were blurring and softening, even though the terebinth trees were still spiky and completely bare of leaves.

I set myself up in the outside study area, alone in the tranquil sun and worked on unfinished gouaches of the painted stones, wrapped and stored with column fragments and architectural marbles under the row of trees, the palm, olive, and bay tree. People passed along the road, greeting me without surprise, and a woman came to pick a bunch of bay leaves.

13. AMATHUS

27 January

With two friends, Glynnis and Cressida, I walked up the steep acropolis of Amathus in a tearing wind, through mounds of stones and low carob trees. The stone heaps were blowing with myriad white cyclamens, a galaxy of flowers, heart-shaped leaves under and between the stones. Amathus is on the edge of the sea near Limassol, a voracious city that seems to be swallowing the coast, eating up small-scale ways of life and agriculture. The site was scoured by a cold wind, and from its heights you looked out on a vast luminous ocean. Traffic noise murmured from the freeway far below. Floors of the temples were clearly seen, but the maze of overlapping foundations interrupted any clear interpretation.

The old kingdom of Amathus has a complex history, bringing together indigenous Cypriot language with Homeric Greek, Phoenician and Egyptian influences. The eastern elements of its culture were as strong as the Greek ones, even though the Greek language was dominant. Aphrodite had a large and renowned temple here, but she was an Aphrodite blended with Hathor, the Egyptian goddess. Extraordinary objects were found here by antiquarians in the nineteenth century: a giant statue of the grotesque Egyptian dwarf god, Bes, which I had seen in Istanbul; inscriptions in Eteocypriot now in the British Museum; wonderfully archaic carvings in New

York. A gigantic carved stone vase, nearly two metres high and weighing twelve tons was shipped to the Louvre in 1865. This small city has fed the great world with its vibrant images.

The acropolis is enclosed by a sixth-century wall from Justinian's time – and is high, higher than Palaepaphos. I've noticed how Aphrodite loved high temple sites overlooking her domain of the sea. Amathus had ties both to indigenous Cypriots and to Homer and a persistent connection to the Ariadne story has brought me here. Plutarch in the second century in his *Life of Theseus* relates that Theseus abandoned Ariadne in Amathus, not in Naxos, and that she died in childbirth here. He mentions a sacred grove associated with the worship of Aphrodite and Ariadne. The French and Cypriot archaeologists who have excavated the site since the 1970s report that there is no important male deity yet discovered on the acropolis. The nursing mother image, the *kourotrophos* figure, turns up as votive figurines near the temple of Aphrodite.[33]

The massive stone vase is the dominant feature, taller than I am, poised on the site among low foundation walls and floors, with a carved relief of bulls between palmettes. One of the original two vases was taken to Paris, but the cast is here, and a fragmentary stone original vase, looking settled and yet surprising. They may have contained water to restore fertility, and cleanse.

The wind blew harder as we walked over the basilica floor of exquisite marble geometric patterns of *opus sectile* towards the very edge of the site, above a cliff. This was where the so-called Tomb of Ariadne had been excavated. It was already 4 p.m. Suddenly a cool haze came over the sun, and it became very cold. My friends left the acropolis to walk down to the sea at the edge of the submerged harbour before dusk, and I started to examine the tomb. It took the form of a key-shaped hole perhaps three metres long, and two metres deep, an Iron Age tomb, possibly eleventh century BC, where a stone slab carved with small hollows (for ritual purposes?) had been found. The hole, lined with stones looked inconsequential, but it is unusual to have a tomb within the city gates. For this reason the archaeologists tentatively identify it with the tomb of Ariadne mentioned by Plutarch.

I sat alone on the site and drew in the wind, the sketchbook almost blown out of my hand. The place was evocative in its unassuming naturalness, a depression in the rocky soil lined with stones on the edge of a steep cliff, its significance almost unimaginable after three thousand years. One version of the momentous journey of Ariadne ended here, in a city devoted to the eastern understanding of the mother goddess, similar to that of Crete, Ariadne's homeland. The tomb cult may have related to the pain and danger of childbirth for both the child and the mother, in this case a refugee mother. There is no way of knowing, except to sift through the texts and the material evidence for tiny indications of possibilities.

The wonderful Hathor heads from Amathus are not at all like women who were abandoned to die in childbirth. They are confident and sexy, holding their breasts in their hands, with weighty swathes of hair curling over their shoulders. A friend of Cressida's had been a draughtswoman for the French excavation. Later she had drawn at the site of Kourion. Once while standing outside having a smoke she had stared at the Byzantine walls criss-crossing the site and noticed a slightly familiar form among the irregular stones. She found two sculptured Hathor heads from column capitals in this way, by observing the oddness of the stones in a Byzantine wall. (Maybe smokers are the new environmental observers, forced to stand and contemplate in the open air, in a way that allows intuitive faculties of vision to emerge, just as Neoptolemos found the gold earring.)

Looking down from the acropolis to the sea, you can see the trapezoid dark shape of the old harbour floating in the blue, now sunk below water level. The patterns of myths and ceremonies, of deities and saints are like that dark shape below the surface of the water. *Mythemes*, referred to in anthropology, form recurring themes that reverberate across generations, like grammar in a language. Both 'myth' and 'mouth' are derived from the same linguistic root. Myth is 'what is spoken', and we walk over the site of Amathus still intrigued and held by the shape of stories. The myth of Ariadne makes something haunting and exceptional out of human pain.

14. THE SEVENTH SEASON

4 November

When I saw the theatre site again eleven months later I remembered how Geoff, the patient and thorough architect of the dig, had described the excavation of the theatre to me as like the episode of the 'perforated sheet' in Salman Rushdie's novel *Midnight's Children*. The young doctor is allowed to see through a seven-inch circle, cut in a sheet, different parts of a young woman's body on every visit. The 'phantasm of the partitioned woman' comes to haunt him, and the sheet becomes something sacred and magical because of the glimpses revealed. The earth of the site is like the sheet – broken and pushed away in places, giving tantalising clues but still not revealing the whole.

It looked as if the sheet of earth was seriously torn when I arrived half way through the season. The theatre site was swarming with more people than I had ever seen working there – it looked like a Brueghel painting of figures building the tower of Babel, except this was a dismantling. Everyone was intent on his or her tasks, scraping, trowelling, wheeling barrows, drawing.

Craig, as the field supervisor, took me on a tour of all the new trenches. Wells and lime kilns were emerging near the stage building, perhaps a 'post-medieval' homestead. Mel was continuing to explore the top of the seating, endeavouring to define the outer perimeter of the theatre. A breathtaking discovery had been made when Brush was investigating the great marble threshold stone lying near the western entrance to the *orchestra*. The top surface of the stone had been revealed for years, but its underside had not been thought of – another instance of the importance of detailed scrutiny. He scraped away earth from underneath it, and felt ridges with his fingers; it was an inscription, the first substantial inscription found on the site. It records the dedication and rebuilding of the theatre by the emperors Antoninus Pius and Marcus Aurelius. By a marvellous chance, the other half of the inscription was in the storerooms of the Paphos Museum.

Similarly, what was thought to be part of a column base in an indistinct context turned out to be a *cippus*, a columnar altar, similar to those lined up in the museum garden. 'In its own way it is just as important as the inscription,' Craig said.

I was very moved to have the name of the emperor Marcus Aurelius, who ruled from AD 161 to 180, associated with the theatre. I had been reading his rather melancholy *Meditations*, written while on endless military duty at the far reaches of Empire, on the Danube. He constantly urged himself to be true to 'what is woven in the pattern of your destiny', and advised a kind of archaeology of self: 'Dig within. There lies the wellspring of good: ever dig and it will flow.'

15. CHANCES

7 November

Today there was an extraordinary chance find in the rubble in Anthoula's trench from the foundation period of fourth-century BC Nea Paphos, or before. The Attic rim of a cup had a shiny black glaze of exceptional quality, and its fabric was a deep close-grained red. It stands out amongst the unglazed Roman domestic pottery like an aristocrat, glowing expensively, an elusive fragment from the golden age of Greek drama. Many of the recent finds have been Late Roman or medieval, and it is good to be reminded of the long trajectory of the theatre.

Edna Stern, the Israeli pottery expert who had recently been working at the medieval site of Acre, was studying the main deposits of medieval glazed ware. As well as one piece from the fourteenth century she identified a fragment of Ming Dynasty porcelain from China, which had made its way across the slow and inevitable trade routes through Asia to Cyprus. Similar ware had been found in Acre, so by chance she was familiar with the type, otherwise it would have slipped past unnoticed.

I was called over to describe for the inventory a torn fragment of earth-coloured fabric that had survived in the stone rubble around the well. It could be of any period – a coarse plain woven linen. Like bone awls, spindles and pins, like plain ware pottery, it is profoundly ordinary. The structure of such a cloth could equally be Roman or woven in the village in the early twentieth century.

Dislocated fragments of conversations from the constantly shifting groups of site workers floated to me where I sat outside documenting the *parodos* plaster, sitting on a column drum. Fran was sorting pottery with Sam; Claudia and Tim cleaned coins with sharp probes and with a wire brush.

'Dick, was the earthquake in 1303 on August 9?'

'Has anyone seen the other two bags of deposit 1206? I know I put them there.'

'If I electroform this coin any more it will disintegrate.'

'Can't you sing something else Fran?'

'Mark, I need to talk to you about those inventory numbers, they haven't been drawn.'

'Do you know how long a Roman foot is?'

A loud exclamation from the site – the well in Jenny's trench has yielded an architectural stone of the Hellenistic period, carved with a meander.

Theatre and Tomb: Cyprus 353

'Do you think this deposit with cooking ware might really be Ottoman plain ware?'

'Hey, I've found two joins!'

Another shout from Kerry's trench – a beautiful fragment of white translucent marble with fragmentary letters – an E? Possibly a P, an L?

The large table is constantly spread with new grids of potsherds brought out from former seasons to establish sequences and connections. The words scattering around me are like the multitudinous fragments of pottery, not joining, in some context that is not quite apparent without further study.

The light pours down from an unclouded sky of a lofty and unvarying blue, and seems to stretch out time, as if it made the minutes pass almost in slow motion.

The archaeologists' fascinated absorption is reflected in children's play. On a vacant block near an apartment building close to the theatre I saw a group of small children, six or seven years old, playing with stones and bits of rubbish. They'd made a square 'house' of stones, and were saying, 'Here is a cigarette box, this can be the father'. 'Here's a stick for the *yaya*, the grandmother.' They had made a rough square out of stones, that familiar tawny limestone, and bits of tile, with a circular hearth full of sticks. Four smaller stones served as seats. The focus of the children's attention is the house and the family, the first space of imagination.

The vacant lot where the children play is opposite the old domed Turkish baths. They too are made from recycled Roman stones, and a marble fragment of an Ionic column spiral lies like a fossilised shell within a rough and battered rectangular foundation wall. The remnants of the foundations are like the children's line of stones outlining the boundaries of the house. I played with the idea of reading the site entirely from the children's viewpoint. That large stone with the mason's V mark must be the grandfather, here is the grandmother, and a whole range of family relationships, sons and daughters and all their children, nieces, nephews and cousins in lines. The stones are a metaphor for all those generations of families that have passed through this place. Under the children's house lies more of the old town of Paphos, and the road they play beside is orientated close to the line of the south-eastern pilgrim road to Palaepaphos.

16. THE TEREBINTH TREE

10 November

This morning I woke to the caw of crows – a sign of mortality. Magpies were flying noisily in and out of the terebinth tree, wheeling above the site all morning, as if to communicate something. The Romans were intensely superstitious about the omens of the natural world, and performed divinatory sacrifices. Here is Propertius:

> I do haruspication with entrails or read
> What the flight of birds portends, or do hydromancy with ghosts
> That show up in bowls of water to tell the future.
> The stars and all the planets, the five zones of the earth
> Are an open book if you know how to read them right.[34]

The terebinth tree stood indomitably amidst all the turbulence of excavation, its leaves turning bronze in the warm autumn sun. It is like a symbol of Dionysos in a tenacious vegetative form providing foliage and shade, looking after his Antipodean performers, this team of celebrants from even further away than India. Every season it has been threatened with destruction, but it is still intact after seven years. Part of the tree is stressed, where its roots have been cut, excavating the actor's tunnel. The naturalist and archaeologist Paul Croft thinks it may be 250 years old, so it could have been planted in 1750, in Ottoman times, before the settlement of Australia.

Sometimes called the turpentine tree, the use of its medicinal qualities and fragrant resin is a classical tradition.

Dr Sophocles Hadjisavvas, the director of the Department of Antiquities, came to the site today unexpectedly, to look at the bulldozing which is changing the shape of the theatre so dramatically and so quickly. It does seem that most of the tiered seating was quarried in antiquity, because no more seating is emerging. Sophocles said firmly that the terebinth tree was doomed in the interests of archaeology. 'The stones hold dampness from the tree,' he said looking across at it. 'The roots go so very deep. To preserve and restore the theatre, it must go.'

As he spoke I watched two magpies balanced atop the bare branches, swaying in the wind. It is like the pupil, the eye of the theatre, a living, breathing entity rooted in the fabric of the ruin.

Standing later under the terebinth tree, the natural point for discussion and meetings, I asked Geoff the architect for his thoughts on the progress of the dig. He nodded towards the entrance hole beneath the boughs of the tree, cutting through the layers of the *orchestra* floor. 'The actors popped up from under the stage into the centre of the *orchestra*,' he said. The tunnel under the tree was mentioned by some people who had lived in the farmer's house (now used as dig accommodation) during the war – they had sheltered under it. The tree is central to all the memories of the people living here.

Yesterday when our medieval food expert, William Woys Weaver, visited the site he gave us two types of terebinth berry to try, black and green. One was oily, one like peppercorns. 'It's cooked with mushrooms to give a flavour like truffles.' The berries are also used in a hard flat bread called *tremithotes*. He produced some, bought in the Limassol market, that looked like the rations of poverty and survival.

11 November

I had a long conversation with Kyria Eleni in her house poised on the edge of the deep trench, a talk about old parents, grandchildren, being a great aunt, and the two *mora* or babies she is looking after. They look very alike, but are cousins, Stelios and Stelios, born from two sisters. The team calls them Castor and Pollux, very delicate looking children, always with long trousers, shoes and socks and little jackets, like miniature adults. They are very unlike the barefoot and physically adventurous Australian toddlers – they remind me of the tiny Christ with large eyes in a waxen face who stands like a miniature man on Mary's lap on the icon just down the road, in the chapel to St John the Baptist, Prodromos.

The little boys stare at me with great seriousness, and slowly smile. 'I have had this one since he was four months old, I am like his mother,' said Kyria Eleni.

I said, 'I often wonder where the little boys went, where is that baby that was constantly on my hip, on my lap?'

'Exactly,' she replied, putting her arms around one of them who had been pushed over by the other. 'That is why I look after them.' The boy laid his sobbing face on her green-shirted breast and half closed his eyes as if this was where he would like to rest forever.

'Stop crying, *agapi mou, stammata*, stopping, stopping,' she soothed.

Meanwhile the other Stelios wept in a corner of the yard as if the end of the world had come, because she had chided him and he was away from that embrace. She smiled and winked at me above his bent head – the centre of that primal drama of giving and denying love. Both the little boys looked up with fascination as her son, a very handsome man of twenty-six, crossed the yard with a nod and a smile to me, moving with energy and intent, immensely self-contained. The two middle-aged women and the babies looked at him, the flower of the family. My son too, is twenty-six.

'Have you grandchildren? I have a tiny one,' Kyria Eleni said with great satisfaction. I had seen Kyria Eleni's mother, stiff and dark-clothed, in her eighties, walking slowly beside her up the road, stopping to peer into the ever deeper hole just beside the road, like an entrance to Hades, her expression said to me. Talking to Kyria Eleni is like having a conversation with people in the tight structures of Aboriginal kinship, where each person is part of a mosaic, a pattern that is essential to life. Without such a net of links, a person does not exist, is a kind of ghost.

Later she walked the tiny boys slowly down the road past the study area, where Sam was patiently teaching a student how to describe and recognise Roman pottery types. Sam is in charge of organising the system of finds across the dig and thinks of many things simultaneously. Seeing the children, she stopped her instruction to give them each a biscuit.

17. THE TOMB IN IKAROU STREET

13 November

Today Eustathios Raptou from the museum rushed in wearing gumboots and holding a hard hat. He suggested that I come with Dave the photographer to help document the paintings in the Odos Ikarou tomb, a few minutes walk from the theatre. I left my close work willingly, eager to see the paintings I had only seen sketches of.

It may have been a Hellenistic tomb originally, with many layers of use. The tomb was actually used as a dwelling in the twelfth to fourteenth centuries, when it was associated with beautiful glazed bowls and stemmed plates. This remarkable medieval pottery from the tomb has become important evidence for Holly's study into the glazed ware from the theatre. The tomb is a deep gash in the middle of the tarmac road, once again found through excavation for laying sewerage pipes. The resources of the Paphos Museum are impossibly stretched by the problems of rescue digs, such as documenting a tomb that cannot be left as a dangerous hole in the middle of the street.

Last winter Dr Raptou showed me the drawings and photographs of the painted tomb in Odos Ikarou with great excitement – a bird, a pomegranate, and scattered flowers very like our flower sprigs. Four arched *loculi* or niches to hold bodies have individual decoration, including a delicately drawn arc of myrtle with berries above the curved niche. The tomb had filled with water and mud but now, at the end of summer the water had drained away and it was possible to enter.

You descend a four-metre ladder into the *dromos* or entrance, taking a powerful halogen light to enter the spacious vaulted tomb, very quiet and dark below the street. The air felt dense and unvisited. The light was attached to a generator in the museum truck. We measured, made notes, photographed, moving with difficulty in the gluey mud on the floor of the tomb. The museum people had to leave quickly, so I returned later to spend time trying to understand the images and the space. Fortunately I knew Martha, the kind and energetic butcher whose small shop was right beside the hole in the street. (We occasionally bought thirty kilos of pork and lamb from her for Australian barbeques.) She allowed me to attach the electric cord of the light to an outlet in her shop, refusing to accept payment and offered me a coffee later, so she could hear about the treasures of the tomb. She will be very glad when the deep hole is sealed up.

I carefully set up the light and organised camera, measuring tools, and tracing paper so that they would be out of the mud. I stood there in the heavy silence and scrutinised the images, vanishing under the encrustations that are the enemies of fresco. I now recognise the two kinds, the crystalline encrustation like a thick varnish, and the thinner black stain that mimics paint. On one wall, just visible under the opaque encrustation of salts were loops of garlands and the outline of two peacocks facing inwards. It was like looking at an image through water that constantly shimmers and breaks your focus.

Being in the tomb, having to move so deliberately in the thick mud, reminds me of being underwater, of trying to draw in a horizontal position in scuba gear. The mud squelched around my gum boots, making it difficult to move, so that every movement to change pencils, to find a clean piece of tracing paper had to be carefully thought out. There was a damp and musty smell. The gauze binding that the conservators placed over the fresco to stabilise it had gone black and mouldy.

The painted surface was in the arch of one of the four *loculi* immediately above where the body must have lain in the sarcophagus, now just an empty bench. The painting was not visible on entering the space – I had to bend over awkwardly inside the arched niche to peer up at the painting. This suggests that the imagery may have been designed primarily for the dead person lying directly below.

The original Hellenistic or Roman sarcophagi and their contents were probably removed in the medieval period, when the beautifully constructed vault was used as a stable for animals, yet parts of the painting has been vividly preserved. Crouching awkwardly I traced with difficulty a pomegranate, a bird, some heart-shaped flowers in pink and red, some long emerald cucumber fruits, a bunch of grapes. Could the shallow rectangle shape be a basket? Tendrils seem to emerge from it. Circles with crosses, and more flowers – all these motifs sprinkled almost arbitrarily over the viewing area of the corpse, like a folk carpet, to give comfort and a place in the tradition. The brush strokes are spontaneous, vigorous, the eye that guided the hand had watched partridges, had held pomegranates and grapes, and was bound by traditional formulas.

Months later, I showed drawings of the images to Jasleen Dhamija, who has spent her life studying the variety and meaning of Indian textiles. 'From my viewpoint,' she said, 'the bird is a spirit bird that speaks for the dead. The pomegranate indicates fertility, or the breasts and ova of women. The heart shaped flower is the poppy, symbolising blood or the heart, with the touch of black pain in the centre.'

Left alone in the thick atmosphere of the tomb, the fierce halogen light burning so warmly that steam rose from the mud, I remembered visiting graves with Tiwi friends in northern Australia earlier in the year. They had called out, with a high pitched yodelling sound, warning cries to the spirits: 'It's alright old man, we're friends, don't worry yourself about us coming on to your land.' You feel the bush listens and acquiesces. There may have been many presences in the Ikarou tomb, used and reused over the centuries, even as a byre for animals. The air was dense with associations and superstitions.

It would be intriguing to find the relationship between the theatre and the tomb, linked through the images of the paintings to Dionysian signs – the myrtle wreaths, pomegranates and red poppy flowers. Looking at catacomb paintings of early Christian art I imagined that the long gourd-like fruits are associated with the Bible story of Jonah and the whale. Because he was disgorged from the whale alive, he was a symbol for rebirth. Could the paintings show the overlap between Christian and pagan in Paphos? All this is speculation, until a detailed study is done.

14 November

On a serene blue day the bulldozer moved in on the eastern entrance to the theatre, a part of the site that is badly preserved. With a grinding roar it uncovered stones and parts of the wall with bewildering rapidity after all the careful slowness of archaeology. The earth of this part of the site has been so disturbed that it was decided, after much deliberation, that such a strategy was justified. Part of the supporting wall that had held up the seating, the *analemma* wall, suddenly appeared, with remains of a well, and a granite column upside down, and a column base. There were even traces of plaster, suggesting another decorated entrance parallel to the western one, but the evidence is slight so far.

Further up at the top of the theatre, with the bulldozer in action, the great arc of seating is becoming apparent – there's an exciting echo of the original breadth. The driver is very careful with his vast machine, trying not to disturb the fragile remains of walls and seats. He is removing centuries of rubble and sculpting the earth into something like the original shell-like space of the seating, making me gasp with the imaginative scope and force of the original concept of the curved seating facing the *orchestra* and stage building. Some kind of restoration of the building may be possible through the Department of Antiquities and the Municipality of Paphos.

Vitruvius famously listed three main principles of architecture: firmness, commodity, and delight or beauty, *venustas*, derived from Venus. He wrote his innovative book in the first century BC about the body of architecture as part of a new world order of Augustan civilisation, based on the universal idea of reason. Beauty, he wrote, was a persuasive force, a civilising emotion. Our involvement with the dissection and excavation of the ruined theatre may be a kind of seduction, I thought, a subversive tactic of Venus-Aphrodite to hold us in sway. Just as we might follow a beloved person, obsessed and unable to keep away, we pursue the excavation of the theatre until we have investigated its boundaries and associations as far as our understanding allows.[35]

Archaeologists must keep within the grid of science but sometimes the grid is shaken. Emily Vermeule points out that archaeologists, like poets, critics and historians spend their working lives as necromancers, 'raising the dead in order to enter into their imagination and experience'.[36]

15 November

I went down to the stretch of sea at dawn – the transparent water held the stones on the sea floor of the harbour as if embedded in glass, like the mosaic *tesserae* touched with gold found in the deep cutting of Carina's trench. The excavation is now sculpting the whole side of Fabrika Hill with convoluted trenches, walls and cuttings.

Early anatomists like Vesalius explored the *fabrica*, the cloth of the human body, with increasingly deeper dissections, uncovering layers of tissues, nerves, blood vessels and at last, bones. The site is like some grotesque dinosauric body. The early anatomists, like archaeologists, probed the dead body in order to understand the living one, progressively peeling away fleshly organs. The theatre is a dark mirror to our own sense of physical self, not reflecting or mirroring us clearly but still related to our own performative architecture. We can sit where they once sat, and gaze out at the sea above the *orchestra*.

Perhaps the physicality of all those people who used the theatres and built them leaves a memory of transient flesh in the absences and the negative spaces of the stone, the worn ruts in trodden marble of hearth or road, and in the round dimples and grooves where sacrifices were made on altars. The theatre site is full of cavities, like eye holes or nose holes in the skull. The ruined blocks of walls scattered by earthquake are like vertebrae across a field after the death of an animal. People formed these immense stony theatres exact to the millimetre, laid stone by stone, ton upon ton. Knowing we die, they built stone tombs at last, exquisitely carved and inscribed with curses on those who might trespass or rob them. The vast, listening theatres seen all across the old Greek routes of the Mediterranean, are voice boxes, places to shout.

As we dig deeper, many different layers are revealed simultaneously, blurring boundaries of time over the great historical span of the ancient theatre, and making it a space entirely specific to the twenty-first century. It would now be unrecognisable to the vast crowds who must have moved through it in different periods of its use, with medieval farm walls rising from the Roman foundations of the stage building, and once hidden cisterns and wells now open to the sky.

The sense of recognition and empathy with ancient inhabited places is common to archaeologists and artists. Richard, the director of the excavation, had been insistent from the beginning that the two approaches were complementary. There is a hunger in the imagination of the artist wanting to find something missing or just on the edge of experience, outside language, some visual clue that might be found in a mark, in a wash of colour or a tracery of threads. The interaction with the things excavated on the site is gripping and profound. Sometimes I wake in the night with an unbearable sense of loss in an empty space without objects, stripped of everything familiar. Walking around the archaeological site of the theatre brings a dawning recognition – of what? The day the painted fresco fragments were brought up into the light from the narrow entrance to the theatre, clogged with earthquake rubble and debris, I recognised them in some kind of epiphany that moved me inexplicably. The colours evoked an unclear emotion, speaking in a language still to be understood.

Always at the last moments of the season, something comes to light – and more painted stones were raised this morning from the western trench, faintly marked with red and indigo. I dreamt the other night that the clue to meaning was in the half-deciphered inscription, the nearly rubbed-out pattern on the fresco fragment. I'll never know the whole design, the complete picture. The obsession is with the vivid fragment, the whisp and trace of the past, an intimation of the great imaginary flowerings of the theatre.

NOTES, BIBLIOGRAPHY
AND INDEX OF PROPER NAMES

NOTES TO PART I

1. Constantine A. Trypanis (ed.), *The Penguin Book of Greek Verse* (Penguin Books, Middlesex, 1988), 134.
2. Lawrence Durrell, *Bitter Lemons*, Faber and Faber (London, 1957, new ed. 1986), 171.
3. Alexander Tzonis and Liane Lefaivre, *Classical Architecture: The Poetics of Order* (MIT Press, Cambridge. Mass., 1988), 28.
4. Christos Ch. Georgiades, *Flowers of Cyprus: Plants of Medicine* (Nicosia, 1992), vol. II, 47.
5. W.A. Daszewski and D. Michaelides, *Guide to the Paphos Mosaics* (Bank of Cyprus Cultural Foundation, 1988), 18.
6. Dimitrios Michaelides, *Cypriot Mosaics* (Department of Antiquities, Proodos Printing and Publishing Co. Ltd, Nicosia, 1992), 35.
7. Demos Christou, *Kourion, its Monuments and Local Museum* (Filokipros Publishing Co. Ltd., Nicosia, 1996), 27.
8. Ibid., 30.
9. Ibid.
10. Fourth meeting of the CIAM, 1933, cited in Tzonis and Lefaivre, *Classical Architecture*, 1.
11. Aristotle, *The Poetics,* ch. VII, para. 35, cited in Tzonis and Lefaivre, *Classical Architecture*, 5.
12. Pindar, *Nemean* VIII, 40-2, cited in Martha C. Nussbaum, *The Fragility of Love,* Cambridge University Press, Cambridge, 1986), 1.
13. Herodotus, *The History of Herodotus.* Edited by E.H. Blakeney and translated by George Rawlinson. 2 vols. (J.M. Dent & Sons, London, 1949), 1, 199.
14. Homer, *Iliad* xiv, 201. Cited in Robert Graves, *The Greek Myths* (Penguin Books, 1960 (first ed. 1955)), 30.
15. Sappho in Trypanis (ed.), *Greek Verse*, 144.
16. G.F. Maier, *A Brief History and Description of Old Paphos (Kouklia)* (Printing Office, Republic of Cyprus, n.d.), 5.

17 Colin Thubron, *Journey into Cyprus* (The Atlantic Monthly Press, New York, 1975), 11.
18 Ibid.
19 Jolanta Mlnarczyk, *Nea Paphos in the Hellenistic Period* (Nea Paphos III Éditions Géologiques, Warsaw, 1990), 25.
20 *The Classic Greek Dictionary* (Follett Publishing Company, Chicago, 1949), 489.
21 Richard Sennett, *Flesh and Stone: The Body and the City in Western Civilization* (Faber and Faber, London, 1994), 106.
22 Elizabeth Bronfen, *The Knotted Subject: Hysteria and its Discontents* (Princeton University Press, New Jersey, 1998), 19.
23 Mlnarczyk, *Nea Paphos*, 80.
24 Artemidorus, *Interpretation of Dreams: Oneirocritica*. Translation and commentary by Robert J. White (Original Books Inc., Torrance, California, 1975), 77.
25 Michael S. Roth with Claire Lyons and Charles Merewether, *Irresistible Decay: Ruins Reclaimed* (Paul Getty Institute, Los Angeles, 1997), 1.
26 Michel de Certeau, *The Practice of Everyday Life*, translated by Stephen Rendall (University of California Press, Berkeley, 1988).
27 Ian McLean, 'Under Saturn: Melancholy and the Colonial Imagination' in Nicholas Thomas and Diane Losche (eds), *Double Vision: Art Histories and Colonial Histories in the Pacific* (Cambridge University Press, 1999), 131-62.
28 Claude Levi-Strauss, *Triste tropiques*, translated by John and Doreen Weightman (Atheneaum, New York, 1974), 37-8, cited in Peter Brunt, 'Clumsy Utopias: an Afterword' in Thomas and Losche (eds), *Double Vision*, 257.
29 Italo Calvino, *Invisible Cities*. William Weaver (trans.). (Vintage Books, London, 1997. First published Italy, 1972), 11.
30 In Roth with Lyons and Merewether, *Irresistible Decay*, 61.
31 Artemidorus, *Interpretation of Dreams*
32 Peggy Phelan, *Mourning Sex: Performing Public Memories* (Routledge, London and New York, 1997).

33 Artemidorus, *Interpretation of Dreams*.
34 Trypanis (ed.), *Greek Verse*. Euripides, *The Bacchae*, 251.
35 *The Vatican Collections: The Papacy and Art* (Metropolitan Museum of Art, New York, 1982), 27.
36 John Schneid and Jasper Svenbro, *The Craft of Zeus: Myths of Weaving and Fabric* (Harvard University Press, Cambridge, Mass., 1996), 13.
37 Sophocles Sophocleous, *Icons of Cyprus* (Museum Publications, Nicosia, 1994), 120, pl. 1A.
38 Gwynneth der Parthog, *Byzantine and Medieval Cyprus: A Guide to the Monuments* (Interworld Publications, 1995; new ed. forthcoming Moufflon Publications, 2004), 48. Andreas Stylianou and Judith A. Stylianou, *The Painted Churches of Cyprus: Treasures of Byzantine Art* (A.G. Leventis Foundation, Nicosia, Cyprus. Second Edition 1997), 349.
39 Sophocleous, *Icons of Cyprus*, 9.
40 Kyriacos C. Markides, *The Mountain of Silence* (Doubleday, New York, 2001), chapter 6, 'Icons and Idols'.
41 D. Talbot Rice, *The Icons of Cyprus*, with chapters by Rupert Gunnis and Tamara Talbot Rice (George Allen and Unwin, London, 1937), 174.
42 *The Confessions of St Augustine*, III, ii, 2 and 4 in Peter Brown, *Augustine of Hippo: a Biography* (Faber and Faber, London, 1967), 39.
43 Sennett, *Flesh and Stone*, 42.
44 Trypanis (ed), *Greek Verse*, 282. Menander, *Vanitas Vanitatum*.
45 der Parthog, *Byzantine and Medieval Cyprus*, 41-3.
46 Sennett, *Flesh and Stone*, 99.
47 Rhea Galanaki, *Heat* 7, 72.
48 Judith Herrin, Margaret Mullett and Catherine Otten-Froux (eds), *Mosaic: Festschrift for A.H.S. Megaw* (British School of Athens Studies 8, London, 2001), 11, and Rita C. Severis, *Travelling Artists in Cyprus 1700-1960* (Philip Wilson Publishers, London, 2000), 241.
49 Durrell, *Bitter Lemons*, 109.

50 Herrin et al., *Mosaic: Festschrift for A.H.S. Megaw*, 11.
51 Christou, *Kourion*, 19.
52 Libanius, *Oration* 23.
53 Charalambos G. Christodoulides, *Saint Neophytos Monastery: History and Art* (Nicosia, 1989), 16.
54 Androula Hadjiyiasemi, *Lefkara Lace Embroidery* (Charalambos I. Philipides and Son Ltd., Nicosia, 1987), 22.
55 Mary R. Lefkowitz and Maureen B. Fant, *Women's Life in Greece and Rome* (Duckworth, 1992), 221-4.
56 The full story is told in Diana Wood Conroy, 'Oblivion and Metamorphosis: Australian Weavers in Relation to Ancient Artefacts from Cyprus' in Sue Rowley (ed.), *Re-inventing Textiles*, vol. 1, *Tradition and Innovation* (Telos Art Publishing, Winchester, 1999), 111-31.
57 K. Nicolaou, 'Excavations at Nea Paphos: The House of Dionysos, Outline of the Campaigns 1964-65' (Report of the Department of Antiquities in Cyprus, 1967), 108.
58 I am indebted to Anton Veenstra for this reference. Porphyry, *On the Cave of the Nymphs*, translated by Thomas Taylor with an introduction by Kathleen Raine (Phanes Press, Grand Rapids 1991), 37-8.
59 Ian Todd, 'Excavations at Sanida' (Report of the Department of Antiquities in Cyprus, 1992), 75-193.

NOTES TO PART II

1 Klaus Wessel, *Coptic Art* (Thames and Hudson, London, 1965), 46, 181.
2 Herodotus, *The History of Herodotus* in 2 vols., edited by E.H. Blakeney, translated by George Rawlinson (J.M. Dent & Sons, London, 1949; original ed. 1910), II, 5-29.
3 Stephen Barker (ed.), *Excavations and Their Objects: Freud's Collection*

of Antiquity (State University of New York Press, Albany, 1996), 10.

4   Sextus Propertius, *Propertius in Love: The Elegies*, translated by David R. Slavitt (University of California Press, Berkeley and Los Angeles, California, 2002), IV, 5, 27.

5   *One of Their Gods* in Edmund Keeley and Philip Sharrard (trans), *Four Greek Poets: C.P. Cavafy, George Seferis, Odysseus Elytis, Nikos Gatsos* (Penguin Books, 1966), 20.

6   Jane Lagoudis Pinchin, *Alexandria Still: Forster, Durrell and Cavafy* (Princeton University Press, Princeton, 1977), 163.

7   William La Riche, *Alexandria: the Sunken City* (Weidenfeld and Nicholson, London, 1996).

8   Plutarch *Demetr.* 12, 3, quoted in W.A. Daszewski, *Corpus of Mosaics from Egypt. I: Hellenistic and Roman Period* (Verlag Philipp von Zabern, Mainz am Rhein, 1985).

9   Athenaeus Book XIII, chapter 86, cited in John Marlowe, *The Golden Age of Alexandria* (Victor Gollancz, London 1971), 115.

10 Jolanta Mlynarczyk, *Nea Paphos in the Hellenistic Period* (Nea Paphos III Éditions Géologiques, Warsaw, 1990), 118-9.

11 Strabo, *Geography*. G.P. Goold (trans) (The Loeb Classical Library, London, 1996), 17:8.

12 E.M. Forster, *Alexandria: A History and Guide* (Anchor Books, Doubleday, New York, 1961), 56 (first ed.1922).

13 Luciano Canfora, *The Vanished Library*, translated by Martin Ryde (Vintage, London, 1989), 83.

14 John Marlowe, *The Golden Age of Alexandria* (Victor Gollancz, London, 1971), 203.

15 Keeley and Sharrard (trans), *Four Greek Poets*, 14.

16 Ibid., 13.

17 Jean-Yves Empereur, *Alexandria Rediscovered* (British Museum Press, London, 1998), 100.

18 Aristotle, *The Poetics*, 45, 91. Translated by W. Hamilton Fyfe and W. Rhys Roberts. With Longinus, *On the Sublime* and Demetrius,

      On Style (Harvard University Press, Cambridge, Mass. and London, England, 1991; first ed. 1927).
19 Diodorus Siculus, Book XVI, 84, 1-5.)
20 Andrew Stewart, *Art, Desire and the Body in Ancient Greece* (Cambridge University Press, 1997), frontispiece.
21 Donald Attwater and Catherine Rachel John, *The Penguin Dictionary of Saints* (Penguin Books, London, 3rd ed. 1995), 322.
22 Diodorus Siculus, Book XVI, 92.3-93.3, 94, pp. 95 and 101.
23 Theocritus, *Idyll I*, in Constantine A. Trypanis (ed.), *The Penguin Book of Greek Verse* (Penguin Books, Middlesex, 1988), 289.
24 Aristotle, *The Poetics* xxii, 16-xxiii, 3, 91.
25 Keeley and Sherrard, *Four Greek Poets*, 15.
26 Euripides, *Hecuba*, l. 444 in James Morwood (trans), *Hecuba, The Trojan Women, Andromache* (Oxford University Press, Oxford, 2000), 13.
27 Arrian, Book I:11 in *Anavasis Alexandri* Books I-IV. Translated by P.A. Brunt (Harvard University Press, Cambridge, Mass. and London, England, 1989).
28 Diodorus Siculus, Book XVII, 17.3-5.
29 E.H. Blakeney (ed.) George Rawlinson (trans), *The History of Herodotus* in 2 vols (J.M. Dent & Sons, London, 1949; original ed. 1910), II.5-29.
30 Vitruvius. *De Architectura*. Translated by Frank Granger (Loeb Classical Library, 2 vols. Cambridge, Mass., 1934), Book V, 3:7, p. 127.
31 Theocritus, *Idyll XV* in Trypanis (ed.), *The Penguin Book of Greek Verse*, 306.
32 Ibid., *Idyll II*, 295.
33 Volker Michael Strocka, *Die Wandmalerei der Hanghäuser in Ephesos* (Verlag der Österreichischen Akademie der Wissenschaften, Wien, 1977).
34 Lucan, *The Splendour of the Palace of Alexandria*, Book X, 1-24. Translated by J.S. Duff (Heinemann, London, 1969).

35 John R. Clarke, *The Houses of Roman Italy 100 BC−AD 250: Ritual, Space, and Decoration* (University of California Press, Berkeley, 1991), 66.
36 Theocritus, *Book XV,* 'The Women at the Adonis Festival', translated by J.M. Edmonds (The Loeb Classical Library, London, 1996), lines 78-95.
37 Oliver Sachs, Australian Broadcasting Commission Radio interview, 1999.
38 Athanasius, Book XIII, ch. 86, cited in John Marlowe, *The Golden Age of Alexandria* (Victor Gollancz, London, 1971), 115.

NOTES TO PART III

1 Freya Stark, *Alexander's Path: from Caria to Cilicia* (Century Publishing Company, London, 1984; original ed. John Murray, 1958), 54
2 Richard Chandler, *Travels in Asia Minor 1764-1765* (Trustees of the British Museum, London, 1971), 6.
3 Kayhan Dortluk, *Guide to Side, Aspendos and Perge* (Keskin Color Kartpostalcilik Ltd., Istanbul and Antalya, 1997).
4 Reinhard G. Hubel. (translated by Katherine Watson), *The Book of Carpets* (Barrie and Jenkins, London, 1971), 14.
5 Apuleius, *The Golden Ass.* Translated by Robert Graves (Penguin Books, 1950, new ed. 1972), 64.
6 Jean-Pierre Vernant and Pierre Vidal-Naquet, *Myth and Tragedy in Ancient Greece* (Zone Books, New York, 1988), chap. XVII, 393.
7 Lucretius, *On the Nature of Things. De rerum Natura.* Translated and edited by Anthony M. Esolen (Johns Hopkins University Press, Baltimore and London, 1995), 23, 2-9.
8 Peter Brown, *Augustine of Hippo: a Biography* (Faber and Faber, London, 1967), 167, quoting Augustine *Conf.* V, viii, 15.
9 Lucretius, *On the Nature of Things,* 4, 75, 124.

10 Mustafa Uysal and Azmi Buyruk. *Termessos: a Pisidian Mountain Town of Antiquity.* Graphics, Antalya, Turkey, 1990.
11 Freya Stark, *Alexander's Path.*
12 Version by Edward Storer, 1915, in Margaret Reynolds (ed.) *The Sappho Companion* (Vintage, London, 2001), 60.
13 May Sarton, *Journal of a Solitude* (The Women's Press, London 1973), 79.
14 Sextus Propertius, David R. Slavitt (trans), *Propertius in Love: The Elegies* (University of California Press, Berkeley and Los Angeles, California, 2002), BC III.13 7.
15 Toni Morrison, 'The Site of Memory' in Russell Ferguson (ed) *Marginalisation and Contemporary Culture* (MIT Press, Cambridge, Mass. and London, England, 1990), 299-305.

NOTES TO PART IV

1 Gilles Deleuze, 'The Mystery of Ariadne according to Nietzsche' in *Essays Critical and Cultural*, translated by Daniel W. Smith and Michael A. Greco (University of Minnesota Press, Minneapolis, 1997), 67.
2 Jolanta Mlynarczyk, *Nea Paphos in the Hellenistic Period* (Nea Paphos III Éditions Géologiques, Warsaw, 1990), 119.
3 Sextus Propertius, translated by David R. Slavitt, *Propertius in Love: The Elegies* (University of California Press, Berkeley and Los Angeles, California, 2002), 1.3.
4 Apuleius, *The Golden Ass.* Translated by Robert Graves (Penguin Books, 1950, new ed. 1972), 222
5 Elizabeth Barber, *Prehistoric Textiles: The Development of Cloth in the Neolithic and Bronze Ages, with Special Reference to the Aegean* (Princeton University Press, New Jersey, 1990), 239.
6 Wikto Andrzej Daszewski, *La Mosaïque de Thésée* (Nea Paphos II. Centre d'Archéologie Méditeranéene de L'Académie Polon-

aise des Sciences. Éditions Scientifiques de Pologne, Warsaw 1977).
7   Ibid. *Corpus of Mosaics from Egypt 1: Hellenistic and Roman Period* (Verlag Philipp von Zabern, Mainz am Rhein, 1985), 150.
8   Demetrios Michaelides, *Cypriot Mosaics* (Department of Antiquities, Nicosia, Cyprus, 1992), 6.
9   Daszewski, *La Mosaïque de Thésée*, 59-63.
10 *De cat. Rud.* xxv, 48. Cited by Peter Brown, *Augustine of Hippo: a Biography* (Faber and Faber, London, 1967), 213.
11 Susan Guettel Cole, 'Procession and Celebration at the Dionysia. Tragedy and Ritual' in Ruth Scodel (ed.), *Theater and Society in the Classical World* (Ann Arbor, University of Michigan Press, 1993).
12 Maria Teresa Marabini Moeus, 'Ephemeral Alexandria: the Pageantry of the Ptolemaic Court and its Documentation' in Russell T. Scott and Ann Reynolds Scott, *Eius Virtutis Studiosi: Classical and Postclassical Studies in Memory of Frank Edward Brown (1908-1988)* (National Gallery of Art, Washington, University Press of New England, Hanover and London. 1993), 123-48.
13 Euripides, *The Bacchae*, translated by H. Milman (J.M. Dent. London, 1947).
14 Michaelides, *Cypriot Mosaics*.
15 Augustine, *De civ. Dei* XXII 24, 175, quoted in Peter Brown *Augustine of Hippo*, 329.
16 Libanius in A.F. Norman (trans), *Libanius. Selected Works*, vols. I and II (Harvard University Press, Cambridge, Mass. and Heinemann, London, 1969), 60.
17 Brown, *Augustine of Hippo*.
18 Robert Calasso, *The Marriage of Cadmus and Harmony*, translated from the Italian by Tim Parkes (Vintage, Sydney, 1994), 289.
19 Homer, *Iliad* Book VI, 147, translated by E.V. Rieu (Penguin Books, London, 1951).
20 Marcus Aurelius, *Meditations*, translated by Maxwell Staniforth (Penguin Books, London, 1964), Book 10:34.

21 Artemidorus, *Interpretation of Dreams: Oneirocritica*, translation and commentary by Robert J. White (Original Books Inc., Torrance, California, 1975).
22 Kerameikos Museum, Athens. See also John Gage, *Colour and Culture* (Thames and Hudson, London, 1999).
23 Ursula Knigge, *The Athenian Kerameikos* (Krene Editions, Athens, 1991).
24 Plutarch, *Moralia*. Quoted by Gage, *Colour and Culture*, 30.
25 Knigge, *The Athenian Kerameikos*.
26 Vincent J. Bruno, 'Mark Rothko and the Second Style: the Art of the Color-Field in Roman Murals' in Russell T. Scott and Ann Reynolds Scott (eds), *Eius Virtutis Studiosi: Classical and Post-Classical Studies in Memory of Frank Edward Brown* (National Gallery of Art, Washington. University Press of New England, New Hampshire, 1993), 235-7.
27 Lucretius, *On the Nature of Things. De rerum Natura*. Edited and translated by Anthony M. Esolen (Johns Hopkins University Press, Baltimore and London, 1995).
28 Apuleius, *The Golden Ass,* 222-5
29 *A Dragoman's House: The House of Hadjigeorgakis Kornesios in Nicosia. A Study of its Background and Architecture* (Cyprus Museum and The Royal Danish Academy of Fine Arts, Copenhagen, 1993).
30 Rose Macaulay, *Pleasure of Ruins* (Thames and Hudson, London, 1984), 427.
31 Christos Ch. Giorgiades, *Flowers of Cyprus: Plants of Medicine* (Nicosia, 1992), 50.
32 Lucretius, *De Rerum Natura,* Book 1, l. 305, p. 33.
33 Pierre Aupert, *Guide to Amathus* (The Bank of Cyprus Cultural Foundation, Nicosia, 2000), 58.
34 Propertius III. 128-32.
35 Indra McEwan, *Vitruvius: Writing a Body of Architecture* (MIT Press, Mass., 2003).
36 Emily Vermeule, *Aspects of Death in Early Greek Art and Poetry.* Sather

Classical lectures, vol. 42 (University of California Press, Berkeley, 1981), 4. 'Kathleen Raine' in Anne Bancroft, *Weavers of Wisdom: Women of the Twentieth Century* (Arkana, Penguin Group, London, 1989).

BIBLIOGRAPHY

Andronicos, Manolis. *Vergina: the Royal Tombs and the Ancient City.* Endotike Athenon, Athens, 1984.

Apuleius. *The Golden Ass.* Translated by Robert Graves. Penguin Books, 1950 (new ed. 1972).

Arrian. *Anavasis Alexandri* Books I-IV. Translated by P.A. Brunt. Harvard University Press, Cambridge, Mass. and London, England, 1989.

Artemidorus. *Interpretation of Dreams: Oneirocritica.* Translation and commentary by Robert J. White. Original Books Inc., Torrance, California, 1975.

Attwater, Donald and Catherine Rachel John, . *The Penguin Dictionary of Saints.* Penguin Books, London, 3rd ed. 1995

A Dragoman's House: The House of Hadjigeorgakis Kornesios in Nicosia. A Study of its Background and Architecture. Cyprus Museum and The Royal Danish Academy of Fine Arts, Copenhagen, 1993.

Åström, Paul. 'Cyprus and Troy.' *Opusculensa Atheniensa,* Vol.13 (3), 1980.

Aupert, Pierre. *Guide to Amathus.* Translated by Diane Buitron-Oliver and Andrew Oliver. The Bank of Cyprus Cultural Foundation, Nicosia, 2000.

Aydingun, Sengul Gundogan. *Ancient Pearl of the Toros, Sagalossos. Skylife,* Turkish Arlines, June 2000.

Barker, Stephen, ed. *Excavations and Their Objects: Freud's Collection of Antiquity.* State University of New York Press, Albany, 1996,

Barber, Elizabeth. *Prehistoric Textiles: The Development of Cloth in the Neolithic and Bronze Ages, with Special Reference to the Aegean.* Princeton University Press, New Jersey, 1990.

Boardman, John, Hammond, N.G.L, Lewis, D.M., Ostwald, M. (eds). *The Cambridge Ancient History,* vol. IV. Cambridge University Press, Cambridge, 1988.

Boardman, John. *The Great God Pan: The Survival of an Image.* Thames and Hudson, New York, 1997.

Blegen, Carl. *Troy and the Trojans*. Thames and Hudson, London, 1964.

Bronfen, Elizabeth. *The Knotted Subject: Hysteria and its Discontents*. Princeton University Press, New Jersey, 1998.

Brown, Peter. *Augustine of Hippo: a Biography*. Faber and Faber, London, 1967.

Bruno, Vincent J. 'Mark Rothko and the Second Style: The Art of the Color Field in Roman Murals' in Russell T Scott and Ann Reynolds Scott (eds) *Eius Virtutis Studiosi: Classical and Post Classical Studies in Memory of Frank Edward Brown (1908-1988)*. National Gallery of Art, Washington. University Press of New England, New Hampshire 1993.

Burkert, Walter. *Greek Religion*. Translated by John Raffan. Harvard University Press, Cambridge, Mass., 1994 (first ed. 1977).

Byatt, A.S. *The Djinn in the Nightingale's Eye: Five Fairy Stories*. Vintage, London, 1995.

Calasso, Robert. *The Marriage of Cadmus and Harmony*. Translated from the Italian by Tim Parkes. Vintage, Sydney, 1994.

Calvino, Italo. *Invisible Cities*. Translated by William Weaver. Vintage, London, 1997. First published in Italy, 1972.

Canfora, Luciano. *The Vanished Library*. Translated by Martin Ryde. Vintage, London, 1989.

de Certeau, Michel. *The Practice of Everyday Life*. Translated by Stephen Rendall. University of California Press, Berkeley 1988.

Chandler, Richard. *Travels in Asia Minor 1764–1765*. Edited by Edith Clay. Trustees of the British Museum, London, 1971.

Charbonneaux, Jean, Martin Roland and François Villard. *Hellenistic Art (350-50 BC)*. Translated by Peter Green. George Brazilier, New York, Editions Gallimard, France, 1973.

Christou, Demos. *Kourion: Its Monuments and Local Museum*. Filokipros Publishing, Nicosia, Cyprus 1996.

Christodoulides. Charalambos G. *Saint Neophytos Monastery: History and Art*. Nicosia, Cyprus 1989.

Clarke, John R., *The Houses of Roman Italy 100 BC–AD 250: Ritual, Space, and Decoration*. University of California Press, Berkeley, 1991.

The Classic Greek Dictionary. Follett Publishing Company, Chicago, 1949.

Coldstream, J.N. *Knossos, the Sanctuary of Demeter.* Supplementary vol. no 8. British School of Archaeology in Athens. Thames and Hudson, Oxford, 1973.

Cole, Susan Guettel. 'Procession and Celebration at the Dionysia. Tragedy and Ritual' in Ruth Scodel (ed.), *Theater and Society in the Classical World.* Ann Arbor, University of Michigan Press, 1993.

Conroy, Diana Wood. *Textile Artefacts and a Fragment of Cloth from Pafos, Cyprus.* Report of the Department of Antiquities, Cyprus 2000.

Daszewski, Wikto Andrzej. *Corpus of Mosaics from Egypt. I: Hellenistic and Roman Period.* Verlag Philipp von Zabern, Mainz am Rhein, 1985.

Daszewski, Wikto Andrzej. *La Mosaïque de Thésée. Nea Paphos II.* Centre d'Archéologie Méditerranéene de L'Académie Polonaise des Sciences. Editions Scientifiques de Pologne, Warsaw, 1977.

Daszewski, Wikto Andrzej. 'La Ville de Thesée et la Maison d'Aion. Fouilles de Nea Pafos' in *Chronique des Fouilles et Decouvertes Archeologiques a Chypre en 1989.* A. Papageorghiou, Bulletin des Correspondences Hellenique 114, 1990.

Daszewski, Wikto Andrzej. *Polish Excavations at Kato (Nea) Pafos in 1970 and 1971.* Report of the Department of Antiquities 1972.

Daszewski, W.A. and Michaelides, D. *Guide to the Paphos Mosaics.* Bank of Cyprus Cultural Foundation, 1988.

Deleuze, Gilles. 'The Mystery of Ariadne according to Nietzsche' in *Essays Critical and Cultural,* translated by Daniel W. Smith and Michael A. Greco. University of Minnesota Press, Minneapolis, USA 1997.

Diodorus of Sicily. *Books XVI 66-95 and XVII.* Translated by C. Bradford Welles. Harvard University Press, William Heinemann, London, 1983.

Dorigo, Wladimiro. *Late Roman Painting.* Translated by James Cleugh and John Warrington. Praeger Publishers, NY, Washington, 1970.

Dortluk, Kayhan. *Guide to Side, Aspendos and Perge.* Keskin Color Kartpostalcilik Ltd., Istanbul and Antalya, 1997.

Durrell Lawrence. *Bitter Lemons.* Faber and Faber, London, Boston 1986 first ed. 1957)

Easterling, P.E. 'Tragedy and Ritual' in Ruth Scodel (ed.), *Theater and Society in the Classical World.* The University of Michigan Press, Ann Arbor, 1993.

Empereur, Jean-Yves. *A Short Guide to the Graeco-Roman Museum, Alexandria.* Serapis Publishing, Alexandria, 1995.

Empereur, Jean-Yves. *Alexandria Re-discovered.* British Museum Press, London, 1998.

Ellis, Marianne and Jennifer Wearden. *Ottoman Embroidery.* V&A Publications, London, 2001.

Erdemigil, Selahattin. *Ephesos (Guide).* Net Turistik Yayinlar A.S, Istanbul. 3rd edition 1994.

Euripides. *The Bacchae.* Translated by H. Milman, J.M. Dent, London, 1947.

Ferrua, Antoni. *The Unknown Catacomb: A Unique Discovery of Early Christian Art.* Translated by Iain Inglis. Geddes and Grosset, Nardini Editore, Florence, 1991.

Flourentzos, P. A. *Guide to the Larnaca District Museum.* Department of Antiquities, Nicosia 1996.

Forster, E.M. *Alexandria: A History and a Guide.* Anchor Books, Doubleday, New York, 1961. (First ed. 1922).

Fyfe, W. Hamilton and W. Rhys Roberts. *Aristotle, the Poetics; Longinus, On the Sublime; Demetrius, On Style.* Harvard University Press, Cambridge, Mass. and London, England, 1991. (First ed. 1927).

Gadbery, Laura M. *Roman Wall Painting in Corinth: New Evidence from East of the Theater.* Journal of Roman Archaeology (Supplementary Series no. 8, Ann Arbor, MI, 1993).

Gage, John. *Colour and Culture.* Thames and Hudson, London, 1999.

Galanaki, Rhea. 'Things Visible and Invisible'. Translated from the Greek by Alexandra Büchler, in *Heat* no 7. Giramondo Press, Sydney, 1998.

Gelder, Ken and Jane M. Jacobs. *Uncanny Australia: Sacredness and Identity in a Postcolonial Nation.* Melbourne University Press, Melbourne, 1998.

Gero, Joan M. and Margaret W Conkey. *Engendering Archaeology: Women and Prehistory.* Basil Blackwell, Cambridge, Mass., 1991.

Giorgiades. Christos Ch. *Flowers of Cyprus: Plants of Medicine.* Nicosia, 1992.

Goddio, Frank et al. *Alexandria: The Submerged Royal Quarters.* Periplus, London, 1998.

Graves, Robert. *The Greek Myths.* Penguin Books, Middlesex, 1960 (first ed. 1955).

Green, J.R. and Eric Handley. *Images of the Greek Theatre.* British Museum Press, London, 1995.

Green, J.R. 'Motif-Symbolism and Gnathia Vases'. *Beitrage zur Ikonographie und Hermeneutik. Festschrift für N. Himmelmann-Wildschutz.* P. von Zabern, Mainz, 1989.

Green, J.R. and G.H.Stennett. *The Architecture of the Ancient Theatre at Nea Pafos.* Report of the Department of Antiquities, Cyprus, 2002.

Gullberg, Elsa and Paul Åström. *The Thread of Ariadne: a Study in Ancient Greek Dress.* Studies in Mediterranean Archaeology XXI, Goteborg, Sweden, 1970.

Harrison, Jane Ellen. *Themis. A Study of the Origins of Greek Religion.* London, Merlin Press, 1989. First published 1963.

Hadjiyiasemi, Androula. *Lefkara Lace Embroidery.* Charalambos I. Philipides and Son Ltd., Nicosia, Cyprus, 1987.

Herodotus. *The History of Herodotus.* Edited by E.H. Blakeney and translated by George Rawlinson. 2 vols. J.M. Dent & Sons, London, 1949. Original ed. 1910.

Herrin, Judith, Michael Mullett, and Catherine Otten-Froux, (eds). *Mosaic: Festschrift for A.H.S. Megaw.* British School of Athens Studies 8. London, 2001.

Hinks, R.P. *Catalogue of the Greek, Etruscan and Roman Paintings in the British Museum.* British Museum, London, 1933.

Homer. *The Iliad*. Translated by E.V. Rieu. Penguin Books, London, 1951.

Hubel, Reinhard G. *The Book of Carpets*. Translated by Katherine Watson. Barrie and Jenkins, London, 1971.

Jobst, Werner. *Römische Mosaiken aus Ephesos I. Die Hanghäuser des Embolos. Forschungen in Ephesos VIII/2*. Verlag der Österreichischen Akademie der Wissenschaften, Wien 1977.

Karageorghis, Vassos. *Greek Gods and Heroes in Ancient Cyprus*. Commercial Bank of Greece, Athens, 1998.

Keeley, Edmund and Philip Sharrard (trans). *Four Greek Poets: C.P. Cavafy, George Seferis, Odysseus Elytis, Nikos Gatsos*. Penguin Books, 1966.

Kern, Hermann. *Through the Labyrinth: Designs and Meaning over 5,000 Years*. Prestel, Munich, London and New York, 2000.

Keshishian, Ruth. *In the Footsteps of Freya Stark*. Cultural Centre of the Popular Bank, Nicosia, Cyprus, 1998.

Kinross, Lord. *Atatürk, the Birth of a Nation*. Weidenfeld and Nicolson. London, 1966.

Kondoleon, Christine. *Domestic and Divine: Roman Mosaics in the House of Dionysos*. Cornell University Press, Ithaca and London, 1994.

Knigge, Ursula. *The Athenian Kerameikos*. Krene Editions, Athens, 1991.

La Riche, William. *Alexandria the Sunken City*. Weidenfield and Nicholson, London, 1996.

Lefkowitz, Mary R. and Maureen B. Fant. *Women's Life in Greece and Rome*. Duckworth, 1992.

Lehmann, Phyllis W. *Roman Wall Paintings from Boscoreale in the Metropolitan Museum of Art*. Cambridge, Mass., 1953.

Levi, Doro. *Antioch Mosaic Pavements*, vol. 1. Princeton University Press, Oxford University Press, 1947.

Ling, Roger. *Roman Painting*. Cambridge University Press, New York and Melbourne, 1991.

Lonsdale, Stephen H. A. 'Dancing Floor for Ariadne (*Iliad* 18.590-592) Aspects of Ritual Movement in Homer and Minoan Religion' in Jane B. Carter and Sarah P. Morris, *The Ages of Homer: a Tribute to Emily Vermeule*. University of Texas Press, Austin, 1995.

Lucan. *The Splendour of the Palace of Alexandria. The Civil War X*. Translated by J.S. Duff. The Loeb Classical Library, 1928.

Lucretius. *On the Nature of Things. De rerum Natura*. Edited and translated by Anthony M. Esolen. Johns Hopkins University Press, Baltimore and London, 1995.

Lysaght, Patricia. *Food and the Traveller. Migration, Immigration, Tourism and Ethnic Food*. Proceedings of the 11th Conference of the International Commission for Ethnological Food Research, Cyprus, June 8-14, 1996. Intercollege Press, Cyprus, 1998.

Macaulay, Rose. *Pleasure of Ruins*. First ed. 1954, Thames and Hudson, London, 1984.

Marcus Aurelius. *Meditations*. Translated by Maxwell Staniforth. Penguin Books, London 1964.

McDonald, William. *Architecture of the Roman Empire*. 2 vols. Yale University Press, New Haven and London, 1965, 1982 and 1988.

McEwan, Indra. *Vitruvius: Writing a Body of Architecture*. MIT Press, Massachusetts, 2003.

McLean, Ian. 'Under Saturn: Melancholy and the Colonial Imagination' in Nicholas Thomas and Diane Losche (eds), *Double Vision: Art Histories and Colonial Histories in the Pacific*. Cambridge University Press, UK and USA, 1999.

Maier, G.F. *A Brief History and Description of Old Paphos (Kouklia)*. Printing Office, Republic of Cyprus, n.d.

Maier, G.F. and V. Karageorghis. *Paphos: History and Archaeology*. A.G. Leventis Foundation, Nicosia, Cyprus, 1984.

Libanius. *Selected Works*, vols. I and II. Translated by A.F. Norman. Harvard University Press, Mass., Heinemann, London, 1969.

Mainstone, Rowland J. *Hagia Sophia. Architecture, Structure and Liturgy of Justinian's Great Church*. Thames and Hudson, 1988.

Markides, Kyriacos C. *The Mountain of Silence*. Doubleday, New York, 2001.

Marlowe, John. *The Golden Age of Alexandria*. Victor Gollancz, London, 1971.

Mau, August. *Pompeii, its Life and Art*. Translated by Francis W. Kelsey. Caratzas Bros. Publishers, New Rochelle, NY, 1982. Reprint of the revised edition published in 1902.

Michaelides, Dimitrios. 'Food in Ancient Cyprus' in Patricia Lysaght, *Food and the Traveller: Migration, Immigration, Tourism and Ethnic Food*. Proceedings of the 11th Conference of the International Commission for Ethnological Food Research, Cyprus, June 8-14 1996. Intercollege Press, Cyprus 1998.

Michaelides, Demetrios. *Cypriot Painted Tombs and Their Ceilings*. Unpublished manuscript, Nicosia, 2002.

Michaelides, Demetrios. *Cypriot Mosaics*. Department of Antiquities, Nicosia, Cyprus, 1992.

Mlynarczyk, Jolanta. *Nea Paphos in the Hellenistic Period*. Nea Paphos III Éditions Géologiques, Warsaw, 1990.

Moeus, Maria Teresa Marabini. 'Ephemeral Alexandria: the Pageantry of the Ptolemaic Court and its Documentation' in Russell T. Scott and Ann Reynolds Scott, *Eius Virtutis Studiosi: Classical and Postclassical Studies in Memory of Frank Edward Brown (1908-1988)*. National Gallery of Art, Washington. University Press of New England, Hanover and London, 1993.

Mora, P. L. *Conservation of Wall Paintings*. Butterworths, London, Sydney, 1984.

Morrison, Toni. 'The Site of Memory' in Russell Ferguson (ed.) *Marginalisation and Contemporary Culture*. MIT Press, Cambridge, Mass., London, England, 1990.

Nicolaou, K. *Excavations at Nea Paphos: The House of Dionysos, Outline of the Campaigns 1964-65*. Report of the Department of Antiquities in Cyprus, 1967.

Nussbaum, Martha. *The Fragility of Goodness*. Cambridge University Press, 1986.

Ösgür, M. Edip. *Perge. Guidebook*. Net Turistik Yayinlar A.S. Turkey. 3rd edition 1992.

Ösgür, M. Edip and A. Esin Kuleli. *The Church of Saint Nicholas in Myra and its Environs.* Donmez Offset Basimevi, Ankara, 1995.

der Parthog, Gwynneth. *Byzantine and Medieval Cyprus: A Guide to the Monuments.* Interworld Publications, UK, 1995. New edition forthcoming 2004, Moufflon Publications, Nicosia, Cyprus.

Pehlivaner, Metin (ed.). *Sculptures of the Museum of Antalya.* Antalya Museum Publication 1, Antalya, Turkey, 1996.

Pensabene, Patrizio and Bruno Matthias. *Il Marmo e il Colore. Guida Fotografica: I Marmi della Collezione Podesti.* L'Erma di Bretschneider, Rome, 1998.

Phelan Peggy. *Mourning Sex: Performing Public Memories.* Routledge, London and New York, 1997.

Pinchin, Jane Lagoudis. *Alexandria Still: Forster, Durrell and Cavafy.* Princeton University Press, Princeton, 1977.

Porphyry. *On the Cave of the Nymphs.* Translated by Thomas Taylor with an introduction by Kathleen Raine. Phanes Press, Grand Rapids, USA, 1991.

Pratt, Pamela. 'Wall Painting 223-231' in Donald Strong and David Brown (eds) *Roman Crafts.* New York University Press, 1976.

Propertius, Sextus. *Propertius in Love: The Elegies.* Translated by David R. Slavitt. University of California Press, Berkeley and Los Angeles, California, 2002.

Rabinowitz, Nancy Sorkin and Amy Richlin (eds). *Feminist Theory and the Classics*, Routledge New York, 1993.

Reynolds, Margaret (ed.). *The Sappho Companion.* Vintage, London 2001.

Richter, Gisela M. *Korai: Archaic Greek Maidens.* Phaidon Press, London 1968.

Roberts K.B. and J.D.W. Tomlinson. *The Fabric of the Body: European Traditions of Anatomical Illustration.* Oxford University Press, Oxford, 1992.

Rose, Charles Brian. 'The 1991 post-Bronze Age Excavations at Troia.' *Studia Troica,* Band 2, 1992. Verlag Philipp von Zabern, Mainz am Rhein.

Rostovtzeff, M. *The Social and Economic History of the Hellenistic World.* Clarendon Press, Oxford, 1941.

Roth, Michael S. with Claire Lyons and Charles Merewether. *Irresistible Decay: Ruins Reclaimed.* Paul Getty Institute, Los Angeles, 1997.

Roueché, Charlotte. *Performers and Partisans at Aphrodisias in the Roman and Late Roman Periods.* Society for the Promotion of Roman Studies, Journal of Roman Studies, monograph no. 6, 1993.

Rushdie Salman. *Midnight's Children.* Jonathan Cape, London, 1981.

Sarton, May. *Journal of a Solitude.* The Women's Press, London, 1973.

Scheid, John and Jasper Svenbro. *The Craft of Zeus: Myths of Weaving and Fabric.* Translated by Carol Volk. Harvard University Press, Cambridge, Mass., 1996.

Scott, Russell T. and Ann Reynolds Scott (eds) *Eius Virtutis Studiosi: Classical and Post-Classical Studies in Memory of Frank Edward Brown (1908-1988).* National Gallery of Art, Washington. University Press of New England, New Hampshire, 1993.

Semper, Gottfried. *The Four Elements of Architecture and Other Writings.* Translated by Harry Francis Mallgrave and Wolfgang Herrmann. Cambridge University Press, Cambridge, 1989.

Sennett, Richard. *Flesh and Stone. The Body and the City in Western Civilization.* Faber and Faber, London, 1994.

Seferis, George. *Collected Poems 1924-1955.* Translated and edited by Edmund Keeley and Philip Sherrard. Jonathan Cape, London, 1967.

Severis, Rita C. *Travelling Artists in Cyprus 1700-1960.* Philip Wilson Publishers, London, 2000.

Spector, Janet D. 'What This Awl Means: towards a Feminist Archaeology' in Joan M. Gero, Margaret W. Conkey, *Engendering Archaeology: Women and Prehistory.* Basil Blackwell, Cambridge, Mass. 1991.

Shelmerdine, Cynthia W. 'Shining and Fragrant Cloth in Homeric Epic' in Jane B. Carter and Sarah P. Morris, *The Ages of Homer: a Tribute to Emily Vermeule.* University of Texas Press, Austin 1995.

Smith, R.R.R. *Hellenistic Sculpture: a Handbook*. Thames and Hudson, London, 1991.
Sophocleous, Sophocles. *Icons of Cyprus*. Museum Publications, Nicosia, 1994.
Staniforth, Maxwell (trans). Marcus Aurelius. *Meditations*. Penguin Books, London 1964.
Stewart, Andrew, *Art, Desire and the Body in Ancient Greece*. Cambridge University Press, Cambridge and New York, 1997.
Stark, Freya, *Alexander's Path: from Caria to Cilicia*. Century Publishing Company, London 1984, original ed. John Murray, 1958.
Strabo, *Geography*. Translated by G.P Goold. The Loeb Classical Library, London, 1996.
Strocka, Volker Michael. *Die Wandmalerei der Hanghäuser in Ephesos*. Verlag der Österreichischen Akademie der Wissenschaften, Wien, 1977.
Stylianou, Andreas and Judith A. Stylianou. *The Painted Churches of Cyprus: Treasures of Byzantine Art*. A.G. Leventis Foundation, Nicosia, Cyprus. 2nd Edition 1997.
Talbot Rice, D. *The Icons of Cyprus*. With chapters by Rupert Gunnis and Tamara Talbot Rice. London, George Allen and Unwin, 1937.
Thomas, Nicholas and Diane Losche (eds). *Double Vision and Colonial Histories in the Pacific*. Cambridge University Press, Cambridge, UK, 1999.
Thubron, Colin. *Journey into Cyprus*. The Atlantic Monthly Press, New York, 1975.
Toynbee, J.M.C. *Death and Burial in the Roman World*. Cornell University Press, Ithaca, New York, 1971.
Trendall, A.D. *The Shellat Mosaic and other Classical Antiquities in the Australian War Memorial, Canberra*. Australian War Memorial, Canberra. 1973.
Trypanis, Constantin A. (ed). *The Penguin Book of Greek Verse*. Penguin Books, Middlesex, England, 1971.

Tzonis, Alexander and Liane Lefaivre. *Classical Architecture: The Poetics of Order*. MIT Press, Cambridge. Mass., 1988.
The Vatican Collections: The Papacy and Art. Catalogue. Metropolitan Museum of Art, New York, 1982.
Uysal, Mustafa and Azmi Buyruk. *Termessos: a Pisidian Mountain Town of Antiquity*. Graphics, Antalya, Turkey, 1990.
Vermeule, Emily. *Aspects of Death in Early Greek Art and Poetry*. Sather Classical Lectures, vol. 42. University of California Press, Berkeley 1981, 4.
Vermeule, Emily D. T. and Florence Z. Wolsky. *Toumba tou Skourou: A Bronze Age Potter's Quarters on Morphou Bay in Cyprus*. The Harvard University Museum of Fine Arts, Boston, Cyprus Expedition, 1990.
Vernant, Jean-Pierre and Pierre Vidal-Naquet. *Myth and Tragedy in Ancient Greece*. Zone Books, New York, 1988.
Vitruvius. *De Architectura*. Translated by Frank Granger. Loeb Classical Library, 2 vols. Cambridge, Mass., 1934.
Warner, Marina. *The Leto Bundle*. Chatto and Windus, London 2001.
Webb., Pamela. *A Hellenistic Architectural Sculpture*. The University of Wisconsin Press, Wisconsin and London, 1996.
Wessel, Klaus. *Coptic Art*. Thames and Hudson, London. 1965.

INDEX OF PROPER NAMES

Achilles, 178, 191, 321
Adonis, 45, 51, 52, 84, 94,
    100-103, 214
Aeneas, 51, 190
Aeschylus, 190
Agamemnon, 190
Alexander the Great, 91, 131,
    142-143, 145, 170, 176, 178,
    180-184, 190-191, 205,
    243, 245-247, 249-250,
    282, 289, 345
Amphitrite, 213
Amun, 143
Anaxilas of Naxos, 170
Antony, Mark, 152
Anubis, 158
Aphrodite, 17, 22, 26-27, 35,
    43-53, 60, 74, 82, 88,
    94, 100, 102, 106, 114,
    146-147, 217, 250-251, 271,
    299, 301, 348-349, 362
Apollonios of Rhodes, 207
Ares, 100
Ariadne, 144-145, 298-303,
    308, 313, 325, 349-351
Aristotle, 37, 159, 184, 190, 212
Arrian, 191
Arsinoe, 146
Artemidorus, 51, 68, 70, 325
Artemis, 60, 94, 207, 215,
    217-218, 221, 250-251, 257,
    281, 285

Astyanax, 190
Atatürk, Mustafa Kemal, 187,
    193, 195, 197, 208, 287-288
Athanasius, 222
Athena, 30, 39, 42, 65, 146,
    169, 191, 200
Athenaeus, 146, 213
Attalos I, 208
Attalos II, 243

Beethoven, Ludwig van, 260,
    262, 264
Berenike, 146, 304
Bes, 147, 348

Caesar, Julius, 157
Calvino, Italo, 57
Cavafy, Constantine, 141, 152,
    154, 189
Chandler, Richard, 248
Cheiron the Centaur, 94
Circe, 33, 71
Cleopatra, 157, 181
Clytemnestra, 190
Constantine (Emperor), 192,
    306
Cronus, 43

Daedalus, 299
Daphne, 71
Daszewski, Viktor, 145, 153,
    304

391

da Vinci, Leonardo, 123
Demeter, 94, 101-102, 169, 182
Demetrios Poliorcetes, 146
Dinocrates, 143
Diocletian, 157
Dionysos, 29, 33-34, 60, 63, 70-71, 126, 144, 153, 158, 173, 210, 249, 253, 263, 273, 275, 298-300, 302, 304, 308-310, 315, 321, 325, 345, 355
Dioscurides, 31
Dufy, Raoul, 101
Durrell, Lawrence, 27, 105-106, 142, 149

Eros, 46-47
Euripides, 71, 190, 309, 314

Flavius Severanus, 290
Freud, Sigmund, 68, 136, 138

Gunnis, Rupert, 83

Hadrian (Emperor) 190, 272, 317
Harpalus, 191
Hathor, 138, 348
Hector, 190
Hecuba, 190
Heracles, 135, 249
Herodotus, 44-45, 134, 192, 259

Hermes, 94, 100, 169, 249, 255, 270, 310
Homer, 46, 100, 188, 190, 197, 201, 243, 250, 298-299, 325, 349
Horus, 158
Hypatia, 151

Iphigeneia, 190

Jason, 207
Jonah, 361
Justinian, 221

Kandinsky, Wassily, 259

Lazarus, 313
Le Carré, John, 96
Le Corbusier, Charles-Édouard, 37
Levi-Strauss, Claude, 55
Libanius, 115, 319-320
Lucan, 212-213
Lucretius, 276, 329, 347

Maillol, Aristide, 101
Marcus Aurelius, 261, 325, 352
Matisse, 155-156
Medea, 207
Medusa, 159, 256, 271, 276, 345
Menander, 92
Michelangelo, 249
Mimnermos, 22
Minerva, 42

Miro, 280
Muses, 205, 216, 218-219, 256

Narcissus, 70, 101, 216
Nike, 169, 205, 255
Nikokles, king of Paphos, 49
Nikokreon, last king of Salamis, 91, 183
Noah, 223

Odysseus, 189
Oedipus, 175
Oppenheim, Meret, 46
Osiris, 158
Ovid, 34

Pan, 184
Paris, 329
Pasiphäe, 299
Peleus, 321
Persephone, 94, 101-102, 169, 182
Phaedra, 299
Philip the Great, 180
Picasso, Pablo, 172, 259
Pindar, 41
Piranesi, Giambattista, 62, 254
Plancia Magna, 251, 252, 257
Plato, 76, 212
Plutarch, 146, 152, 299, 301
Poseidon, 94, 192
Poussin, Nicholas, 58
Propertius, Sextus, 137, 300

Proust, Marcel, 54
Ptolemy, 91, 141, 157, 165, 183, 223, 304
Ptolemy Philadelphus, 146
Purcell, Henry, 38
Pyramos, 22, 34-35, 71
Pythagoras, 28, 31

Rothko, Mark, 328
Rushdie, Salman, 351
Russell, Bertrand, 131

Sachs, Oliver, 219
St Augustine, 85, 220, 272, 304, 307, 319, 321
St Barnabas, 250
St Francis of Assisi, 334
St George, 337
St Janoufrios, 314
St John, 220-222, 357
St Mamas, 314
St Marina, 314
St Mark, 133
St Nicholas, 277
St Paul, 44, 114, 250
St Simeon the Stylite, 174
Sappho, 46, 218-219, 284
Schliemann, Heinrich, 188
Scylla, 33, 70, 94
Shakespeare, William, 34, 141
Siculus, Diodorus, 173, 180, 191
Sobek, 148, 158

Sophocles, 56, 79, 190, 356
Sostratus, 143
Stark, Freya 243, 246, 260, 270, 280, 291
Strabo, 107, 147
Sybil, 50

Theocritus, 182, 206-207
Theodosius (Emperor), 114
Thetis, 320-321
Thisbe, 34, 71
Thoth, 136
Triton, 213
Tyche, 42, 275

Uranus, 43

Vesalius, 363
Vitruvius, 189, 204, 214, 265, 362

Winckelmann, Johann Joachim, 29

Xerxes, 192, 243

Zeus, 102, 174, 182, 200-204, 208, 218, 281, 285, 299